*Shakespeare's Universe of Discourse*

# Shakespeare's Universe of Discourse

## Language-Games in the Comedies

KEIR ELAM

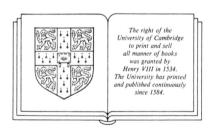

The right of the
University of Cambridge
to print and sell
all manner of books
was granted by
Henry VIII in 1534.
The University has printed
and published continuously
since 1584.

CAMBRIDGE UNIVERSITY PRESS

*Cambridge*
*London   New York   New Rochelle*
*Melbourne   Sydney*

Published by the Press Syndicate of the University of Cambridge
The Pitt Building, Trumpington Street, Cambridge CB2 1RP
32 East 57th Street, New York, NY 10022, USA
296 Beaconsfield Parade, Middle Park, Melbourne 3206, Australia

First published 1984

Printed in Great Britain at
the University Press, Cambridge

Library of Congress catalogue card number: 83–18892

*British Library cataloguing in publication data*
Elam, Keir
Shakespeare's universe of discourse.
1. Shakespeare, William – Language
I. Title
822.3'3   PR3072
ISBN 0 521 22592 2 hard covers
ISBN 0 521 27734 5 paperback

WV

*To Silvana*

# Contents

CONTENTS

viii

# Illustrations

# Acknowledgments

I would like to thank the following friends and colleagues who generously read and commented on this work, or on parts or earlier versions of it, during the various stages of its composition: Basil Greenslade, Terence Hawkes, Marcello Pagnini, Jane Roberts, Vivian Salmon, Alessandro Serpieri. Special thanks are due to Nicholas Brooke, whose sharp but patient reading helped remove at least some of the flaws. For the flaws that remain, of course, the responsibility is the author's alone.

# Abbreviations

The following abbreviations of the titles of Shakespeare's comedies have been adopted:

AWW  *All's Well that Ends Well*
AYLI  *As You Like It*
CE  *The Comedy of Errors*
LLL  *Love's Labour's Lost*
MA  *Much Ado about Nothing*
MM  *Measure for Measure*
MND  *A Midsummer Night's Dream*
MV  *The Merchant of Venice*
MWW  *The Merry Wives of Windsor*
TG  *The Two Gentlemen of Verona*
TN  *Twelfth Night*
TS  *The Taming of the Shrew*

# Editions

Act, scene and line references are all to the respective Arden editions of the plays.

# Introduction: Games and frames

## (1) 'EXCELLENT DISCOURSE'

This is a study of the self-consciousness of Shakespeare's language. Or more specifically, of Shakespeare's discourse. The term 'discourse', now fashionable again in literary studies, is Shakespeare's own favourite linguistic word in the comedies. 'Language' normally refers in the plays to a given tongue, such as English or Latin, while 'speech' is usually reserved either for the faculty of speaking ('this prerogative of speech') or for an actual oral performance ('I will on with my speech'). 'Discourse' is the general Shakespearean word for language in *use*. Which includes, of course, the language used in the plays themselves. Indeed, discourse is often vividly characterized in the comedies as a tangible presence possessing imposing qualities: 'sweet discourse' *(The Two Gentlemen of Verona)*; 'admirable discourse' *(The Merry Wives of Windsor)*; 'voluble and sharp discourse', 'excellent discourse', 'enchanting . . . discourse' *(The Comedy of Errors)*; 'sweet and voluble . . . discourse' *(Love's Labour's Lost)*, etc. It is just this active and self-advertising presence of language in use, as it were discourse in the comedies and not merely the discourse of the comedies, that this book aims to explore.

The reasons for such an emphasis on the active roles of language within Shakespearean comedy are primarily historical. The philosopher Ernst Cassirer, in a brilliant commentary on the comedies, identifies what he calls the 'game of the pure self-activity of the word' as their main motive force (1932: 176). And he relates this verbal self-activity, surely correctly, to the obsessive cultivation of linguistic forms in the Renaissance. Shakespeare's was an age in which language occupied a central place in all areas of cultural endeavour and of socio-political conflict: in religious controversy (e.g. the dispute over 'sacred' verbal formulae that underlay the Reformation); in geographical exploration (the contact with unknown tongues); in philosophical debate (e.g. the competing Aristotelian and Platonic conceptions of the linguistic sign); in the politics of education (the benefits or otherwise of instruction in rhetoric); in the new science (the reliability of language as a cognitive tool); in the new national consciousness (the affirmation of the vernacular); and of course in the arts, not least in the theatre itself (the debate on the morality of plays and their discourse). There can be no question that the intense linguistic consciousness of the Elizabethan period influenced in turn the very linguistic make-up of the Elizabethan drama, not only in its rhetorical complexity but in its very concern with language in its manifold aspects.

Discourse – this is the main thesis of this study – occupies the same kind of centrality in Shakespearean comedy as it does in Elizabethan culture at large. It is a centrality not simply as privileged semiotic means (language as the communicative medium *par excellence*, not least on the Elizabethan stage), but as direct dramatic and comic object. In other words, in an age that elects language as both primary channel and primary target for its enthusiasms, for its suspicions, and even for its wars, the dramatic and theatrical potential of verbal events in themselves becomes virtually limitless. In this sense the 'self-activity of the word' that characterizes the comedies of Shakespeare (or for that matter the comedies of Lyly or of Jonson) amounts not so much to the autonomy of verbal form as to the identity of that form with the dramatic concerns of the plays. This is nowhere more evident than in *Love's Labour's Lost,* the comedy that serves as the main point of reference for this study.

Now our own age, like Shakespeare's, is one of intense linguistic awareness. The central importance of language in contemporary thought, manifested most directly in the growth of linguistics, of semiotics, of the philosophy of language and of language-oriented sociology, raises the problem of how to approach, from our late twentieth-century standpoint, the language and the linguistic culture produced in other ages, a problem which is at once historical and methodological. In what ways do the modes and instruments of contemporary linguistic enquiry enable us to account for the language of, and the place of language in, texts of the past, and specifically such linguistically formidable texts as Shakespeare's comedies? These introductory comments will be mainly concerned with trying to answer this question, and so with sketching a methodological and historical framework for the critical analysis of the roles of discourse in the plays, setting out from a rapid review of the critical tradition with respect to the language of the comedies, and then proposing some alternative critical criteria.

### (II) SHAKESPEARE'S LANGUAGE, SHAKESPEARE'S COMEDIES, SHAKESPEARE'S CRITICS

Studies, especially book-length studies, of Shakespeare's language run two main risks. The first is the risk of tautology, or, what amounts to the same thing, of getting lost in a virtually limitless terrain. In the textual form in which we have received it, Shakespearean drama is *all* language, however great its potential for becoming, in performance, a communicative event that goes quite beyond merely *verbal* discourse. And so to elect as object of study 'Shakespeare's language' is to take on the drama *tout court*. Everything and (this is the danger, at least) nothing. The second risk is the opposite one, namely of too severe a delimitation of the critical and dramatic territory. Whatever its descriptive value, criticism that abstracts from the plays a given linguistic function or level - Shakespeare's syntax, Shakespeare's imagery, Shakespeare's lexicon, etc. – will not normally be able to integrate its findings into an overall account of linguistic structure.

It is this second danger that has been most often courted in the history of language-oriented Shakespeare criticism. We possess a considerable corpus of valuable studies dedicated to each of the respective linguistic 'strata' of the comedies and of the dramas in general: the phonetic (from Kökeritz 1953, to Cercignani 1981); the grammatical (from Abbott 1881, to Wikberg 1975); the rhetorical (from Clemen 1951, to Vickers 1970); the social or sociolinguistic (from Schlauch 1965, to Krieger 1979), etc. But each delimited level of analysis has tended to remain isolated from, or, to use an appropriate metaphor, non-communicating with the rest. Descriptive syntheses are rare and dangerously close to extinction.

Such efforts as have been made to characterize the overall roles of language in these plays have more often than not created insuperable critical problems for themselves by bringing to the task unhelpfully restrictive pseudo-Aristotelian criteria. Particular difficulties have arisen from the principle, derived from the *Poetics* but widely applied to Shakespearean comedy, that 'Diction is only one of the elements of the drama, and no matter how brilliant it may be, it is still properly *one of the lesser elements*. It must be *subordinated* to the interests of character and plot, or at least not permitted to override them' (Bonazza 1966: 74, my italics). A dramaturgic dogma that insists *a priori* on the dutiful self-effacement of 'diction', that 'lesser' ingredient of dramatic structure, can only lead to critical embarrassment before the unclassical and indecorous linguistic *in*subordination that marks the comedies in their livelier moments.

One encounters such embarrassment throughout the critical history of the comedies. It appears, for example, in the recurrent strategy of dividing the comic canon into two distinct and opposing phases – 'early' versus 'late' – so as to separate off for special treatment 'those inferior early works in which a great comedian gives away his predilections'

3

(Cody 1969: 126). Thanks to this move it is not the 'great comedian' himself but that lesser figure, the 'early Shakespeare', who sins against the classical dramaturgic code in his 'failure to subordinate means to ends' (Phialas 1966: 84), that is in allowing language too prominent a role.

It was probably Coleridge who set the prevailing terms and tone of this critical tradition in his condescension towards the divinely gifted but, as yet, verbally ill-disciplined author of the first comedies: 'Sometimes you see this youthful god of poetry connecting disparate thoughts purely by means of resemblances in the words expressing them' (1960 ed., 1: 86). Both the terms and the tone survive in a good deal of influential later criticism, such as Harley Granville-Barker's: 'To many young poets of the time their language was a new-found wonder; its very handling gave them pleasure. The things it could be made to do! [Shakespeare] had to discover that they were not much to his purpose; but it is not easy to stop doing what you do so well' (1927: 8).

Now it is scarcely surprising that of all 'those inferior early works' whose supposed failure to subordinate linguistic means to structural ends is repeatedly lamented by commentators, it is *Love's Labour's Lost* – by general consent the 'linguistic' comedy *par excellence* – that has served as the preferred butt for contemptuous critical dismissal. Dryden's 'meanly written' is echoed in Johnson's 'unworthy of our poet' and amplified in Hazlitt's resounding 'If we were to part with any of the author's comedies, it should be this.' This unceremonious refusal of the play is unequivocally due to its putative structural imbalance or verbal top-heaviness. Thus Swinburne likens the structure of the comedy to 'that of a house of cards which the wind builds and unbuilds at pleasure. Here we find a very riot of rhymes, wild and wanton in their half-grown grace' (1880: 47). Twentieth-century evaluations have tended to take up H. B. Charlton's judgment of the work as 'merely a verbal display', and thereby 'deficient in plot and characterization' (1938: 276, 270). So we are told that 'plot and action [are] submerged in tides of words' (Calderwood 1969: 79), that 'the diction of melody and words is all that we ... remember' (Hamilton 1967: 130), or, more bluntly, that the comedy is vitiated by 'too much talk' (Bonazza 1966: 64).

A number of assumptions underlying this lengthy evaluative tradition are likely to be challenged in any critical engagement with the texts that aims to do more than apply inherited judgmental yardsticks. The first of these yardsticks has to do with the conveniently binary opposition itself ('early'/'late'). A division which, apart from the all too familiar chronological uncertainties it evokes (how early *is Love's Labour's Lost*? Is *A Midsummer Night's Dream* still early enough to be considered 'early' or already late enough to be deemed 'late'?), entails a highly questionable assessment of the structural disposition of the plays within the two respective groups. It is by no means self-evident that 'One of the points in which *Twelfth Night* and *As You Like It* are superior to *Love's Labour's Lost* is that in these the role of language is made properly subordinate' (Phialas 1966: 71), even if we feel able to determine what a 'properly subordinate' role should be. There are good reasons, on the contrary, for claiming that the language of the two 'late' texts in question – as, indeed, of *Much Ado about Nothing, The Merry Wives of Windsor, The Merchant of Venice* and others – manifests a vitality and a dramaturgic conspicuousness that in no sense correspond to the dull and humble subservience approvingly attributed to it by Phialas and others.

Harder still to sustain is what might be termed the 'layer cake' conception of the drama betrayed in much of the critical reception met by the comedies. A rigid scale of dramatic 'components', in which plot, character, theme and diction are assigned to their proper places according to their relative dramaturgic value, does not merely recognize the existence of different structural levels in the dramatic text but supposes the absolute distinctness of these levels, as if 'plot' in no way depended on 'diction' nor 'character' on 'theme'. At its most reductive, this form of dissection is purely quantitative, a simple question of more and less ('too much talk'). It is not to be wondered at that such criteria have failed spectacularly to come to terms with texts in which the unfolding of discourse, action and thematic issues is of a richly dialectical rather than rigidly stratified nature.

A related obstacle to any detailed consideration of Shakespeare's comic language is the widely shared moralistic abhorrence at the showing-off of the plays' verbal 'means'. The complaint that in Shakespeare's more 'self-indulgent' plays words 'too often exist for their own sake' (Bonazza 1966: 74) is based on a misconception of the roles of discourse in comedy, and especially in Elizabethan comedy. The generic constraints on tragedy tend to set severe limits on the play of discourse, whose narrative duties are normally too pressing to leave much space for self-propagating freeplay (although the language of *Hamlet* can scarcely be said to be modestly and soberly transparent). But one of the salient characteristics of much comic drama from Aristophanes to Stoppard has been the foregrounding, or bringing to prominence, of the linguistic sign itself as phonetic, syntactic or semantic presence, a material factor to be bandied or toyed with or tortured or otherwise offered as immediate object of audience attention. This is Cassirer's 'pure self-activity of the word'. And it need scarcely be underlined that the Aristotelian principle of dramaturgic decorum, according to which language is judged 'one of the lesser elements' in the structural hierarchy, and which is so often and uncritically applied to comedy, was not formulated with that genre in view.

In order to find more appropriate and constructive criteria for the analysis of Shakespeare's comic discourse, we have to look beyond the critical tradition proper.

## (III) LANGUAGE AS ACTION: THE SPEECH ACT

The opposition derived from the *Poetics* that underlies critical resistance to dramatic 'talk' is that between *lexis* (verbal expression) and *praxis* (action, found at the apex of the Aristotelian hierarchy, *Poetics* 38a. 15). Only if dramatic language is reduced to the status of mere 'diction', the verbal dressing-up of an action level that is in itself non- or pre-linguistic, can its absolute subordination to that level be upheld. But what if *lexis* itself, as many linguists and philosophers of language have insisted in recent years, may instead be viewed as an exemplary form of *praxis*? And what if, correspondingly, the principal mode of *praxis* in Shakespearean comedy lies in what Pirandello called 'spoken action', that is in direct *acts* of language rather than in some verbally decorated extra-linguistic substance?

This alternative perspective on language and language-use is offered by the theory of speech acts, developed over the past two decades in the wake of the pioneering work of J. L. Austin (1962). In the light of such 'a theory of language [as] part of a theory of action' (Searle 1969: 17), the speaking of language is not merely the conveying of some conceptual content (Aristotle's *dianoia*) in variable syntactic and stylistic garb, but is primarily a mode of *doing* in its own right, namely the performing of acts 'such as making statements, giving commands, asking questions, making promises, and so on; and more abstractly, acts such as referring and predicating' (Searle 1969: 17). Here priority is given to the dynamic interpersonal role of speech, thereby throwing into question any absolute polarity between linguistic representation and social practice.

A number of theorists of the drama have proposed the application of speech-act theory to dramatic discourse (Chambers 1980; Ohmann 1971, 1973; Serpieri 1978a; Elam 1980; Savona 1980; Short 1981), and indeed the immediate implications of such an application are clear and considerable. If we are able to approach the dialogue not as the 'lexical' representation or reporting of some non-linguistic action, but as a network of direct verbal deeds, that is, of *illocutions* ('the performance of an act *in* saying something' (Austin 1962: 99): thus questions,

6

commands, affirmations, denials, promises, etc.) and *perlocutions*
('what we bring about or achieve *by* saying something, such as
convincing, persuading, deterring, and even, say, surprising or misleading', 109), then we may begin to come to terms with the dynamic
discourse structure of the drama in its moment-by-moment unfolding.
'In a play', claims Richard Ohmann, 'the action rides on a train of
illocutions' (1973: 83); and Ross Chambers is still more confident of the
central importance of the illocutionary act within the dramatic
narrative at large: 'in the great majority of cases, the dramatic action
appears, in its unfolding, as a story composed of a series of speech acts,
and the basic unit of all narrative analysis of drama can thus only be the
speech act' (1980: 401, my translation). What are in play in the dialogic
exchange, according to this proposal, are no longer static 'characters'
represented by their 'diction', but interpersonal forces responsible for
carrying forward the narrative dynamic.

With such a shift in analytic focus, unproductive critical scruples
regarding the appropriate or decorous *quantities* of speech in the
comedies might give way to a more fruitful concern with what comes
actually to be *done* with words in a given play. To illustrate both the
immediate dialogic and the overall narrative role of the speech-act
continuum in Shakespearean comedy, one might take a conspicuous
and consequential 'dramatic' (rather than playful) dialogic exchange,
such as the first encounter between Isabella and Angelo in *Measure for
Measure* (2. 2. 26ff.). Isabella's would-be perlocutionary campaign (her
attempt to persuade Angelo to spare her brother Claudio's life), which
unfolds through a series of individual *illocutionary* moves, meets with
resistance from her interlocutor. Or in terms of speech-act jargon, her
plea fails at first to achieve the desired 'perlocutionary effect':

| | |
|---|---|
| *Ang.* | Y'are welcome (1): what's your will (2)? |
| *Isa.* | I am a woeful suitor to your honour (3); |
| | Please but your honour hear me (4). |
| *Ang.* | Well (5): what's your suit (6)? |
| *Isa.* | There is a vice that most I do abhor, |
| | And most desire should meet the blow of justice; |
| | For which I would not plead, but that I must; |
| | For which I must not plead, but that I am |
| | At war 'twixt will and will not (7). |
| *Ang.* | Well: the matter (8)? |
| *Isa.* | I have a brother is condemn'd to die (9); |
| | I do beseech you, let it be his fault, |
| | And not my brother (10) ... |
| *Ang.* | Condemn the fault and not the actor of it (11)? |
| | Why every fault's condemn'd ere it be done (12). |

7

The exchange can be broken down into the following constituent acts (as indicated):

| | |
|---|---|
| (1) | Greeting |
| (2) | Question to discover Isabella's intent |
| (3) | (= 'illocutionary sequel') Statement of Isabella's illocutionary/perlocutionary intentions as speaker ('suitor') |
| (4) | Request for a hearing (a 'turn signal', see p. 189 below) |
| (5) | (= 'perlocutionary sequel') Request granted |
| (6) | Question to discover the exact nature of Isabella's would-be perlocution |
| (7) | (= illocutionary sequel) Statement, by way of a preamble, qualifying and justifying the suit in advance (note the *meta*-illocutions – 'I would not plead'/'I must not plead' – dramatizing the speaker's ethical agonies in making the plea) |
| (8) | Question prompting Isabella to come to the object of her plea |
| (9) | (= illocutionary sequel) Statement of object |
| (10) | The plea (explicitly indicated through the 'performative' verb phrase 'I do beseech', see p. 201 below) |
| (11) | (= Lack of perlocutionary sequel) Rhetorical question, by way of a rejection of the suit (thus an example of what John Searle (1975a) terms *indirect* speech acts) |
| (12) | Statement elaborating and justifying the rejection |

Even from so rudimentary an anatomy, the skeletal pattern of the interaction emerges clearly enough. And so does the fact that any divorce within the scene between *discursive* and *dramatic* development is purely notional. Isabella's attempted persuasion and Angelo's albeit brief gesture of opposition, like his later attempt at counter-persuasion against Isabella's vows of chastity, are exemplary speech *events* rather than instances of decorative lexical dressing. And it is this very exchange, of course, that generates the main plot (Aristotle's *mythos*) of the comedy as a whole.

At this point, however, a number of objections might be raised against the kind of utterance-by-utterance breakdown of the dialogue sketched here. One may be able legitimately to splinter the drama into a succession of well-defined little 'local' acts when, as in the cited passage, the dialogue comprises a rapid give and take of antithetical moves. But just as there will be episodes of linguistic interaction (say, the opening dialogue between Egeon and the Duke in *The Comedy of Errors*) that do not unfold in so neat a 'micro'-illocutionary fashion, so there will be larger stretches of discourse (monologues, orations, verbal performances of various kinds) whose illocutionary definition is either problematic (for example, what type of illocutionary act does Launce perform in his monologic reconstruction of his dog Crab's disgrace in *The Two Gentlemen of Verona* (4. 4. 1ff.)?: scarcely the simple act of 'narrating' or 'reporting') or otherwise tautological and banal: in illocutionary terms, Jaques's 'seven ages of man' speech (*As You Like It* 2. 7. 139ff.) is a somewhat lengthy statement, but this tells us less than nothing about its characteristics as a verbal happening.

And what are we to make, similarly, of those dramatic language-events that are definable not so much according to illocutionary content as according to dramaturgic and literary convention? In *The Taming of the Shrew*, as everyone knows, Katherina and Petruchio engage in mutual maltreatment of a more or less ritual nature:

| | |
|---|---|
| *Kath.* | Let him that mov'd you hither |
| | Remove you hence. I knew you at the first |
| | You were a movable. |
| *Pet.* | Why, what's a movable? |
| *Kath.* | A joint-stool. |
| *Pet.* | Thou hast hit it. Come, sit on me. |
| *Kath.* | Asses are made to bear, and so are you. |
| *Pet.* | Women are made to bear, and so are you. |
| *Kath.* | No such jade as you, if me you mean. (2. 1. 195ff.) |

Now it might be said, not altogether unjustly, that the main point of this kind of verbal brawl (compare Beatrice and Benedick or the lords and ladies in the wood in *A Midsummer Night's Dream*) is the insult-exchange itself, whereby the sequence might safely be labelled in 'illocutionary' forms as a piece of squabbling or reciprocal vilifying or the like. But this is to ignore the main defining feature of the sequence: its strict observance of the rules governing what Margaret Galway rightly describes (1935: 183) as 'the oldest of all laughter-provoking devices in native English drama', namely the *flyting* (the device first appears in the Wakefield *Processus noe cum filiis*). The decisive characteristics of the flyting – sustained vituperation, direct statement on the part of the man, sarcastic insinuation on the part of the woman, etc. – are themselves merely secondary illocutionary rules, but the overriding and implicit convention, that which makes the contest a worthy spectacle, is that the insults should be wittily and inventively varied. It is this witty inventiveness, and not the vilification as such, that is on show.

It would be quite superfluous to catalogue here all those more or less conventional and non-illocutionary units of discourse that contribute so decisively to the verbal make-up of many of the comedies: poems, songs, *lazzi*, punning exhibitions, declamations, readings, and so on.

What is important to emphasize, as a more general rule of the poetics of Shakespearean comedy (and indeed of much English comic drama from Jonson to Shaw to Stoppard), is that language may figure as a dramatic-theatrical 'event' at levels altogether different from that of directly 'pragmatic' interaction. Take the all too conspicuous example of Holofernes's alliterative folly in *Love's Labour's Lost*:

> I will something affect the letter; for it argues facility.
> The preyful princess pierc'd and prick'd a pretty pleasing pricket;
> Some say a sore; but not a sore, till now made sore with
> shooting. (4. 2. 53ff.)

There can be no question that the pedant's little poem represents a well-defined linguistic 'happening' in its own right, ceremoniously marked off from its dialogic context. And there is likewise little doubt that the kind of speech act it purports to perform, the narration of the shooting, is of minor importance: indeed, difficult to decipher. The real event is indicated unambiguously in Holofernes's own prefatory comments: the display of letter-affecting itself as a sign of 'facility'. What is being brought to the foreground is the factor that Austin terms (1962: 96) the *'phonetic* act', i.e. the sheer material production of English phonemes. An event that in Austin's system is merely a requisite (part of the base 'locutionary' act *of* saying something) of the speech act proper (the illocution performed *in* saying something).

What these examples seem to suggest is that an adequate account of the 'active' functions of Shakespeare's comic discourse requires a more flexible analytic framework, a framework that includes Austin's speech-act apparatus without, however, reducing all verbal events to a single action level. What is needed, in other words, is a conception of language not only *as* action but more generally *in* action at any and all of its constitutive levels.

### (IV) LANGUAGE IN ACTION: THE LANGUAGE-GAME

One way of going forward in this direction might be to go back chronologically, i.e. to a proposal that actually pre-dates Austin's system but which, unlike speech-act categories, has been singularly neglected in literary and dramatic theory and criticism. The proposal in question is Wittgenstein's notion of the language-game *(Sprachspiel)*, expounded in the *Brown Book* (1933–5; published 1958) and more decisively in the *Philosophical Investigations* (1941–8; published 1953). Wittgenstein, in the latter work particularly, employs the term 'game' in a very special sense, namely to indicate any distinct form of language-use subject to its own rules and defined within a given behavioural context. Thus rather like Austin's 'act', the concept of the linguistic *Spiel* is intended 'to bring into prominence the fact that the *speaking* of language is part of an activity, or a form of life' (1953: § 23). Like Austin, moreover, Wittgenstein appears to set out from a reflection on the 'illocutionary' range of sentences: 'But how many kinds of sentence are there? say assertion, question, and command?' *(ibid.)*. But Wittgenstein's emphasis – and this is the crucial difference for our critical purposes – is placed on the multiformity and fluidity of language-uses or 'kinds of sentence': 'There are *countless* kinds: countless different kinds of use of what we call "symbols", "words", "sentences". And this multiplicity is not something fixed, given once for all; but new types of language, new language-games, as we may say, come into existence, and others become obsolete and get forgotten' *(ibid.)*.

As a result, Wittgenstein's 'games' prove far more heterogeneous or many-levelled than Austin's illocutions and perlocutions. In the *Philosophical Investigations* he provides a (very partial) list that may be instructive here (some seventy-three language-games are listed at the beginning of the *Brown Book*): 'Review the multiplicity of language-games in the following examples, and in others:

> Giving orders, and obeying them –
> Describing the appearance of an object, or giving its measurements –
> Constructing an object from a description (a drawing) –
> Reporting an event –
> Speculating about an event –
> Forming and testing a hypothesis –
> Presenting the results of an experiment in tables and diagrams –
> Making up a story; and reading it –
> Play-acting –
> Singing catches –
> Guessing riddles –
> Making a joke; telling it –
> Solving a problem in practical arithmetic –
> Translating from one language into another –
> Asking, thanking, cursing, greeting, praying.' *(ibid.)*

The listed games, it might be noted, do include speech acts proper (giving orders, reporting an event, asking, thanking . . .), but extend quite beyond the illocutionary sphere to embrace modes of verbal play

(play-acting, guessing riddles), forms of language-use with specific points of departure or arrival (describing the appearance of an object, forming and testing a hypothesis, presenting the results . . .), and most significant, linguistic activities that directly entail *non*-verbal actions (constructing an object from a description . . .). It is this 'mixed' semiotic character of Wittgenstein's language-games that makes them particularly inviting to the student of drama. 'Words', writes Anthony Kenny, paraphrasing Wittgenstein himself, 'cannot be understood outside the context of the non-linguistic human activities into which the use of the language is interwoven: the words plus their behavioural surroundings make up the language-game' (1973: 14). Nowhere is this truer than in the case of dramatic discourse, which is always destined, if not on the page then at least potentially on the stage, to interact with its physical and behavioural surroundings, and especially with the body and its movements, in the production of meaning. Indeed, the dramatic representation itself is an extreme and large-scale instance of a communicative event in which words cannot be understood outside 'the context of the non-linguistic human activities' of which they are part. The language of Shakespearean comedy in particular always presupposes the theatrical activity or 'form of life' in which it is bound to participate.

It is for these reasons – because of its flexibility and multiformity, because of its mixed semiotic status, because of its dependence on a physical and behavioural context – that Wittgenstein's notion of the language-game has been adopted here as the most promising descriptive category for the study of Shakespeare's discourse. Each of the chapters that follow will be dedicated to exploring one of the main contexts or 'forms of life' in which the comedies' eminently multiform verbal activities are defined. It might therefore be useful at this point to review, in Wittgensteinian fashion, some of the more recurrent language-games in Shakespearean comedy, grouped here into the five main areas that this book's five chapters will investigate.

### (1) Theatrical games

The first class of linguistic activities in the plays – let us christen them 'theatrical' games – has to do with the very potential of Shakespeare's language for participating in the stage performance. Which is to say that while Shakespeare's discourse at all its levels is obviously destined to contribute to the theatrical representation, there are specific uses of language in the comedies that very powerfully presuppose the physical, vocal, gestural and scenic conditions of their stage delivery. These aspects of verbal structure are particularly responsible for the irresistible performability of the texts. They include:

> Indicating objects, verbally with possible accompanying gestures ('One can refer to an object when speaking', observes Wittgenstein, 'by pointing to it. Here pointing is part of the language-game', 1953: 669) –
> Describing objects presumably present on stage –
> Displaying objects, with accompanying verbal comments –
> Using and referring to stage properties –
> Requesting or indicating verbally a particular movement –
> Employing a particular pitch, volume or intonational colouring of the voice –
> Employing particular idiosyncrasies of pronunciation –
> Putting on stage performances (within the drama), etc.

This particularly marked allegiance of dramatic discourse to the stage context is the subject of the first chapter ('Performances').

### (2) World-creating games

The second of 'the kinds of case where we say that a game is played according to a definite rule (or rules)' (Wittgenstein 1953: § 54) brings into play not the 'real', if potential, physical context of the stage but the represented fictional context of the dramatic world. Whatever its allegiance to the actors and their theatrical performance, the language of the plays is in the first instance bound to the dramatic speakers and their universe: the realm, say, of Ephesus, with its pre-dramatic history, its changing spatial and temporal circumstances, its set of inhabitants and their characteristics, its set of fictional events, etc. Now as in the case of 'theatrical' games, it is of course true that the discourse of the comedies as a whole participates in the creation of the dramatic fiction. But again there are a number of uses of language – particularly those of an expository and 'referential' kind – that have an especially important role in setting up the dramatic world. These linguistic functions might be baptized, borrowing a term from logic and linguistics (see McCawley 1978), 'world-creating' games. They comprehend, among others:

> Expounding, directly or indirectly, the facts and antefacts of the drama –
> Referring to oneself as speaker (as 'I') –
> Referring to the addressee (as 'you') –
> Referring to third persons (as 'he'/'they') –

13

Naming oneself, the addressee, third persons, etc. –
Referring to moments in time –
Referring to space and place –
Referring to the physical qualities of the dramatic world –
Picking up references made by others –
Misunderstanding references made by others –
Predicating the attributes of an individual ('Shylock *the Jew*') –
Speculating, hypothesizing, supposing, predicting about the world (i.e. creating 'possible' worlds) –
Inventing, fabricating or lying about individuals, events, properties, etc.

The world-creating duties of the dialogue, which are brought to particular prominence in *The Comedy of Errors*, in *Love's Labour's Lost* and in *As You Like It*, are the main concern of chapter two ('Universes').

### (3) Semantic games

The business of producing meaning, or as it were of making sense, is the source not only of the plays' very comprehensibility but also of a good part of their comic and theatrical vitality. Verbal doings that bring directly into force the sense and meanings of words and other units are among the most potent modes of linguistic 'self-activity' in Shakespearean comedy. This group of language-games, which are explored in chapter three ('Signs') may be generically labelled, *faute de mieux*, 'semantic'. They concern in general the nature and make-up of the linguistic sign, its relationship with the extra-linguistic world and the sense relationships *between* signs. The most significant (in more senses than one) are:

Taking the sign for the object –
Taking the sign as the direct effect of the object –
Taking the name as the natural counterpart of its bearer –
Taking the common name as a proper name –
Taking the sign as a magical force over the world –
Taking the proper name as a common noun –
Bringing together unrelated words with identical sounds –
Bringing together unrelated words with closely similar sounds –
Using the word as empty sound, etc.

14

*(4) Pragmatic games*

Within the fictional world itself the dramatic *personae* are taken to be directly engaged in talk. This, of course, is the chief institutional difference between drama and narrative: the dramatic fiction is not so much narrated as *conversed*. It is this founding principle of dramatic narrative – what we might term the conversation fiction – that allows the plot of the play to unfold as a series of direct speech acts rather than as an external reporting or narrating of acts (see discussion above, p. 6. As a consequence, much of the dramatic and comic energy of the plays is invested in the maintenance of the fictional conversational exchange, involving alternating turns at talking and various forms of illocutionary-perlocutionary interaction within a series of dynamic speaking situations. These conversational and interactional functions, which are the subject of the fourth chapter ('Acts'), can best be termed 'pragmatic' games. Some of the most important are:

Requesting a turn at talk –
Granting, inviting, prompting a turn at talk –
Taking an uninvited or unwanted turn at talk –
Denying or interrupting another's turn –
'Hogging' the conversational floor –
Performing an illocutionary act –
Performing a perlocutionary act –
Failing to achieve a perlocutionary act (failing to persuade, etc.) –
Performing an 'unhappy' speech act (insincere, unauthorized, etc.) –
Failing to make one's illocutionary intentions understood (failing to achieve 'uptake') –
Performing an illocutionary sequel (responding appropriately) –
Failing to perform an illocutionary sequel –
Performing a perlocutionary sequel (obeying a command, etc.) –
Predicting a future speech act –
Hypothesizing about possible speech acts, etc.

*(5) Figural games*

Rhetorical figures have long been a staple of the literary critical industry in its Shakespearean branch. More often than not, however, figural devices have attracted critical attention either as formal literary-stylistic options (in a word, as aspects of diction), or alternatively as vehicles for thematic motifs ('imagery'). But it is possible – as chapter five ('Figures') aims to demonstrate – to see the figure as a strategic *move* within the discursive, dramatic and even theatrical make-up of the comedy. And indeed Renaissance rhetoricians conceived of the figures precisely as persuasive *doings* with words. Review the multiplicity of Shakespeare's figural games in the following examples, and in others:

> Repeating the initial word or phrase of verses or sentences ('anaphora') –
> Repeating the final word or phrase of verses or sentences ('epistrophe') –
> Altering customary word order ('hyperbaton') –
> Altering logical clause order ('hysteron proteron') –
> Interrupting one's speech and changing its direction ('parenthesis') –
> Placing epithets in crescendo ('climax') –
> Reversing the order of the foregoing sentence or phrase ('chiasmus') –
> Repeating initial phonemes ('alliteration') –
> Adding a sound to the end of the word ('paragoge') –
> Adding a sound to the beginning of a word ('prosthesis') –
> Adding a sound to the middle of a word ('epenthesis') –
> Omitting a sound from the beginning, middle or end of a word ('apostrophus') –
> Substituting one phoneme for another within a word ('antisthecon') –
> Accumulating epithets ('congeries') –
> Varying synonymous terms ('synonymia') –
> Coining (synonymous) neologisms –
> Joining words into compounds –
> Omitting words from a sentence ('ellipsis') –
> Substituting a foreign word for a native one ('soriasmus') –
> Substituting an archaic term for a current one –
> Citing proverbial expressions ('paroemia') –
> Breaking up or paraphrasing proverbial expressions –
> Taking A as B ('metaphor') –
> Taking A as standing for B ('metonymy') –
> Taking A as the whole of which it is part ('synecdoche') –
> Comparing A to B ('simile') –
> Giving an unfaithful description, known to be unfaithful, of A ('metalogisms': hyperbole, irony, etc.)

This, then, is the conceptual point of departure for the present study: the notion that the various levels of language in the comedies are directly 'activated' as specific dramatic and comic doings rather than remaining inert elements of verbal structure. Now of course, every godfather, as Berowne complains in *Love's Labour's Lost*, can give a name, and other earthly godfathers may well wish to suggest alternative names, or offer additional ones, or eliminate some of the names proposed here, for Shakespeare's linguistic games. There is an inevitable degree of arbitrariness in the naming and in the groupings, especially since the very conception of the language-game, as we have seen, supposes its flexibility and mutability: the name of the game, in Wittgenstein's terms, 'is not something fixed'.

And by the same token – by virtue, that is, of their multiform character – it is evident that any number of language-games can be played *simultaneously* in the plays. Wittgenstein's observation that 'There are ... countless kinds of use of what we call "symbols", "words", "sentences"' can be taken in precisely this sense. 'One kind of sentence', as Anthony Kenny says in commenting on this passage, 'may have more than one use' (1973: 166). Take, as one more or less casual example among an almost limitless set, Eglamour's brief time-and-place-setting description which opens the fifth act of *The Two Gentlemen of Verona*:

> The sun begins to gild the western sky,
> And now it is about the very hour
> That Silvia at fair Patrick's cell should meet me.

In 'theatrical' terms, Eglamour's description provides pseudo-visual information which may or may not be confirmed by non-verbal (e.g. scenographic) means on stage; its 'pragmatic' (illocutionary) force is that of a descriptive statement; at a 'world-creating' level it provides essential spatio-temporal and expository narrative details (the time, the dramatic location, the imminence of Silvia's arrival, etc.); figurally, the speech employs hyperbolic metaphor ('gild'); and 'semantically' – and this may be the most important, if not the most immediately evident, aspect of the speech – it represents a certain 'pastoral' mode of description that bears particular implications for the relationship between language and the natural landscape (see pp. 136–40 below).

Now this 'vertical' co-operation of different forms of language-use (the co-existence of different 'kinds of sentence') is not especially problematic in itself. We are quite used to doing several things at once in our normal talk. But it does raise the question, a question of vital importance here, of the dominance of a particular linguistic level. How are we – as auditors, or as critics – to know what is 'really' being done with words, or to know the name of the game that is really being played at a given point in a given play? What is it, in other words, that foregrounds (i.e. attracts our attention to) one game in progress, be it theatrical or world-creating or semantic or pragmatic or figural, rather than another?

## (v) FRAMES FOR THE GAMES

One answer to these questions is that many of Shakespeare's language-games mark themselves out by their own unmistakable dramatic or comic conspicuousness, a conspicuousness due as a rule to one of three factors:

*Heightening.* Verbal activities that would normally be more or less 'transparent', being the flour-and-water ingredients of all our linguistic doings, may be brought to audience attention as happenings in their own right when performed in an exaggerated, or insistent or burlesque or otherwise de-automatizing fashion. Phonetic, syntactic or referential functions (Austin's 'locutionary' acts) may be put on display in themselves if and when they become sufficiently obtrusive. Holofernes's already quoted 'preyful princess' performance, foregrounding the phonetic act, is a good instance. But much the same heightening procedure is at work in all 'figural' games of a phonetic or syntactic kind: compare the frequent anaphora of *The Two Gentlemen of Verona* with its insistent lexical iterations ('Some to the wars . . . /Some, to discover islands . . . /Some, to the studious universities', see p. 246 below). Similarly, in *The Taming of the Shrew* the act of referring comes to dominate over – or, as it were, tame – other functions in Petruchio's obstinate misnaming of the world:

> Good Lord, how bright and goodly shines the moon! . . .
> I say it is the moon that shines so bright . . .
> It shall be moon, or star, or what I list . . . (4. 5. 2ff.; see p. 96 below)

Here underlining, or overemphasizing, is the key.

*Suspension.* At an extreme of obtrusiveness, a given game may mark itself out by virtually *blocking off* altogether other forms of dramatic or semantic information. Certain kinds of more or less nonsensical *lazzi*, as in *Twelfth Night* ('I did impeticos thy gratillity'); malapropistic slips (Mistress Quickly's 'She's as fartuous a civil wife . . .'); phonetic aberrations (Caius's 'do not tell-a me dat . . .' in *The Merry Wives of Windsor*); vertiginous code-switching (the pedants' bursts of bad Latin in *Love's Labour's Lost*); gratuitous neologizing (Armado's 'excrement'

18

for 'moustache' in the same play); spells of manic punning (the ladies' 'light heart . . . more light . . . mar the light . . . light wench' display in the same comedy); speaking in invented languages (the 'throca movousos, cargo, cargo, cargo' of *All's Well that Ends Well*) or in emptily modish jargon (Nym's obsessive 'humours' in *The Merry Wives*): these are all uses and abuses of language that tend to banish, or at least relegate to the margins, mere conceptual or illocutionary or dramatic content. The main information conveyed by the game to the audience is the *playing* itself.

*Connotation.* Modes of discourse that powerfully connote their own allegiance to a particular stylistic or cultural origin will usually come to advertise the game-type to which they belong. Examples are proverb-quoting (especially of biblical, euphuistic or other strongly recognizable sayings); emblem-citing; the use of 'magical' verbal formulae or practices; the adoption of a 'pastoral' style of description (as in the Eglamour passage above); the performance of literary burlesques (e.g. the 'Thisbe, the flowers of odious savours sweet' of *A Midsummer Night's Dream*), and so on.

But there are also more direct ways in which the active roles of discourse in Shakespearean comedy are brought to notice. One of the most striking and significant, if least studied, aspects of Shakespeare's dramaturgy is the frequency with which attention is called explicitly to the verbal goings-on. This is no longer a question simply of conspicuous uses of language but of overt commentary on those uses within the plays themselves. Frames, as it were, are placed around the games. A very considerable part of the verbal business in all the comedies is dedicated not so much to an immediate 'doing things' with words as to the indicating, defining or disputing what is being or has been or is about to be done. Direct commentary of this kind offers language itself as the proper object of dramatic or comic interest. This crucial aspect of Shakespeare's poetics merits the most serious critical consideration.

Language used to comment directly on language itself is generally know as *metalanguage* ('In order to speak *about* any *object language* . . . we need a *metalanguage*', Carnap 1947: 4), 'meta' having here the Greek sense of a secondary or parasitic 'going beyond'. And by analogy, a use of language which in turn frames, or 'goes beyond', language *in use* can be termed *metadiscourse*. The extraordinary metadiscursive density of Shakespeare's comedies is one of the chief sources of their formidable rhetorical complexity and formal self-awareness. To the multiplicity of games corresponds a multiplicity of frames. Discourse at all its levels in the plays may be taken up as urgent dramatic issue or as direct comic butt. Thus it is possible to classify the 'meta' or framing functions of

Shakespeare's language precisely in terms of the types of language-game taken as object, thus following the grouping of games outlined above (pp. 12–16):

### (1) Theatrical and dramatic frames

The term 'metatheatre' was coined by Lionel Abel (1963) to indicate all modes of theatrical self-consciousness in the drama. 'External' presentational devices – the induction to *The Taming of The Shrew* and the epilogues to *A Midsummer Night's Dream, As You Like It* and *All's Well that Ends Well* – and 'internal' theatrical displays, such as the Worthies' parade in *Love's Labour's Lost* and the Mechanicals' tragic performance in *A Midsummer Night's Dream*, represent the fullest and most conventional means of framing the theatrical game at large. Most relevant here are the theatrical functions of language that it includes: e.g. the relations between language and the actors' bodies or stage props in the Mechanicals' representation. There are in addition, however, numerous moments within the main drama proper, in *Love's Labour's Lost* and *Twelfth Night* especially, in which the theatricality of the verbal proceedings is explicitly vaunted, toyed with or otherwise gone beyond.

Closely related in function is the meta*dramatic* framing of language (on Shakespearean 'metadrama' in general, see Calderwood 1969, 1979). Often enough the same external and internal devices framing theatrical games bring to consciousness also the verbal artifices and rhetorical rules of the comic drama, as with the modes of exposition cruelly exposed, as it were, in the Worthies fiasco (see pp. 44–6). But again the specifically dramatic or dramaturgic self-awareness of discourse in the comedies extends also to the language of the main play in progress, as the dénouement of *Love's Labour's Lost* demonstrates. (On theatrical and dramatic frames, see chapter one.)

### (2) World-creating frames

The expository and 'referential' construction of the dramatic universe and its inhabitants is subject to, or object of, a deal of earnest, ironic or burlesque commentary. The dramatic reference act – 'something', as Rosalind puts it in *As You Like It*, 'that hath a reference to my state' – is game in more senses for the frame (see chapter two).

### (3) Semantic frames

Biondello's complaint against his master in *The Taming of the Shrew*,

'But he has left me here behind to expound the meaning or morals of his signs and tokens' (4. 4. 76–7), might be the insignia for much of what is done and said about, rather than directly with, words in the comedies. An impressively dense and intense concern with meaning and its production, with the status of the linguistic sign, and with the relationship of language to the world, marks the entire comic canon, although it receives its most evident and extensive comic-dramatic treatment in *Love's Labour's Lost* (chapter three).

## (4) Pragmatic frames

Jürgen Habermas observes (1970) that human communication is made possible only by the simultaneous operation of *meta*communication, which serves to keep the communicative exchange going, to control the passage of information, to repair damages etc. (on 'metacommunicative messages' see also Bateson 1972). Shakespeare exploits such semiotic check-ups to the full for their dramatizing and ironizing potential. Pragmatic or metacommunicational framing in the plays takes as objects both the interactional force of discourse itself (the kinds of speech act performed, or aborted) and the fictional communicative exchange at large: the speaking situation and its elements, the progress of the conversation etc. (chapter four).

## (5) Figural frames

It is scarcely surprising, given the rhetorical consciousness of the Elizabethan age, that figural devices are among the favourite objects of Shakespearean commentary. Holofernes's meta-rhetorical question 'What is the figure? What is the figure?' is not, in this sense, an isolated moment of pedagogic pedantry.

## (VI) SHAKESPEARE AND THE ELIZABETHAN UNIVERSE OF DISCOURSE

It is, then, the game-frame dialectic, exploiting language as activity and as object, that lends Shakespearean comedy much of its discursive momentum and depth. And it is this same dialectic that is the object of this study and *its* metalanguage. Now for as long as the discussion of Shakespeare's discourse and metadiscourse is limited to formal mechanisms, the accusation might well arise that such an approach fatally reduces the plays to a rarefied playing with rhetorical mirrors. Discourse, that is, can only fulfil the double role of game and frame, or of 'means' and 'theme', by emptying the play of all its dramatic-thematic content and interest. This accusation has indeed already been voiced by at least one Shakespearean critic, Neal Goldstein, in his summary dismissal of certain 'linguistic' – or, better, metalinguistic – readings of the comedies, especially *Love's Labour's Lost:* 'The fact that language cannot play this dual role without a consequent warping of the play's thematic concerns is ... too obvious to warrant correction' (1974: 335-6). Goldstein's impatience at the verbal means/verbal theme coupling is shared by Peter Phialas with reference to the same comedy: 'Language ... is not the theme of *Love's Labour's Lost* any more than it is the theme of *Twelfth Night* or *As You Like It*' (1966: 84).

One answer to such an objection is that the other two comedies mentioned by Phialas do indeed have linguistic themes, among others: i.e. they are more directly concerned with language than he acknowledges. But the issue is obviously broader than this, and raises the question of whether it is possible to elect the 'means' itself as 'theme' without thereby creating a disastrous dramaturgic short-circuit. This possibility can be fruitfully discussed only with reference to the 'thematic' potential of discourse itself within Elizabethan culture, which brings us back to the historical framework adopted here.

Each of the areas of Renaissance linguistic or metalinguistic enquiry indicated above (pp. 1–2) – the religious, the geographical, the philosophical, the educational, the national-political, the artistic, etc. – is marked by passionately and at times violently conflicting views as to the make-up and proper ends of language itself. It is in this powerfully controversial nature of the linguistic 'object' that Shakespeare's dramatization or thematization of discourse finds its non-formal correlatives. If the word in its very make-up, in its God-given or man-made origins, in its representational powers and in its social and ethical duties is the single most problematic and far-reaching question of the period, then its status as dramatic and comic topic is anything but paradoxical. In this sense the exploration of linguistic concerns in the comedies, far from representing a formalistic involution, can be seen as a powerful response to the most important epistemological crisis of the Elizabethan age.

For this reason frequent and at times extensive reference will be made, in the discussion that follows of the game-frame play of Shakespeare's discourse, to Renaissance theories of language and language-use: in particular to conceptions of the linguistic sign (chapter three); to Renaissance 'conversation' rules and ethical 'speech-act' models (chapter four); to controversies over the rhetorical figure, and especially the figurality of theatre itself (chapter five). In this fashion the use here of contemporary modes of linguistic analysis with its particular technical metalanguage – borrowed eclectically from linguistics, semiotics, literary theory, sociology of language and the philosophy of language – is married with or, better, filtered through Renaissance models and Renaissance terminology. And in order to avoid undue confusion or mystification *à la* Holofernes, a glossary is provided at the end of this mixed feast of languages (pp. 309–16), bringing together the respective metalinguistic vocabularies of both periods.

## (VII) THE SHAKESPEAREAN BAROQUE: LANGUAGE 'EN ABYME'

But there is a further historical dimension to Shakespeare's verbal self-mirroring, a dimension that is not so much theoretical as cultural and artistic. Formal self-reflection is one of the dominant features of baroque art in all its forms, and there is no question that the poetics of Shakespearean comedy, in its pursuit of structural and rhetorical complexity, is governed by the spirit of the baroque. The pleasures of Shakespeare's eminently self-interrogating dramatic art are in this respect the same pleasures derived from the mirroring games of the visual and other art forms of the period – pleasures that André Gide reflects upon in a happily neologistic moment in the *Journal*:

> What I like in a work of art is when one finds the very subject of the work transposed, with specific reference to the characters in it . . . Thus, in certain paintings by Memling or by Quentin Metzys a small convex dark mirror reflects on its own the interior of the room where the painted scene occurs . . . Then, indeed, in literature, in *Hamlet*, the scene of the play; and in a lot of other theatre plays as well. (quoted in Kowzan 1976: 67)

In the attempt to find an adequate label for this extremely recurrent phenomenon, typical of the baroque in general, Gide turns to heraldry: '[one can] compare it to a coat of arms where one image places a second one in a *subjugated* position (*en abyme*)' (*ibid.*). Gide's fortunate, and usefully generic, notion of the *mise en abyme* – literally the placing within the central blazon of the coat of arms elements of the outer structure – includes in practice all modes of self-mirroring, self-commentary, texts-within-texts, structures-within-structures, and Russian-doll effects in general. And it can be usefully extended, without undue distortion, to the game-framing of Shakespearean comedy. What the plays offer, in effect, is language placed (structurally, thematically, theatrically) *en abyme*.

Shakespeare's particular linguistic or metalinguistic version of the

23

baroque is, of course, related to a number of Elizabethan comedies which similarly present language in the central thematic 'blazon': not only such academic logomachies as Tomkis's *Lingua* or the *Parnassus* plays but structurally sophisticated linguistic satires like Jonson's *Every Man In / Out of His Humour*. Shakespeare's formal contribution to this tradition is undoubtedly the range and vitality of his *abyme* techniques – techniques that call into play the two closely related principles of recursion (or embedding) and reflexivity. Since these principles are so crucial to the poetics of Shakespearean discourse, it is worth reviewing rapidly their most recurrent forms in the plays.

### (1) Modes of recursion

Recursion in grammar is the principle that allows complex syntactic structures to be built up: phrases embedded within phrases within indefinitely extendible and hierarchically organized sentences ('This is the cat that killed the rat that ate the malt . . .'; see Lyons 1977: 388f.; Hofstadter 1979: 127ff.). Analogously, dramatic discourse achieves rhetorical or semiotic complexity through the embedding of different kinds of discursive and textual units: games nesting in other (framing) games in a potentially infinite regressive series.

### (a) Embedded events

The emblematic instance of the recursive and hierarchical framing of speech events in the comedies is the 'overspying' scene in *Love's Labour's Lost* (4.3), in which each of the aristocratic male lovers betrays himself by reading a love poem to his inamorata in the unacknowledged presence of one or more of his fellows. The framing hierarchy in question can be represented graphically as a simple system of nested boxes:

(Berowne overhears the other three, Navarre two, Longaville only Dumain and Dumain, of course, nobody). This 'structural' or situational scheme is translated into direct metadiscursive frames as each overspier comes forward – in reverse order – to castigate his inferior in the hierarchy. Thus Longaville to Dumain: 'I should blush, I know, / To be o'erheard and taken napping so'; Navarre, sarcastically, to Longaville: 'as his your case is such / You chide at him, offending twice as much . . . Longaville/Did never sonnet for her sake compile'; and finally (or apparently so) Berowne to Navarre: 'Now step I forth to whip hypocrisy / . . . what grace hast thou, to reprove / These worms for loving, that art most in love'. Each framing comment (each act of reproval), it might be noted, is in its turn framed or picked up. The scene ends with the complete overthrowing of the hierarchy when Berowne himself is exposed before all three colleagues (he is demoted, as it were, to the most internal box) and has in turn to suffer their comments ('What! did these rent lines show some love of thine?').

### (b) Embedded conversations

Overhearing and eavesdropping episodes may place *en abyme* entire speaking situations and exchanges, most conspicuously of course in *Much Ado about Nothing*, where the frame – Beatrice's and Benedick's respective acts of 'accidental' listening – becomes, so to speak, the main game (see pp. 180–2 below). Similarly, although in quite unsimilar fashion, the reporting of conversational exchanges, true or fabricated, 'on-stage' or 'off-' (pp. 183–5 below).

### (c) Embedded speech acts

Reports of illocutions and perlocutions performed in an earlier dramatic or extra-dramatic exchange (pp. 205–7).

### (d) Embedded styles

Description (imitation, illustration, anatomy) by one speaker of another's style of speech (or *idiolect*) (pp. 238–41).

### (e) Embedded texts

Most of the comedies include at least one internal 'textual' event – the reading of a poem, say, or of a letter – placed in a 'boxed' position within the main text and within the main performance, and generally accompanied either by metadiscursive commentary on the text itself ('soft! here follows prose', *Twelfth Night* 2. 5. 142; 'This is the very false gallop of verses', *As You Like It* 3. 2. 111; 'Here are only numbers ratified', *Love's Labour's Lost* 4. 2. 116–17) or by metacommunicative framing of the recital, as a special 'bracketed-off' event ('You find not the apostrophus, and so miss the accent', *Love's Labour's Lost* 4. 2. 115–16; I would be loath to cast away my speech', *Twelfth Night* 1. 5. 173–5; 'I pray you mar no more of my verses with reading them ill-favouredly', *As You Like It* 3. 2. 257–8).

Particular weight attaches, in *Love's Labour's Lost* especially, to the recited letter, which becomes one of the comedy's more recurrent discursive happenings. It would be mistaken to see this epistolary density as a necessarily 'literary' concession. The dramatic and theatrical potential of the letter lies first in its material stage presence as object of exchange (note the business, in *Love's Labour's Lost*, over finding, misreading and deciphering the epistles, and the jokes on ink, paper, calligraphy, etc.); then in the infinite possibilities of its interruption, interpretation, effects on the present listeners, especially if directly referred to (Costard's 'Me? . . . Still me?', see pp. 77–8); and, at a comic-narrative level, in the trouble that the letter may provoke as a 'detached' communicative vehicle perfectly capable of going astray (which is what seals the fate of Berowne), and thus epitomizing all the 'pragmatic' problems of miscommunication and misinterpretation on which Shakespearean comedy draws for a good deal of its comic vitality (see chapter four; on the theatricality of Armado's first letter see pp. 251–2).

### (f) Intertextual debts

An intimately related but quite distinct mode of textual embedding has to do not with original 'internal' compositions but with other ('external' but imported) literary or dramatic or non-fictional texts and text-fragments. This more or less overt kind of intertextuality may take any of five main forms in Shakespeare:

(i) *Quotation.* Direct quoting within the plays is limited in frequency and still more in extension. A certain 'explicit' intertextual licence is permitted to the pedants in *Love's Labour's Lost* as part of the pedagogic show: Holofernes's '*Facile precor gelida quando pecus omne sub imbra Ruminat*, and so forth', duly marked out by a schoolmasterly acknowledgment ('Ah! good old Mantuan') being the most obtrusive instance (4. 2. 90–1). A species of 'false' quotation is offered in *The Two Gentlemen of Verona* as direct borrowing, signalled by Proteus's and Valentine's 'writers say' (1. 1. 42, 45): the 'writers' are perfectly identifiable (George Pettie and John Lyly), but the attributed text-fragments prove in fact to be 'euphuistic' proverbs that vary somewhat from their sources ('as in the sweetest bud . . .'; see pp. 287–9 below).

The one recurrently quoted – and paraphrased – extra-textual text is, naturally, the Bible, for example, anachronistically, in Ephesus: 'it is written, they appear to men like angels of light' (*The Comedy of Errors* 4. 3. 53ff.; see p. 286 on the 'proverbial' status of this quotation).

*(ii) Allusion*. More common is the passing literary reference, which may have the role of acknowledging, as it were, certain stylistic or dramaturgic or narrative allegiances, as in Valentine's 'some shallow story of deep love, / How young Leander cross'd the Hellespont' (*The Two Gentlemen of Verona* 1. 1. 21–2), which, despite the alluder's scornful terms, does suggest one of the 'romantic' models for the scene and for Proteus's amorous style; or the parade of literary lovers produced by Lorenzo and Jessica as their direct antecedents in love ('In such a night/Did Thisbe fearfully o'ertrip', etc., *The Merchant of Venice* 5. 1. 6–7). Or it may have the purpose of lending supposed *auctoritas* to the performing of a particular game, as in Armado's citing – as a pre-text for his love and for his love-letter ('More authority, dear boy') – of the 'ballad . . . of the King and the Beggar' (*Love's Labour's Lost* 1. 2. 102–3), or Feste's mystifying allusive back-up to a piece of 'proverbial' nonsense ('for as the old hermit of Prague . . . very wittily said to a niece of King Gorboduc, "That that is, is"', see p. 278). Or it may simply have the effect of suggesting the alluder's bookish pretensions: Slender's longing for Surrey, perhaps as a source of quotation itself ('I had rather than forty shillings I had my book of Songs and Sonnets here', 1. 1. 179–80), or Holofernes's spurious point of comparison in his deprecation of Berowne's sonnet ('Ovidius Naso was the man', 4. 2. 118ff.). 'The allusion', claims the pedant himself optimistically, 'holds in the exchange' (4. 2. 40).

*(iii) Parody*. As a mode of placing an 'alien' text *en abyme*, parody lies halfway between direct (if unacknowledged) quotation and indirect (i.e. implicit) commentary, since the heightening of stylistic features that renders the parodied source at once recognizable and ridiculous is in itself, of course, a kind of critical statement. Touchstone has to exaggerate only slightly the pseudo-taxonomic fastidiousness of the duelling-etiquette manual *à la* William Segar (with a probable glance, also, at the 'Englished' figural typology *à la* Puttenham, see p. 241) to win the critical Jaques's admiration for his satirical virtuosity ('this is called the Quip Modest . . . that is called the Reply Churlish', etc.: '*Jaq*. Is not this a rare fellow my Lord?', 5. 4). The stylistic, and especially prosodic, exaggeration in Bottom's 'The raging rocks, / And shivering shocks / Shall break the locks' performance is less restrained, although the parodied text itself (almost certainly, as W. J. Rolfe first noted (1877 ed. of play), and as Bottom's 'This is Ercles' vein' comment suggests, John Studley's translation (1581) of Seneca's *Hercules Octaeus*) has an almost self-burlesquing thumping and hyperbolic grotesqueness of its

own ('The roaring rocks have quaking stirred, / And none thereat have pushed; / Hell's gloomy gates I have brast ope'; see note to Arden edition).

*(iv) Hypertextual signals.* Gérard Genette (1982) introduces the category of the 'hypertext' to characterize any 'secondary' text that transforms – derives from, adapts, dramatizes, etc. – a source or *hypo*text. None of the cases within the comic canon of extensive narrative one-to-one or one-from-one derivation makes direct acknowledgment, even in the title, of its debt, but within the texts of various of the comedies certain hypertextual verbal (as opposed to narrative) clues are discernible to a reader or spectator with a fresh knowledge of the source. These clues take the form of:

*Discursive borrowings. The Two Gentlemen of Verona* is so full of verbal echoes from its main source (Bartholomew Yong's translation of Montemayor's *Diana*) as virtually to declare its own (partial) 'secondary' status: Proteus's 'living sluggardis'd at home' in the play's opening lines (1. 1. 7: compare Yong's 'spende his youth idly at home'); Julia's 'how now, minion?' (1. 2. 88: 'an impudent and bold minion'); Lucia's 'she makes it strange' (1. 2. 103: 'in making the matter strange'), etc.

*Contextualized allusion.* Lucentio, in the final act of *The Taming of the Shrew*, announces to Baptista his secret marriage to Bianca, revealing to him at the same time the disguises and subterfuges of which the 'Bianca' plot has been composed:

> That have by marriage made thy daughter mine,
> While counterfeit *supposes* blear'd thine eyne.
>
> (5. 1. 106–7, my italics)

Lucentio's announcement is a confession not only of the deviousness of his means, but – in a more or less occult fashion within the dialogic context – of the very derivation of the secondary plot (in which he participates) and its complications. The prologue to the source, Gascoigne's Ariostan *Supposes*, expounds the sense of the titular key term: 'But understand, this our suppose is nothing else but a mistaking or imagination of one thing for another. For you shall see the master supposed for the servant, the servant for the master', an explanation that is taken for read in Lucentio's cryptic reference.

*Burlesque.* Probably the heaviest narrative dependence in the canon is the debt – for its *fabula* and for a good part of the plot – of *As You Like It* towards Lodge's *Rosalynd*. But this dependence emerges most powerfully – apart from occasional echoes – in the travestying maltreatment, in the comedy's opening act, of the narrative source and of its very narrativity; namely in Le Beau's attempt to narrate, *à la*

Lodge, the background events to the wrestling match (1. 2. 84ff.).
Lodge's narrative propositions ('taking his forest bill on his neck, he
trudgeth in all haste') become fair game for the witty 'pick-up' game:

| | |
|---|---|
| *Le Beau.* | Three proper young men, of excellent growth and presence – |
| *Ros.* | With bills on their necks: 'Be it known unto all men by these presents'. (1. 2. 111–14) |

(Rosalind squeezes two senses out of 'bill', in addition to Lodge's
innocuous hedging tool: 'label' and 'legal bill', senses which quite
destroy the quaintly 'rural' character of the source scene. On this
ungrateful abusing of the hypotext, see pp. 73–5 below.)

*(v) Interdiscursive links.* A distinction has to be drawn between
intertextual allegiances proper and what Cesare Segre (1982) usefully
baptizes as inter*discursive* relations; regarding, that is, those discourse
units which, without necessarily having a single definable 'origin',
come to have a 'shared' trans-textual life of their own. Examples are
certain kinds of polygenetic proverb, or expressions that evoke a
particular textual tradition: Navarre's 'wonder of the world' (*Love's
Labour's Lost* 1. 1. 12), with its 'Hermetic' pedigree, for example (see
pp. 148–51 below). The recognition of such links depends, naturally, on
familiarity with the cultural context within which the play itself is
broadly 'framed': a form of 'historical' competence to which the
Shakespearean critic, among others, presumably aspires.

### (g) 'Mal mise': misframing

Virtually all of the strategies discussed so far presuppose a more or less
perfect harmony or symmetry between frame and game: what is said or
implied about language really does correspond with what is being done
with it. Yet one of the more productive sources of verbal comedy – or
better, verbal farce – in Shakespeare is precisely the business of getting
it all wrong: errors in framing that set up a comic divide between meta-
and object languages (placing language not so much *en abyme* as *en
abysse*). An entire scene of *The Merry Wives of Windsor* (4.1) is
structured on Mistress Quickly's grotesque misreading of Evans's Latin
quiz as a series of straightforward utterances in the Queen's English:

| | |
|---|---|
| *Evans.* | What is 'fair', William? |
| *Will.* | Pulcher. |
| *Quick.* | Polecats? There are fairer things than polecats, sure. |
| *Evans.* | You are a very simplicity 'oman. (27ff.) |

The running squabble that breaks out between Evans and Mistress
Quickly around William's efforts is a ludicrous version of what the
sociologist Erving Goffman calls the 'frame dispute', in which 'the

parties with opposing versions may openly dispute with each other on how to define what has been or is happening' (1974: 322). All too clearly the mis-framing itself (product of a particular species of linguistic *incompetence*), together with the angry 'corrective' reactions it provokes, takes over altogether from the rather colourless embedded happening (the dull lesson) as the main dramatic event.

### (h) Metalinguistic reflection

In the more 'philosophical' moments of certain comedies (especially the 'dark' ones), the elected object of commentary ceases to be a particular use or unit of language and becomes, so to speak, language at large: words, i.e., in their very phenomenal or social or ethical nature, as in Isabella's lament on the politically abusable power of speech ('O perilous mouths, / That bear in them one and the self-same tongue', *Measure for Measure* 2. 4. 171ff.), which lexicalizes this play's central concern with the verbal *ethos* of the public figure (see pp. 220–3 below).

### (2) Modes of reflexivity

'One of the most characteristic features of natural languages', writes John Lyons (1977: 5) '. . . is their capacity for referring to, or describing themselves. The term we will employ for this feature, or property, of language, is reflexivity. Language can be turned back on itself, as it were.' In the sentences ' "William" is very common' and ' "Shakespeare" is disyllabic', the names are employed not referentially but reflexively or, according to a well-established distinction, they are not directly *'used'* but *'mentioned'* or referred to: it is 'William' as a proper name and 'Shakespeare' as a phonetic structure, not an individual or individuals named William and Shakespeare, that are brought into play.

### (a) The Shakespearean mention

Reflexive (citational) 'mentions' of this kind appear recurrently in the plays as one of the most direct means of bracketing off language – usually single words or brief stretches of discourse – as object of commentary. The effect is often that of a dramatic or ironic underlining of the denotative or connotative force of a particular lexical item or phrase: ' "Was" is not "is" ', notes Celia, commenting on Orlando's possible apostasy in love (*As You Like It* 3. 4. 27), while Bertram in *All's Well that Ends Well* complains of the arguments used to keep him from the wars: 'I am commanded here, and kept a coil with / "Too young" and "The next year" and " 'Tis too early" ' (2. 1. 27–8).

*(b) Textual hook-ups*

The reflexive mention alone tends to frame – to put, as it were, in quotation marks (literally so within the text) – de-contextualized language: 'was' and 'is', say, as general indicators of past and present states. Direct commentary on the language of the comedy – on some speech event or on some aspect of structure or choice of words within the play – usually calls upon a related reflexive device, one of the most frequent 'meta' functions in Shakespeare. Consider the Countess of Rossillion's 'turning back' on her own expository speech at the beginning of *All's Well that Ends Well*: 'This young gentlewoman had a father – O, that "had", how sad a passage 'tis!' (1. 1. 16–17); or later in the same comedy, the King's picking-up of Lafew's (ambiguous) reference to Helena: '*Laf.* . . . And write to her a love-line./*King*. What "her" is this?' (2. 1. 77); or Tranio's response to Gremio's proposal in *The Taming of the Shrew* (playing on the different senses of the mentioned 'only'): '*Gre.* . . . If whilst I live she will be only mine./*Tra.* That "only" came well in' (2. 1. 355–6). In each of these instances, the framing 'mention' is reinforced by demonstrative hook-ups to the preceding utterance: 'that' or 'this', examples of what Lyons (1977: 607) terms *textual deixis*, i.e. the direct indication of the cited fragment of discourse (on the 'world-creating' functions of textual deixis, see pp. 81–3 below). It is important to stress that any language-game may be deictically 'pointed to' in this overt fashion: in the examples cited, the Countess indicates her own exposition and the significance of its tense; the King takes up Lafew's act (and object) of reference; and Tranio plays with Gremio's lexical choice – an identical framing strategy for quite distinct linguistic 'objects'. The textual deictic pointer, as we will repeatedly see, is perhaps the most fundamental means of linguistic raising-to-consciousness in Shakespeare.

*(c) Simultaneous reflexes*

A final and more subtle reflexive move: in certain of the plays (*Love's Labour's Lost* is as usual the prime instance), a given utterance will have a *self*-framing reflexive force by adopting a 'metalinguistic' term that refers to the very language-game in progress. A clear instance is the use by Armado of the verb 'enfranchise' ('Sirrah Costard, I will enfranchise thee', 3. 1. 118), one of whose current Elizabethan senses was precisely the foreign word importing that the Spaniard – not least in the use of this 'hard' word as synonym for 'free' – is putting on display in order to mystify Costard (see p. 272 below and chapter five in general for other instances of 'simultaneous' rhetorical reflexivity).

Such, then, are the main framing modes found throughout the comic canon. And it is because of the insistent and richly varied ways in which it places language *en abyme* that *Love's Labour's Lost* is the central point of reference for this study; a key text or textual key for the reading of the canon as a whole. It is without question the comedy that best exemplifies Shakespeare's baroque poetics not only in the complexity of its framing techniques but in the manner in which it exploits to the extreme the possibilities contained in the framed games themselves, as Ugo Volli, quoting Borges, notes:

> Borges says in one of those observations of his that are subtle to the point of irony, 'the baroque is the style that knowingly attempts to exhaust all its own possibilities and that borders on its own caricature'. In this sense, certainly, *Love's Labour's Lost* is the most baroque of Shakespeare's comedies. Nowhere else, in fact, does one find in this author such an unrestrained taste for the language game, such an extreme desire to take it to its limits . . . And never has the question of the borders of caricature been so closely tested. (1982, my translation)

The Russian formalist critic Viktor Schlovsky once remarked that *Tristram Shandy*, in its anomalous and self-conscious narrative game-playing, is the most 'typical' (i.e. form-exemplifying or -exasperating) of novels. *Love's Labour's Lost* can equally be described as the most 'typical' of Shakespeare's comedies, but only in the sense that it presents in heightened and obsessive form linguistic practices and issues in some degree common to the other plays. Among the individual comedies linguistic and metalinguistic emphases vary considerably: thus *The Comedy of Errors* is extensively taken up with 'referential' problems; *A Midsummer Night's Dream* with metatheatrical, metadramatic and ontological issues; *The Merry Wives of Windsor* with adventures and misadventures in the vernacular; *Measure for Measure* with the ethics of speech, and so on. The underlying poetics, however, has certain fixed points of return. Like all successful feasts, Shakespeare's great feast of languages – to use Costard's happy, if often misquoted, phrase – is made up of the most varied fare, but for all that it is best appreciated (within the limits of digestibility) whole.

# 1    *Performances*

(I) LANGUAGE BETWEEN PAGE AND STAGE

Language leads a double life in the drama. In performance, the words spoken by the actor will register as a physical event in the theatre but will also be processed by the audience as a speech event within the dramatic world. In a reading, vice versa, the dialogue is perceived immediately as a dramaturgic phenomenon, but any theatrically competent and experienced reader will at the same time create his own mental voices for the parts. These two allegiances – the theatrical and the dramatic – have to do with quite different levels of linguistic production and reception, each with its own logic. In the theatrical game, the actor has the tasks, in Austin's terms, of 'uttering certain noises (a "phonetic" act)' and of 'uttering certain vocables or words, i.e. noises of certain types belonging to . . . a certain vocabulary, in a certain construction', i.e. he performs the 'locutionary' act of making sense in a certain language (1962: 92). In the dramatic game, instead, these noises and constructions, or their textual equivalents, are interpreted as full speech acts within a fictional speaking situation (see Urmson 1972).

But in practice the two allegiances are inevitably and perfectly reciprocal: the dramatic dialogue bears the traces of its potential stage enunciation, while the actor's physical uttering of 'noises' and 'vocables' on stage is what allows their dramatic interpretation by the audience. This reciprocity gives rise in Shakespearean comedy to tensions, to comic business, and to a good deal of ironical commentary. It is with the comedies' explorations of the double duty of words in the drama that this chapter is concerned.

Considerable critical attention has been paid to the general theatrical and dramatic reflexivity of Shakespearean comedy, from Anne Righter's charting of the 'idea' of the play in the comic as in the general canon (1962), to James L. Calderwood's interpretations of *MND* and *LLL* as allegories of the dramatist's art (1969), to William Dodd's reading of *MM* as a showing-forth of the mechanisms of comedy (1979), etc. But the specific point of interest here is the place of language in the comedies' metatheatrical-metadramatic reflexions and reflections. The page-to-stage career of discourse, with its logical and ontological ambiguities, with its aspirations to glory and its risks of public disaster, is, especially in the earlier plays, an inexhaustible object of dramatic enquiry.

### (II) PRESENTATIONAL FRAMES: THREE AND A HALF EPILOGUES AND ONE INDUCTION

Both historically and structurally, the first function of language in dramatic performance is the definition of drama and performance *as such*. Historically, the marking-out of the representation from its non-theatrical context was one of the main semiotic tasks of the early English drama: 'at the very beginning one finds dramatists having to deal with the problem of defining the play as a play, of separating it from the current of ordinary living by what amounts to proclamation' (Burns 1972: 41). And structurally, these demarcational labours are for the most part entrusted, in the same early drama, to pre- or para-dramatic devices such as prologues, choruses and inductions.

Not that the entire pre-Shakespearean history of the presentational frame is reducible to a crude defining convention. If a medieval morality play like *Everyman*, performed in the open, requires a directly attention-requesting and drama-signalling prologue:

> I pray you all give your audience,
> And hear the matter with reverence,
> By figure a moral play:
> The *Summoning of Everyman* called it is

an interlude such as Medwall's *Fulgens and Lucrece* (c. 1497), performed in a hall to a more select audience, is able to offer a sophisticated induction that makes considerable play with its own para-dramatic status, pretending not to be a formal presentational device at all:

> A.      But I pray you tell me that again,
>            Shall here be a play . . . ?

An early Elizabethan comedy of the rhetorical agility of Gascoigne's *Supposes* (1566) uses the prologue device primarily for relaxed pseudo-conversational toying with its own Ariostan theme and title, bringing directly into play the audience's (supposed) suppositions and expectations:

> I suppose you are assembled here, supposing to reap the fruit of my travails.

And by the time of Lyly's *Campaspe* (1584), the prologue (to the Court, and thus to the Queen) has become simply a polite and oblique exercise in literary modishness, an autonomous performance with no demarcational pretensions at all:

> We are ashamed that our bird, which fluttered by twilight seeming a Swan, should be proved a bat, set against the sun, but as Jupiter placed Silenus' ass among the stars

(although in contrast, Marlowe's tragedy *Tamburlaine I* (1587) still makes use of the initial address in an explicational and scene-setting fashion: 'We'll lead you to the stately tent of war / Where you shall hear the Scythian Tamburlaine').

This progressive rhetorical enrichment of presentational conventions culminates, within the Elizabethan period, in the para-dramatic virtuosity of Shakespeare and Jonson. Of the two, Shakespeare is decidedly more sparing in his use of pre- and post-narrative affixes. Not a single comedy is furnished with a prologue and only three (*AYLI*, *MND* and *AWW*) with epilogues, if one excludes the two-line reference to the play incorporated in Feste's song at the end of *TN*. The elaborateness of the induction scenes tacked on to *TS* might seem to compensate for such thrift, but they remain something of an anomaly, 'Shakespeare's only concession, a concession that is curiously incomplete', as Anne Righter puts it, 'to the popularity of Kyd's Don Andrea and the whole idea of the play within a frame' (1962: 94). It is not even strictly accurate, indeed, to describe the main action of *TS* as a play contained within a frame. The transformation of Sly, an episode practically complete in itself, can be said to frame the main play to the extent that the performance is supposedly given for his benefit; but apart from Sly's single expression of somnolent impatience after the opening scene – "Tis a very excellent piece of work, madam lady. Would 'twere done' – the framing is rapidly abandoned and quite forgotten with the unfolding of the comedy proper.

What theatrical and dramaturgic force does the little microdrama of the induction have, then, apart from that of providing a curtain-raiser in the form of innocent burlesque? The two scenes, with their 'local' colouring, might be thought to furnish a stepping-stone rendering access to the remoter italianate world of the main comedy somewhat easier ('a bridge', in Righter's words, 'between the two realms of reality and illusion', 1962: 55). Or the entire episode might be seen, on the contrary, as a distancing or alienating mechanism, an implicit acknowledgment of the facticity of the main performance. But in either of these perspectives, it remains at best a half-hearted effort, never developed into a challenging commentary on the main play or into an ironical reflection on its performance conditions, as in the induction to Jonson's *Every Man In His Humour*, say.

35

The teasing of Sly acquires a precise dramaturgic point only if it is seen as a playful parable on the very business of constructing a fictional world, and in particular on the status of linguistic reference in the drama. Sly, it will be noted, is forced willy nilly into the role of actor, having been dressed up and being made to play a part alien to what he takes, at first, to be his true personality. But at the same time he is also in the position of the naïve spectator unable to distinguish one level of reality from another. The ludic Lord and his servants are able to create, through a few hyperbolic references, a new and all too seductive context for him ('Thou art a lord and nothing but a lord. / Thou hast a lady far more beautiful/Than any woman in this waning age', Ind. 2. 62–4), causing him to lose his albeit drunken cognitive hold on things ('Am I a lord? and have I such a lady?/Or do I dream? or have I dream'd till now?', 69–70). And when Sly attempts to recall his own past discourse – 'These fifteen years! . . . But did I never speak of all that time?' (82–3) – his transformers deny its referential value:

> O yes, my lord, but very idle words,
> For though you lay here in this goodly chamber,
> Yet would you say ye were beaten out of door,
> And rail upon the hostess of the house,
> And say you would present her at the leet,
> Because she brought stone jugs and no seal'd quarts.
> Sometimes you would call out for Cicely Hacket. (84–91)

Sly is quite ready to renounce his familiar but paltry universe of discourse in favour of the more alluring one sketched out by the Lord and his helpers. The moral, apparently, is that the referential status of the second world constructed for the audience is similarly limited to the discourse-based universe in question, and that only the Slys in the playhouse will take it for something more immediately present. A modest point, no doubt, but, as dramatized, a lively enough (and oblique enough) variation on the conventional 'This is but a play' warning.

An analogous, though more direct, disclaimer is contained in the epilogue to *MND*, i.e. in Puck's acknowledgment of the merely oneiric constitution of his world:

> If we shadows have offended,
> Think but this, and all is mended,
> That you have but slumber'd here
> While these visions did appear. (5. 1. 409–12)

Now the epilogue, of course, has quite a different conventional status with respect to that of the prologue. The defining duties of post-dramatic address, even in its most ingenuous early forms, are very limited, except in clumsy and anomalous cases such as Medwall's interlude *Nature* (Part I, c. 1495), where direct address actually marks, *ex abrupto*, the end of the dramatic proceedings: 'And for thys seson / Here we make an end / Lest we shuld offend / Thys audyence' (see Potter 1980: 158–9). Epilogues tend to fulfil, within the pre-Shakespearean English tradition, one or more of five optional roles:

(1) That of narrative appendix, giving news of the post-textual destinies of the dramatic persons (rather like the information provided at the end of certain Hollywood films – 'Mary did eventually marry'); an example is Arden of Faversham (1591):

> As for the ruffians, Shakebag and Black Will,
> The one took sanctuary, and, being sent for out,
> Was murther'd in Southwark

(2) That of moral summary, making explicit the allegorical content of what has gone before:

> Then to our reason God give us His grace,
> That we may follow with faith so firmly
> His commandment. (John Heywood, *The Four PP*, c. 1520)

(3) That of polite apology, imploring an act of clemency on the part of the audience towards the company and its offering ('If we shadows have offended'):

> Yet the author hereof desireth
> That for this season
> At the least ye will take it in patience;
> And if there be any offence ...
> It is only for lack of cunning. (*Fulgens and Lucrece*)

(4) That of applause-signal:

> Since at our last ending thus merry we be,
> For Gammer Gurton's needle's sake, let us have a plaudite!
> (*Gammer Gurton's Needle*, c. 1553)

(5) That of a wittily and knowingly discursive curtain-closer. Like the prologue, the epilogue acquired increasingly, during the Elizabethan period, the status of a legitimate stage 'turn' capable of considerable variation and elaboration. The lengthy dialogic epilogue to Nashe's *Summer's Last Will and Testament* (1600) – comparable in intent and in literary sophistication to the prologue to Lyly's *Campaspe* (see above) – is little more or less than a show of the author's formidable stylistic resources:

Boy.    Ulysses, a dwarf and the prolucutor for the Grecians, gave me leave (that am a pigmy) to do an embassage to you from the cranes.

Shakespeare's contribution to this tradition, within the comic canon

37

at least, is to heighten the rhetorical knowingness of the final address and to render more or less overt its claim to attention as a rule-bound event in its own right. All three (or three and a half) epilogues have the nominal function of a formal request for indulgence, but in the event their strategic courting of the plays' patrons takes a patent second place to their self-referentiality as discursive constructs. The main topic becomes the peculiar illocutionary strategy involved in the change of orientation from indirect to direct communication with the auditors.

Thus the King at the end of *AWW*, while marking, superfluously, the end of the drama, draws attention to his change of illocutionary stance, from that of regal command (within the dramatic communicational exchange) to that of humble supplication (within the theatrical transaction):

> The king's a beggar, now the play is done.

He proceeds – with a passing glance at the play's title – to look forward to the perlocutionary success of his would-be persuasion. All this is by way of an elegant applause signal:

> All is well ended if this suit be won,
> That you express content;

before promising, as incentive, future gratification:

> which we will pay
> With strife to please you, day exceeding day.

Rosalind's version of the 'introspective' address at the close of *AYLI* is a veritable essay on the epilogue convention and on the violations she supposedly subjects it to. Her speech falls into a series of distinct and clearly signalled moves, which can be roughly summarized as follows:

(1) Playing on her dramatic – as opposed to the actor's – gender, she notes ironically the indecorum and unmodishness of her present speaking role (with a stab at patriarchal sexism):

> It is not the fashion to see the lady the epilogue; but it is no more unhandsome than to see the lord the prologue.

(2) She confesses the redundancy of the address itself – thereby acknowledging the redundancy of the device at this late stage in the history of the English drama – but at the same time argues for its supplementary and decorative value:

> If it be true that good wine needs no bush, 'tis true that a good play needs no epilogue. Yet to good wine they do use good bushes; and good plays prove the better by the help of good epilogues.

(3) She declares her embarrassment at her position as vehicle of the inadequate apology for an inadequate play (this, of course, being in itself a conventional disclaimer):

> What a case am I in then, that am neither a good epilogue, nor cannot insinuate with you in the behalf of a good play?

(4) She claims to reject – here with an eye to her stage garb rather than her dramatic *persona* – the supplicatory attitude adopted, for example, by the King in *AWW*:

> I am not furnished like a beggar, therefore to beg will not become me.

(5) Resorting, for the first time, to direct pronominal address ('you'), she warns of her intended persuasion, again looking back to her recent dramatic guise (as 'magician'), and identifies the precise target of her would-be feminine enchantment:

> My way is to conjure you, and I'll begin with the women.

(6) She issues her first 'spell-binding' command, but it turns out to be merely a take-it-or-leave-it invitation of the kind perhaps contained in the play's title:

> I charge you, O women, for the love you bear to men, to like as much of this play as please you.

(7) With a sharp change in locutionary and sexual orientation, and with an ironical passing shot at male amorous behaviour (invoking the love scenes behind her), she launches another pseudo-command, which this time is revealed as a simple request for audience favour:

> And I charge you, O men, for the love you bear to women – as I perceive by your simpering none of you hates them – that between you and the women the play may please.

(8) 'She' becomes 'he', renouncing the dramatic sex asserted in (1), and assuming instead the theatrical identity of 'male actor', but only in order to describe his/her possible behaviour as hypothetical female. This, naturally, recalls the sexually ambiguous games of the comedy:

> If I were a woman, I would kiss as many of you as had beards that pleased me, complexions that liked me, and breaths that I defied not.

(9) And finally she resorts to a formal request for the expected audience applause:

> And I am sure, as many as have good beards, or good faces, or sweet breaths, will for my kind offer, when I make curtsy, bid me farewell.
> (*Exit*)

39

It is interesting to observe how the modest and codified plea that the actor / Rosalind has to convey ('kindly applaud') is repeatedly suspended and refracted by means of a succession of ironical, playful or self-contradictory verbal manoeuvres that dramatize the ambiguous status of the speech. Its 'halfway' position between the fictional and the immediate theatrical contexts is reflected in the speaker's sudden change of identity and gender and in the references at once to the play-world and the playhouse. The uncertainty of the locutionary terrain here is particularly marked in the pronominal (I–you) relationship: just as it is never clear precisely who is really speaking (the character, the actor, the dramatist, the company, the text . . .?) so the addressee is at once fictional – a 'model' audience projected by the text – and actual, the physically present auditors who in some measure identify themselves with the offered 'you'. The odd speaking situation thus created – a kind of semiotic no-man's land – is cannily exploited for such piquancy as it yields.

Plainly, the address's amused self-exploration here as communicational *tour de force,* a species of linquistic tightrope-walking between different ontological zones, quite removes it from any simply 'parasitic' framing function. What is framed, if anything, is the speech's own involuted accomplishing of its ends.

## (III) PRESENTATION FRAMED, OR THE AGONIES OF EXPOSITION

Shakespeare, then, finds use for expository presentational contrivances only inasmuch as he is able to transform them into something quite else, namely into elegant exhibitions of discursive bravura. But a negative image of actual Shakespearean practice – i.e. a version of those deadly defining exertions, external to the main play, that Shakespeare avoids – is impressed *internally,* in the various disastrous dramatic representations offered within the comedies, and in particular within *LLL* and *MND.* These meta-performances and their reception reflect, more than anything else, the perils attending ingenuous performer–audience address.

It is the prologue, conspicuously absent from the comedies as external prefix, that forms the dramaturgic staple of the internal performances. The most ardent faith is invested in it. The metalanguage of all the plays' dramatists, directors and performers expresses conviction as to the diplomatic necessity and theatrical efficacy of the device. Both of the inner spectacles in *LLL* come accoutred with carefully planned and rehearsed preambles designed to win the respective theatrical days. In

Boyet's report to the ladies of the lords' preparations for the Muscovite masque, it is Moth's rehearsal of his expository speech that dominates the account. He is directed collectively by the lords, who are attentive to posture and delivery – 'Action and accent did they teach him there / "Thou must thus speak, and thus thy body bear"' (5. 2. 99–100) – and who congratulate themselves on their joint workmanship:

> One rubb'd his elbow thus, and fleer'd, and swore
> A better speech was never spoke before;
> Another, with his finger and his thumb,
> Cry'd 'Via! we will do't, come what will come';
> The third he caper'd, and cried, 'All goes well.' (5. 2. 109–13)

The creators of the Worthies' pageant, instead, resort to explicit presentation as a means of remedying the discrepancies between the physical stature of one of their stage vehicles (Moth, again) and the represented *dramatis persona* (Hercules). A verbal gloss is thought sufficient to reconcile representer and represented:

*Hol.*    . . . he shall present Hercules in minority: his enter and exit shall be strangling a snake; and I will have an apology for that purpose.
*Moth.*   An excellent device! (5. 1. 125–8)

The remedial value of the 'excellent device' is similarly advocated by Bottom during the first rehearsal scenes of *MND*. The problem here is not the feared inverisimilitude of the representation, but on the contrary, the possible excess of mimetic power in the portrayal of Pyramus's suicide. The play-makers doubt the auditors' (especially the ladies') capacity to make the simple cognitive distinctions necessary for the serene appreciation of the stage doings. The answer is automatic: write a 'device', here to be entrusted with the full 'This is but a play' signalling duty:

*Bot.*    I have a device to make all well. Write me a prologue, and let the prologue seem to say we will do no harm with our swords, and that Pyramus is not killed indeed; and for the more better assurance, tell them that I, Pyramus, am not Pyramus, but Bottom the weaver. This will put them out of fear. (3. 1. 15–21)

And once established as a convention, of course, the 'ontological' exposition rapidly becomes for the Mechanicals the *sine qua non* of theatrical spectacle. Since the assumption (regarding the audience's theatrical incompetence, by analogy with the performers') remains constant, so too must the device, whereby every element of the representation is to be suitably pre-glossed, until the entire performance becomes the prospective framing of a display that barely has the chance to get under way:

*Snout.*  Therefore another prologue must tell he is not a lion.
*Bot.*  Nay, you must name his name, and half his face must be seen through the lion's neck; and he himself must speak through, saying thus, or to the same defect: 'Ladies . . . If you think I come hither as a lion, it were pity of my life. No, I am no such thing; I am a man, as other men are.' (3. 1. 33–43)

And so, indeed, it proves on the occasion. Access to the first dramatic interaction, between Pyramus and the wall, is provided through a triple-level orgy of prologuing. First, Quince's version of the formal plea for indulgence on the grounds of the performer's well-meaning offensiveness: 'If we offend, it is with our good will' (5. 1. 108) (compare the 'if there be any offence . . . It is only for lack of cunning' of *Fulgens and Lucrece*, p. 37 above); then the canonical play-defining address – for the benefit of the predicted theatrical virgins, liable to be merely bemused by the proceedings ('Gentles, perchance you wonder at this show; / But wonder on, till truth make all things plain', 126–7). This leaves no room for misreadings of the representation since it renders explicit both the stage vehicle / dramatic object relationships ('This man is Pyramus, if you would know; . . . This man, with lime and rough-cast, doth present / Wall . . .; This man, with lantern, dog, and bush of thorn, / Presenteth Moonshine', 128ff.) and the entire narrative. And third comes the specifically wall-identifying preamble, carefully distinguishing the two levels of reality at work in Snout's performance ('In this same interlude it doth befall / That I, one Snout by name, present a wall', 154–5). And so the expository feast continues, with Lion and Moonshine being presented rather than represented and an epilogue planned as the final *coup*, presumably designed to give a retrospective explication of the explication.

But the allocutionary density of the Mechanicals' play does not end here. A gently ironical remark by Theseus, the spectator-in-chief ('The wall, methinks, being sensible, should curse again') provokes a zealous correction from Bottom: Bottom's riposte is a notable instance of what Goffman (1974) calls frame-breaking, an illicit stepping-out of the bounds of the dramatic performance; but only, in his case, in order to *uphold* the order of things imposed by the text and so ensure the successful progress of the drama. Bottom, with a degree of condescension, lets the non-initiate into one of the mysteries of the art, namely the determining role of the cue:

*Pyr.*  No, in truth sir, he should not. 'Deceiving me' is Thisbe's cue: she is to enter now, and I am to spy her through the wall. You shall see it will fall pat as I told you: yonder she comes. (5. 1. 182–5)

42

Thus another level of the performance, its textual basis, is generously exposed.

The spectators' running commentary, like the play-makers' enthusiastic discussions during rehearsals, focuses primarily on the presentational strategies at work. Quince's breathlessly distressed opening plea is immediately subjected to an amused, if restrained, anatomy:

| | |
|---|---|
| *Lys.* | He hath rid his prologue like a rough colt; he knows not the stop. A good moral, my lord: it is not enough to speak, but to speak true. |
| *Hip.* | Indeed he hath played on this prologue like a child on a recorder; a sound, but not in government. |
| *The.* | His speech was like a tangled chain; nothing impaired, but all disordered (5. 1. 119–25); |

while the offered 'if there be any offence' closing address is kindly but pointedly declined as a redundancy:

| | |
|---|---|
| *The.* | No epilogue, I pray you; for your play needs no excuse. Never excuse; for when the players are all dead, there need none be blamed. (341–3) |

Such comments mark not only the class and cultural distinctions between performers and audience, but also the historical and dramaturgic distance between the main play, with its exquisite narrative and rhetorical artifices, and the still remembered (and occasionally still practised) canons of the old Tudor drama, very much as the thumping prosody and pathetic exclamations of Quince's script measure the stylistic distance. For in the explicatory zeal, typical of the Tudor model (such as popular Mummers' plays – 'I am the Dragon, here are my jaws', Oxfordshire St George play, in Manly 1897, I: 291; see Barber 1959: 151–2), but also of a relatively sophisticated interlude such as Heywood's *Four PP* ('I am a palmer, as you see'), and in their fear of letting the verbal interaction define itself and its own dramatic context, the Mechanicals not only render the visual spectacle an awkward tautology but even upstage such modest dialogue as there is by *anticipating* it metalinguistically:

| | |
|---|---|
| *Wall.* | a crannied hole, or chink, |
| | Through which the lovers, Pyramus and Thisbe, |
| | Did whisper often, very secretly. . . . |
| | And this the cranny is, right and sinister, |
| | Through which the fearful lovers are to whisper. (157–63) |

And the simultaneous doubling of speaking roles (explanatory/representational), triumphant solution to the feared confusion of levels, places a strain on the already precarious fiction which the auditors

43

cannot concede without at least a pinch of irony. Overplaying the part of undiscriminating innocents, the spectators fail to make the requested ontological distinctions and perceive instead a gallery of prodigies, speaking walls and lions:

*The.*   Would you desire lime and hair to speak better?
*Dem.*   It is the wittiest partition that ever I heard discourse, my lord.
         (164–6)

*The.*   A very gentle beast, and of a good conscience.
*Dem.*   The very best at a beast, my lord, that e'er I saw. (222–3)

The reception given to the various presentational efforts in *LLL* is a good deal harsher. Even at its best and most sophisticated, direct address works only when the audience is predisposed towards acting as (first silent and then vocally appreciative) addressee, and towards accepting the conventional meeting between real and fictional worlds. Neither of the displays in *LLL* is of the best or most sophisticated, and each meets with an uncooperative and unforgiving public.

Moth's hyperbolic prologue to the Muscovite masque, a quasi-dramatic performance to the extent that the lords are in disguise, carries with it the unhelpful connotations of facticity associated with the device, and is all too easily dismissed by the ladies as a hollow fiction. As such it represents a piece of extreme communicational ingenuousness on the part of the men, the worse for their literary pretensions, rather than the miraculously persuasive pseudo-theatrical *coup* they had envisaged. Pre-informed and ill-disposed, the ladies are able to play havoc with the textual references, refusing to identify themselves with the 'you' of the speech and rendering, by their behaviour, the catalogue of compliments conspicuously non-referential, despite Moth's efforts to improvise and save his masters' faces:

*Moth.*   All hail, the richest beauties on the earth!
*Boy.*    Beauties no richer than rich taffeta.
*Moth.*   A holy parcel of the fairest dames,
                    (*The Ladies turn their backs to him.*)
          That ever turn'd their – backs – to mortal views!
*Ber.*    'Their eyes,' villain, 'their eyes'.
*Moth.*   . . . Not to behold –
*Ber.*    'Once to behold,' rogue. (5. 2. 158ff.)

The ambiguous status of the address (as a premeditated text delivered in the guise of direct communication), so knowingly exploited in the epilogue to *AYLI*, becomes here a trap into which the men fall headlong, since their 'prologue vilely penn'd' (305) fails to go beyond elementary and earnest entreaty. It is a dangerous device when left unguarded.

The humiliated lords, however, have a chance soon enough to recover a little lost pride by showing off their superiority as auditors towards the humble Worthies' parade, although the poverty of rhetorical means shown by Holofernes and company is, in reality, little different from the compositional naïveté they themselves have recently demonstrated. The problem, again, is that the presenters, in setting up a pseudo-relationship with their audience, invite them to intervene (it is the situation that music-hall artists know how to turn to advantage). As a result the actors' simple affirmations of their dramatic identities are either rejected, as part of the non-acceptance-of-the-frame game:

*Cost.*      I Pompey am, –
*Ber.*                   You lie, you are not he. (5. 2. 541)

*Nath.*      My scutcheon plain declares that I am Alisander, –
*Boy.*       Your nose says, no, you are not; for it stands too right (560–1)

or taken literally with mock-shock:

*Hol.*       Judas I am, –
*Dum.*     A Judas! (590–1)

Inevitably, the presentation turns into a continual fight for the floor, since in fact it is the lords who wish to give the real verbal show, with consequent frame-breaking by the presenters in order to claim their performing rights (see the discussion of turn-taking, pp. 185–99):

*Hol.*       I will not be put out of countenance. (602)

*Arm.*      But I will forward with my device. Sweet royalty, bestow on me the sense of hearing (655–7);

to correct the spectators' feigned misframings:

*Hol.*       Not Iscariot, sir.
            Judas I am, ycleped Maccabaeus (592–3);

to protest at their lack of co-operation in the game:

*Hol.*       This is not generous, not gentle, not humble (623);

or even, taking up the auditors' mock-literalness, to defend the illustrious *dramatis personae* from the assault:

*Arm.*      The sweet war-man is dead and rotten; sweet chucks, beat not the bones of the buried; when he breathed, he was a man. (653–5)

But only Costard is able to deflect the barbs by becoming, like Bottom, an enthusiastic commentator on the theatrical and dramatic games in progress:

45

'Tis not so much worth; but I hope I was perfect. I made a little fault in 'Great'. (554–5)

There, an't shall please you: a foolish mild man; an honest man, look you, and soon dashed! He is a marvellous good neighbour, faith, and a very good bowler; but, for Alisander, – alas! you see how 'tis, – a little o'erparted. But there are Worthies a-coming will speak their mind in some other sort. (575–81).

And it is Costard himself who finally destroys what is left of the shaky dramatic context by mixing actual with the fictional references, and so overthrowing Armado–Hector:

Cost.     Faith, unless you play the honest Troyan, the poor wench is cast away: she's quick; the child brags in her belly already: 'tis yours.

Arm.      Dost thou infamonize me among potentates? Thou shalt die. (667–71)

This is the way an overworked convention meets its doom: in a brawl.

### (IV) THE PRESENCE OF THE VOICE

Between the stage performance and the written text there is one immediate point of contact: the actor's voice. In assuming the roles of physical source and vehicle of the lines assigned to him, the actor is responsible not only for materializing the utterances but also for lending them sufficiently marked vocal colouring to personalize the represented speaker. The vocal work of the actor ranges from the phonetic and prosodic handling of those aspects of the dialogue predicted both by the text and by the rules of the language (intonation, stress, rhythm) to the more optional overlaying of so-called paralinguistic features (pitch, volume, tempo, timbre, non-vocal sounds, etc.) that give his speech its particular attitudinal colouring and present it as a phonic event worthy of the auditor's attention (see Trager 1958; Lyons 1977: 63–7; Elam 1980: 78–83).

Logically, of course, the discourse of the dramatic speakers and the actual vocal qualities of the performer belong to absolutely distinct realms, and their 'meeting' in performance remains a fictional expedient. The actor, what is more, has a good deal of freedom with regard to the precise pitch, loudness, punctuation and modulation that he gives to his delivery. But this does not mean that the vocalization of the utterances is simply *separate from* and *posterior* to the linguistic make-up of the written text itself. In the first place, the speaker's voice (however actually concretized) is always fully implicit in the 'disembodied' speech of the text (and provided by the mind's ear in the case of a silent reading). And still more, certain of the language-games on show in the comedies depend precisely on the *exaggeration* by the performer of vocal traits, signalled more or less specifically in the text, that connote regional, foreign or idiosyncratically personal colouring. The obvious instance is the parade of accents in *MWW*, marked by an approximate phonetic annotation:

Evans.    Od's plessed will, I will not be absence at the grace. (1. 1. 242–3)

Caius.    By gar, he has save his soul, dat he is no come; he has pray his Pible well, dat he is no come. (2. 2. 6–7)

To underline the point, and to render even more central to the game the vocal realization of their speech, Evans's and Caius's pronunciational deviations are ironically picked up, notably by Falstaff:

Evans.    *Pauca verba*; Sir John, good worts.
Fal.      Good worts? Good cabbage. (1. 1. 112–13)

Evans.    Seese is not good to give putter; your belly is all putter.
Fal.      'Seese' and 'putter'? Have I lived to stand at the taunt of one that makes fritters of English? (5. 5. 141–4)

Such paralinguistic signals assert, in performance at least, identity between the articulation of speech on stage and its production in the dramatic world. The presence of the voice in the dramatic utterance is confirmed by the concurrence between the actor's vocal characteristics on the one hand and direct references by the dramatic speakers on the other. And of the different elements of vocal production, it is the two fundamental components, *pitch* and *volume*, that are brought most often into play.

Voice pitch enters directly into the 'transvestite' performances in such plays as *TG*, *AYLI*, *MV* and *TN*. Given the three-tier complexity of the disguise scenes on the Elizabethan stage (male playing young woman playing adolescent boy), the ambiguous character of the speaking voice (feminine or pre-pubescent masculine or even adult male?) is both one of the bases of the trick and the irresistible object of irony within the play. In *TN*, for instance, Viola–Cesario's boyish-girlish tones are anatomized in all their androgynous indeterminacy by Orsino:

> For they shall yet belie thy happy years,
> That say thou art a man; Diana's lip
> Is not more smooth and rubious: thy small pipe
> Is as the maiden's organ, shrill and sound,
> And all is semblative a woman's part (1. 4. 30–4)

while Malvolio emphasizes the uncertainty of the speaker's age:

47

> 'Tis with him in standing water, between boy and man. He is very
> well-favoured, and he speaks very shrewishly. One would think his
> mother's milk were scarce out of him. (I. 5. 160–4)

In part, of course, what is happening here is a pointed toying with the
danger, inherent in the transvestism ploy, of the character's betraying
his/her 'real' gender in the very act of speaking. But at the same time,
the ambiguity underlined here is a clear reflection of the *actor's*
necessary vocal disguise in undertaking 'semblative a woman's part'.
The point is made explicit in the induction to *TS*, where the boy charged
with playing Sly's invented wife is to 'bear himself/ . . . With soft low
tongue and lowly courtesy' and to 'usurp the grace,/ Voice, gait and
action of a gentlewoman' (Ind. I, lines 108ff.), and in the rehearsal scenes
of *MND*, where the bearded Flute is ordered to 'play it in a mask; and you
may speak as small as you will', while the vocally versatile Bottom
boasts, in a paralinguistic paradox, 'And I may hide my face, let me play
Thisbe too. I'll speak in a monstrous little voice' (I. 2. 45ff.). Portia, in
*MV*, meanwhile, ironizes on her own vocal 'dressing up', which she
undertakes with some spirit:

> I'll prove the prettier fellow of the two . . .
> And speak between the change of man and boy,
> With a reed voice. (3. 4. 64–6)

It must be stressed that the exploitation of sexual-vocal ambiguity is
anything but an overworn dramatic convention of the period. Despite
the fundamental importance of 'transsexual' disguise to the Elizabethan
stage in general, very little play with gender roles appears outside
Shakespeare (Jonson's *Epicoene* being a conspicuous exception), and
indeed outside the comedies within the Shakespearean canon.

Volume, instead, is a more general histrionic and dramatic problem,
not limited with respect to age or sex. For the actor, the control of vocal
intensity is a central factor in the art of delivery: he has to achieve
maximum audibility without excessive loudness or shouting. For the
dramatic speaker, the limits on volume have to do, rather, with social
decorum or, at times, the need for secrecy. But again, the two spheres of
vocal sound appear to ratify one another in performance. Loudness is
one of the range of behavioural vices attributed to Gratiano in *MV*, and
is perhaps the one most directly under the mimetic control of the actor.
The excess emerges, immediately following Gratiano's opening words,
in Bassanio's complaint:

> but hear thee, Gratiano,
> Thou art too wild, too rude, and bold of voice,

> Parts that become thee happily enough,
> And in such eyes as ours appear not faults –
> But where thou art not known; – why there they show
> Something too liberal (2. 2. 171–6)

and is confirmed in Shylock's sarcastic retort to Gratiano's uncontrolled insults:

> Till thou canst rail the seal from off my bond,
> Thou but offend'st thy lungs to speak so loud. (4. 1. 139–40)

And the same form of vocal intemperance is, of course, a major ingredient of Katherina's shrewishness in *TS*:

*Hor.* Tush, Gremio. Though it pass your patience and mine to endure her loud alarums, why, man, there be fellows in the world ... would take her with all faults, and money enough. (1. 1. 126–30)

*Pet.* For I will board her though she chide as loud
As thunder when the clouds in autumn crack. (1. 2. 94–5; see also p. 292 below)

The second dramatic constraint, the supposed desire to hide what is said from some potential listener or overhearer, is, for obvious reasons, closely associated with the convention of the aside, and may, indeed, be invoked in order to motivate the device and the corresponding adoption of *sotto voce* tones by the actor, as in the case of Olivia's professed fear of being heard by Malvolio or others:

*Oli.* *(Aside)* I have sent after him, he says he'll come:
How shall I feast him? What bestow of him?
For youth is bought more oft than begg'd or borrow'd.
I speak too loud. – (3. 4. 1–4)

Pitch, volume, stress, rhythm, timbre and the rest become, in co-operation, traces above all of the subjectivity or individuality of the speaker. And it is, of course, the *subjectivity* of the fictional speaker which the actor's performance, oral and otherwise, is immediately designed to affirm in the idiosyncrasies he brings to the representation. Such vocalic individuality, or the lack of it, is at times registered within the drama itself. Egeon, in *CE*, for example, expresses dismay at the non-recognition of his speech by one of the Dromios at their reunion:

> Not know my voice? O time's extremity,
> Hast thou so crack'd and splitted my poor tongue
> In seven short years, that here my only son
> Knows not my feeble key of untun'd cares? (5. 1. 307–10)

The text-based identity of the *dramatis persona* is tied, at the same time, to an orality that at every point invites stage materialization.

## (V) EXTRA-LINGUISTIC RELATIONS: VERBAL INDICES

In the meeting between stage and page a crucial position is occupied by the body. Or more accurately, by the conventional coincidence of *three* logically distinct bodies, one fictional (that of the speaking or listening *dramatis persona*), one physical (that of the actor on stage) and a third, 'virtual' or ideal, the intervening body of the actor *as indicated in the text*. That is to say, in order to be genuinely performable, the dramatic text will leave space for the movement and self-display of the body and its accessories on stage, pointing to them explicitly through direct reference or calling upon them implicitly through the 'gaps' left by the incomplete linguistic references.

Indication of the (virtual) presence of the actor's body in the dramatic text takes the primary form – apart, of course, from stage directions – of the 'pointing' signs that C. S. Peirce (1931–58) termed *indices*, and specifically of verbal indices or 'indexical symbols'. Peirce gives as the chief type of indexical symbol the deixis (personal and demonstrative pronouns and adjectives, adverbs of time and space, etc.). Deictic reference, inasmuch as it 'points to' rather than fully describes or specifies the object, presupposes its actual presence. As such, it serves as a bridge between dramatic language-games and the performance, since it is the actor's body, costume and accessories, or the space around him, that are displayed at the moment of the utterance.

Indexical relations with the potentially present body are a constant feature of the comedies' linguistic exchanges. Apart from the 'disembodied' *I* and *you* of the dialogue – which call, as it were, for stage incarnation – the principal means of indicating the participation of the actor as physical vehicle in the production of speech is through the demonstrative. Enraged at his wife's apparent involvement in a plot against him, Antipholus of Ephesus in *CE* resorts to verbal violence which embraces parts of the two main bodies in the exchange:

> But with *these* nails I'll pluck out *these* false eyes
> That would behold in me this shameful sport. (4. 4. 102–3)

(Italics in the extracts on pp. 50–2 are mine.) In his first meeting with Isabella in *MM*, Lucio immediately points verbally to his interlocutor's face, which in turn is taken as an index of her sexual innocence:

> Hail virgin, if you be – as *those* cheek-roses
> Proclaim you are no less. (1. 4. 16–17)

And it is through indexical reference that the crucial presence of Antonio's (and the actor's) body in the trial scene of *MV* is established:

*Por.*      A pound of *that* same merchant's flesh is thine:
            The court awards it, and the law doth give it. . . .
            And you must cut *this* flesh from off his breast:
            The law allows it, and the court awards it. (4. 4. 300–4)

References of this kind, among the commonest features of Shake-spearean discourse, set up a vital reciprocity between language and physical stage vehicles, which come to complement each other in showing forth the represented world. The actor's costume may similarly be included deictically in the exchange, as in the repeated indications of Petruchio's eccentric wedding garb (clearly calling for a visual co-ordinate) in *TS*:

*Pet.*      Were it not better I should rush in *thus*? . . .
*Bap.*      Fie, doff *this* habit, shame to your estate,
            An eyesore to our solemn festival. . . .
*Tra.*      See not your bride in *these* unreverend robes,
            Go to my chamber, put on clothes of mine.
*Pet.*      Not I, believe me. *Thus* I'll visit her,
*Bap.*      But *thus*, I trust, you will not marry her.
*Pet.*      Good sooth, even *thus*. (3. 2. 89–114)

Indispensable props, as opposed to those added for decorative purposes or at any rate not essential to the action, are likewise signalled indexically at the moment of their stage appearance; the discovery of the means of Valentine's proposed elopement with Silvia in *TG* provides such a moment:

*Duke.*     I pray thee let me feel thy cloak upon me. . . .
            What's *here*?
                *Silvia, this night I will enfranchise thee.*
            'Tis so; and *here's* the ladder for the purpose. (3. 1. 136–52)

Often enough, indexical references will be accompanied in per-formance by manual or other gestures towards the stage vehicles representing the objects in question ('Here pointing is a part of the language-game', Wittgenstein 1953: 669), thereby further involving the body of the actor as indicating, in addition to indicated, agency. Gesture may indeed be quite essential to the completion of the reference contained in the utterance. The 'There, take you *that*, sir knave' (1. 2. 92) and 'Think'st thou I jest? hold, take thou *that*, and *that*' (2. 2. 23) of *CE* are banal cases in point. The struggle between Orlando and Oliver in the opening scene of *AYLI* provides a more elaborate example:

*Oli.*      (*Striking him*) What, boy!
*Orl.*      (*Putting a wrestler's grip on him*) Come, come, elder brother, you are
            too young in *this*.
*Oli.*      Wilt thou lay hands on me, villain?

51

*Orl.*      ... Wert thou not my brother, I would not take *this* hand from thy throat till *this* other had pulled out thy tongue for saying so. (1. 1. 52–61)

Indispensable as bond between dramatic fiction and stage representation, the verbal index is also a notable source of comic (stage) business as autonomous event. This is true particularly where indexical reference and the simultaneously displayed stage object are blatantly at odds, giving rise to a reciprocal tension that is readily exploitable for farcical effect. This is the case with Petruchio's paradoxical referential games directly entailing stage vehicles (body, costume, prop). Katherina's new gown, which will invariably be represented in performance by a costume of some elegance, is transformed through Petruchio's indexical perversity into shoddy frippery:

*Pet.*      O mercy, what masquing-stuff is *here*?
           What's *this*? a sleeve? 'tis like a demi-cannon,
           What! up and down, carv'd like an apple-tart?
           *Here's* snip and nip and cut and slish and slash,
           Like to a censer in a barber's shop.
           Why what a devil's name, tailor, call'st thou *this*? (4. 3. 87–92);

while the face of the aged Vincentio becomes a haven of feminine charms:

           Tell me, sweet Kate, and tell me truly too,
           Hast thou ever beheld a fresher gentlewoman?
           Such war of white and red within her cheeks!
           What stars do spangle heaven with *such* beauty,
           As *those* two eyes become *that* heavenly face? (4. 5. 28–32)

The very 'incompleteness' of deictic reference, particularly of the demonstrative pronoun ('this' / 'that') and the spatial adverb ('here' / 'there'), which may remain ambiguous until specified through gesture, leaves it open to comic trouble deriving from the interlocutor's misconstruing – deliberately or otherwise – of the reference. The most striking instance, literally, occurs again in *TS*, namely in Grumio's insistent interpretation of his master's simple scenic reference as a bizarrely masochistic bodily index:

*Pet.*      I trow *this* is his house.
           *Here*, Sirrah Grumio, knock, I say.
*Gru.*      Knock, sir! whom should I knock? is there any man has rebused your worship?
*Pet.*      Villain, I say, knock me *here* soundly.
*Gru.*      Knock you *here*, sir? why, sir, what am I, sir, that I should knock you *here*, sir?
*Pet.*      Villain, I say, knock me at *this* gate,
           And rap me well, or I'll knock your knave's pate.

| | |
|---|---|
| *Gru.* | My master is grown quarrelsome. I should knock you first, |
| | And then I know after who comes by the worst. (1. 2. 4–14) |

In the early comedies the body is fair game for the deconstructive play of the word. Body movement is assimilated as a form of 'discourse' into the dialectic of language and metalanguage. This often strife-ridden marriage of linguistic and gestural factors as part of the united unfolding of discourse is overtly demonstrated in *TG*, where a head movement and a (tautological) monosyllabic affirmation by Speed are wittily interpreted as morphemes making up a single unflattering lexeme, and the interpretation itself in turn subjected to earnest glossing:

| | |
|---|---|
| *Pro.* | But what said she? |
| *Spe.* | (*First nodding*) Ay. |
| *Pro.* | Nod – ay: why, that's 'noddy'. |
| *Spe.* | You mistook, sir: I say she did nod; and you ask me if she did nod, and I say 'Ay'. |
| *Pro.* | And that set together is 'noddy'. |
| *Spe.* | Now that you have taken the pains to set it together, take it for your pains. (1. 1. 107–14) |

Speed himself is later the victim of a bad 'referential' pun by his fellow-clown involving not only body movement but, more critically, a stage prop promoted to the position of intelligent dramatic listener:

| | |
|---|---|
| *Lau.* | . . . when it stands well with him, it stands well with her. |
| *Spe.* | What an ass art thou, I understand thee not. |
| *Lau.* | What a block art thou, that thou canst not! My staff understands me. |
| *Spe.* | What thou say'st? |
| *Lau.* | Ay, and what I do too: look thee, I'll but lean, and my staff understands me. |
| *Spe.* | It stands under thee indeed. |
| *Lau.* | Why, stand under and understand is all one. (2. 5. 20–9) |

Elsewhere, gesture is attributed, within playful or ironical commentary on the exchange in progress, the status of full-blown illocutionary act, for example in Dromio of Syracuse's reception of his unmerited beating in *CE* as a quip in bad taste:

| | |
|---|---|
| *Syr. Ant.* | Think'st thou I jest? hold, take thou that, and that. (*Beats Dromio*) |
| *Syr. Dro.* | Hold sir, for God's sake; now your jest is earnest: Upon what bargain do you give it me? (2. 2. 23–5); |

or the 'narrative' reading of the same act in *TS*:

| | |
|---|---|
| *Gru.* | . . . and thereby hangs a tale. |
| *Cur.* | Let's ha't, good Grumio. |
| *Gru.* | Lend thine ear. |
| *Cur.* | Here. |

| Gru. | There. (*He strikes him*) |
| Cur. | This is to feel a tale, not to hear a tale. |
| Gru. | And therefore 'tis called a sensible tale. (4. 1. 50–7) |

But it must be stressed that however much licence they concede to the play of the word at the expense of the body, its metonymies and its movements, such games in no sense promote a self-sufficient and all-exclusive 'verbalism'. On the contrary, departing from the very possibility of their delivery in performance, they implicate the stage and its physical vehicles in an integral fashion.

The same cannot be said, alas, for the linguistic pointers put to such wide and conspicuous use in the internal performances within *MND* and *LLL*. Indeed, one of the chief metatheatrical morals to be drawn from them regards this very question of the relations between language and stage signs. For while the verbal indices at work in the Mechanicals' tragedy and the pageant of the Worthies certainly indicate, and all too directly, the simultaneously displayed stage vehicles, they do so only in order to label them and fully specify their properties and functions. As a consequence, far from remaining 'incomplete' deictic references which invite the complementary presence of body and prop, the pointers in both cases altogether pre-empt the vehicles' stage appearance ('the player, when he cometh in', complains Sidney of contemporary English performances, 'must ever begin with telling where he is, or else the tale will not be conceived', 1595: 134; and compare again the Mummers' play and its explicatory deictic redundancy: 'I am King Alfred and this here is my bride / I've a crown on my pate and a sword by my side', in Manly 1897, I: 289–90):

| Nath. | My scutcheon plain declares that I am Alisander (*LLL* 5. 2. 560) |

| Hol. | Great Hercules is presented by this imp, |
| | Whose club kill'd Cerberus, that three-headed *canus*; |
| | And, when he was a babe, a child, a shrimp, |
| | Thus did he strangle serpents in his *manus*. (*LLL* 5. 2. 583–6) |

| Wall. | This loam, this rough-cast, and this stone doth show |
| | That I am that same wall; the truth is so. (*MND* 5. 1. 160–1) |

| Moon. | This lantern doth the horned moon present; |
| | Myself the Man i' th' Moon do seem to be. (*MND* 5. 1. 235–6) |

It is quite striking that in each instance the performers' indexical labours are undermined by counter-indices from the audience, cruelly exploiting the distance between linguistic reference and stage mimesis. Nathaniel's claim regarding the indicative force of his scutcheon is belied by other involuntary signs that he carries (namely his personal features); Boyet pitilessly points out the chasm that divides the 'virtual' body of the script ('that I am Alisander') from the actual physical presence:

Boy.    Your nose says, no, you are not; for it stands too right. (*LLL* 5. 2. 561)

And when Holofernes attempts unhappily to defend himself and his representation by means of an extra-textual reference (here functionally 'incomplete') to his own face, he is bombarded with rival interpretations both of his verbal pointer and of its physical object, whereby he loses, precisely, face and the entire indexical game:

Hol.    I will not be put out of countenance.
Ber.    Because thou hast no face
Hol.    What is this?
Boy.    A cittern-head.
Dum.    The head of a bodkin.
Ber.    A death's face in a ring.
Long.   The face of an old Roman coin, scarce seen.
Boy.    The pommel of Caesar's falchion.
Dum.    The carved bone face on a flask.
Ber.    Saint George's half-cheek in a brooch.
Dum.    Ay, and worn in the cap of a toothdrawer.
        And now, forward; for we have put thee in countenance.
Hol.    You have put me out of countenance.
Ber.    False: we have given thee faces. (5. 2. 603–16)

Faces are saved in *MND* mainly because of the performers' thicker skins, since very similar treatment is given to their verbal pointers, in particular the attempt to foist off a rustic and rusty prop as the most sublime of celestial symbols by means of simple assertion. Again the presentation is ironically countered by the spectators' pointing to the stage vehicles and their inverisimilitude, although here the presenter persists:

Moon.   *This lantern doth the horned moon present –*
Dem.    He should have worn the horns on his head.
The.    He is no crescent, and his horns are invisible within the circumference.
Moon.   *This lantern doth the horned moon present;*
        *Myself the Man i' the Moon do seem to be.*
The.    This is the greatest error of all the rest; the man should be put in the lantern. How is it else the Man i' the Moon? . . .
Moon.   All that I have to say is, to tell you that the lantern is the moon; I the Man i' the Moon, this thorn-bush my thorn-bush; and this dog my dog.
Dem.    Why, all these should be in the lantern, for all these are in the moon.
        (5. 1. 231–51)

Yet the most singular and extensive excursus on the perilous relations between language and physical stage bodies occurs not in any of the 'official' dramatic performances but in the frustrated attempts by the clown Launce, in *TG*, to re-enact his 'off-stage' farewell to his family. Launce's monologue – or, better, monodrama – in which he elects himself *dramatis persona*, dramatist, director, actor and finally commentator, begins as a straightforward narrative account ('my mother weeping; my father wailing', 2. 3. 6) until Launce, addressing not so much the actual auditors as a 'possible' audience of his own inventing, decides to demonstrate directly rather than recount the events ('Nay, I'll show you the manner of it', 13–14). This move, naturally, raises all the problems of theatrical ostension or display ('I'll *show* you'), as Launce endeavours to indicate his stage vehicles and their signified parts. The first question regards the distribution of roles among the few paltry bodies he has at his disposition, all the more problematic since some – namely he and his dog – have to double as actors and characters: can they represent themselves or are they bound, as stage signs, to stand for something else? Like the other performers, he has to make do with the indexical label to signal his choice:

> This shoe is my father. No, this left shoe is my father; no, no, this left shoe is my mother; nay, that cannot be so neither. Yes, it is so, it is so: it hath the worser sole. This shoe with the hole in it is my mother; and this my father. A vengeance on't, there 'tis. Now, sir, this staff is my sister; for, look you, she is white as a lily, and as small as a wand. This hat is our maid. I am the dog. No, the dog is himself, and I am the dog. O, the dog is me, and I am myself. Ay; so, so. (14–23)

But this is only the beginning of Launce's mimetic troubles. For he is not content with merely presenting the chosen bodies, but determines to set them to work, engaging them in the dialogic reproduction of the tearful scene of greetings. The result is another grotesque and laborious tautology, with Launce as commentator doing all the work of 'showing' the exchange:

> Now come I to my father: 'Father, your blessing.' Now should not the shoe speak a word for weeping; now should I kiss my father; well, he weeps on; now come I to my mother. O that she could speak now, like a wood woman! Well, I kiss her. Why, there 'tis: here's my mother's breath up and down. Now come I to my sister: mark the moan she makes. Now the dog all this while sheds not a tear; nor speaks a word; but see how I lay the dust with my tears. (23–32)

The pointer all too rapidly loses its point.

## (VI) 'TROMPE L'OREILLE': VERBAL ICONS

Launce's toilsome stage management throws light on a further and fundamental aspect of the interplay between language and other semiotic factors on stage. His desire to establish a sign relationship linking a group of present objects ('this shoe', etc.) to a number of absent agents ('my father', etc.) presupposes not only that the slightest similarity between the two will suffice ('she is . . . small as a wand'), but that indeed any one of the objects, more or less, can come to stand for any given figure. Hence Launce's uncertainty. And in any case, the appointed sign vehicles themselves prove, in the event, anything but indispensable, since practically all the hard labour of representation is borne by linguistic description.

The principle at work here is what the Prague School semioticians termed the *transformability* or *dynamism* of the theatrical sign (see Bogatyrev 1938; Honzl 1940; Elam 1980: 12–16). There is no limit, in theory, to the range of signifying roles that any stage vehicle can play. Even the *dramatis persona* is not invariably figured by the human figure: all that is required is 'something real . . . able to assume this function'; so that 'the actor is not necessarily a man; it can be a puppet, or a machine . . . or even an object' (Honzl 1940: 75).

Honzl extends this principle to the operations of discourse, and particularly to certain 'visual' functions fulfilled by linguistic description, or what he calls *'acoustic scenery'* (1940: 75). The roles of those stage vehicles which register along the visual channel – thus sets, props and even, at an extreme, bodies – can be to some extent usurped by the evocative force of linguistic reference, so that the actual embodiment of the scene on stage is not always obligatory. This is precisely what Launce discovers, but a little late.

Honzl's 'acoustic scenery' takes us out of the realm of the index (which supposes the physical presence of the thing referred to, the referent) and into that of the *icon*, that species of sign which evokes an image of the object through similarity of some kind. 'Anything whatever, be it quality, existent individual, or law', declares Peirce' 'is an Icon of anything, in so far as it is like that thing and used as a sign of it' (1931–58: 2. 247). Iconism is most clearly exemplified in the representation of the human body by the human body, costume by costume, weapons by the equivalent stage props, and so on. But the criterion of being 'like that thing' is sufficiently general and flexible to allow more schematic iconic relations to be formed (Peirce terms them 'diagrams'): a green backcloth figures a country scene or a wooden staff Launce's sister (the 'similarity' here consisting in the common trait of slenderness).

And indeed, inasmuch as 'anything whatever ... is an Icon of anything' provided that it be 'used as a sign of it', the principle of similarity involved may be purely metaphorical (Peirce, in fact, considers metaphor a subclass of icon). The actor's body may stand iconically for a table, or the stage area for a court or field, to the extent that they succeed in evoking the appropriate images in the spectator's mind or in being accepted, in any case, as substitutes.

By the same token, language, which normally has the general task of standing iconically for the discourse of the *dramatis personae*, may come to assume other iconic duties in the theatre, including that of representing scenes and persons, providing that it successfully provokes the corresponding image. A sign, as Peirce puts it, 'may be iconic, that is, may represent its object mainly by its similarity, no matter what its mode of being' (2. 276). Thus signs perceived *temporarily*, like the linguistic, can come to represent 'by similarity' objects defined *spatially* and *visually*. It is on the basis of such metaphorical iconism that Honzl's 'acoustic scenery' works, producing, so to speak, an auditory illusion or *trompe l'oreille* in conjuring up a 'visual' image by purely verbal means.

Now far from being the brainchild of twentieth-century semioticians, the category of the icon is present in the taxonomies of the classical (including Elizabethan) rhetoricians, and precisely as a metaphorical or similitudinous 'visualizing' of the object. Henry Peacham's definition is the fullest: 'Icon, when the image of a thing or person, is painted out by comparing and resembling forme with forme, quallitye with quallity, and one likenesse with another, I may paint forth a ravinous and venemous person after this manner, even like a cressed Dragon' (1577: Vii[r]). As such, verbal iconism falls under the general rhetorical rubric of *energia*, the mode of vivid description (or in Puttenham's Englished terms, 'counterfait representation') whereby discourse is enlivened and the auditor's imagination stimulated to reproduce an image ('counterfait') of the described object.

In Elizabethan drama, iconic counterfeit representations occupy a prominent place not merely as scene-setting or narrative devices, but, in accordance with the rhetoric books, as efficacious means of vivifying dramatic discourse and of striking the auditor's fantasy. And in Shakespearean comedy, the verbal icon, sparingly used, often appears as a monologic set-piece, a luxurious *tour de parole* developed beyond its immediate information-bearing utility.

The forest scenes of *AYLI* are obvious occasions for verbal evocation of the dramatic landscape by means of the particular subset of icons known to the rhetoricians as *topographia* (Puttenham's 'counterfait place'). The first speech in Arden, the Duke's emblematic essay on the pastoral life, sets the pattern (it might be noted here that the icon extends and fleshes out an initial indexical reference to the present scene):

> Are not these woods
> More free from peril than the envious court?
> Here feel we not the penalty of Adam,
> The seasons' difference, as the icy fang
> And churlish chiding of the winter's wind (2. 1. 3ff.)

while the maximum of topographic intensity is reached a few lines later in the First Lord's meticulous description of the preposterously picturesque forest spectacle witnessed by Jaques (in this case the object is a scenic 'elsewhere' allowing a full-blown and autonomous descriptive show):

> Under an oak, whose antique root peeps out
> Upon the brook that brawls along this wood,
> To the which place a poor sequester'd stag,
> That from the hunter's aim had ta'en a hurt,
> Did come to languish. (2. 1. 31ff.)

Scenes normally contain events, and the topographic icon is readily extendible into a form of pseudo-narrative reproducing or mimicking of off-stage or earlier on-stage action. The narrative version of the device, *pragmatographia* ('counterfait action'), permits the actor to intervene gesturally and paralinguistically in showing forth the physical and linguistic behaviour of the described agent, while conserving the full 'painterly' force of the description. A conspicuous example occurs in *LLL*, in Boyet's reporting of the lords' masque-rehearsal:

> Under the cool shade of a sycamore
> I thought to close mine eyes some half an hour,
> When, lo! to interrupt my purpos'd rest,
> Towards that shade I might behold address
> The king and his companions: warily
> I stole into a neighbour thicket by,
> And overheard what you shall overhear: ...
> With that all laugh'd and clapp'd him on the shoulder,
> Making the bold wag by their praises bolder.
> One rubb'd his elbow thus, and fleer'd, and swore
> A better speech was never spoke before;
> Another, with his finger and his thumb,
> Cry'd 'Via!' – (5. 2. 89ff.)

(Note again how the iconic account includes indexical elements which secure its full incorporation into the present speaking and acting situation: Boyet's 'rubb'd his elbow *thus*' calls inescapably for gestural mimicry of the event.)

But the strongest claim that time-bound language makes to 'usurping' the mimetic force of spatially perceived stage signs is in its relations with the most imposing of vehicles, and physical source of speech itself, namely, the body. Cameo sketches of both present and absent bodies or their parts and accessories tend to 'outdo' the actor's embodying power in the figural intensity of their descriptions. The precise object is often enough the most representative and character-betraying body part, the face, figured in the description labelled rhetorically as *prosopographia* ('counterfait countenance'), as in Aegeon's hyperbolic depiction of his own physical decay in *CE*:

> Though now this grained face of mine be hid
> In sap-consuming winter's drizzled snow,
> And all the conduits of my blood froze up (5. 2. 311ff.)

or the Prince of Morocco's tropical apology for his negritude in *MV*:

> Mislike me not for my complexion,
> The shadow'd livery of the burnish'd sun,
> To whom I am a neighbour and near bred. (2. 1. 1ff.)

The verbal representation of the whole human figure and its metonymies, *prosopopeia* or 'counterfait in Personation', achieves an unparalleled degree of detail and extensiveness in *TS*, where Petruchio's much-indicated wedding apparel is fully catalogued immediately prior to his arrival, so that the actor's entry on stage may have the effect of straightforward confirmation or of comic contradiction:

*Bio.* Why, Petruchio is coming in a new hat and an old jerkin; a pair of old breeches thrice turned; a pair of boots that have been candle-cases, one buckled, another laced; an old rusty sword ta'en out of the town armoury, with a broken hilt, and chapeless; with two broken points; his horse hipped – with an old mothy saddle and stirrups of no kindred. (3. 2. 41ff.)

Undoubtedly, these categories possess a very relative analytic value and in part reflect the classical rhetoricians' passion for name-giving (thus they provide such highly useful labels as *dendographia*, the description of a tree and *hydrographia*, the description of water – and why not *podographia*, the representation of a foot, or *kynographia*, the 'counterfait dog'?). The point is, rather, that however we christen the devices and even if we prefer to give them no name at all, for the Elizabethans the 'pictorial' use of words constituted a well-defined rhetorical game much recommended for its efficacy as locutionary *coup* upon the ear and the mind's eye. And it is as such, i.e. as a mode of 'graphic' virtuosity, that the verbal icon is normally presented in the comedies.

This emerges clearly enough from the frames placed around certain of the verbal pictures, whose double allegiance (acoustic and 'optical') is either directly vaunted or scornfully criticized. In *AYLI*, for example, the Duke's idyllic scene-setting is in turn praised by one of his listeners as a stylistic feat justly rendering its personified object in linguistic terms:

*Ami.*                          Happy is your grace
             That can translate the stubbornness of fortune
             Into so quiet and so sweet a style (2. 1. 18–20);

1     'D'un amore incurabile', emblem from Gabriele Symeone, *Le sententiose imprese.*

while the First Lord's account of Jaques's encounter with the deer (p. 59 above), the plight of which was a commonplace of contemporary iconography (Figure 1; see Uhlig 1970), is commented as the paraphrase of a standard emblem, from which Jaques – in emblem-book fashion – goes on to draw suitable allegorical conclusions. Here, then, the reported verbal icon bears explicit pictorial connotations of dubious cultural prestige.

*Duke S.*                       But what said Jaques?
             Did he not moralize this spectacle?

*First L.*    O yes, into a thousand similes.
          First, for his weeping into the needless stream,
          'Poor deer', quoth he, 'thou mak'st a testament
          As worldlings do, giving thy sum of more
          To that which had too much.' (2. 1. 43ff.).

Portia, in *MV*, elects the *descriptio* game as a pastime worthy of filling part of the long wait prior to the discovery of the identity of her husband-to-be. Having set up the terms of the exercise, she proceeds to furnish a veritable gallery of cameos representing her various suitors (the very men who, in succeeding scenes, are to be confronted with a series of icons allegorizing the felicity or otherwise of their choice of casket):

*Por.*    I pray thee, over-name them, and as thou namest them, I will describe them; and, according to my description, level at my affection.
*Ner.*    First, there is the Neapolitan prince.
*Por.*    Ay, that's a colt indeed, for he doth nothing but talk of his horse. (1. 2. 39ff.)

Not all the frames echo the rhetoricians' enthusiasm for the iconic display. More scathing comments associate it with trite poetasting or with facile substituting for wit. This is clearly the force of Orlando's counter to Jaques's accusation of cliché-peddling:

*Jaques.*    You are full of pretty answers. Have you not been acquainted with goldsmiths' wives, and conned them out of rings?
*Orl.*    Not so; but I answer you right painted cloth, from whence you have studied your questions (3. 2. 266–70)

as it is of Rosaline's judgment regarding Berowne's simile-ridden sonnet in *LLL* (she plays, it might be noted, on the ambivalently 'graphic' nature of the composition, i.e. as portrait rendered through calligraphic signs):

*Ros.*    I am compared to twenty thousand fairs.
          O! he hath drawn my picture in his letter.
*Prin.*    Any thing like?
*Ros.*    Much in the letters, nothing in the praise. (5. 2. 37–40; on 'graphic' games, see also pp. 262–4 below)

Such commentary reminds us that however effectively it brings off the acoustic-visual illusion, the icon not only remains exquisitely linguistic but almost invariably advertises its own discursive status. Indeed, more often than not, the description falls into one or more topics more or less codified in the books of *inventio*, adages, proverbs or emblems of the time. A prominent example is what Peacham and his

colleagues would have termed the 'dendographic' (or tree-describing)
element recurrent in many of the scenic representations. Two of the
more vivid descriptions in *AYLI* begin in similar fashion:

> Under an oak, whose antique root peeps out
> Upon the brook that brawls along this wood (2. 1. 31ff.)

> Under an old oak, whose boughs were moss'd with age
> And high top bald with dry antiquity (4. 3. 104ff.);

an opening which (in addition to Amiens's 'Under the greenwood tree'
song) Boyet's report in *LLL* closely parallels:

> Under the cool shade of a sycamore
> I thought to close mine eyes some half an hour. (5. 2. 89ff.)

At its most intensely figural, indeed, the device becomes less
functional description than literary conceit in the Petrarchan mould,
the natural exponent of which is the effusive lover and the natural form
of which the hyperbolic compliment, such as Navarre's in *LLL*:

> So sweet a kiss the golden sun gives not
> To those fresh morning drops upon the rose,
> As thy eye-beams when their fresh rays have smote
> The night of dew that on my cheeks down flows. (4. 3. 24ff.)

And as rhetorical construct lending itself readily to banality and excess,
the icon is easily burlesqued. *LLL* is replete with bombastic, failed or
parodied versions of the pictorial display, from Armado's narcissistic
*narratio* of his simple walk in the park ('So it is, besieged with
sable-coloured melancholy, I did commend the black oppressing
humour to the most wholesome physic of thy health-giving air', 1. 1.
227ff.) to the lords' ironical contest in painting 'by comparing and
resembling forme with forme, quallitye with quallity, and one likenesse
with another':

| | |
|---|---|
| *Ber.* | And therefore is she born to make black fair. |
| | Her favour turns the fashion of the days, |
| | For native blood is counted painting now: |
| | And therefore red, that would avoid dispraise, |
| | Paints itself black to imitate her brow. |
| *Dum.* | To look like her are chimney-sweepers black. |
| *Long.* | And since her time are colliers counted bright. |
| *King.* | And Ethiops of their sweet complexion crack. |
| *Dum.* | Dark needs no candles now, for dark is light (4. 3. 257ff.) |

and the Princess's gentle travesty of earnest scene-setting, undertaken
purely as an occasion for a quibble:

| | |
|---|---|
| *Prin.* | Was that the king, that spurr'd his horse so hard |
| | Against the steep-up rising of the hill? |

63

*For.*      I know not; but I think it was not he.
*Prin.*     Whoe'er a' was, a' show'd a mounting mind. (4. 1. 1–4)

*Pragmatographia*, a counterfeit action, becomes *paronomasia*, an authentic pun.

It is difficult, then, to agree with that critical tradition (concerning 'verbal scenography' and the like: see Stamm 1954; Bellinghausen 1955; d'Amico 1974) which sees the aspiration of language to metaphorical visuality as an attempted substitution for the equivalent stage vehicles. A. M. Nagler, emphasizing the richness of mimetic scenic means in the Elizabethan theatre, justly objects to so naïve an assessment of Shakespearean description: 'One of the many widespread myths about the Elizabethan theatre is that the dramatists of the time made up for the lack of illusionistic elements by more or less poetic description from the mouths of their characters. Poetry, by this theory, becomes a substitute for scenery' (1958: 32).

While no one would wish to deny the essential informational and representational roles that it often plays on stage, it is nevertheless more accurate to see the Shakespearean icon primarily as a species of verbal virtuosity which acquires particular weight just *because* of its co-operation with literal visual signs. Indeed, the more 'visual' it becomes, the more it betrays its linguistic constitution. For the same reason, the claim that the play scenes in *MND* offer 'a parody of the author's own use of verbal scenography' ('O grim-look'd night! O night with hue so black!', etc., Stamm 1954: 33) is highly questionable, since ingenuous scene-painting for purely expository purposes has little to do with actual Shakespearean practice. The Mechanicals' tragedy, indeed, actually manages to confuse the visual with the auditory channel:

*Pyr.*     I see a voice; now will I to the chink,
          To spy and I can hear my Thisbe's face. (5. 1. 190–1).

Shakespeare's comedies, instead, exploit the distance between them. More often than not, the descriptive exposition turns out to be a discursive exhibition (on the semantic implications of verbal iconism, see pp. 139–40 below).

(VII) ALL THE WORLD'S A DIALOGUE: SPEAKING AS PERFORMANCE

The manner in which the different theatrical and dramatic functions discussed so far – epilogues, indices, icons and the like, apart from the inner dramas proper – tend, as we have seen, to turn into local shows, instead of remaining transparent vehicles for expository material, can be taken as a symptom of a more general principle. The progress of the linguistic action and the unfolding of dramatic information in the comedies are in part brought about through a series of happenings apparently contrived for the benefit of some internal audience or for the self-gratification of the speaker, and which are best described as *performances*. The very act of speaking, however banal its actual 'dramatic' content, assumes a directly theatrical character.

This *mise-en-scène* of speech-production within the plays not only dramatizes the speaking situation but increases the 'listenability' of the speech event itself. The simplest and most automatic act – the reading of a letter, the posing or answering of a question, the relating of a recent event, the naming of an individual, the defining of a term – may be stage-managed as a star turn requiring particular improvisational and histrionic skills. And the intensity of the production has little or nothing to do with the actual importance of the event, or rather, is often inversely proportional to it. This is seen most clearly in *LLL*, where the speaking–performance equation is rapidly established as the norm, conspicuously in the long and idle repartee between Armado and Moth and the wandering periphrastic exchanges between Holofernes and Nathaniel, in which every empty utterance becomes a show number, commissioned or announced beforehand and duly applauded afterwards:

| | |
|---|---|
| *Arm.* | I will hereupon confess I am in love; . . . Comfort me boy. What great men have been in love? |
| *Moth.* | Hercules, master. |
| *Arm.* | Most sweet Hercules! More authority, dear boy, name more. (1. 2. 53ff.) |
| | |
| *Arm.* | Define, define, well-educated infant. |
| *Moth.* | My father's wit and my mother's tongue assist me! |
| *Arm.* | Sweet invocation of a child; most pretty and pathetical! (88ff.) |
| | |
| *Arm.* | Sing, boy; my spirit grows heavy in love. (115) |
| | |
| *Arm.* | Warble, child: make passionate my sense of hearing. |
| *Moth.* | (*Sings*) Concolinel. |
| *Arm.* | Sweet air! (3. 1. 1ff.) |
| | |
| *Moth.* | A wonder, master! here's a costard broken in a shin. |
| *Arm.* | Some enigma, some riddle: come, thy l'envoy; begin. (67–8) |
| | |
| *Hol.* | I will something affect the letter; for it argues facility. The preyful princess pierc'd . . . |
| *Nath.* | A rare talent! (4. 2. 53ff.) |
| | |
| *Hol.* | Let me hear a staff, a stanze, a verse: *lege, domine*. (100) |

*LLL* has been described as a 'medley' (Granville-Barker 1927: 14 and Swinden 1973: 43) and as 'such stuff as . . . a revue-maker would offer us' (Charlton 1938: 45). This suggests that the succession of stage-turns it presents has indeed been perceived as such, even if in automatically pejorative terms. The continual invitations to take the stage or to attend to the offered proceedings ('*King.* Will you hear this letter with attention? / *Ber.* As we would an oracle', 1. 1. 212–13; '*Prin.* We will read it, I swear. / Break the neck of the wax and every one give ear', 4. 1. 59–60; '*Jaq.* I beseech your grace to let this letter be read . . . / *King.* Berowne, read it over', 4. 3. 190–2); the direct requests for the stage floor ('*Hol.* Shall I have audience?', 5. 1. 125); the reception of repartee as a form of sporting exhibition ('*Prin.* Well bandied both; a set of wit well played', 5. 2. 29); and the acclaim given to worthy demonstrations, including one's own ('*Ros.* Finely put off!', 4. 1. 111; '*Boy.* Finely put on!', 113; '*Cost.* By my troth, most pleasant: how both did fit it! / *Mar.* A mark marvellous well shot, for they both did hit it', 131–2) not only underline unmistakably the 'variety'-like nature of the goings-on but create a constant shifting in the inner performer–spectator dynamic. Each character is called now to be witness, now to be 'on'; even the rustics have the chance to do their piece:

| | |
|---|---|
| *Moth.* | I will tell it sensibly. |
| *Cost.* | Thou hast no feeling of it, Moth: I will speak that l'envoy. |
| | I, Costard, running out, that was safely within, |
| | Fell over the threshold and broke my shin. (3. 1. 110–14) |
| | |
| *Dull.* | You two are book-men: can you tell me by your wit |
| | What was a month old at Cain's birth, that's not |
| | five weeks old as yet? (4. 2. 33–4) |

Elsewhere, the utterance-spectacle is less consistently affirmed but certainly present, particularly in the early plays. The flyting in *TS*, for example, is perceived and received by the non-participants as a rhetorical wrestling match:

| | |
|---|---|
| *Bap.* | How likes Gremio these quick-witted folks? |
| *Gre.* | Believe me, sir, they butt together well (5. 2. 38–9); |

and in *TG* as a shooting competition:

| | |
|---|---|
| *Sil.* | A fine volley of words, gentlemen, and quickly shot off. (2. 4. 30–1) |

A phenomenon equally common to early and later comedies, however, is the direct application of theatrical metaphors to the characterization of the speaking situation or of the utterance itself. The speaker is no longer generically a *performer* but specifically a *stage actor*. It is not simply – this must be emphasized – the character and his general behaviour which is presented in stage terms, but precisely his intervention in the *linguistic* action. Rosalind leaves no doubt about the nature of this equation in her declared intention to participate in the

love scene between the shepherds Silvius and Phebe (itself framed as a
stage spectacle):

Corin.   If you will see a pageant truly play'd
         Between the pale complexion of true love
         And the red glow of scorn and proud disdain,
         Go hence a little, and I shall conduct you
         If you will mark it.
Ros.                      O come, let us remove.
         The sight of lovers feedeth those in love.
         Bring us to this sight, and you shall say
         I'll prove a busy actor in their play. (AYLI 3. 4. 48–55)

Likewise Puck suggests that his vocal mimicry of the Mechanicals is
essentially a histrionic ploy:

                    I'll be an auditor;
       An actor too perhaps, if I see cause (MND 3. 1. 75–6)

Examples are legion; but it is especially interesting to note that the
already many-layered overspying scene in LLL is further framed, at one
point, as a sorry and outmoded dramaturgic contrivance:

Ber.    All hid, all hid; an old infant play.
        Like a demi-god sit I in the sky,
        And wretched fools' secrets heedfully o'er-eye. (4. 3. 75–7)

  Not surprisingly, to the extent that such theatrical framing is applied
to verbal discourse, the play metaphor regularly takes a metadialogic
form. A given exchange is conceived, either by the agents themselves or
by some self-appointed observer, as a quasi-dramatic dialogue. This is
especially the case with those speaking situations deliberately set up to
trap or deceive some unknowing and unrehearsed outsider. The
stratagems used against Falstaff by the merry wives of Windsor are
consciously concocted in such terms:

Mrs F.   Mistress Page, remember you your cue.
Mrs P.   I warrant thee; if I do not act it, hiss me (3. 3. 33–4)

as, in MA, are the conversational ruses devised in order to provoke the
eavesdropping Benedick and Beatrice into amorous union:

Hero.    When I do name him, let it be thy part
         To praise him more than ever man did merit:
         My talk to thee must be how Benedick
         Is sick in love with Beatrice: ...
Urs.     Fear you not my part of the dialogue. (3. 1. 18–31)

The equally premeditated torturing of Parolles in AWW is relished in
advance as a dialogic diversion:

| *Ber.* | But shall we have this dialogue between the Fool and the Soldier? Come, bring forth this counterfeit module has deceiv'd me like a double-meaning prophesier. |
| *Second L.* | Bring him forth. (4. 3. 94–8) |

But the fullest and most ironical acknowledgment of the fact or act of speaking according to pseudo-dramatic constraints is unquestionably found in *TN*, and namely in Viola's feigned concern over the progress of her text-based message to Olivia. Proudly confessing the composed and rehearsed quality of her performance ('I pray you tell me if this be the lady of the house, for I never saw her. I would be loath to cast away my speech: for besides that it is excellently well penned, I have taken great pains to con it', 1. 5. 172–5), Viola hints at her quasi-histrionic position and thus her absolute dependence on her lines:

| *Oli.* | Whence came you, sir? |
| *Vio.* | I can say little more than I have studied, and that question's out of my part. Good gentle one, give me modest assurance if you be the lady of the house, that I may proceed in my speech. |
| *Oli.* | Are you a comedian? |
| *Vio.* | No, my profound heart: and yet, by the very fangs of malice I swear, I am not that I play. (178–85) |

Her interlocutor, however, refuses to abide by the same dramaturgic canons:

| *Oli.* | Come to what is important in't: I forgive you the praise. |
| *Vio.* | Alas, I took great pains to study it, and 'tis poetical. |
| *Oli.* | It is the more like to be feigned . . . 'tis not that time of moon with me to make one in so skipping a dialogue. (193–203) |

Now it is tempting to view references to the dialogic or dramatic constitution of the linguistic action as means of exposing, reflexively, the genuinely composed and rehearsed nature of the theatrical performance. Anne Righter claims that 'Essentially a technique for maintaining contact with the spectators, the play image also became in mature Shakespearian drama a meditation upon the nature of the theatre' (1962: 81). But while it is undoubtedly true that theatrical and dramatic metaphors bring into play audience consciousness of the drama-as-artifice, they depend equally on the convention according to which the dramatic persons do not share this privileged cognitive viewpoint, so that the 'this is like a dramatic dialogue' affirmation is charged with a certain irony for the playhouse auditor, but not for the play's speaker. Paradoxically, the metatheatrical frame may actually serve to authenticate the linguistic exchange, rather than define the play as such: in positing a hypothetical drama, the 'like a play' simile presupposes a point of reference which is in itself non-dramatic. A patent case in point is Fabian's comment on the programmed duping of Malvolio in *TN*:

> If this were played upon a stage now, I could condemn it as an improbable fiction. (3. 4. 128–9)

In asserting the speech–performance equation, furthermore, the comedies might be said to reflect not only 'upon the nature of theatre' but equally upon the nature of speech in its social manifestation. For if dramatic performance is the mimesis of social intercourse, the reverse is also true, as Goffmanian sociology has been at pains to demonstrate:

> All in all, then, I am suggesting that what talkers undertake to do is not to provide information to a recipient but to present dramas to an audience. Indeed, it seems that we spend most of our time not engaged in giving information but in giving shows. . . . The point is that ordinarily when an individual says something, he is not saying it as a bald statement of fact on his own behalf. He is recounting. He is running through a strip of already determined events for the engagement of his listeners. (Goffman 1974: 508)

This reflective force of the commentary is most apparent when it is amplified into the full-blown *theatrum mundi* topic. For example, the *locus classicus* of the Shakespearean version of this commonplace, Jaques's 'All the world's a stage' set-piece, gives a central place, in the behaviour it surveys, to the modes of discourse characteristic of each histrionic generation:

>                         . . . And then the lover,
> Sighing like furnace, with a woeful ballad
> Made to his mistress' eyebrow. Then, a soldier,
> Full of strange oaths, and bearded like the pard,
> Jealous in honour, sudden, and quick in quarrel, . . .
>                         And then, the justice, . . .
> Full of wise saws, and modern instances,
> And so he plays his part. The sixth age shifts . . .
>                         and his big manly voice,
> Turning again toward childish treble, pipes
> And whistles in his sound (2. 7. 147–63);

and when Antonio invokes the *topos* – somewhat mechanically – in *MV*, it is taken up and developed by Gratiano precisely as a framework within which to consider the contrasting speech habits (or silence) of the mundane players:

Ant.   I hold the world but as the world Gratiano,
       A stage, where every man must play a part,
       And mine a sad one.
Gra.                        Let me play the fool,
       With mirth and laughter let old wrinkles come, . . .

69

> There are a sort of men whose visages
> Do cream and mantle like a standing pond, . . .
> As who should say, 'I am Sir Oracle,
> And when I ope my lips, let no dog bark.'
> O my Antonio, I do know of these
> That therefore only are reputed wise
> For saying nothing; when I am very sure
> If they should speak, would almost damn those ears
> Which (hearing them) would call their brothers fools.
>
> (I. I. 77–99)

Thus, to adapt Petronius and the Globe motto, it is not only that *totus mundus agit histrionem* ('all the world acts like a player'), but, more specifically, that *totus mundus loquitur ut histrionem* ('all the world speaks like a player'). The dramatic world may be figured as 'This wide and universal theatre' (*AYLI* I. I. 136) to the extent that its speakers are bound continually to perform within it, but it is on these very grounds that dramatic discourse most directly reflects the quotidian.

## (VIII) 'TOO LONG FOR A PLAY': THE WORK IN PROGRESS

From the simple *equation* of the speaking situation with a drama to the open *acknowledgment* of the comedy or its performance in progress is a bigger step, logically, than it might seem. Unlike some of Jonson's (and, later, Pirandello's) plays, Shakespeare's comedies never toy consistently with the ontological barrier whereby the spectator can 'see into' the world of the *dramatis persona* but not vice versa, and whereby the dramatic figures cannot know of their own fictional status. Shakespeare's speakers, on the whole, are left serenely blind to their own textual origins.

Yet there is one instance where the dramatic trope is so extended as virtually to abandon its merely hypothetical character ('as if it were a play') and to take on, instead, the force of a direct framing of *the* play. The references in question occur in the final scene of *LLL*, a scene in which concern for the theatrical goings-on within the play (the masque, the pageant) is gradually transformed into an apparent awareness of the narrative progress of the main comedy. This radical shift of axis is first signalled in Berowne's discovery of the plot against the masquers (although here the trope is still a definite simile):

> I see the trick on't: here was a consent,
> Knowing aforehand of our merriment,
> To dash it like a Christmas comedy. (5. 2. 459–61)

The change in point of view (moving from within, as it were, to without) is further marked by Berowne's curious identification of the pageant presenters with their *commedia dell'arte* stock equivalents, thus suggesting that the speakers are as much codified stereotypes as the historical roles they are about to assume:

> The pedant, the braggart, the hedge-priest, the fool,
> and the boy:–
> Abate throw at novum, and the whole world again
> Cannot pick out five such, take each one in his vein. (536–9)

But it is the interruption of the pageant by Marcade that definitively secures the transference of focus from the inner spectacle to the comedy proper. Again it is Berowne who registers the effect of Marcade's news, displacing the dramatic scene from the pageant stage to the wider fictional context:

> Worthies, away! The scene begins to cloud. (714)

Since the close of the comedy follows rapidly on the dissolution of the pageant – the two endings being separated by the ladies' refusal to marry the lords immediately – this paralellism is developed into a confession and critique of the play's own convention-breaking incompleteness. Berowne not only accurately defines the kind of fictional structure in which he is involved, but insists that, if he and his fellows must be governed by comic canons, then at least those canons (notably that old neoclassical straitjacket, the unity of time) should be applied in full, with no false finishes:

> Ber.     Our wooing doth not end like an old play;
> Jack hath not Jill: these ladies' courtesy
> Might well have made our sport a comedy.
> King.     Come, sir, it wants a twelvemonth and a day,
> And then 'twill end.
> Ber.                                    That's too long for a play. (866–70)

Berowne's vain attempt to steer the concluding linguistic action along the prescribed illocutionary course (i.e. to convert the ladies' striking refusal into a conventional acceptance) is all the more elegant an irony for the fact that the overall dramatic frame, that which keeps the speakers in their fictional places, is never unambiguously broken. Berowne does not fully emerge from the action in order to comment on it, but, more interestingly, is allowed to be at once its victim and its dramaturgically competent analyst. The game may be up, but that does not mean that it is over.

# 2  Universes

WORLD-CREATING STRATEGIES: CONTEXTS AND
CO-TEXTS

All the hard linguistic labours – presentational, vocal, descriptive, indicative, etc. – reviewed in the last chapter have to do with the delicate relationship between two distinct but interdependent domains, the theatrical and the dramatic. But the dramatic realm is at the same time subject to a logic of its own, and the purpose of this chapter is to explore some of the ways in which the fictional world is created in the comedies, together with the dramatic, comic and self-exploratory uses to which this very creating is put.

The drama, as Aristotle teaches us, sets up its fictional domain not by narration from 'without' (*diegesis*) but by the direct representation of events 'within' the dramatic world (*mimesis*). This means that narrative information will normally be provided to the audience through the interactions of the very persons who make up the fictional realm. The dramatic world defines itself, so to speak, as it goes along. Here lies the peculiar reflexivity of dramatic discourse, which has to convey expository content regarding the individuals who supposedly issue and receive it (say, Shylock and Portia), the circumstances in which it is supposedly issued (Venice, the courtroom) and the action which its very issuing constitutes (the demanding, for example, of a pound of flesh). In the comedies, however, this world-creating reflexivity of the dialogue is much more than a conventional narrative short cut (or way of expelling the story-teller, as it were, from the story-telling). It becomes a major source of rhetorical vitality in itself.

The operations of the dialogue in setting up the world of the drama can be usefully seen as a dynamic triangle, involving a triple discursive orientation. First, there is an orientation to the dramatic universe itself and its individuals, taken as *objects of discourse*. Second comes the *context of utterance* as it emerges directly from the dialogue (the I–you and here–now of the speech exchange). And the third element is an orientation towards the *co-text*, i.e. the *verbal* context of the discourse with its internal semantic and syntactic structure (see Petöfi 1975). It is

72

with these three axes of linguistic activity that the following discussion is primarily concerned.

An inviting point of departure may be found in the comparison of two directly related fictional worlds and their construction: those of *AYLI* and of its main source, Lodge's *Rosalynd*. At the levels both of *fabula* (or underlying story) and actual plot, Shakespeare follows the inherited narrative pattern with an unusual degree of fidelity. But any parallel episode – the wrestling match is a good instance – will reveal the radical divergences not only in the elaboration of the narrative material, but more particularly in the disposition of discourse along the three axes of orientation.

Lodge presents the event through classical narration of the most ingenuously 'transparent' kind: a mixture of straightforward diegesis ('it chaunced that *Torismund* King of *France* had appoynted for his pleasure a day of Wrastling and of Tournament'), direct character portrayal ('a Champion there was to stand against all commers – a *Norman*, a man of tall stature and of great strength'), *oratio obliqua* ('He went to young Rosader . . . and began to tell him of this Tournament and Wrastling') and quoted direct speech ('now brother (quoth he) for the honour of Sir John of Bourdeaux'). The only elements indicating a distinct narrative voice – and at that a collective proverbial voice – are the parenthetic and moralistic Latin tags punctuating the account ('The *Norman* desirous of pelfe, as (*Quis nisi mentis inops oblatum respuit aurum?*)'). In other words, all but eliminating the indices of the context of utterance – at most dimly implied in the narrative point of view – Lodge's narration places all its weight on the orientation, from without, towards its objects of discourse, namely the individuals and events described. As for the co-text, it remains both self-effacingly outward- and backward-looking, since references are always to the past fictional domain, never to the discourse in progress.

Shakespeare's dramatization of this incident is set – typically for this comedy – within an apparently rambling series of more or less playful colloquies, ushered in by the ladies' resolution to defeat despondency through verbal pastimes (*'Cel.* Therefore, my sweet Rose, my dear Rose, be merry. / *Ros.* From henceforth I will, coz, and devise sports', 1. 2. 21–3). Only after a lengthy warm-up in the guise of a wit contest with Touchstone is preliminary information regarding the scene's central event introduced. And what is made of it is quite instructive. Shakespeare resorts to the conventional solution of the messenger, allowing the ladies' recreation to be strategically interrupted by the 'real' topic of the day, clearly signalled as a piece of tellable and listenable, if gossipy, intelligence:

| | |
|---|---|
| *Cel.* | Here comes Monsieur Le Beau. |
| | (*Enter Le Beau*) |
| *Ros.* | With his mouth full of news. |
| *Cel.* | Which he will put on us, as pigeons feed their young. |
| *Ros.* | Then shall we be news-crammed. |
| *Cel.* | All the better; we shall be the more marketable. |
| | Bon jour, Monsieur Le Beau. What's the news? (84–91) |

Le Beau appears to represent an internal or introjected version of Lodge's narrator, ready to impart equivalent details with similar diegetic earnestness ('Fair Princess, you have lost much good sport'). But he is never permitted to fulfil so innocent an information-bearing role. From the outset his attempts to orient his and the ladies' discourse to the other scene, that spatiotemporal elsewhere in which the wrestling tournament has already got under way, are frustrated by the continual intervention of his interlocutors, who are decidedly less co-operative than Lodge's implicit readers. The ladies seize his every outward-looking reference as just another occasion for their *intra*referential semantic diversions, until the messenger, in order to get his account out, takes refuge in the conditional (what he might have related in a now hypothetical report):

| | |
|---|---|
| *Le Beau.* | . . . good sport. |
| *Cel.* | Sport? Of what colour? |
| *Le Beau.* | What colour, madam? How shall I answer you? |
| *Ros.* | As wit and fortune will. |
| *Touch.* | Or as the Destinies decrees. |
| *Cel.* | Well said! That was laid on with a trowel. |
| *Touch.* | Nay, if I keep not my rank – |
| *Ros.* | Thou losest thy old smell. |
| *Le Beau.* | You amaze me, ladies. I would have told you of good wrestling, which you have lost sight of. (92–102) |

And when the ladies finally concede to Le Beau a certain licence as raconteur ('*Ros.* Yet tell us the manner of the wrestling'), they insist nevertheless on maintaining the dominion of the discourse in progress over the described individuals and events by interrupting with a running analysis of the narration itself and its constituent moves:

| | |
|---|---|
| *Cel.* | Well, the beginning that is dead and buried. |
| *Le Beau.* | There comes an old man and his three sons – |
| *Cel.* | I could match this beginning with an old tale. |
| *Le Beau.* | Three proper young men, of excellent growth and presence – |
| *Ros.* | With bills on their necks: 'Be it known unto all men by these presents'. (108–14) |

The episode is an exemplary essay in the referential poetics of Shakespearean comedy: direct narrativity of the kind originally intended by Le Beau (sent in good faith, as it were, as delegate of the source romance) is refused in favour of a dialogic telling which privileges the current communicative context, and still more the brilliantly self-propagating co-text, over the proposed objects of discourse. And as if to cap the point, the absent other place – the scene of the wrestling – becomes shortly afterwards the here and now of the dialogue not because the present speakers, or the audience, are taken to it, but because *it* is brought, mountain-to-Mohammed- or Birnam Wood-to-Dunsinane-like, to them, in order to be duly subjected to the ladies' commentary:

Le Beau.  . . . and if it please your ladyships, you may see the end, for the best is yet to do, and *here where you are* they are coming to perform it. . . .
Cel.  Yonder sure they are coming. Let us now stay and see it. (104–37, my italics)

It is important to emphasize that what is meant by context here is not the dramatic scene at large within which the speech event arises: this is better termed, following an established linguistic tradition, the situation of utterance (see p. 179). Context, instead, comprises only 'the factors which, by virtue of their influence upon the participants in the language-event, systematically determine the form, the appropriateness or the meaning of utterances' (Lyons 1977: 572). As the emblematic scene of frustrated narration from *AYLI* amply illustrates, the context of utterance is the first and main point of dialogic orientation. At the outset, before any reference is made to the situation, local or global (i.e. the dramatic world beyond the scene), what is established is, as it were, an *internal model* of the most influential external factors, namely the participants and their relationship, at first purely pronominal but immediately afterwards, and within the same utterance, fleshed out as an actual kinship:

Cel.  I pray thee, sweet my coz, be merry. (1. 2. 1)

If the primary and most evident contextual clues here are the deictic terms (I–thee), this simple utterance also traces most of the essential semantic and pragmatic parameters within which the ensuing colloquy develops. These can be summarily outlined as follows:

*Role.* Over and above the alternating deictic roles assumed (I–you), the participants' social role relationship emerges through the actual choice of pronoun (*thee*). The suggestion of equality is confirmed by 'my coz'.

*Status.* Again the actual social status of the interlocutors, determining their reciprocal attitudes and styles, appears at once parallel; this is confirmed and amplified through successive bits of oblique information (the speakers' sex, age and noble origins, their similar nubile state, etc.).

*Province* (see Crystal and Davy 1969). It becomes rapidly clear that the girls are engaged not in any specific occupation- or activity-geared exchange, and that the pragmatic province within which the dialogue unfolds is that of 'conversation' (thus not directed towards any agreed end or task and not constrained by any particular professional lexicon).

*Degree of formality.* In the terms of M. Joos (1962; see also Lyons 1977: 580), the initial utterance indicates that the conversation will be placed on the bottom rung of the formality scale, i.e. will be 'intimate' in style. This is a decisive factor in the choice of lexemes and syntax (NB '*sweet* my coz') (my italics).

*Pragmatic presupposition.* Much is obviously presupposed as 'shared knowledge' between the participants, and is thus to be inferred by the auditor rather than being overtly stated. Not only their existing relationship, Rosalind's sadness and the events responsible for it, but the entire social sphere in which they both move (roughly equivalent to the domain described by Lodge) is taken as a conversational given, and is partially reconstructible only later, from references made, as it were, from within.

*Topic.* The conversational topic or subject-matter that underlies the dialogue until, and even, to some extent, after, the entry of Le Beau, paraphrasable as 'smiling in the face of adversity', is partially lexicalized at once ('be merry').

*Illocutionary intentions.* Celia's performative verb phrase ('I pray thee') and the actual request she produces first indicate her own and then imply her interlocutor's illocutionary stance in the exchange, i.e. supplication and lament respectively. The opposition between these two positions is maintained for the first twenty-five lines and reappears sporadically thereafter.

*Propositional attitude.* While implying the 'actual' state of affairs (Rosalind's misfortune and misery), Celia's request also creates a possible world – the world of her wants – in which all is felicity. This world-creating act not only anticipates the eventual narrative development of the comedy (its inevitable happy ending) but manifests an attitude which is of some dramatic significance in itself: Celia's desire to bring about the happy state of affairs is a major propulsive influence in the play, in part determining later actions (the flight to Arden, etc.).

Now, the point of this micro-analysis is not really or merely to reveal the informational overloading of one fairly modest line. It is, rather, to demonstrate a more general principle of Shakespearean poetics: the dramatic world is in the first instance an implicit network of contextual constraints on a speech event at once defined within and defining of that world. Wider-ranging propositional acts (the acts of referring and predicating: see section (v) below) are invariably filtered, as it were, through the communicative context, which, however variable the actual speaking situations, remains constant.

Precisely because of its omnipresence, the context of utterance does not usually come to prominence as a definite component of the comedies' world-creating activities. It lays the groundwork, rather, for other more articulate and conspicuous referential games. There are, nevertheless, instances of context being brought into the foreground as the main linguistic business or even as the main metalinguistic topic. This is especially true in *CE*, where the doubling of names and faces, and the consequent swapping of conversational partners, play havoc with the whole range of contextual constraints on the dialogue: presupposed shared knowledge is found not to be shared at all, social roles are confused, styles suggesting close acquaintanceship are inappropriately applied, and so on. The resulting perplexities are registered above all through emphatically stressed and reiterated personal pronouns:

*Eph. Dro.*  To me, sir? why, you gave no gold to me. (1. 2. 71)

*Syr. Ant.*  Plead you to me, fair dame? I know you not. . . .
*Syr. Dro.*  By me?
*Adr.*  By thee. . . .
*Syr. Dro.*  I, sir? I never saw her till this time. . . .
          I never spake with her in all my life. (2. 2. 147–65)

In exasperation, one of the two Dromio twins, when they finally meet, accuses the other of usurping not only his proper name but also his role (social, deictic and the rest):

*Eph. Dro.*  O villain, thou hast stol'n both mine office and my name. (3. 1. 44)

Otherwise, it is the *meeting* of contexts that draws attention to the linguistic means in force. Where, for example, the objects of discourse of a detached text (poem, letter) correspond to the participants in the ongoing exchange, the result is a proud or surprised pronominal claim on the part of the doubly involved individual:

*King.*  (*Reading*) . . . there did I see that low-spirited swain, that base minnow of thy mirth, –
*Cost.*  Me?
*King.*  that unlettered small-knowing soul, –
*Cost.*  Me?
*King.*  that shallow vassal, –
*Cost.*  Still me?
*King.*  which, as I remember, hight Costard, –

| | |
|---|---|
| *Cost.* | O! me. (*LLL*, 1. 1. 243–50) |
| *Mal.* | (*Reading*) 'Besides, you waste the treasure of your time with a foolish knight' – |
| *Sir And.* | That's me, I warrant you. |
| *Mal.* | 'One Sir Andrew.' |
| *Sir And.* | I knew 'twas I, for many do call me fool. (*TN* 2. 5. 77–81) |

The social status implicit in pronoun choice is, of course, central to practically all the exchanges, be they between equals or between superiors and inferiors (see Quirk 1970), and indeed it constitutes the prime index of the speakers' relationship. Above all, what Roger Brown and Albert Gilman christened the 'power semantic' underlying the T/V (in English, thou/you) opposition, whereby 'the superior says T and receives V' (1960: 255), is as much in play in the comedies as it is in the more obviously power-dominated realms of the tragedies and history plays, although it bears less dramatic weight. The connotations at stake are brought to consciousness in *TN*, where Sir Toby ironically recommends the power-enhancing effect of a well-placed 'T' or three in Sir Andrew's otherwise less than imposing challenge to Viola:

| | |
|---|---|
| *Sir To.* | Taunt him with the licence of ink. If thou thou'st him some thrice, it shall not be amiss. (3. 2. 42–4) |

The principles of the dialogic 'contextualizing' of narrative material, together with the mental labours this calls for on the part of the theatrical spectator, are vividly illustrated in the opening scene of *MV*, which presents an apparently leisurely – though in fact tension-charged – discussion between Antonio and two friends. The amount of actual dramatic intelligence to be given is fairly modest and is limited almost exclusively to Antonio himself, despite his relative silence: his name, his melancholy state, his social role and status (as merchant), his investment in argosies and their uncertain fate. These few informational 'bits', the first items in the auditor's stock of knowledge regarding the fictional realm, have to be processed through a kind of synthetic paraphrase from a fairly extensive weave of affirmations, speculations and denials. It is not, in other words, one world that is presented, ready defined, but a series of alternative 'belief' worlds projected by Antonio's interlocutors on the basis of his opening declaration ('In sooth I know not why I am so sad'). Thus Salerio fantasizes over Antonio's mental activities, hypothesizing his anxiety regarding the argosies as the cause of his sadness ('Your mind is tossing on the ocean', 8ff.); Solanio attempts to put himself in Antonio's position through a highly elaborate counterfactual conditional, confirming Salerio's hypothesis ('Believe me sir, had I such venture forth,/The better part of my affections would / Be with my hopes abroad', 15ff.); Salerio proceeds to extend the same counterfactual reverie ('My wind cooling my broth / Would blow me to an ague when I thought / What harm a wind too great might do at sea', 23ff.); Antonio succinctly dismisses this speculation ('Believe me no, I thank my fortune for it', 41ff.), which immediately provokes the creation of another possible state of affairs ('*Sol.* Why then you are in love', 46), in turn denied; after the elimination of these suppositions, the exchange finishes with a tautological restatement of the opening move ('*Sol.* Then let us say you are sad / Because you are not merry', 47–8).

A very tortuous, and essentially dialectical, way of encoding a few details, then. What has to be left out of a 'narrative' paraphrase of this scene is considerably greater than what we can put in (including, it might be noted, the apparent centrality of Antonio himself), although even the rejected hypotheses do contain precious grains of intelligence, regarding Antonio's commercial activities for example. But the fact remains that the spectator *does* decode the exchange without undue difficulty, sorting out the 'actual' from the merely 'possible'. And that he is able to initiate, on the basis of so circuitous and negative an exposition, his conceptual construction of Antonio's Venice and Antonio's troubles is indicative of the sure sense of textual direction constraining the seemingly idle talk.

These, in brief, are the most important world-creating principles of the drama, nowhere so vividly exemplified as in Shakespearean comedy: what for the audience is new information has to be transmitted as if in part known or 'given' to the dramatic speakers (at the very least their own identity; on the 'given' and the 'new' see Clark and Haviland 1977); and while for the audience the information-bearing references in question must be readily followable and processable – and so well-ordered – they are encoded as if emerging from an untidy and unpremeditated dialectic of possible worlds, some of them confirmed, others abandoned.

All of this leads to a central, and probably only too obvious, moral: the factors which appear to determine the dialogic co-text in the drama (including the speakers themselves, putative sources of the utterances) are instead determined by it. Or put another way: within the bounds of the dramatic fiction (as opposed, of course, to the theatrical representation), elements of the communicational context, of the speaking / doing situation and of the dramatic world at large, referred to or implied in the dialogue, are, in the first instance, internal textual points of reference disguised as pre-existing extra-textual entities. So that whereas in our non-fictional speech events the co-textual structure is the final product of a series of reductions (namely from the world to the speaking situation to the context of utterance to the co-text itself), in the drama the process is reversed. The main effect of the dramatic illusion, however, is precisely to suggest otherwise.

In the realm of the verbal co-text what reigns is not so much reference as *co*-reference. It is the successive 'picking up' of the objects of discourse – once named or otherwise referred to – that holds the dialogue together as a coherent structure. And the chief agent of this semantic continuity is anaphora. Consider the scene in *AWW* where the Countess of Rossillion learns of Helena's love for Bertram (1.3). Her interrogation of the messengerial Steward begins with a reference to the main object of discourse, Helena ('What say you of this gentlewoman?'), which is already a glance *back* to a previously introduced entity: the demonstrative *this* is anaphoric here, being co-referential with a presupposed antecedent ('Helena'). Once established, the object of discourse can be repeatedly returned to anaphorically, as, in this scene, it is more than ninety lines later, after a long disgression by the Clown:

*Count.*　　Her father bequeath'd her to me, and she herself, without other advantage. (97ff.)

At the end of the interrogation, and prior to Helena's actual appearance, the Countess reflects upon this news, picking up this time not merely the immediate point of reference but the Steward's report as a whole again through 'backward-looking' anaphoric means:

*Count.*　　Even so it was with me when I was young;
　　　　　　If ever we are nature's these are ours; this thorn
　　　　　　Doth to our prose of youth rightly belong. (123ff.)

This, then, is how the 'referents' within the co-text are kept in play, forming, in Andrea Bonomi's words, 'an ensemble of points – objects of discourse – ordered in a relationship founded on anaphoric chains' (1979: 28, my translation).

Now the importance of these 'introvert' functions in the comedies is not limited to their more or less 'hidden' structural role within the dialogue in general. They emerge – the chains, as it were, are strategically rattled – in much of the more intensely and exclusively self-perpetuating verbal sport, the 'game of the pure self-activity of the word ... charged with inner tensions' so admired by Cassirer (1932: 176). This turning and twisting of anaphoric chains at the expense of the 'outward' referential content of the utterance is best exemplified, of course, in the punning *lazzi* of the earlier plays. For the early clowns, co-reference – in the guise of backward-looking pick-ups reinforced by the repetition of the theme word, but in a changed sense – is the instrument mainly responsible for that gamut of semantic tortures that included *paronomasia, antanaclasis* and other forms of punning:

| | |
|---|---|
| *Spe.* | How now, Signor Launce! What news with your mastership? |
| *Lau.* | With my master's ship? Why, *it* is at sea (*TG* 3. 1. 277–9); |

while in the more aristocratic wit matches sense-distorting backward reference more commonly takes the form of *asteismus*, the 'civill jest':

| | |
|---|---|
| *Ber.* | One word in secret. |
| *Prin.* | Let *it* not be sweet. |
| *Ber.* | Thou griev'st my gall. |
| *Prin.* | Gall! bitter. |
| *Ber.* | Therefore meet. |
| *Dum.* | Will you vouchsafe with me to change a word? |
| *Maria.* | Name *it*. |
| *Dum.* | Fair lady, – |
| *Maria.* | Say you *so*? Fair lord, – |
| | Take *that* for your fair lady. (*LLL* 5. 2. 236–40) |

(Italics in the extracts in this section are mine.) A single initial proposition may spawn an indefinitely protractable series of 'parasitic' returns and variations: this is the generative principle behind the close-knit interweaving of move and countermove in the flyting. Textual continuity fosters textural perpetuity:

| | |
|---|---|
| *Pet.* | Come, come, you wasp; i'faith, you are too angry. |
| *Kath.* | If I be waspish, best beware my sting. |
| *Pet.* | My remedy is then, to pluck *it* out. |
| *Kath.* | Ay, if the fool could find *it* where *it* lies. |
| *Pet.* | Who knows not where a wasp doth wear *his* sting? |
| | In *his* tail. |
| *Kath.* | In *his* tongue. |
| *Pet.* | Whose tongue? |
| *Kath.* | Yours, if you talk of tales, and so farewell. |
| *Pet.* | What, with my tongue in your tail? nay, come again. (*TS* 2. 1. 209–16.) |

But of all modes of reflexive pick-up, what gives the co-text most emphatically a certain referential autonomy and dignity in these plays is a function often confused with the anaphoric return, namely the textual deixis (see Introduction, p. 31), which 'refers to, but is not co-referential with, a preceding linguistic form' (Lyons 1977: 668). Co-text-oriented indices, whose sphere of operation is restricted to the very dialogue in progress, promote 'inward' reference to the status of open (thus 'outward') dramatic topic. A decidedly earnest instance is provided by Hero's incredulous taking-up of the accusations against her in *MA*:

O God defend me, how am I beset!
What kind of catechizing call you *this*? (4. 1. 77–8)

while the periodic running commentary on the development of the
discourse in *MWW* uses the indexical hook-up to less solemn effect:

Evans.   What phrase is *this*, 'He hears with ear'?
         Why, *it* is affectations. (1. 1. 135–6)

Anne.    What is your will?
Slen.    My will? Od's heartlings, *that*'s a pretty jest indeed. (3. 4. 55–7)

Textual deictics can equally operate prospectively ('*Ford*. . . . experience
. . . hath taught me to say *this*: "Love"', 2. 2. 218–20) and, at
self-analytic extreme, within a given utterance and even in the same
sentence ('*Bass*. And she is fair, and (fairer than *that* word)', *MV* 1. 1.
162). The generative power of so modest a linguistic feature is easily
underestimated. Entire scenes or situations – those of a more intensely
logomachic nature – are structured on the propagating force of the
textual pointer, as in the pattern of avowal and uncomprehending
rebuttal amongst the lovers in *MND*:

Lys.    Why should you think that I should woo in scorn? . . .
Hel.    *These* vows are Hermia's: will you give her o'er? . . .
Dem.    O Helen, goddess, nymph, perfect, divine! . . .
Hel.    If you were civil, and knew courtesy,
        You would not do me *thus* much injury. . . .
Lys.    You are unkind, Demetrius; be not so.
        For you love Hermia; *this* you know I know: . . .
Her.    You speak not as you think; *it* cannot be!
Hel.    Lo, she is one of *this* confederacy.
        Now I perceive they have conjoin'd all three
        To fashion *this* false sport in spite of me.
        Injurious Hermia! Most ungrateful maid!
        Have you conspir'd, have you with these contriv'd
        To bait me with *this* foul derision?
Her.    I am amazed at your passionate words: . . .
Hel.                    Wherefore speaks he *this*
        To her he hates? . . .
Her.    I understand not what you mean by *this*.
Hel.    *This* sport, well carried, shall be chronicled.
        If you have any pity, grace, or manners,
        You would not make me *such* an argument. . . .
Her.                    Sweet, do not scorn her *so*. . . .
        Lysander, whereto tends all *this*?
        Why are you grown so rude? What change is *this*,
        Sweet love? . . .
Hel.                    What, will you tear
        Impatient answers from my tongue?
        Fie, fie, you counterfeit! You puppet you!

82

*Her.*     'Puppet'! Why *so*? Ay, *that* way goes the game! (3. 2. 122ff.)

That way goes the game indeed; in these plays the world-creating game begins and, often enough, ends with the infinitely extendible chain.

## (II) 'THE WORLD'S LARGE TONGUE': UNIVERSES OF DISCOURSE

'I hold the world but as the world': Antonio's tautology begs a sizeable question. For while the world that his analytic proposition brings to *our* minds may be our own 'actual' or 'real' world, *he* as a fictional being is clearly in no position to hold any opinion about it at all, nor even to refer to it. This is one of the central ambiguities regarding the 'referential' status of all fictional discourse. For dramatic and other 'possible' fictional realms may be limited to what we learn about them, but they nevertheless continually assume, and at times directly invoke, an epistemic background that goes quite beyond the ontologically circumscribed zone of the play or story proper, appearing to coincide with what we take to be our own universe and its history.

'O wicked, wicked world' (*MWW* 2. 1. 20–1); 'Is the world as it was, man?' (*MM* 3. 2. 49); 'O, what a world is this' (*AYLI* 2. 3. 14): the assumption that the dramatic *hic et nunc*, while at an obvious and inviolable remove from that of the audience, is in some larger sense the same 'world' is automatic. It is reinforced, of course, by the picking up from the actual world of familiar geographical points of reference: the Vienna, Verona, Athens or Windsor imported into the text. And although in the comedies the question of the actual referentiality of the *dramatis personae* and their proper names does not arise with such urgency as in the history or Roman plays (the Duke of Verona or the Princess of France having a less 'extensionally' verifiable identity than Julius Caesar or King Richard III of England), there are nonetheless numerous passing mentions of historical, mythical or literary figures whom we take to be the same as those that people our own reference world rather than mere for-the-nonce simulacra: 'I was never so berhym'd since Pythagoras' time' (*AYLI* 3. 2. 173–4); 'Or so devote to Aristotle's checks/ As Ovid be an outcast quite abjured' (*TS* 1. 1. 32–3); 'So I say – both of Galen and Paracelsus' (*AWW* 2. 3. 11); etc.

Such apparent cracks in the fictional barrier cause no perplexity or discomfort in themselves: they fall under the general rubric, common to all the arts, of what Marcello Pagnini (1980) has called the 'introjection of the referent'. Rosalind's Pythagoras is also our (or the Elizabethans') Pythagoras, but his mere introduction into her pastoral domain in no sense threatens its integrity: it is sanctioned, rather, by the conventional dramatic licence to 'cheat' in allowing the fictional figures to assume real personages as objects of discourse, provided the closed-circuit autonomy of the representation is not disrupted.

But however untroublesome and codified the trespassing of the dialogue beyond its fictional bounds, it does raise a question of some importance here: just what *are* the limits of the world-creating game? Or better, if the dramatic world is necessarily created and supported by what the co-text attributes to it, can the two properly be said to coincide? Or again, more crudely, is the dramatic world greater or lesser in extent than what is said within and about it in the dialogue?

The broad answer is that the world, say, of MA is both more and less extensive than the sum of the speech acts, propositions, references and predications that constitute it. It is more extensive, first because any number of added properties can be attributed to it ostensively in performance, and second because in any case what is manifested and referred to is taken as non-exhaustive, a synecdochic reduction of the dramatic Messina and Italy (with its wars and the rest) as a whole: in Benedick's words (2. 1. 192–3), 'Beatrice puts the world into her person' (and into her tongue above all), standing for an indeterminately larger sphere of individuals and their intercourse, since, as Benedick again puts it 'the world must be peopled' (2. 3. 236). And it is less extensive, not merely because Beatrice, Benedick and their co-citizens are allowed to 'look out' to the audience's reference world and its cultural patrimony, but more particularly because the dialogue creates, as we have seen, any number of hypothesized, invented, believed, desired and deliberately falsified states of affairs (notably the one in which Hero betrays Claudio) that are indeed referred to but that do not make up part of the 'actual' course of dramatic events. There are more things dreamt of in the co-text than are found in the heaven and earth of the play.

It is for this reason that it is useful to introduce a concept first formulated by the logician Augustus De Morgan (1847) and made current by C. S. Peirce, namely that of the *universe of discourse*. Broadly, a language-created universe is a structured set of objects of discourse held together by the co-text in force: 'It may be now the physical universe, now the imaginary "world" of a play or a novel, now a range of possibilities' (quoted in Jakobson 1956: 96, my translation). The objects or 'referents' within it can be real, imaginary or both, provided that they are located within the same 'anaphoric space' (see Bonomi 1979: 26):

> It is not of course the referent itself that is in the text or co-text. The
> referent is in the universe-of-discourse, which is created by the text

and has a temporal structure imposed upon it by the text; . . . To say that the referent has a textual location implies, then, that it will be found in a certain part of the universe-of-discourse as this is structured, temporally, by the text; and subsequent reference to this referent by means of an anaphoric expression will identify the referent in terms of the textual location of the antecedent. (Lyons 1977: 670)

This, in brief, is what each of Shakespeare's texts creates: a discourse-based universe from which the individuals, properties and events making up the dramatic world are inferred (and, in performance, represented), but which goes beyond it to include the 'possible' worlds created by the dramatic speakers and, at times, objects picked up from the actual or reference world of the audience. These text-created universes are in practice broken up into what might be called sub-universes – those appertaining to single speakers or particular groups, or those set up in given scenes – which do not coincide completely. Each has its own objects and its own 'anaphoric space', although there is always sufficient overlap, obviously, to ensure certain firm points of reference throughout the play: the central individuals, locations, happenings. It might be helpful, at this point, to examine more closely where Shakespeare's universes of discourse begin and end, how they are filled and in what ways the very filling attracts trouble or attention.

## (III) 'AN APPERTINENT TITLE'

In a sense, of course, they begin before their beginnings. Or at least, they get off to some kind of start, however false or uncertain, with the titular tags hung on or around them. Not that the allegiance of each title to the universe of the play is unambiguous; and not that they all have the same effect or function. Part of the play's discourse or external to it? Game or frame? Authorial label or independent pre-text (or 'paratext': Genette 1982: 9)? There is no one answer, and indeed it is possible to construct a modest typology of the twelve textual fragments in question, on the grounds of the modes of discourse they embody.

### (1) The title as utterance

Two of them tell us nothing at all about the respective dramas, adopting, instead, the 'contextualized' form of apparent speech acts. Even as an utterance, 'As you like it' is incomplete and ambiguous, mainly because of the uncertain status of the second pronoun. If the 'it' refers reflexively to the very business of 'entitling', then the speech act

85

must be taken as a command roughly equivalent to 'invent your own' or 'do it yourself'. If it refers anaphorically to the audience's preferences, then the expression is interpretable as a casual 'take it or leave it'. But if, instead, it is a form of textual deixis indicating the comedy itself, then the illocution becomes a direct promise, completable as 'I assure you, this play is exactly as you like it.' In any event, whether as would-be command, dismissal or promise, it is an incomplete or 'unhappy' act, since while it is plainly enough directed towards the play's patrons, we have no idea who lies behind the missing 'I' (perhaps it is the text itself boasting or shrugging its shoulders?). What kind of order or undertaking is it if we do not know who is responsible for it? The result is a small irony: an indeterminable illocution that in any case has no authority (as a locutionary orphan) to present itself as such.

As for the other utterance-title, 'Twelfth night: or what you will' offers *two* contexts, marked off by the colon: the first possibly theatrical (the occasion of the first performance) and the second generically communicational. Here there is little doubt that the second phrase reflects upon the act of entitling that produced the first: the main title is so scandalously irrelevant to the comedy that the 'you'-patron can most probably do better himself.

In neither case, therefore, does the detached 'speech' fragment anticipate the discourse of the drama proper. What each traces, instead, is an interlocution between a phantom and a possibility, the speaker being hidden and the addressee a potential collectivity. The final effect, perhaps, is that of an invitation to interact 'dialogically' (as audience) with the play itself. (Pre-Shakespearean dramatic titles-as-utterance, it might be noted, are very rare, William Wager's 'The Longer Thou Livest the More Fool Thou Art', c. 1559, being an exception. Compare, among more or less contemporary instances, Marston's 'What You Will', 1601, Rowley's 'When You See Me You Know Me', 1604, and Heywood's 'If You Know Not Me, You Know Nobody', 1604–5. There are, of course, no Shakespearean instances outside the comic canon.)

### (2) The title as saying

One step nearer to an engagement with the play-world, we find two proverbial titles, which not only seem to hint at the ethics in force in the plays but mimic the more sententious aspects of their style. The biblical origin of 'measure for measure' does not constitute an unarguable guarantee of its authority as a prospective moral weighing-up of the events, since its simultaneous status as codified catch-phrase suggests, on the contrary, a judgmental facility that the comedy itself questions.

Again, the question of point of view arises: as applied to the ethical juggling practised by Angelo, the saying acquires a satirical tinge, but as echoed in the Duke's parallelistic pronouncement in the final act ('An Angelo for Claudio; death for death/Haste still pays haste, and leisure answers leisure; / Like doth quit like, and Measure still for Measure', 5. 1. 408–10), it takes on a certain ethical complexity, suggesting that the original biblical force of the phrase prevails over its easy utilization as ready-made justification for unscrupulousness, but not in the equally automatic 'eye for an eye' sense, Angelo's 'punishment' being an altogether different kind of measure. What the title comes – if only *retro*spectively – to imply, perhaps, is that its own 'measured' parallelism is in reality an antithesis, and that inherited topical formulae may conceal problematic contradictions.

The all too evident shallowness of 'all's well that ends well', meanwhile, immediately suggests ironic distance from the text. In this case, the more 'polygenetic' and popular character of the proverb might be taken as equivalent with the easily contentable obtuseness of public morality, were it not for the fact that in the comedy itself the proposition is repeated twice by the female protagonist in circumstances that indicate a serious and indeed solemn application. But in both instances, it might be noted, Helena has an eye to securing in time the comic ending she has been preparing through the machinations of the bed-trick and the rest ('All's well that ends well; still the fine's the crown./Whate'er the course, the end is the renown', 4. 4. 35–6; 'All's well that ends well yet, / Though time seem so adverse and means unfit', 5. 1. 25–6). In this light, the object of the titular irony becomes, instead, the desperate appropriate-end-securing machinery of the plot, pre-announced as a piece of bottom-heavy machinery designed to save the conventional framework of the genre at all costs. (Non-Shakespearean proverbial titles are again relatively few, and tend to belong to an earlier period of English drama: William Wager's 'Enough is as Good as a Feast', c. 1560; Ulpian Fulwell's 'Like Will to Like', c. 1568, George Wapull's 'The Tide Tarrieth No Man', c. 1576, etc.)

### (3) The title as 'fabula'

The most generous tags – in terms of direct dramatic information, at least – are those (again there are two of them) which offer a paraphrase of the main narrative pattern, a form of *reductio ad extremum*, if not necessarily *ad absurdum*, of the narrative *fabula* (they are among the more common titular forms in Tudor drama: 'The Marriage of Wit and Science', c. 1568, Peele's 'The Arraignment of Paris', c. 1581, Hughes *et al.*'s 'The Misfortunes of Arthur', 1588, etc.). Of the two Shakespearean instances, 'The taming of the shrew' is as accurate a representation in miniature as one could wish for of the albeit simple dynamic structure of the comedy, identifying, as it does, not only the intended central act but also the stocktype of its victim and even, implicitly, the dominant male viewpoint from which the whole procedure is defined in the play-world. If 'Love's labour's lost' is decidedly more synthetic, it does, on the other hand, represent in addition a kind of stylistic advertisement, its alliterative form prefiguring (in various senses) the predominance of the linguistic signifier in the play.

### (4) The title as comic mode marker

A more strictly 'framing' type of titular gloss singles out what is to be the mode not of the *fabula* but of plot and discourse. 'The comedy of errors' specifies the generative principle of both action and dialogue, the game of the 'pragmatic' error being what most strongly characterizes the exchanges. 'Much ado about nothing' is more general, since both the empty 'ado' and the focal 'nothing' might take any form, while the implication of frivolity is scarcely borne out by the main plot. But on the other hand such lightness is indeed registered at the level of the wit combats, as the *antanaclasis* on nothing/noting similarly forewarns. The pun, furthermore (underlined as it is in the text: 'Note notes, forsooth, and nothing!', 2. 3. 57), pinpoints the main source both of trouble and of the romantic dénouement in the comedy, the act of overhearing. (There are two more or less contemporary titles that identify the main comic element of the plot: 'A Knack to Know a Knave', 1592, and Middleton's 'A Trick to Catch the Old One', 1605; there are no earlier instances to speak of.)

### (5) The title as designator of agent and scene

Simple nomination of the protagonist, the titular strategy common to much Tudor and Jacobean drama (from 'Gorboduc' to 'Catiline') and to all Shakespeare's tragedies, history plays and Roman plays, is never employed in the comic canon. The simplest type of world-initiating label here is that which selects the agent(s) in terms of social status and designates the location of the main action: 'The two gentlemen of Verona'; 'The merchant of Venice'; 'The merry wives of Windsor'. The effect is to signal the allegiance of the fictional sphere to the laws of the mundane (compare Robert Wilson's 'The Three Ladies of London', 1581, and Porter's 'The Two Angry Women of Abingdon', 1588, etc.).

## (6) The title as modal frame

In contrast, 'A midsummer night's dream' is a clear invitation to apply the canons of the fantastic, functioning as an indicator of the fictional modality in force while also singling out a central dramatic event: the comedy is an oneirically 'impossible' world and so exempt from the more literal and this-worldly criteria of verisimilitude. (Points of comparison are Gascoigne's 'Supposes', Peele's 'The Old Wives Tale', 1590, and Shakespeare's own 'The Winter's Tale'.)

### (IV) BEGINNINGS

'Well, the beginning that is dead and buried': the ladies' mockery in *AYLI* of the naïve narrative starting-point rightly implies that Shakespeare's own opening gambits are more artful affairs. As, of course, they have to be, since the unashamed opening *ab ovo* ('There dwelled adioyning to the citie of Bourdeaux') is not, as it were, open to dramaturgy in any case. Dramatic beginnings, Shakespeare's more so than most, are necessarily overdetermined, if not overloaded, given the number of simultaneous functions they have to fulfil: roughly, the setting-up of context, the identification of agents and location, the securing of attention through the apparent 'tellability' of the initial information and the indicating of a pre-dramatic 'history'. In addition, however – and this, perhaps, is what most powerfully characterizes the 'comic' Shakespearean *incipit* – many of the comedies trace, in one way or another, an anterior co-text and its corollary, a partially pre-existing universe of discourse. They begin, that is to say, not only *in medias res* but, more strikingly, *in media verba*.

Over and above other more or less invariable ingredients of the first utterance – i.e. nomination of the addressee or indication of his relationship to the speaker, indexical reference to the speaker himself plus a certain interest-exciting propositional content – the impression that the text presents but a *fragment* of an indefinitely more extensive dialogic continuum is created, in more cases than not, by a metadiscursive reference back to some pre-textual speech act. Two of the comedies open with what look more like closings, i.e. attempts to put an end to the interlocutor's would-be perlocutionary efforts, apparently in progress for some time:

Val.     Cease to persuade, my loving Proteus; (*TG*)

Shall.   Sir Hugh, persuade me not; I will make a star-chamber matter of it. (*MWW*)

89

This, of course, creates the occasion or pretext for the speaker's *counter*-argument to the failed persuasion, and so motivates more or less straight exposition of the given topic (note the anaphoric 'it' indicating the topic, unknown but already powerfully characterized as a matter of urgent interest, in *MWW*). *CE*, instead, starts off with a curious inversion of the persuasion-arresting persuasion, namely with Egeon's invitation to the Duke of Ephesus to *continue* in his pronouncement of the sentence against him, a request which the Duke himself, however, interprets as a supplication:

*Ege.*      Proceed, Solinus, to procure my fall,
             And by the doom of death end woes and all.
*Duke.*     Merchant of Syracusa, plead no more.

This sets the pattern for the rather contorted expository dialectic that follows, in which Egeon's reluctant narration has to be virtually dragged out of him by the frequently intervening Duke.

If the form of the 'parasitic' hooking-up to an unheard previous utterance varies elsewhere, the principle remains the same. Antonio, in *MV*, invokes an earlier pronouncement on the topic of his melancholy:

> In sooth, I know not why I am so sad,
> It wearies me; you say it wearies you

and Navarre's inaugural narration in *LLL* recalls the men's collective vow, so central to later development:

> You three, Berowne, Dumain, and Longaville,
> Have sworn for three years' term to live with me

while the pre-dramatic act, in this case the act of writing, is externalized in *MA* in the guise of the information-bearing letter that Leonato holds up and paraphrases:

> I learn in this letter that Don Pedro of Arragon comes this night to
> Messina.

Of course, this feature of the texts is in part attributable to the general direction-through-indirection that the 'conversationalized' exposition adopts in order to conceal itself, a strategy that is seen clearly enough in Duke Vincentio's planting of the opening topic of *MM* ('good government') within a discursive disclaimer, a *refusal* to broach the subject:

> Of government the properties to unfold,
> Would seem in me to affect speech and discourse.

But it may equally be taken as a signalling of the precedence, both 'chronological' and structural, of discourse and its universe over the represented drama and its world. Both in and before the beginning is the word, and if in the comedies, as we shall see, the word is often allowed its way with the world, this is a strategic exploitation of a textual priority rather than the structure-destroying product of a dramaturgic vice.

It is instructive, in this respect, to compare Shakespeare's opening moves in other genres. Of the tragedies, only *Othello* begins with a metadiscursive reference back to a preceding act ('Tush, never *tell* me') – appropriately enough for a play in which the purely *rhetorical* background (Iago's preparation of the terrain for his verbal dominion over Roderigo and Othello) is of direct dramatic import – while in the history and Roman plays initial reference to discourse is invariably *pro*spective, serving as it were to *inaugurate*, almost ritually, the dramatic universe of discourse, either by inviting a speech act ('*King John*. Now, *say*, Chatillon, what would France with us?'; '*Flavius. Speak*, what trade art thou?' *Julius Caesar*), or by declaring an intention to speak ('*Canterbury*. My Lord, I'll *tell* you', *Henry V*); or by requesting a turn at speaking ('*First Citizen*. Before we proceed any further, *hear me speak*', *Coriolanus*) (my italics). So that if the comic *incipit* suggests an infinitely extendible continuity of speech (see also 'Endings' below), the history play appears on the contrary to establish from the outset a sense of discursive limit and self-sufficiency.

Moving beyond the opening lines to consider the initial exchange at large, it is notable that metadiscursive reference often acts as a direct clue to what are destined to become the chief rhetorical registers and issues in the respective comedies (even though, of course, this is revealed only *retro*spectively, with critical hindsight). Valentine and Proteus in *TG* exchange literary reflections and allusions on the topic of the 'love-discourse', thereby not only declaring the intertextual or interdiscursive debts of their own language, but also anticipating the shallow and callow rhetorical attitude of Proteus towards love itself (see pp. 223–6 below); the insistent references within the opening configuration in *LLL* to the scholarly vow and to the necessity of its fulfilment introduce the central dramatic topic of the 'felicity' of language, especially in its would-be 'performative' guise (see pp. 226–9 below); in *MM* the Duke declares himself reluctant, and perhaps unfit, to speak on the subject of power ('Of government the properties to unfold / Would seem in me t'affect speech and discourse'), a clue to the difficult and dangerous relationship between language and executive power that underlines the play's central ethical conflicts (pp. 220–3 below); the first exchange in *AWW* displays an explicit preoccupation with its own lexical make-up ('*Countess*. O, that "had"'', etc.) and with the business of nomination ('*Lafew.* How called you the man you speak of, madam?'), a preoccupation that is registered throughout the comedy in the recurrent *topoi* of the untrustworthy word and of the devalued name (pp. 172–3). And so on. The beginning, in this sense, is never properly dead and buried, since, in looking at once backwards and forwards, it presents itself as part of an unbroken and unbreakable rhetorical continuum.

(v) 'SOMETHING THAT HATH A REFERENCE TO MY
STATE': REFERRING AND PREDICATING

Once under way, the discourse-created universe can only be replenished with those objects and properties progressively put into it by the co-text. This means that a good portion of the dialogic activity will necessarily be given over to the fundamental universe-stocking acts of referring and predicating: 'Here comes Beatrice. By this day, she's a fair lady', *MA* 2. 3. 234; 'By my troth, Nerissa, my little body is aweary of this great world', *MV* 1. 2. 1–2; 'Sirrah, your lord and master's married', *AWW* 2. 3. 238. This is the workaday stuff of all our linguistic dealings with the world: object-establishing 'singular definite' referring expressions ('Beatrice', 'my little body', 'your lord and master') coupled with property-attributing predicative expressions ('is a fair lady', 'is aweary', 'is married'). While the very 'definiteness' of the references here is the apparent guarantor of the objects' actual existence (singular definite referring expressions being founded on existential presupposition), its characteristic colouring is descriptively bestowed by the predicative follow-up.

Of course, expressions as such do not refer to anything: it is *speakers* who refer by means of them. And in the act of referring to one another, to themselves and to the things around them the *dramatis personae* further manifest and define themselves *as* speakers. Each referring act presupposing the existence of the object or referent equally presupposes the existence of the referrer: this referential doubleness is an essential factor in the economy of the dialogue. But the 'existence' at either end of the act is a fairly precarious quantity, residing in two points of textual return held together and apart by the same discursive thread. Or to put it another way, that point of textual reference (the speaker) which constitutes the sole authority testifying to the existence of the other point (the object), is in reality held in position by the very act of which he is the supposed source, until taken up in turn as object of some other existence-confirming reference (thus the 'fair lady' Beatrice of Bene-dick's singular definite reference reverses the roles and returns the referential favour ('And Benedick, love on, I will requite thee', 3. 1. 111) in what can be described as a 'you verify me and I'll verify you' reciprocation).

Surprisingly much is at stake, then, in even the humblest referential move. And correspondingly much is made of it. In *LLL* the singular definite referring act is elevated by the pedants to the rank of solemn public ceremony or earnest scholarly exercise, an occasion for the parading of indefinitely extendible synonymous variations for the same elementary referential content (see also pp. 267–8 below):

(Arm.)    Now for the ground which? which, I mean, I walked upon: it is ycleped thy park. Then for the place where? where, I mean, I did encounter that obscene and most preposterous event, that draweth from my snow-white pen the ebon-coloured ink, which here thou viewest, beholdest, surveyest, or seest. But to the place where: (1. 1. 234ff.)

Arm.    Do you not educate youth at the charge-house on the top of the mountain?
Hol.    Or *mons*, the hill.
Arm.    At your sweet pleasure, for the mountain.
Hol.    I do, sans question. (5. 1. 74ff.)

Dull.    What was a month old at Cain's birth, that's not five weeks old as yet?
Hol.    Dictynna, goodman Dull; Dictynna, goodman Dull.
Dull.    What is Dictynna?
Nath.    A title to Phoebe, to Luna, to the moon.
Hol.    The moon was a month old when Adam was no more. (4. 2. 34ff.)

Rival exponents of the *recherché* referring expression are prompted to take note of, and congratulate, however reluctantly, each other's choicer finds:

Arm.    Sir, it is the king's most sweet pleasure and affection to congratulate the princess at her pavilion in the posteriors of the day, which the rude multitude call the afternoon.
Hol.    The posterior of the day, most generous sir, is liable, congruent, and measurable for the afternoon. (5. 1. 79ff.)

The consequence, and indeed the advertised intention, of such rhetorically 'rhetic' overworking is to privilege act and expression (and, by the same token, the referrer himself) over the humble object and its due placing in the dramatic universe. Throughout the comedy, Navarre's park is only very sketchily characterized as a scenic point of reference, and serves, more often than not, as a kind of textual *locus ludicer*, the pseudo-spatial grounds for the more pressing adventures in the *anaphoric* space of the co-text. Even relatively straightforward spatial references offered in apparent good faith are deflected from their course and robbed of their content:

93

| | |
|---|---|
| *Arm.* | I will visit thee at the lodge. |
| *Jaq.* | That's hereby. |
| *Arm.* | I know where it is situate. |
| *Jaq.* | Lord, how wise you are! (1. 2. 126ff.); |

while the few meagre scene-setting details that are imparted have to emerge from – and are rapidly reassimilated into – those vertiginous semantic spirals that virtually constitute the locutionary norm of the play:

| | |
|---|---|
| *Cost.* | The manner of it is, I was taken with the manner. |
| *Ber.* | In what manner? |
| *Cost.* | In manner and form following, sir; all those three: I was seen with her in the manor-house, sitting with her upon the form, and taken with her into the park; which, put together, is in manner and form following. (1. 1. 201ff.) |

The park, then, is more rhetorical than physical *topos*. Like the 'curious-knotted garden' of Armado's description (1. 1. 242) – one of its few specified zones – it is a figured space for the play of figures, human and rhetorical (the directly figural nature of the knotted garden itself is testified to in Francis Bacon's horticultural advice on 'the *Making of Knots*, or Figures', 1625: 137ff.). Even its proprietor and his followers treat the park (and, indeed, the court) as the topical support for their tropical endeavours, the metaphorical and hyperbolic character of their spatial references being consistently mocked by the ladies, who insist, instead, on a certain referential fidelity:

| | |
|---|---|
| *King.* | Say to her, we have measur'd many miles<br>To tread a measure with her on this grass. |
| *Boy.* | They say, that they have measur'd many a mile<br>To tread a measure with you on this grass. |
| *Ros.* | It is not so. Ask them how many inches<br>Is in one mile: if they have measur'd many,<br>The measure then of one is easily told. (5. 2. 184ff.) |

The ladies' reprimands may serve to remind us – like certain critics' complaints against the comedy's 'verbalism' – of the more solemn outward-looking duties of the dialogue, but they are in turn, of course, a figural camouflage for the textual basis of the reprimanders and reprimanded themselves: an invitation, as it were, to disguise better the inner topological space traced by the parabolic career of the rhetorical figure ('many a mile') as the outer topographical space charted by the physical career of the human figure ('how many inches').

The Forest of Arden, that other venue of continous *ludi*, both scenic and linguistic, impinges more definitely and more consistently on the dialogue as spatial construct and constraint. But it is, nonetheless,

94

equally victim of referential burlesque, and its presence in the drama is registered, as often as not, as a local stimulus to witty repartee or semantic equivocation. Rosalind–Ganymede's jokey simile on its boundary is a good instance:

| | |
|---|---|
| *Orl.* | Where dwell you pretty youth? |
| *Ros.* | With this shepherdess my sister; here in the skirts of the forest, like fringe upon a petticoat. (3. 1. 328–30) |

The specific physical feature most readily prey to playful rhetic reduction is that scenic synecdoche (part for the woodland whole) *par excellence,* the carved-upon, leaned-upon and discoursed-upon tree. The arboreal is an occasion for the arbitrary, sanctioning the careless self-promotion of the pseudo-referential act iself, as in Rosalind's quip on Orlando's location:

| | |
|---|---|
| *Cel.* | I found him under a tree like a dropped acorn. |
| *Ros.* | It may well be called Jove's tree, when it drops forth such fruit (3. 2. 230–3) |

or her show of aphoristic strength with Touchstone on the matter of Orlando's tree-borne love verses:

| | |
|---|---|
| *Ros.* | Peace you dull fool! I found them on a tree. |
| *Touch.* | Truly the tree yields bad fruit. |
| *Ros.* | I'll graff it with you, and then I shall graff it with a medlar. Then it will be the earliest fruit i' th' country; for you'll be rotten ere you be half ripe, and that's the right virtue of the medlar. |
| *Touch.* | You have said; but whether wisely or no, let the forest judge. (3. 2. 112–20) |

The two aspects of comic pastoralism expressed here, an easy relationship with the natural scene on the one hand and a romantic relationship between the pseudo-shepherds on the other, produce throughout the forest scenes the characteristic spinning out, lazy and effusive by turns, of a strictly limited propositional material based on the stock topics of the landscape and Eros. The form of the referring expression bears more weight than the more or less predictable object. As Celia ironically points out, Rosalind, in her role as pastoral lover, unleashes a flood of propositions, all geared to the same amorous co-referent but offered in a range of formal and predicative variations:

| | |
|---|---|
| *Ros.* | What said he? How looked he? Wherein went he? What makes he here? Did he ask for me? Where remains he? How parted he with thee? And when shalt thou see him again? Answer me in one word. ... But doth he know that I am in this forest, and in man's apparel? Looks he as freshly as he did the day he wrestled? |
| *Cel.* | It is as easy to count atomies as to resolve the propositions of a lover. (3. 1. 216–29) |

95

The situation is somewhat different in *TS*, where Petruchio's insistent referential tyranny appears not as an affectionate toying with the dramatic landscape but as a form of determined verbal swashbuckling. His ostentatious and muscular manhandling of the textual point of reference presumes its relative robustness and stability, and since the pre-announced strategic purpose of his designational caprices is the subordination of his wife to his will rather than the subjugation of the world to his word, little enough threat is offered to the object and its supposed exteriority. Nevertheless, in a comedy whose induction, as we have seen, gives a working demonstration of what can be done with a few tawdry pseudo-references, a vigorous dispute over whether one point in the universe of discourse is to be designated as the sun or the moon may legitimately be seen – at least by the non-Slys in the audience – as an amused estranging of one of the more rudimentary semantic operations of the dialogue:

| | |
|---|---|
| *Pet.* | Good Lord, how bright and goodly shines the moon! |
| *Kath.* | The moon? The sun! It is not moonlight now. |
| *Pet.* | I say it is the moon that shines so bright. |
| *Kath.* | I know it is the sun that shines so bright. |
| *Pet.* | Now by my mother's son, and that's myself, |
| | It shall be moon, or star, or what I list . . . |
| | I say it is the moon. |
| *Kath.* |                     I know it is the moon. |
| *Pet.* | Nay, then you lie. It is the blessed sun. |
| *Kath.* | Then, God be blest, it is the blessed sun. |
| | But sun it is not, when you say it is not, |
| | And the moon changes even as your mind. |
| | What you will have it nam'd, even that it is, |
| | And so it shall be so for Katherine. (4. 5. 2–22) |

'What you will have it named, even that it is': this is the principle of the progressive fixing of a number of points of textual orientation and return out of an initial void. But it is, of course, an overstatement. Like Petruchio's moon, not everything that is named *is*, even in comedy. Reference to what is defined for the auditor as *non*-actual within the drama is an important source both of the vicissitudes of plot and of certain modes of verbal play and linguistic consciousness. It is the species of referential game, above all, that dominates and generates *MA*, whose titular 'nothing' is in effect an interplay of distinct and contraposed nothings, i.e. of merely 'possible' states which clash, overlap and cancel one another, exciting a great deal of non- and pseudo-referential 'ado' along the way.

The central nothing, the story of Hero's infidelity, is knowingly created as a false point of reference likely to undermine predicted events in the 'actual' dramatic world, i.e. Hero's marriage to Claudio. Its originator, Borachio, not only invents events, but imagines likely reactions and effects ('to vex Claudio, to undo Hero, and kill Leonato', 2. 2. 28–9). Borachio is expressly aware that the fortune of his invention lies in the consistency and coherence of Don John's references to it, establishing it as a firm point of discursive return:

> Be you constant in the accusation, and my cunning shall not shame me. (2. 2. 54–5)

And so it proves, since Don John's object (the dark deed) is taken up and taken over by Claudio and Don Pedro with even greater insistence. Their accusations prior to the planned wedding ceremony are framed from different viewpoints – as oneiric hallucinations ('*Leonato.* Are these things spoken, or do I but dream?', 4. 1. 66) or as affirmations of the actual ('*Don John.* . . . these things are true', 67), etc., tracing a gamut of propositional attitudes towards the same matter from simple belief to knowing deceit to incredulity.

The pattern of invention, projection and confirmation established here becomes the norm. Borachio's fabrication is directly countered by Friar Francis's fiction of Hero's death, similarly set up as the object of insistent reference ('And publish it that she is dead indeed', 4. 1. 202) and of speculation as to probable reactions ('When he shall hear she died upon his words, / Th'idea of her life shall sweetly creep / Into his study of imagination', 4. 1. 222ff.), in turn verified by events. The main plot is structured on the conflict between the two fictional 'worlds' and the affirmations relative to each, while its dénouement lies in their successive cancellation and the fulfilment of the originally projected course of events (the wedding).

This specular relationship between complementary possible worlds and references to them is reproduced in the romantic subplot, where the love and eventual marriage between Benedick and Beatrice is similarly the product of fabrications and confirmed predictions. Here the fictional worlds are created dialogically, through two microdramas whose eavesdropping auditors are also the respective referents, Benedick and Beatrice themselves. Their responses are again projected beforehand, with some relish ('*Don P.* If we can do this, Cupid is no longer an archer; his glory shall be ours', 2. 1. 362–3). And the false references – to the supposed love of Benedick for Beatrice or vice versa, according to the auditor – are ironically framed by the listeners' absolute acceptance of the acts as genuine, thereby confirming the predictions:

*Ben.*     This can be no trick. The conference was sadly borne.
            They have the truth of this from Hero. (2. 3. 212ff.)

Thus, while the main plot is resolved through the dismantling of the contraposed worlds, the subplot concludes with the mutual verification of the two 'possible' situations (Benedick's fictional love for Beatrice provoking requital, and vice versa), although not without a final and sardonic glance back towards the linguistic machinery responsible:

| | |
|---|---|
| Ben. | Do you not love me? |
| Beatr. | Why, no, no more than reason. |
| Ben. | Why then your uncle, and the prince, and Claudio, Have been deceiv'd – they swore you did. |
| Beatr. | Do you not love me? |
| Ben. | Troth, no, no more than reason. |
| Beatr. | Why then my cousin, Margaret, and Ursula, Are much deceiv'd, for they did swear you did. |
| Ben. | They swore that you were almost sick for me. |
| Beatr. | They swore that you were well-nigh dead for me. |
| Ben. | 'Tis no such matter. Then, do you not love me? |
| Beatr. | No, truly, but in friendly recompense. (5. 4. 74–83) |

As if infected by the devise-an-object spirit of the upper two strata of the play, the participants in its lowest and most farcical sphere, i.e. the local police, chief agents of truth in the comedy as exposers of Don John's machinations, manage to come up with a pseudo-referent of their own. Again, the source of the trouble is an overheard dialogue (the same one in which Don John's followers give the game away), where an idle epithet from Borachio is converted by the eavesdropping watchmen into a definite reference to some monstrous villain, personification of the evil that motivates the conspirators:

Bor.           But seest thou what a deformed thief this fashion is?
Sec. Watchman. (Aside)
                  I know that Deformed; a' has been a vile thief this seven year; a' goes
                  up and down like a gentleman: I remember his name. (3. 3. 121–4)

As is the rule, the object, once created, is tenaciously kept alive and his properties extended by later acts:

Sec. Watchman. And one Deformed is one of them; I know him, a' wears a lock
                                                        (3. 3. 163–4)

Sec. Watchman. You'll be made bring Deformed forth, I warrant you. (166–7)

Dogberry. And also the watch heard them talk of one Deformed; they say he
          wears a key in his ear and a lock hanging by it, and borrows money in
          God's name, the which he hath used so long and never paid, that
          now men grow hard-hearted and will lend nothing for God's sake:
          pray you examine him upon that point. (5. 1. 301–7)

Dogberry's 'point', by now a character in its own right, introduces another and more general point, namely the comic uses to which *predicating,* as opposed to referring, is put in the plays. The same kind of farcical error, mistaking predication for reference, is committed by members of the lower social ranks in other comedies, notably *LLL*:

| | |
|---|---|
| *Arm.* | Sirrah Costard, I will enfranchise thee. |
| *Cost.* | O! marry me to one Frances. (3. 1. 118–19) |

| | |
|---|---|
| *Nath.* | . . . but, sir, I assure ye, it was a buck of the first head. |
| *Hol.* | Sir Nathaniel, *haud credo.* |
| *Dull.* | 'Twas not a *haud credo,* 'twas a pricket. (4. 2. 9–12) |

| | |
|---|---|
| *Nath.* | A rare talent. |
| *Dull.* | If a talent be a claw, look how he claws him with a talent. (4. 2. 61–3) |

The wittily 'intentional' version of the same transformation (epithet into definite description), turned against the predicator himself, is part of the stock-in-trade of the 'early' clowns:

| | |
|---|---|
| *Spe.* | How now, Signor Launce! What news with your mastership? |
| *Lau.* | With my master's ship? Why, it is at sea (*TG* 3. 1. 277–9) |

and the agency for a winning move in the flyting:

| | |
|---|---|
| *Kath.* | I knew you at the first You were a movable. |
| *Pet.* | Why, what's a movable? |
| *Kath.* | A joint-stool. |
| *Pet.* | Thou hast hit it. Come, sit on me. (*TS* 2. 1. 196–8) |

If the fate of reference, then, is often to be treated with amused or cavalier lightness, it is the frequent destiny of predication to be taken only too literally, although with similarly subversive results. The trick is usually based on a sylleptic shift between different senses of the same lexeme, normally from an abstract secondary application in the original predicating expression to a more concrete primary sense in the co-referential pick-up, bringing into play the denotatum (or class of objects) involved:

| | |
|---|---|
| *Cost.* | Pray you, which is the head lady? |
| *Prin.* | Thou shalt know her, fellow, by the rest that have no heads. (*LLL* 4. 1. 42–5) |

A still more drastic form of predicative upset, again practised nowhere so eagerly and insistently as in the clowning scenes of *TG*, involves a kind of slipping on a well-placed dialogic banana skin, i.e. a slide between quite distinct but homonymic lexemes (*antanaclasis*) or near homonyms (*paronomasia*) in the two utterances, an operation that radically transforms the properties ascribed to the object by the original expression:

| | |
|---|---|
| *Spe.* | Sir, your glove. |
| *Val.* | Not mine: my gloves are on. |
| *Spe.* | Why, then this may be yours; for this is but one. (2. 1. 1–3) |

| | |
|---|---|
| *Spe.* | But, Launce, how say'st thou that my master is become a notable lover? |
| *Lau.* | I never knew him otherwise. |
| *Spe.* | Than how? |
| *Lau.* | A notable lubber, as thou reportest him to be (2. 5. 36–40) |

While referring, in its many modes and mutations, has to do above all with the place or placing of entities in the textual universe, the predicating game puts on show (or puts in question) their further characterization. Homonymy and polysemy replace synonymy as the specific local rules. But the general principles remain the same: repetition and variation. Thus the heightened predicating act will usually result in some kind of list, catalogue or adjectival running on the spot, permitting the pattern of varied or reiterated epithets to make itself felt. Speed's ringing of a single and somewhat feeble punning change is a fairly nonsensical case in point:

| | |
|---|---|
| *Pro.* | Gavest thou my letter to Julia? |
| *Spe.* | Ay, sir; I (a lost mutton) gave your letter to her (a laced mutton) and she (a laced mutton) gave me (a lost mutton) nothing for my labour. |
| *Pro.* | Here's too small a pasture for such a store of muttons (1. 1. 94–8) |

while the clowns' endless annotated list of the properties ascribed to Launce's inamorata ('the cate-log of her conditions') in the same play carries the act to the limits of both descriptive and physical exhaustion:

| | |
|---|---|
| *Spe.* | 'Imprimis, she can milk.' |
| *Lau.* | Ay, that she can. |
| *Spe.* | 'Item, she brews good ale.' |
| *Lau.* | Thereof comes the proverb: 'Blessing of your heart, you brew good ale.' |
| *Spe.* | 'Item, she can sew.' |
| *Lau.* | That's as much as to say, 'Can she so?' (3. 1. 295ff.) |

A measure of the changes that the clowns' fooling undergoes from the first plays to the later comedies is given in the comparison between Launce and Speed's 'cate-logs' and the anatomy of a single epithet undertaken by Lavatch in *AWW*. In place of an obsessive fascination with the phonetic closeness or sheer hectic building-up of expressions what we have is a logical picking-apart of their propositional content:

| | |
|---|---|
| *Hel.* | My mother greets me kindly; is she well? |
| *Lav.* | She is not well, but yet she has her health; she's very merry, but yet she is not well. But thanks be given she's very well and wants nothing i' th' world; but yet she is not well. |

| | |
|---|---|
| *Hel.* | If she be very well what does she ail that she's not very well? |
| *Lav.* | Truly, she's very well indeed, but for two things. |
| *Hel.* | What two things? |
| *Lav.* | One, that she's not in heaven, whither God send her quickly! The other, that she's in earth, from whence God send her quickly! (2. 4. 1–12) |

But if these differences are characteristic of a general movement away from the headier forms of lexical fetishism, the more 'dialectical' version of the game is not, nevertheless, the exclusive province of the 'late' clowns. It is anticipated in Moth's pseudo-analytic definitions, masochistically commissioned by his master, in *LLL*:

| | |
|---|---|
| *Arm.* | Who was Samson's love, my dear Moth? |
| *Moth.* | A woman, master? |
| *Arm.* | Of what complexion? |
| *Moth.* | Of all the four, or the three, or the two, or one of the four. |
| *Arm.* | Tell me precisely of what complexion. |
| *Moth.* | Of the sea-water green, sir. . . . |
| *Arm.* | Define, define well-educated infant. (1. 2. 71–88) |

In this comedy, where so humble an ingredient is worked up and decked out in the widest range of dishes imaginable, a good deal of fuss is also made of the simpler forms of adjectival accumulation and variation, particularly by Holofernes (as exponent) and Nathaniel (as commentator):

| | |
|---|---|
| *Hol.* | The deer was, as you know, *sanguis*, in blood; ripe as the pomewater, who now hangeth like a jewel in the ear of *coelo*, the sky, the welkin the heaven . . . |
| *Nath.* | Truly, Master Holofernes, the epithets are sweetly varied, like a scholar at the least: (4. 2. 3–9) |
| *Hol.* | He is too picked, to spruce, too affected, too odd, as it were, too peregrinate, as I may call it. |
| *Nath.* | A most singular and choice epithet. (5. 1. 12–15) |

The predicable may all too easily become the predictable, but it is for all that a considerable source of textual energy.

(VI) 'I AM YOUR THEME': ON BEING AN OBJECT OF DISCOURSE

At the other end of these ceremonial goings-on, their often eclipsed focal points lead a somewhat uneven existence. As Andrea Bonomi's definition emphasizes, objects of discourse need respond to only a very weak 'existential' criterion:

> we need a notion of existence able to account not for the objects of the actual world, but, more simply, for the objects *that we talk*

> *about.* In brief, we need a notion of existence that is relevant
> exclusively for linguistic purposes. . . . According to this weak
> definition, we will say that something exists if it is the object of an
> identifying act within a given context. In this sense, therefore, to
> exist is nothing other than to be identified within a linguistic space.
> (1979: 18, my translation)

But even within this merely linguistic (anaphoric) space, their
stability is a fluctuating affair, the identity of the 'talked-about'
phenomena being at times safely 'given' and at others apparently
threatened or put at issue.

What we might call the crisis of the object is most vividly and
recurrently present in *CE*, in which the virtual norm of the interchanges
becomes the *conflict* between rival linguistic spaces with a consequent
mix-up of the 'individuals' they contain. The doubling of faces and
names, therefore, results at the 'pragmatic' level of speech in a
corresponding doubling of subject-matters and the co-referential
threads on which they are strung out. In its most straightforward form,
this amounts to simple failure on one or both sides to get (i.e. locate) the
'point':

Syr. Dro.   Master, here's the gold you sent me for: what, have you got the
picture of old Adam new-apparelled?
Syr. Ant.   What gold is this? What Adam dost thou mean?
Syr. Dro.   Not that Adam that kept the paradise, but that Adam that keeps the
prison; . . . he that came behind you, sir, like an evil angel, and bid
you forsake your liberty.
Syr. Ant.   I understand thee not. (4. 3. 12–21)

But the trouble is greatly aggravated when there arises between the
clashing spaces sufficient referential (and especially anaphoric) overlap
to create the impression for the speakers that the two points in reality
make up a single object. Take the case of the ambiguous 'marks' given
and received by Antipholus of Syracuse and Dromio of Ephesus
respectively:

Syr. Ant.   Where is the thousand marks thou hadst of me?
Eph. Dro.   I have some marks of yours upon my pate,
Some of my mistress' marks upon my shoulders,
But not a thousand marks between you both.
If I should pay your worship those again,
Perchance you will not bear them patiently. (1. 2. 81–6)

Each speaker's successive experiences within the play, his various
encounters with other 'individuals', human and otherwise, lead to what
is in part a personal and in part a shared discursive space held together by
anaphoric chains. And indeed, what serves as the comedy's chief
emblem of the speaker's experiential and referential difficulties with

objects is, precisely, a chain. Since both the Antipholus twins are familiar with it (one as its frustrated commissioner and the other as its startled receiver), the chain and its career provide ample grounds for the most intricate intertwining of the different catenary series they generate:

| | |
|---|---|
| *Angelo.* | Master Antipholus. |
| *Syr. Ant.* | Ay, that's my name. |
| *Angelo.* | I know it well, sir; lo, here's the chain; |
| | I thought to have ta'en you at the Porpentine, |
| | The chain unfinish'd made me stay thus long. |
| *Syr. Ant.* | What is your will that I shall do with this? |
| *Angelo.* | What please yourself, sir; I have made it for you . . . |
| *Syr. Ant.* | What I should think of this I cannot tell; |
| | But this I think, there's no man is so vain |
| | That would refuse so fair an offer'd chain. (3. 2. 164–80) |

| | |
|---|---|
| *Angelo.* | Have you the chain about you? |
| *Eph. Ant.* | And if I have not, sir, I hope you have, |
| | Or else you may return without your money. |
| *Angelo.* | Nay, come, I pray you, sir, give me the chain; |
| | Both wind and tide stays for this gentleman, |
| | And I, to blame, have held him here too long. |
| *Eph. Ant.* | Good Lord! You use this dalliance to excuse |
| | Your breach of promise to the Porpentine . . . |
| *Angelo.* | You hear how he importunes me; the chain! |
| *Eph. Ant.* | Why, give it to my wife and fetch your money. |
| *Angelo.* | Come, come, you know I gave it to you even now. |
| | Either send the chain or send me by some token. |
| *Eph. Ant.* | Fie, now you run this humour out of breath; |
| | Come, where's the chain? I pray you let me see it. (4. 1. 42ff.) |

Communicational misprision and mystification become so thoroughly associated with the chain and its misadventures that in reporting the arrest of what he takes to be his master as a result of its disappearance, Dromio of Syracuse perpetuates the mistake-the-object pattern as a form of perverse fooling:

| | |
|---|---|
| *Adr.* | Tell me, was he arrested on a band? |
| *Syr. Dro.* | Not on a band, but on a stronger thing; |
| | A chain, a chain, do you not hear it ring? |
| *Adr.* | What, the chain? |
| *Syr. Dro.* | No, no, the bell, 'tis time that I were gone. (4. 2. 50–3) |

Of course, it is not only things that are mixed up in colliding anaphoric spaces, but also and even more so the participants themselves. And one of the consequences of the mistaking of identities is the continual surprise of the talked-to and talked-about strangers at being referred to at all. The very fact of being elected object of discourse becomes a matter of note, as Antipholus's wonder at finding himself Luciana's addressee and topic illustrates:

Syr. Ant.   (Aside) To me she speaks, she moves me for her theme. (2. 2. 181)

The disconcertion at being caught up in a continual intersecting of unconnected messages, of mysterious addresses, of apparently correct but contradictory identifying acts is such as to throw in question their objects' sense of their own *subjectivity*. Dromio of Syracuse, made aware that he depends for the integrity of his very existence on the consistency of the references made to him, appeals to his master for confirmation of his threatened personality:

Syr. Ant.   Why, how now Dromio, where run'st thou so fast?
Syr. Dro.   Do you know me sir? Am I Dromio? Am I your man? Am I myself?
Syr. Ant.   Thou art Dromio, thou art my man, thou art thyself. (3. 2. 71–5)

In other comedies the shocked, baffled or anxious calling of attention to the position occupied at the receiving end of the identifying act usually has the effect of underlining an incongruity (as in Mistress Page's reaction to Falstaff's epistolary compliments: 'What, have I scaped love-letters in the holiday-time of my beauty, and am I now a subject for them?' MWW 2. 1. 1ff.), an irony (the embarrassment of Benedick and Beatrice after the overheard criticisms: 'Ben. I hear how I am censured – they say I will bear myself proudly', MA 2. 3. 219ff.; 'Beatr. Stand I condemned for pride and scorn so much?', 3. 1. 108; or Malvolio's self-identification as target of the false billet-doux: '"I may command where I adore." Why, she may command me: I serve her, she is my lady', TN 2. 5. 116ff.); or discomfort (Antonio's gloomy 'I am th'unhappy subject of these quarrels', MV 5. 1. 238) in the situation, if not an outright humiliation, as in the case of Falstaff. The most prominent talker and talked-about in the canon is forced to thematize his own role as 'theme', as the embarrassed butt of the verbal punishment inflicted by the assembled company:

> Well, I am your theme: you have the start of me. I am dejected; I am not able to answer the Welsh flannel; ignorance itself is a plummet o'er me; use me as you will. (MWW 5. 5. 162–5)

To be confirmed is not always to be comforted.

(VII) 'SO MUCH FOR THE TIME WHEN': THE TEXTUAL-ITY OF TEMPORALITY

When Theseus announces, at the beginning of MND, 'Now, fair Hippolyta, our nuptial hour/Draws on apace: four happy days bring in/Another moon', he is doing several things in the name of a single

presiding deity. Several things, inasmuch as Theseus's fairly straightforward 'Counterfait Time' in fact brings together at least four of the more
or less distinct kinds of temporal constraint co-operative in the drama.
For if what he is immediately concerned with are the 'four happy days'
that have to be filled before the wedding ceremony – i.e. the period
within which dramatic events are to unfold – he also invokes the
moment of the utterance itself ('Now'), the passage of time in general
governing the world ('Another moon'), and not least, though less
directly, the mythical or epic epoch to which the heroic existences of
Hippolyta and himself are to be attributed.

The last of these factors, the supposed historical or chronological
context of events, is only vaguely specified in the comedies. Extra-
textual 'history' is present in most of the plays, rather, in very
occasional and fragmentary references to the distance past, references
which serve not so much to add chronological thickness or verisimilitude as to exploit the familiarity of items within the audience's
epistemic stock for the purposes of some for-the-nonce effect. As a rule,
the historical is equivalent with the hyperbolical: legendary and
mundane eminences are invoked in extravagant similes characterizing
the present scene and *its* personages. In *MV*, for instance, heroic
predecessors are recurrently disinterred, with varying degrees of
earnestness, in order to figure the qualities of the speaker or
spoken-about, whether in Bassanio's mixed bag of classical similitudes
for Portia ('nothing undervalu'd / To Cato's daughter, Brutus'
Portia, / . . . her seat of Belmont Colchos' strond, / And many Jasons
come in quest of her', 1. 1. 165ff.), the Prince of Morocco's exotic
heroizing of his own prowess ('by this scimitar / That slew the Sophy,
and a Persian prince / That won three fields of Sultan Solyman', 2. 1.
24ff.), or Lorenzo and Jessica's parade of romantic precedents for their
own situation ('In such a night as this, / . . . Troilus methinks mounted
the Trojan walls', etc., 5. 1. 1ff.).

The lovers' catalogue of notables here indicates how readily the
extra-textual past becomes an intertextual path, a means of entry into
dramatic and literary tradition rather than a way out of the realm of the
text. Historical similes practically always conjure up the creatures – and
at times the creators – of other texts: the Hercules, Samson and the rest,
together with Ovid, Priscian and Mantuan, of *LLL*; the Robin Hood of
*AYLI* (which similarly sports an Ovid, plus a Gargantua and Julius
Caesar as author of 'I came . . .') and of *TG* (where he keeps company
with a highly literary Leander). Such trespasses into the past of the
spectator's reference world do no more than underline how text-bound
that world is itself.

What is normally meant by 'dramatic' time, however, is that temporal co-ordinate of events (the 'four days' of *MND*) which is at once a construct of and a constraint upon the dialogue: a construct, that is, of temporal reference and a constraint on the sequence of speech and other events. We might better term this factor narrative or *fabula* time. Clearly, the points of reference making up the dramatic universe are held together in a dynamic structure, being modified, added to or removed with the development of the drama, and constantly changing their position with respect to the fictional (speaking) present: 'the universe-of-discourse . . . has a temporal structure imposed upon it by the text; and this temporal structure is subject to continuous modification' (Lyons 1977: 670).

On the whole, the temporal structure of the textual universe remains fairly fluid and not very strongly bounded. *MND* is unusual in so clearly and repeatedly marking out the (lunar) limits of the action (see 1. 1. 1ff., 1. 1. 7–8, 1. 1. 83ff.). For the most part, *fabula* time emerges as a set of past or, more commonly, future points of textual orientation, as in the various appointments anticipated in *MWW* ('between ten and eleven', 2. 2. 80; ''Twixt eight and nine', 3. 5. 121; 'Be you in the Park about midnight', 5. 1. 10–11, etc.), or the single obsessive 'tomorrow' appointed for Claudio's death and referred to some twenty-four times in *MM*, a comedy which is, in Suzanne Langer's words, 'directed towards the future, and is always great with things to come' (1953: 306).

What this means, of course, is that the temporal constitution of the dramatic world is almost invariably measured with respect to the instant of the utterance, the 'now' of discourse, as in the case of Theseus's prolexis or the indexical 'tomorrow' which dominates *MM*. Time in the plays is not a progression through a series of chronological signposts ('the next day'), but a constantly shifting present through which dramatic past and future are gauged. However definitely or weakly characterized the other temporal constraints in the text, the speaking moment or temporal component of the context of utterance – *discourse* time, as it were – is the one constant, although ever-evolving, point of orientation.

The chronological decorum and coherence of the *fabula* will depend, naturally, on a general agreement concerning the 'now', the 'ago', the 'since' or the 'hence' issued at any given moment, and concerning the events located in the text at the respective points of time thus indicated. Even if the overall temporal setting of events is vague or fragmentary, at least discourse time is normally smooth enough and steady enough. The oustanding exception, as always, is *CE* – the most time-conscious and past-dominated of comedies – in which trouble arises on this very score, i.e. the non-coincidence of deictic temporal reference. Conflicting versions of the past produce in the dialogic *hic et nunc* a series of disputes regarding what is to be found at the 'since' (in the sense of 'ago') in question:

| Syr. Dro. | What answer, sir? when spake I such a word? |
|---|---|
| Syr. Ant. | Even now, even here, not half an hour since. |
| Syr. Dro. | I did not see you since you sent me hence. (2. 2. 13ff.) |

| Eph. Ant. | I owe you none, till I receive the chain. |
|---|---|
| Angelo. | You know I gave it to you half an hour since. |
| Eph. Ant. | You gave me none; you wrong me much to say so. (4. 1. 64ff.) |

| Syr. Ant. | Is there any ship puts forth to-night? may we be gone? |
|---|---|
| Syr. Dro. | Why, sir, I brought you word an hour since, that the bark *Expedition* put forth to-night, . . . |
| Syr. Ant. | This fellow is distract, and so am I. (4. 3. 33ff.) |

If the trouble with time in *CE* springs directly from the imperfect convergence, brought about by the plot, between overlapping 'histories', it is aggravated, as with other types of reference, by misinterpretation and contrived play. Thus Dromio of Syracuse's anxious reminder of time passing on is converted by Adriana, through a deliberate or unwitting pun (on/one), into a paradox on its going backwards, this in turn prompting Dromio to a philosophical meditation on time's crimes:

| Syr. Dro. | It was two ere I left him, and now the clock strikes on[e]. |
|---|---|
| Adriana. | The hours come back; that did I never hear. |
| Syr. Dro. | O yes, if any hour meet a sergeant, 'a turns back for very fear . . . Time is a very bankrupt, and owes more than he's worth to season. Nay he's a thief too. (4. 2. 54ff.) |

This introduces a further aspect of temporality in the comedies, particularly prominent in this play, namely the *thematizing* of time not as object or point of reference but as sustained topic. In *CE*, as R. A. Foakes observes (Arden edition, note to 2. 2. 54ff.) the repeated analysis and personification of Time '[relate] to the constant mistiming which is part of the sequence of "errors"'. The delays, missed appointments, untimely interventions and general out-of-phase non-co-ordination of the action result in the avowed anxiety, on the part of the victims (for whom, as Adriana puts it, 'Time is their master', 2. 1. 8), to restore the lost temporal decorum of the dramatic world. Note the frequency of reminders or reproofs such as "'tis dinner time', 'it is two o'clock', 'the hour steals on', etc. 'In good time' becomes the unfulfilled motto, and it is indeed this axiom which leads to the play's most extensive pseudo-logical anatomy ('burlesque dialectics' as Foakes terms it) of a grotesquely anthropomorphized Time and its effects, an analysis which attempts, as it were, to re-establish the speakers' linguistic dominion over a force that, however dependent on their specifications, threatens continually to undo them:

Syr. Ant.   In good time, sir; what's that? . . . Well, sir, learn to jest in good time;
            there's a time for all things. . . .
            By what rule, sir?

Syr. Dro.   Marry, sir, by a rule as plain as the plain bald pate of Father Time
            himself.

Syr. Ant.   Let's hear it.

Syr. Dro.   There's no time for a man to recover his hair that grows bald by
            nature. . . .

Syr. Ant.   Why is Time such a niggard of hair, being (as it is) so plentiful an
            excrement?

Syr. Dro.   Because it is a blessing that he bestows on beasts, and what he hath
            scanted men in hair, he hath given them in wit. . . . Thus I mend it:
            Time himself is bald, and therefore to the world's end will have bald
            followers.

Syr. Ant.   I knew 'twould be a bald conclusion. (2. 2. 56–108; on the proverbial
            character of Father Time's bald pate, see p. 281)

A similar travestying of philosophical meditation on time in *AYLI* has precisely the opposite source: the serene confidence of the exiled lovers that their pastoral pastimes are so much time off, there being 'no clock in the forest'. This sense of atemporal otherworldliness in the woodland scenes governs the mock-romantic make-believe, where chronology is replaced by the freeplay of the language of *amour courtois*, and chronometry by the mechancial predictability of the lover's expressions of passion:

Ros.   I pray you, what is't o'clock?

Orl.   You should ask me what time o' day; there's no clock in the forest.

Ros.   Then there is no true lover in the forest, else sighing every minute
       and groaning every hour would detect the lazy foot of Time, as well
       as a clock. (3. 2. 294–9)

As if to stress the point that in Arden time is strictly at the behest of the forms of expression, optional and variable topic rather than ruling force of the speech continuum, Orlando questions Rosalind's trope, provoking a reflection that, unlike Dromio's, is more sociological than metaphysical:

Orl.   And why not the swift foot of Time? Had not that been as proper?

Ros.   By no means, sir. Time travels in divers paces with divers persons. I'll
       tell you who Time ambles withal, who Time trots withal, who Time
       gallops withal, and who he stands still withal. . . . Marry he trots
       hard with a young maid, between the contract of her marriage and
       the day it is solemnized (3. 2. 300ff.);

while Orlando's violation of the lover's mythical clockwork punctuality calls for a microscopic breakdown of the heart's time-keeping:

*Orl.*   My fair Rosalind, I come within an hour of my promise.
*Ros.*   Break an hour's promise in love! He that will divide a minute into a thousand parts, and break but a part of the thousand part of a minute in the affairs of love, it may be said of him that Cupid hath clapped him o' th' shoulder, but I'll warrant him heart-whole. (4. 1. 40–7)

Although there is, in fact, a clock in the forest – Touchstone's 'dial' – it appears only at a double remove, as the object of the object of a report, namely Jaques's ecstatic account of the clown's temporal moralizing, itself another instance of the mock-philosophical irreverence with which the lazy foot of time is lazily kept at bay in the play:

*Jaques.*   And then he drew a dial from his poke,
And looking on it, with lack-lustre eye,
Says, very wisely, 'It is ten o'clock.
Thus we may see', quoth he, 'how the world wags:
'Tis but an hour ago since it was nine,
And after one hour more 'twill be eleven;
And so from hour to hour, we ripe, and ripe,
And then from hour to hour, we rot, and rot,
And thereby hangs a tale.' When I did hear
The motley fool thus moral on the time,
My lungs began to crow like chanticleer,
That fools should be so deep-contemplative. (2. 7. 20–31)

What the anti-chronological games in the Arden scenes of *AYLI* amount to is a reduction of temporality to the semantic space of the dialogue: the disavowal (itself, inevitably, temporary) of narrative time in order to open up the prospect of the limitless play of discourse. The reduction is illusory, of course, on two accounts: first, because speech itself is inescapably time-bound (it is the most exquisitely temporal of theatrical elements), and then because the proairetic dynamic *does* progress all the while, as the canons of comedy dictate and as the arrival of Jaques de Boys and the subsequent turn of events underline.

A more deliberate stand against the temporal restrictions on language – and in particular on textuality – is taken by the male figures in *LLL* as the founding principle of the projected Academy. Navarre's opening deliberative oration opposes to 'cormorant devouring Time' both long-term Fame inscribed 'upon our brazen tombs' and a shorter-term stasis of textual study, 'still and contemplative in living art'. And in order to demonstrate the ready performative sway of the royal word over cormorant time, Navarre imposes an arbitrary limit on the static humanistic textual space:

> You three, Berowne, Dumain, and Longaville,
> Have sworn for three years' term to live with me. (1. 1. 15–16)

Thereafter, the 'three years' signal becomes an obsessive refrain, creating a 'virtual' temporality the very nomination and renomination of which are equivalent to its enactment: "'tis but three years' fast' (1. 1. 24); 'to live and study here three years' (35); 'for three years space' (52); 'the penance of each three years' day' (115); 'within the term of three years' (129); 'within these three years space' (149); 'to study three years is but short' (179). But that the repetition is a favourite *figura verborum*, an elegant *epimone* rather than an actual commitment, is seen soon enough both in the sardonic confession of one of the swearers ('*Ber.* Necessity will make us all forsworn/Three thousand times within these three years' space', 1. 1. 148–9) and in the comic commutation of the penalty against Costard, first violator of the new code:

*King.*  It was proclaimed a year's imprisonment to be taken with a wench. . . . Sir, I will pronounce your sentence: you shall fast a week with bran and water.

*Cost.*  I had rather pray a month with mutton and porridge. (1. 1. 280–94)

It is notable that Costard himself takes the King's new pronouncement as a 'sentence' more in the syntactic than in the legal sense, a pretext for a jokey antithesis rather than an imposition to be actually observed. The climax in this easy tyranny over chronology, however, is reached in Moth's nonchalantly nominalistic demonstration for his master that the only kind of temporality really at stake in the 'three years' motif is the time it takes to put the components of the expression itself together:

*Arm.*  I have promised to study three years with the duke.
*Moth.*  You may do it in an hour, sir.
*Arm.*  Impossible.
*Moth.*  How many is one thrice told?
*Arm.*  I am ill at reckoning; it fitteth the spirit of a tapster. . . . It doth amount to one more than two.
*Moth.*  Which the base vulgar do call three.
*Arm.*  True.
*Moth.*  Why, sir, is this such a piece of study? Now here is three studied ere ye'll thrice wink; and how easy it is to put years to the word three, and study three years in two words, the dancing horse will tell you. (1. 2. 34–50)

As easy as that, or 'so much for the time when', as Armado's letter puts the matter (1. 1. 234). No more is heard of Navarre's chronological framework, and the only use that the men, in the guise of Petrarchan lovers rather than academicians, find for time is as a counter in their courtship (and as such duly exposed by the ladies: '*Ber.* What time o' day? / *Ros.* The time that fools should ask', 2. 1. 119–20), or as topical material for poetic conceits vaunting the time-defeating efficacy of the beloved object:

*Ber.*   A wither'd hermit, five-score winters worn,
        Might shake off fifty, looking in her eye:
        Beauty doth varnish age, as if new-born,
        And gives the crutch the cradle's infancy. (4. 3. 238–41)

But, as with the foresters of Arden, although far more rudely and abruptly, the would-be atemporal verbal idyll is brought to a close when events from without the closed pastoral scene catch up with the lazy progress of discourse: when the dialogue, that is, is forced back on to a more directly narrative track with Marcade's announcement of death in the 'outside' world. At this point, a second temporal scheme is projected into the (post-dramatic) future: the year's penance which the men are bound to undergo in order to earn their ladies' hands. This new period of planned austerity looks like a corrective counterpart to the first, a lesson, among others, in the overdue subordination of the over-aspiring word to the world and its solemn chronology. The ladies set up another refrain:

*Prin.*   There stay, until the twelve celestial signs
         Have brought about the annual reckoning. (5. 2. 789–90)

*Kath.*                    A twelvemonth and a day
         I'll mark no words that smooth-fac'd lovers say. (819–20)

*Mar.*                     At a twelvemonth's end
         I'll change my black gown for a faithful friend. (825–6)

*Ros.*    You shall this twelve month term from day to day . . . (842)

This is firm enough and decisive enough, an apparently clear reminder that words, even in comedy, cannot have their way altogether with the world, which has to go on developing. Unlike the lords' repeated undertaking, the ladies' reiterations seem insistent rather than merely schematic. But a quiet note of doubt is introduced in Berowne's passing protest ('That's too long for a play', 5. 2. 870; see pp. 70–1 above), throwing into question the performativity (as well as the performability) of this second commitment to 'virtual' time. Is the status of the ladies' 'twelve-month' so different from that of the men's 'three years', each an arbitrarily imposed and conveniently 'round' period, too long at least for *this* play? What is presented as a re-assertion of cormorant time is just, Berowne's objection suggests, another verbal ruse, and one which actually *robs* the comedy of its temporal decorum by projecting final events into an impossible and anti-comic future: so much for the time when, yet again.

(VIII) ENDINGS

If the advertised incompleteness of events in *LLL* is unique within the comic canon, not so is the prospect of something more to come after the close. *CE* and *TS* alone conclude with what are unambiguously last words, backward-looking summaries of the main dramatic pattern in the form of end-marking couplets:

*Eph. Dro.*   We came into the world like brother and brother,
                    And now let's go hand in hand, not one before another.

*Hortensio.* Now go thy ways, thou has tam'd a curst shrew.
*Lucentio.*   'Tis a wonder, by your leave, she will be tam'd so.

The rule otherwise is anticipation, a promise that the rounding-off of the narrative action does not as such signal the outer temporal limit to the represented realm. The something more may be unfinished and untroublesome business, like the definitive defeat of Don John in *MA* ('I'll devise thee brave punishments for him'); unrepresented wedding festivities, as in *AYLI* and *MND*; or, in *MWW*, the ironical fulfilment of Falstaff's undertaking ('To Master Brook you yet shall hold your word, / For he to-night shall lie with Mistress Ford'); but in any case it is more than anything symbolic of general perpetuation, a disclaimer as to the dependence of the fictional intercourse on its mere stage or textual representation.

Yet once the narrative dynamic is exhausted, what is left that can conceivably go on post-dramatically? Another narrative, perhaps (a third Falstaff play, for example)? But that involves a new beginning and another possible world. Or the continuing universe of the play's discourse (which in many cases, as we have seen, gets under way by looking back to a *pre*-dramatic past)? In a majority of instances this is indeed what is prospected: a future speech act that guarantees the continuity of the co-text after the other events are done. In his closing speech in *MM*, for example, Vincentio pre-announces a word in Isabella's ear that any audience member with a minimum of comic competence can safely predict:

> Dear Isabel,
> I have a motion much imports your good;
> Whereto if you'll a willing ear incline,
> What's mine is yours and what is yours is mine.

And Orsino in *TN* commissions a peace-making parley with Malvolio, designed to squeeze out of him the last drop of dramatic intelligence:

> Pursue him, and entreat him to a peace:
> He hath not told us of the captain yet.

Still the future prosperity of the discourse is not fully conceivable, in the absence of new objects and topics thrown up by narrative developments. What three endings propose, however, is not merely some forthcoming utterance or exchange exhausted as soon as enacted, but a full-scale act of narration, a *re-telling* of the dramatic *fabula* itself for the benefit of one of its less informed participants:

*Val.* Please you, I'll tell you, as we pass along,
That you will wonder what hath fortuned.
Come, Proteus, 'tis your penance but to hear
The story of your loves discovered. (*TG*)

*Por.* It is almost morning,
And yet I am sure you are not satisfied
Of these events at full. Let us go in,
And charge us there upon inter'gatories,
And we will answer all things faithfully. (*MV*)

*King.* Let us from point to point this story know
To make the even truth in pleasure flow. (*AWW*)

These metadiscursive endgames create the image of a potentially infinite dialogic regress, endless reworkings within the fiction of the same proairetic material, analogous with the limitless possibilities for new stage representations in the extra-fictional domain. At the close of each new version will be embedded, in Chinese-box recursion, the anticipation of another telling. The progress of discourse 'from point to point' becomes inexhaustible.

# 3   *Signs*

It is one of the more familiar tenets of modern criticism that what animates the language of Elizabethan comedy is, above all, the sheer process of making sense, and especially of making multiple senses. The glossing of semantic slips, tortures and pile-ups has become a major staple of the Shakespeare industry. Somewhat less widely remarked is the amount of excitement and anxiety which the communication or occultation of meaning appears to generate among the dramatic speakers themselves. If *LLL* contains as many as nine semantic 'replay' signals of the 'what mean you?', 'what's your dark meaning?', 'we need more light to find your meaning out' kind, this is just, as usual, the cornucopian overflowing of a metalinguistic mode common to all the comedies, ranging from Katherina's blunt 'A very mean meaning' to Orlando's incredulous 'speak'st thou in sober meanings?' and Benedick's hermeneutical 'there's a double meaning in that'.

Such pointers to hidden or misconstrued senses, or simply to the production of meaning as such, might be thought automatic reflexes in any dialogue fired by puns and quibbles, i.e. codified components of the word-corrupting games themselves. But semantic commentary in the comedies is not limited to the marking of obscure or double meanings, any more than language-games bringing into play the relationship between signs and meanings are restricted to punning wordplay. On the contrary, the range of signifying modes and of types of semantic self-consciousness in the plays is extraordinary. In order to approach either or both, a double perspective, at once broadly semiotic (regarding signs in general, and the place of language within semiosis at large) and synthetically historical (taking up the main semantic theories and some of the more powerful semiotic practices of the Elizabethan age), would seem indispensable.

The sphere of meaning is overtly extended beyond language as such in most of the plays. Attention is called to the signifying power of the body (Duke Vincentio reading the Provost's virtue 'written on your brow'; the 'fair speechless messages' Bassanio deciphers in Portia's eyes; the 'heavenly rhetoric' Berowne discovers in Rosaline's eyes), of costume

(Petruchio's significant wedding gear – 'He hath some meaning in his mad attire' – or Thurio's waistcoat cited by Valentine: 'I quote [your folly] in your jerkin'), of gestural and other forms of behaviour (the 'old signs' displayed by Benedick, betraying his enamoured state; the 'special marks' discerned to similar effect by Speed in Valentine's gestures, similar to the amorous 'marks' supposedly lacking in Orlando's comportment; or the full-blown kinesic code used by Tranio and decoded by Biondello – 'he has left me here behind, to expound the meaning or moral of his signs and tokens'), and even of the natural scene (the Forest of Arden 'translated' or linguisticized by Duke Senior: 'tongues in trees, books in the running brooks').

The direct semiotization of phenomena in the dramatic world constitutes in part an 'internal' version of what occurs on stage, where all theatrical vehicles (and, in particular, precisely the body, costume, gesture and physical scene) acquire a sign function by virtue of their very presence. The status of signs in general is a matter of no minor importance in an art form which draws upon a potentially unlimited range of semiotic means.

It was similarly a matter of no small interest, it is safe to say, to Shakespeare's auditors, theirs being an age in which not only was a vast amount of ingenuity and seriousness expended in the construction and deciphering of symbols of all kinds, but the relationship between signs and their meanings was the object of intense theoretical debate and even warfare, especially of a religious kind. It is surely impossible to appreciate what is done with and said about linguistic and other signs in these plays without some reference to contemporary semantic theory and semiotic practice. And nor is this recourse to history merely an academic duty. The existence of lively, and at times clamorous, controversies over language and other sign systems goes in part to explain how apparently abstract or abstruse issues were accessible to 'dramatization'. If the nature and putative powers of the sign were questions to be fought over or (in the case of heretical theories) to die for, their influence on the drama and its metalanguage is comprehensible enough. At the same time, the very seriousness with which the semantic issues of the day were taken made them eminently eligible butts for burlesque.

Of course, the endeavour to illuminate Shakespeare's language and metalanguage in terms of sixteenth-century semantics is in no sense new. Indeed, Shakespearean criticism has engendered, as one of its many by-products, a long line of confident declarations regarding the Elizabethans' attitude towards words and signs. But this heritage, rather than rendering superfluous further recourse to Renaissance theories of meaning, justifies it all the more. For what the critical tradition amounts to in this regard is a strikingly narrow consensus, a single received and repeated dogma representing at best an incomplete account of a fairly complex body of ideas.

The *locus classicus* of this dogma – its most influential statement, though not, of course, its source – is in Molly Mahood's study of Shakespeare's wordplay (1957), where (p. 169) an unspoken but intuitively perceptible semantic ingenuousness is firmly attributed to Elizabethan Man:

> The Elizabethan attitude towards language is assumed rather than stated, and is therefore much easier to feel than to define. Like Plato, the Elizabethans believed in the truth of names, but whereas, according to Socrates in the *Cratylus*, these right names had been given by 'the legislators', to the sixteenth century ways of thinking the right names of things had been given by God and found out by Adam . . . Names . . . seemed true to most people in the sixteenth century because they thought of them as at most the images of things and at least the shadows of things, and where there was a shadow there must be a body to cast it.

This affirmation does scant justice to all the parties involved: to the Plato of the *Cratylus*, who demonstrates anything but a straightforward faith in 'the truth of names'; to the Elizabethans, who did not share a uniform semantic 'attitude', and whose notions of language and meaning were by no means always 'assumed rather than stated'; and to 'people in the sixteenth century' in general, the century in question being marked, contrary to Mahood's portrait of a monolithic and unchanging linguistic naïveté, by radically opposed positions concerning, among other things, this very question of the 'rightness' of signs.

But such faith in the faith of the Elizabethans is evidently seductive, perhaps because it appears to explain the seriousness with which wordplay was taken. James L. Calderwood takes Mahood's 'good summary' as the basis and authority for his own, still more cursory version of the linguistic credo of *Homo elisabettianus*: 'In Shakespeare's time a belief in word-magic still persisted as part of a more general faith in the inherent rightness of words' (1969: 167). The theme is only very slightly varied by William C. Carroll, who again cites Mahood, in his study of *LLL*: 'The magical energy of language revealed itself to the Renaissance most clearly in the power of names. The prevailing linguistic theory held that there is an inherent rightness in names, that names are not arbitrary signs but are in some sense in themselves the essence of what is named' (1976: 12).

Outside the domain of Shakespearean criticism, and specifically in the field of the history of ideas, a more elaborate and ambitious exposition of what is virtually the same case is given by Michel Foucault in his reconstruction of a sixteenth-century 'episteme'. Foucault discovers in this period a homogeneous epistemological confidence, founded upon the supposed God-given phenomenality of the sign – and of language in particular – perceived as inseparable from the world of things:

> In its raw, historical sixteenth-century being, language is not an arbitrary system; it has been set down in the world and forms a part of it, both because things themselves hide and manifest their own enigma like a language and because words offer themselves as things to be deciphered ... Language partakes in the world-wide dissemination of similitudes and signatures. It must, therefore, be studied itself as a thing in nature. (1966: 35)

Foucault, unlike the Shakespearean critics, does furnish a body of evidence for his generalizations, but it is evidence of a strategically selective and weighted kind (his main source being the Hermetic Paracelsus). What each of these commentators gives us, in effect, is a boiled-down and rudimentary account of one Renaissance semantic tradition, the Neo-Platonic–Hermetic, while ignoring or suppressing not only alternative doctrines of the sign – particularly current towards the end of the century – but the complexities of the Neo-Platonic system itself. It is undeniable, of course, that Neo-Platonic and Hermetic philosophy, whose influence was felt everywhere, has left its traces on the language and linguistic commentary of the comedies, and indeed it is one of the aims of this chapter to examine such traces as closely as possible. But at the same time, contrary (i.e. more sceptical) positions, equally illustrable in terms of contemporary theory, are reflected in the plays. The resulting opposition is an occasion of central importance to the dialogue and to the progress of the comedy.

If in the discussion that follows considerably more space (sections (ii) to (vii)) is dedicated to versions of 'faith' in the sign than to the directly sceptical dismissal or maltreatment thereof in the plays (section (viii)), this is for two reasons. First, the range of Renaissance semio-linguistic practices founded on some form of semantic credulity and reflected directly or obliquely in the plays constitutes a wide and (within Shakespearean circles at least) under-explored cultural terrain. Second, as often as not the 'Cratylan' strain in the plays already implies the opposite semantic option in the irony or playfulness of the assertions of 'faith in the inherent rightness of words'. In the end – and this is the important consideration – the comedies are structured on an open 'exchange' between these opposing semantic positions, an exchange at once profoundly serious (since it involves, *inter alia*, the very nature of dramatic and theatrical representation) and eminently frivolous. Signification is of more than academic significance in these texts.

## (II) 'NOMINA SINT NUMINA': THE MOTIVATED SIGN

In describing certain kinds of 'primitive' language-game, Wittgenstein warns us: 'It is important to note that the word "meaning" is being used illicitly if it is used to signify the thing that corresponds to the word. That is to confound the meaning of the name with the bearer of the name' (1953: § 40). Such an error, such a 'primitive idea of the way language functions' (§ 2) – or in Gilbert Ryle's phrase, the 'Fido'–Fido view of meaning (1957) – is a common enough ground for a simple species of verbal slapstick in comedy. It is a child's-eye-view of language that has its most persistent and articulate dramatic exponent in the clown Costard in *LLL*, who, not content to fall repeatedly into the object = meaning trap, also improvises a kind of theoretical dissertation on the subject along the way. What seduces Costard into the enthusiastic identification of sense with referent is exactly the type of procedure quoted by Wittgenstein, as the point of departure for his own investigations, from Saint Augustine's autobiographical account of language acquisition, namely that of ostensive definition: 'When they [my elders] named some object, and accordingly moved towards something, I saw this and I grasped that the thing was called by the sound they uttered when they meant to point it out. . . . Thus, as I heard words repeatedly used in their proper places in various sentences, I gradually learnt what objects they signified' (*Confessions* I. 8). Costard, confronted with new words, immediately and excitedly associates them, like the infant Augustine, with the simultaneously ostended objects; the results, however, are somewhat less edifying:

| | |
|---|---|
| *Arm.* | There is remuneration; for the best ward of mine honour is rewarding my dependents. . . . |
| *Cost.* | Now will I look to his remuneration. Remuneration! O that's the Latin word for three farthings: three farthings, remuneration. 'What's the price of this inkle?' 'One penny': 'No, I'll give you a remuneration': why, it carries it. Remuneration! why it is a fairer name than French crown. I will never buy and sell out of this word. (3. 1. 128–38) |

| | |
|---|---|
| *Ber.* | There's thy guerdon: go. |
| *Cost.* | Gardon, O sweet gardon! better than remuneration; a 'leven-pence farthing better. Most sweet gardon! . . . Gardon! Remuneration! (3.1. 163–7) |

Costard's rhapsodic gloss on his own interpretation, and still more his fantasies of future glories in vaunting his new acquisition, betray clearly enough the conceptual chain reaction involved: from the assumption – shared, as Wittgenstein observes, by Augustine himself – that 'the individual words in language name objects' (1953: § 1), he proceeds to equate first meaning and then the word itself with the object. Any distinction between the lexical and the monetary units concerned is thereby collapsed (although, to be fair to Costard, they are indeed both means of exchange and commerce). The underlying conviction that all linguistic units are intimately and immediately tied to the physical world of (usually harsh) experience emerges in another of Costard's semantic frenzies, this time prompted by the coincidence of a neologism with the all too pressing reality of his recent injury:

| | |
|---|---|
| Moth. | A wonder, master! here's a costard broken in a shin. |
| Arm. | Some enigma, some riddle: come, thy l'envoy; begin. |
| Cost. | No egma, no riddle, no l'envoy; no salve in the mail, sir. O, sir, plantain, a plain plantain! no l'envoy, no l'envoy: no salve, sir, but a plantain! (3. 1. 67–71) |

The principle of 'if you don't understand, look for the nearest thing' is demonstrated by the second of the play's two main rustics, Constable Dull, in what amounts to a lesson in the 'ostensive' language-learning method. Like Costard, Dull is only too generous in – literally – pointing out the object of his confusion, painstakingly building up a quibble that proves, inevitably, rather dull:

| | |
|---|---|
| Nath. | A rare talent! |
| Dull. | If a talent be a claw, look how he claws him with a talent. (4. 2. 61–3) |

Of course, it is always somewhat arbitrary, in discussing the language of clowns and fools, to make tidy distinctions between the ingenuous and the burlesque, and still more to insist upon a single coherent linguistic practice or 'attitude'. Dull's apparent naïveté here, for example, might equally well be seen as an isolated piece of would-be sophistication, his one attempt at an 'intentionally' witty *antanaclasis*. The same is true of Costard's endeavour in the opening scene to argue his way out of the punishment due to him for violating Navarre's anti-carnal decree. In the light of his general verbal behaviour, Costard's excuses before the King would seem to embody the inevitable and classic result of the meaning–object confusion, namely the conviction that each single lexical item is necessarily tied to a distinct entity, whereby synonymity becomes quite inconceivable. Or is he, instead, archly playing up the rustic role and sophistically mocking both the terms of the decree and its author? –

| | |
|---|---|
| *King.* | It was proclaimed a year's imprisonment to be taken with a wench. |
| *Cost.* | I was taken with none, sir: I was taken with a demsel. |
| *King.* | Well, it was proclaimed damsel. |
| *Cost.* | This was no damsel neither, sir: she was a virgin. |
| *King.* | It is so varied too, for it was proclaimed virgin. |
| *Cost.* | If it were, I deny her virginity: I was taken with a maid. (1. 1. 280–8) |

The question of intentionality is a false track, however, especially with respect to a comedy in which the earnest and the parodic always go hand in hand. What are at issue, rather, are the rules of the game, and there is no doubt that one of the principal verbal activities of *LLL* is that of the hypostasization (whether knowing or guileless) of the word. A further principle in this game: each lexeme (and not only the substantive) is perceived as a proper name, indissolubly linked to its bearer. Again it is Costard who, in his most resolutely literal manner, makes the point in an encounter with yet another neologism:

| | |
|---|---|
| *Arm.* | Sirrah Costard, I will enfranchise thee. |
| *Cost.* | O! marry me to one Frances – I smell some l'envoy, some goose in this. |
| *Arm.* | By my sweet soul, I mean setting thee at liberty, enfreedoming thy person. (3. 1. 118ff.) |

As is often the case, Costard's superstitious mistranslation represents a grotesque travesty of the general treatment received by the linguistic sign in the play. The great paradigm for language at large in *LLL* is the proper name. If, as John Lyons warns, 'the relation which holds between a proper name and its bearer is very different from the relation which holds between a common noun and its denotata' (1977: 216), this does not in the least reduce the force that the name and the rite of nomination exercise as models for all our linguistics dealings with the world, as Lyons himself emphasizes: 'As far back as we can trace the history of linguistic speculation, the basic semantic function of words has been seen as that of naming' (215). In *LLL* the appeal, as it were, of appellation is evident first in the obsessive adamic ceremony of nomination as such and in the very range of names for naming drawn upon:

| | |
|---|---|
| *King.* | This child of fancy, that Armado hight (1. 1. 169) |
| *(Arm.)* | . . . it is ycleped thy park (1. 1. 235)<br>which, as I remember, hight Costard (1. 1. 250)<br>so is the weaker vessel called (1. 1. 265)<br>which we may nominate tender (1. 2. 14–15) |
| *Moth.* | . . . which we may name tough (1. 2. 17)<br>Which the base vulgar do call three (1. 2. 45) |

| | |
|---|---|
| *Arm.* | . . . name more (1. 2. 64) |
| | his disgrace is to be called boy (1. 2. 170) |
| *Ros.* | Berowne they call him (2. 1. 66) |
| *Boy.* | Katherine her name (2. 1. 194) |
| *Ber.* | What's her name in the cap? (2. 1. 208) |
| *Arm.* | Call'st thou my love hobby-horse? (3. 1. 28) |
| *Ber.* | When tongues speak sweetly, then they name her name, |
| | And Rosaline they call her (3. 1. 160–1) |
| *Cost.* | To a lady of France that he call'd Rosaline (4. 1. 106) |
| *Nath.* | A title to Phoebe, to Luna, to the moon (4. 2. 37) |
| *Hol.* | . . . for the nomination of the party writing to the person written |
| | unto (4. 2. 129–30) |
| *Nath.* | . . . who is intituled, nominated, or called Don Adriano de Armado |
| | (5. 1. 7–8) |
| *Prin.* | That he was fain to seal on Cupid's name (5. 2. 9) |
| | You nickname virtue (5. 2. 349) |
| *Cost.* | I Pompey am, Pompey surnam'd the Big (5. 2. 545) |
| *Hol.* | Judas I am, ycleped Maccabaeus (5. 2. 593) |

and then in the carefully cultivated anxiety that the pedants in particular express over nominal propriety: whether for the 'singular and choice epithet', the 'liable, congruent and measurable . . . well culled, chose; sweet and apt' noun, or the proper name proper. The most conspicuous instance is Holofernes's pious exegesis of a particularly prestigious (not to say prominent) surname:

> Ovidius Naso was the man: and why, indeed, *Naso*, but for smelling out the odoriferous flowers of fancy, the jerks of invention? (4. 2. 118–21)

The pedant, it might be noted, *reverses* the superstitious reduction practised by Costard in first interpreting the name as a common noun and then attributing to it a direct bond of perfect semantic appropriateness with the eminent nominee. What Holofernes invokes, quite evidently, is the chimera of a directly motivated linguistic sign, a possibility which also underlies, in burlesque form, Moth's verbal relations with his more credulous master. The page is able to mimic, on commission, the motivate-the-name game for his patron:

| | |
|---|---|
| *Arm.* | . . . name more; and, sweet my child, let them be men of good repute and carriage. |

*Moth.*     Samson, master: he was a man of good carriage, great carriage, for he
          carried the town-gates on his back like a porter (1. 2. 64–8);

just as he is capable of out-exclaiming Armado's passionate preoccupation with appropriate labelling:

*Arm.*     How canst thou part sadness and melancholy, my tender juvenal?
*Moth.*    By a familiar demonstration of the working, my tough Signor.
*Arm.*     Why tough Signor? why tough Signor?
*Moth.*    Why tender juvenal? why tender juvenal?
*Arm.*     I spoke it, tender juvenal, as a congruent epitheton appertaining to
          thy young days, which we may nominate tender.
*Moth.*    And I, tough Signor, as an appertinent title to your old time, which
          we may name tough.
*Arm.*     Pretty, and apt.
*Moth.*    How mean you, sir? I pretty, and my saying apt? or I apt, and my
          saying pretty?
*Arm.*     Thou pretty, because little.
*Moth.*    Little pretty, because little. Wherefore apt?
*Arm.*     And therefore apt, because quick. (1. 2. 7–23)

Moth's apt and quick semantic fluttering about his master; the
pedants' quest for congruous designation; the rustics' enthusiastic
reification of the word: what emerges, albeit in very varied guises, as the
common denominator of the communal denominational frenzy in *LLL*
is the 'naturalistic' hypothesis of an immediate union between sign and
denoted phenomenon. It is with respect to such an atmosphere of ardent
or mock linguistic credulity that the more 'primitive' semantic theories
of Shakespeare's time become an instructive rather than a token point
of reference.

Semantic naturalism – and the mystical and occult theories of the
sign that often went with it – found their most authoritative support in
the Renaissance in a mistakenly literal reading of the *Cratylus*. In
Plato's dialogue, Cratylus champions what may be a form of Hera-
cliteanism (in the philosophy of language often attributed to Heraclitus
the distinction between language (*logos*) and the phenomenal world
(*physis*) is collapsed and the word upheld as 'the eloquent presence of
the thing': see G. S. Kirk's edition of the *Cosmic Fragments*, 1970: 68;
see also Albert Borgmann, 1974: 13). 'He says', complains Cratylus's
opponent Hermogenes of him in the dialogue, 'that [names] are natural
and not conventional; not a portion of the human voice which men
agree to use; but that there is a truth and correctness in them, which is
the same by nature for all, both Hellenes and barbarians' (Jowett ed.,
1953: § 383a). What lent weight to this indefensible opinion for later –
and notably Renaissance – readers of Plato was the apparent, somewhat
modified support given to it by Socrates in the dialogue: his elaborate

etymologies demonstrating the onomatopoeic correctness of certain names and the universal significance of various letters and sounds look, when de-ironized, like a determined rationalization of the 'natural' position. But in reality Socrates reduces both Cratylus's credulous 'correctness' thesis and Hermogenes's equally extreme and preposterous conventionalism *ad absurdum*, and his final position with regard to the putative reproductive power of the *logos* is unmistakable: 'how ridiculous would be the effect of names on the things named, if they were always made like them in every way! Surely we would then have two of everything' (432d; on this subject see Levinson 1957 and Anagnostopoulos 1972).

Socrates's all too evident scorn was lost, however, on most Platonists of the late fifteenth and sixteenth centuries, who, following the lead of Plato's translator and commentator *par excellence*, Marsilio Ficino, embraced the most uninhibited form of Cratylan credence. Ficino's *argumentum in Cratylum, uel de recta nominum ratione* (1561: 67ff.) made respectable the attribution to Plato himself of a belief in a non-arbitrary and non-conventional sign relationship. The gesture was repeated by the most influential of all Renaissance Platonists, Pico della Mirandola, who, in the fifty-third of his Platonic conclusions (part of his heretical Nine Hundred Theses) issued what was to be the classic statement of the naturalist case: 'Similarly regarding names, the fact that they have a natural force is known to everyone. Indeed, they do not have this force inasmuch as they signify by convention (*ad placitum*) but inasmuch as they have certain natural things in them ... Plato agrees with this in the *Cratylus*, namely that they are correctly imposed' (1486a: 42–3, my translation).

What is interesting and important about Pico's affirmation is not the specific account of meaning it expounds, which is philosophically half-baked and interpretatively (the 'Plato agrees') misleading, but its context, the extraordinary syncretistic mélange of Neo-Platonic, Hermetic, Orphic and Cabalistic dogma which during the century following was to be invariably associated with the Cratylan position. The 'Platonic' *nomina sint numina* (name = essence of thing) doctrine as such is crude and rapidly stated: language is made up of individual 'names', each bearing a one-to-one relationship with the *res* or slice of reality denoted, not on the grounds of its conventional sense and the arbitrary bond between that sense and the spoken or written lexical form, but through a direct and natural union with the thing itself, the essence of which is expressed in the very sounds and letters of the name. Such a dogma certainly represents a step backwards with respect to the complex Scholastic semantics of the late Middle Ages (against which, particularly nominalism, the Platonists were indeed reacting). But this simple-minded creed served as the theoretical back-up to a broad compass of mystical and occult precept and *praxis* that greatly enriched its implications. And not least among its claims to pious respect, of course, was its vicinity to the biblical account of the origins of language, an account which facilitated the syncretistic marriage of the mystical pagan with the Christian. The German magus Agrippa Von Nettesheim did more than anyone to popularize this conflation of the *Cratylus* with Genesis under the aegis of the 'occult philosophy':

> The Platonists, therefore, say that in this very voice, or word, or name framed, with its articles, that the power of the thing, as it were some kind of life, lies under the form of the signification. . . . Adam, therefore, that gave the first names to things, knowing the influences of the heavens and properties of all things, gave them all names according to their natures, as it is written in Genesis . . . which names, indeed, contain in them wonderful powers of the things signified. (1533: 209)

That the Neo-Platonic doctrine of names, which became a sixteenth-century commonplace, was well-known in Elizabethan England, along with other favourite tenets of Ficino, Pico and their followers, is scarcely in need of illustration (on the influence of Neo-Platonism in Elizabethan England, see Yates 1979). References to it outside the bounds of philosophy proper are innumerable, and the Englishing of such popular and influential works as *The Examination of Men's Wits* by the Spanish psychologist Juan Huarte (translated 1594) made the Platonists' argument readily accessible to the English public: '[Plato] saith that there are proper names, which by their nature carrie signification of things, and that much wit is requisite to devise them' (1594: 103–4). The general appeal of the naturalist theory – which also, of course, coincided with popular superstition – was immense, and some version of semantic 'primitivism' is to be found among the most respectable (and decidedly non-Platonist) humanist scholars of the time. Erasmus, to cite only the most eminent instance, championed a quasi-mystical semantics, endeavouring to demonstrate on the Socratic model (but quite without Socratic irony) the fixed significance of certain phonemes in Latin: 'If there be not a traceable likeness between the word and the object or action which it symbolises, then there is some *invisible* reason why object or action is named by the word which expresses it . . . words which express *softness* or *slowness* prefer an L sound, *levis* and *labi* are examples' (in Woodward 1904: 141). The natural propriety of native English lexical stock, meanwhile, became a favourite rallying cry for defenders of the vulgar, like Richard Verstegen:

'This our ancient language consisted most at the first of words of monosillable, each having his own proper signification, as by instinct of God and nature they first were received and understood' (1605: 189). William Camden includes among his 'Remains' Richard Cawdray's spirited apology for the vernacular and the inherent rectitude of its morphemes and lexemes:

> Now for the significancy of words, as every *Individuum* is but one, so in our native English-Saxon language, we find many of them suitably expressed by words of one syllable ... Grow from hence to the composition of words, and therein our language hath a peculiar grace, a like significancy, and more short than the Greeks, for example in *Moldwarp* we express the nature of that beast. In handkercher the thing and its use. (1605 ed.: 37–8)

Camden himself, observing that Old English 'could express most aptly', adds a quaint instance of lost native propriety: 'An *Eunuch*, for whom we have no name, but from the Greeks, they could aptly name *Unstana*, that is, without stones' (27).

Now the distance between the reverential asseverations of a Pico della Mirandola and the burlesque inanities of Shakespeare's clowns could scarcely be greater, and any coincidence between the underlying 'philosophies' of language – in one case solemnly manifest and in the other ludically and ludicrously encoded – might seem at best a matter of like superstitiousness. What makes the comic 'naturalism' of *LLL* and its doctrinal implications particularly intriguing, however, is the genuinely philosophical programme proposed, however half-heartedly, in the upper social sphere of the play.

As is only too well-known, Navarre's sententious opening oration (here the tone is suitably grave) inaugurates that modish intellectual institution, 'a little academe'. And like all the French academies of the time, the projected school has, by definition, unmistakable philosophical allegiances. In the words of Pierre de la Primaudaye's *The French Academy* (considered by many as one of the sources of *LLL*), and specifically his Epistle Dedicatory to another King of Navarre, Henri III, it is 'a Platonicall garden ... otherwise called an ACADEMIE' that Shakespeare's Navarre intends to create at his court. That the French academies, on the model of Ficino's original Florentine Platonic Academy, were synonymous with Neo-Platonism and the accompanying Hermetic and Orphic practices, has been amply demonstrated by Frances Yates (1947). As for Navarre's little academe, the implication that it is to be suitably dedicated to mystical researches in the Platonic mould is clear enough in the first exchange between the King and Berowne:

*Ber.*      What is the end of study, let me know?
*King.*     Why, that to know which else we should not know.
*Ber.*      Things hid and barr'd, you mean, from common sense?
*King.*     Ay, that is study's god-like recompense. (1. 1. 55–8)

If the Academy spells Platonism in general, it also implies, more specifically, a Platonist view of language. The evidence for this is not far to seek. In his *Le Second Curieux*, the philosopher Pontus de Tyard, founder member of the Pléiade (the first French academy to be instituted by royal decree), dutifully rehearses the semantic theory of Ficino, Pico and such French predecessors as Symphorien Champier: 'names are substantial, by which I mean that they signify the substance of the named thing' (see Walker 1954: 230, my translation). This is no more than academic orthodoxy.

It is vain, of course, to seek an articulate philosophical platform of any kind in the declarations of Shakespeare's would-be academicians, the more so since Navarre's scheme proves so fragile and ephemeral. But that the male aristocrats in the play (or at least most of them, and at least some of the time) betray, like their social inferiors, a faith in the phenomenal and numinal fullness of the linguistic sign is plain enough. The academic programme itself is founded upon a double optimism regarding the (written) word: in the texts to be studied and, *scripta manent*, 'register'd upon our brazen tombs' in the form of the fame aspired to. And it is officially instituted with the solemn subscribing of the members' names to their 'deep oaths'. A like reverence towards nomination underlying the projected studies is reflected in the sardonic commentary of Berowne, the only reluctant and critical academician of the four ('These earthly godfathers of heaven's lights, / That give a name to every fixed star', 1. 1. 88ff.).

Even after their transformation from would-be ascetic Platonic scholars (with a hint, in the best syncretist manner, of Stoicism: 'Still and contemplative in living art') into pseudo-Platonic lovers, the lords' ardour is still directed towards the name. 'I desire her name', pleads Longaville of Maria (or rather of 'Maria'). He is promptly rebuked by Boyet with a nice irony on the propriety, or at least the proprietorship, of the longed-for name: 'She hath but one for herself; to desire that were a shame' (2. 1. 198–9). And at the height of his amorous frenzy, Berowne rhapsodizes on the euphony of his beloved's name in harmony with the qualities of its bearer: 'When tongues speak sweetly, then they name her name, / And Rosaline they call her' (3. 1. 160–1).

In his defence of their collective infatuation, Berowne gives a direct indication that the lords' amorousness, like their aborted scholarship, is as much as anything a cultivation of language, motivated *by* the linguistic sign as well as oriented towards it. Berowne incites his fellow-lovers 'for love's sake, a word that loves all men' (4. 3. 354), admitting the seductive driving force of the word in question. The immediate issue of this verbal infatuation is, of course, the series of earnest Petrarchan sonnets and odes that the men, in the true style of the Platonic lover, produce. But the effect of their linguistic libido (language serving as the object and motive force of desire) is more generally felt in the lovers' fascinated handling of discourse, and particularly in Berowne's aristocratic version of the punning and self-propagating lexical delirium indulged in at all social levels in the play:

> *Ber.* The king he is hunting the deer; I am coursing myself: they have pitched a toil; I am toiling in a pitch, – pitch that defiles: defile! a foul word. (4. 3. 1ff.)

The most pertinent and acute commentary on this heady enchantment with the linguistic sign is given by Ernst Cassirer in his study of Platonism in Renaissance England (1932). Reflecting on the manifestation of the Neo-Platonic spirit in Shakespeare's early comedies, Cassirer remarks that

> As always, the conception and treatment of speech is but a symptom of a general and fundamental intellectual disposition. . . . The Renaissance does not look upon speech through the medium of the great models of antiquity, only as crystallised form; but the farther it penetrates into these models, the more clearly it perceives the forming energy, the plastic power, which is embodied in language as such. . . . The process of cultivation of the intellect must begin with the cultivation of language, and the two must remain in the closest relationship. This demand for linguistic culture leads finally to an actual cult of linguistic forms. (173–4)

An 'actual cult of linguistic forms' is a fairly precise description of the lords' verbal behaviour from their solemn oath-swearing to their enthusiastic sonnet-writing to their oratorical efforts before the ladies. It is in their various encounters with the ladies, indeed, that their elegantly literary hypostasization of the sign is most brutally exposed, first in the Princess's repudiation of Navarre's empty complimentary forms ('Fair I give you back again; and welcome I have not yet', 2. 1. 91–2), and her equally derisive scepticism towards his 'deep oath' ('*King*. I have sworn an oath. / *Prin.* Our lady help my lord! he'll be forsworn', 2. 1. 96–7), and then in the emblematic 'word-exchanging' scene, in which the men's reification of the name is directly travestied. One by one the suitors are humiliated by means of the satirical literalness with which the ladies take their offers of a conversational 'word'. Berowne's approach is sabotaged by the very identity proposed by the Princess between the qualities of the lexeme and what it denotes:

| | |
|---|---|
| *Ber.* | White-handed mistress, one sweet word with thee. |
| *Prin.* | Honey, and milk, and sugar: there is three. |
| *Ber.* | Nay then, two treys, an if you grow so nice, |
| | Metheglin, wort, and malmsey: well run, dice! |
| | There's half-a-dozen sweets. |
| *Prin.* | Seventh sweet, adieu . . . |
| *Ber.* | Thou griev'st my gall. |
| *Prin.* | Gall! bitter. |
| *Ber.* | Therefore meet (5. 2. 230–7); |

Dumain's 'word' is again understood in its lexical sense, and promptly 'changed' as requested:

| | |
|---|---|
| *Dum.* | Will you vouchsafe with me to change a word? |
| *Mar.* | Name it. |
| *Dum.* | Fair lady, – |
| *Mar.* | Say you so? Fair lord, – |
| | Take that for your fair lady (238–40); |

and, the unkindest cut of all, Longaville's lexical offering is taken as his proper name, which, analysed into its component 'morphemes' (*long/veal*), is found to be only too directly motivated:

| | |
|---|---|
| *Kath.* | Veal, quoth the Dutchman. Is not veal a calf? |
| *Long.* | A calf, fair lady! |
| *Kath.* | No, a fair lord calf. |
| *Long.* | Let's part the word. |
| *Kath.* | No, I'll not be your half: |
| | Take all, and wean it: it may prove an ox. (247–50) |

The women's detached metalinguistic strategy here rests on an agile and ironical textual deictic 'pick-up' ('Name *it*', 'Say you *so*?', 'Take *that*', 'wean *it*') exploiting the suitors' gauche discursive openings. It is especially significant that the men's inept solicitations are directed, in any case, towards the wrong objectives, the ladies having exchanged their distinguishing tokens or 'favours' in order to confound their respective wooers. The heedless persistence of the men in their empty campaign, having failed to spot the trick, not only confirms their commitment to an autotelic 'cult of linguistic forms', but betrays, more directly, a general credulity towards the sign, both linguistic and otherwise. As usual it is Berowne who, looking back on the debacle, explicates the principle of their ingenuousness:

> The ladies did change favours, and then we,
> Following the signs, woo'd but the sign of she. (5. 2. 469–70)

The *wooing of the sign* (including the sign 'she') is exactly what the lords practise as scholars and as lovers. But in neither guise are they conspicuously successful or convincing Platonists. Indeed, the women's accusation against them, by way of a final irony, is not merely that of a facile resort to verbal formulae (their new vows of love substituting the old 'deep oaths') but of an outright linguistic *im*propriety, a fatal *mis*naming at the heart of their oratorical labours:

> King.   Rebuke me not for that which you provoke:
> The virtue of your eye must break my oath.
> Prin.   You nickname virtue; vice you should have spoke. (5. 2. 347–9)

In this academic-amorous context, the semantic naïveté of the rustics and the neologistic fastidiousness of the pedants assume a more particular weight, namely as grotesque variations of the semiotic enthusiasms indulged in by their social and intellectual betters, just as, by the same pseudo-philosophical token, the more outrageous *tours de force* by Moth can be understood in part as witty reductions *ad absurdum* of the adult males' collective precepts. In this light, his demonstration for Armado's benefit of the power of a simple noun phrase over the denoted time period ('how easy it is to put years to the word three, and study three years in two words, 1. 2. 48–50) looks like a sly stab at the elaborate trust placed by the scholars in the empty temporal clause of their decree (see above, p. 110). Or likewise, his deriving of an unflattering portmanteau-word from an idle encounter with the pedants might be seen as a guying of the 'significancy' attributed to 'Moldwarp'-style composites of Germanic monosyllables:

> Arm.   . . . it rejoiceth my intellect; true wit!
> Moth.   Offered by a child to an old man; which is wit-old. (5. 1. 56–7)

It might be argued that the what's-in-a-name game, however recurrent in *LLL*, is never really serious enough to raise authentically philosophical issues. This does not mean, however, that it has nothing directly to do with the epistemology of the age. Indeed, the very lightness with which the 'motivated' name is paraded in the play suggests the degree to which the mystical reification of the sign had become familiar, or even codified, towards the end of the sixteenth century. This is borne out by the more occasional glimpses of linguistic superstition in other comedies, where semantic faith is almost invariably assumed for some ulterior (strategic, clownish, romantic) purpose. Even the one conspicuously sober, not to say macabre, instance, Shylock's determination to 'realize' *a posteriori* the Christians' abuse – 'Thou call'dst me dog before thou hadst a cause, / But, since I am a dog, beware my fangs' (3. 3. 6–7) (a tactical stand confirmed by Shylock's later instance on the one-to-one matching of the terms of the bond with their bodily referents: 'Ay, his breast, / So says the bond, . . . / 'Nearest his heart,' those are the very words . . . / Is it so nominated in the bond?', 4. 1. 248–55) – clearly has more to do with personal than with semantic motivation. The pious scruples of Don John in avoiding the nomination of Hero's sins in *MA*, for fear of a consequent contamination of the lexicon itself –

> Fie, Fie! they are not to be named, my lord,
> Not to be spoke of.
> There is not chastity enough in language,
> Without offence, to name them (4. 1. 94–7) –

in fact disguises, as the audience well knows, the non-existence of what is so nicely unnamed. In comparison, Claudio's reluctance to refer to his crime, in *MM*, on the grounds that the very naming may re-present the misdeed – 'Lucio. What's thy offence, Claudio? / *Claud.* What but to speak of would offend again' (1. 2. 126–8) – seems serious enough, but is presumably attributable to simple prudence.

Otherwise, the travestying of lexical 'propriety' is good for a rhetorical *coup* on the *asteismus* model, as in Adam's sardonic reflection on his new master's treatment of him in the opening scene of *AYLI*:

Oli.     Get you with him, you old dog.
Adam.   Is 'old dog' my reward? Most true, I have lost my teeth in your service (1. 1. 81–3);

just as, for the clowns in *TG*, the feigning of a naïve confusion between the common and the proper name serves as an easy ruse in the endless production of patter:

Spe.     'Item, she hath many nameless virtues.'
Lau.     That's as much as to say 'bastard virtues'; that indeed know not their fathers; and therefore have no names. (3. 1. 311–14)

And while the obstinate insistence of Petruchio, in *TS*, on the adamic rightness of his naming – 'I say it is the moon' – is largely a function of his taming schemes (as Katherina complains, he tyrannically substitutes the word for the thing: 'That feed'st me with the very name of meat', 4. 3. 32), the violent literalness with which the Shrew herself is reported to interpret an unfamiliar term can be put down to the hyperbolic overacting of her pre-taming role:

Hor.     I did but tell her she mistook her frets,
          And bow'd her hand to teach her fingering,

When, with a most impatient devilish spirit,
'Frets, call you these?' quoth she, 'I'll fume with them.'
And with that word she struck me on the head. (2. 1. 149–53)

But if the election of the common name to the status of the 'proper', in its various senses, is good for a passing *bon mot* or sarcastic retort, then the assimilation of the proper name itself with its human bearer is a favourite expedient of the romantic or mock-heroic conceit. At its basis, as we know from *The Golden Bough,* is one of the commonest forms of primitive superstition: 'Unable to discriminate clearly between words and things, the savage commonly fancies that the link between a name and the person . . . denominated by it is not a mere arbitrary and ideal association, but a real and substantial bond which unites the two' (Frazer 1936: 318). Appearing to issue from its owner, the name acquires the value of an effect standing in a direct metonymic relation with its cause, or even of a synecdochic part standing for the whole being. 'The rightness of the name', as Hans-Georg Gadamer puts it, 'is confirmed by the fact that someone answers to it. Thus it seems to be part of his being' (1960: 366). This, dressed up with the intellectual trimmings of Platonism, is the assumption underlying, as we will see, the Cabalistic onomancy of Agrippa and his fellows. In the context of the exclamatory tropical effusions of Shakespeare's 'early' lovers, instead, superstition is transformed into elegant whimsy, of which the fullest and most fanciful instance is Julia's passionate self-castigation, in *TG,* after tearing up her beloved's billet-doux. Prefacing her outburst with a show of conventional piety towards the damaged signifiers themselves, as if the written characters were endowed with the saccharine qualities they express – 'O hateful hands, to tear such loving words; / Injurious wasps, to feed on such sweet honey' / And kill the bees that yield it, with your stings!' – Julia proceeds to expand the conceit into a rapturous parable on nominal incarnation, the use or abuse of the titular body:

Look, here is writ 'kind Julia': unkind Julia!
As in revenge of thy ingratitude,
I throw thy name against the bruising stones,
Trampling contemptuously on thy disdain.
And here is writ 'love-wounded Proteus'.
Poor wounded name: my bosom, as a bed,
Shall lodge thee till thy wound be throughly heal'd;
And thus I search it with a sovereign kiss.
But twice, or thrice, was 'Proteus' written down:
Be calm, good wind, blow not a word away,
Till I have found each letter, in the letter,
Except mine own name: that some whirlwind bear
Unto a ragged, fearful, hanging rock,
And throw it thence into the raging sea. (1. 2. 110–23)

It is, of course, the *writtenness* of the names here that emphasizes their corporality and bestows on them a notionally independent physical interaction – once literally torn from the context of the letter – with and within the world. An irresistible extension of this sentimental gesture, seen in *MA*, is the direct eroticizing of the two graphic bodies, setting up between the names an intimacy not socially permitted to their owners. The joke does not involve, as in *LLL*, the lover's desire *for* the name, but direct desire *between* names, an outright lexical lust:

| | |
|---|---|
| *Clau.* | Now you talk of a sheet of paper, I remember a pretty jest your daughter told us of. |
| *Leon.* | O, when she had writ it, and was reading it over, she found 'Benedick' and 'Beatrice' between the sheet? |
| *Clau.* | That. (2. 3. 132–7) |

This commonplace of the life-incorporating denomination is taken to a logical extreme in *MND*, in Lysander's mock-epic threat of revenge against 'Demetrius'; once animated as a natural part of its owner, the name must by the same token share, even when detached from him, something of his physical vulnerability and mortality:

Where is Demetrius? O! how fit a word
Is that vile name to perish on my sword! (2. 2. 105–6)

Undoubtedly, the onomastic extravagance of Shakespeare's Julia and Lysander may be attributed to the romantic fancy that dominates both the comedies concerned. At the same time, however, the figurative excess of their conceits does have a certain – and specifically, a metadramatic – justification. For the name/bearer relationship is never as simple or as unilateral in the drama as it is in extra-dramatic society. In various ways, the name *is* a synecdoche, or at least a direct metonymy, of the *dramatis persona*. In the first place, quite simply, it belongs to the corpus of language on which the 'life' of the character directly depends. To the extent that 'Demetrius', say, is a construct of discourse (his own and others'), then the name itself is indeed an essential part of him and, what is more, motivates *him*. In this sense Lysander's wrath against the 'word' denoting his rival is a precise indication of the real status of the 'Demetrius' he wishes to assassinate. This principle is equally valid for all drama.

But if we consider Julia's 'Proteus', then other kinds of nominal motivation come into play, typical of Shakespearean and, in general, Elizabethan comedy. The name of the protagonist in *TG* obviously possesses a referential thickness that goes beyond the dramatic context itself and back, to be precise, to a multiform Roman sea-god; and as such it bears a definite sense by antonomasia (already codified in English:

132

'protean'), which allows it to function as a rather crude index of the character of the changeable gentleman of Verona.

Aristotle remarks that 'our comic poets ... assign names to the persons quite arbitrarily' (*Poetics* 51b. 12–13, trans. Else 1967: 33). The same can scarcely be said of the comic poets of the Elizabethan age. And while Shakespeare never reaches the outer limits of significant naming so often vaunted in Ben Jonson's character lists (Jonson's denominations are more like entire phrases or discourse fragments than mere names: Zeal-of-the-Land Busy; In-and-In Medlay; Politic-Would-be; Amorous La Foole, etc.), there is nevertheless in almost every one of his comedies a sprinkling of such 'natural' nominal indices: 'how much of the atmosphere in Shakespeare's plays is already conveyed to us when we scan his dramatis personae!', as Harry Levin comments (1965: 62), 'to state it categorically, the *persona* begins with the name' (64).

There are really several quite distinct kinds of baptismal 'rightness' in Shakespeare's comic nomenclature, although they all have an evident defining role. In the 'Proteus' category – i.e. historical or legendary, picking up some designation from the audience's reference world – one might also place Holofernes of *LLL*, Pompey of *MM* (both ironical) and Adam of *AYLI*, as well as (more seriously) Portia in *MV*. Indeed, the appropriate associations that accompany the latter name – what John Searle terms the '*descriptive backing*' to names from history (1969: 162ff.) – are somewhat heavily underlined at Portia's first mention in the play, in Bassanio's gushing encomium:

> In Belmont is a lady richly left,
> And she is fair, and (fairer than that word),
> Of wondrous virtues, ...
> Her name is Portia, nothing undervalu'd
> To Cato's daughter, Brutus' Portia. (1. 1. 161ff.)

Close to, and indeed overlapping with this group are what we might call *intertextually* motivated names, whose aptness derives from a descriptive backing which is more strictly literary or dramatic than historical. The names of various figures in *AYLI*, from the protagonist Orlando to the woodland shepherds, Corin, Silvius and Phebe, betray an obvious pastoral (in Orlando's case, a specifically Ariostan) ancestry that determines 'genetically', as it were, the more conventionally poetic aspects of their behaviour and language. It is interesting to note that in the same comedy this very issue of onomastic 'heredity' of an intertexual and mythological kind is raised directly in Rosalind's choice of *nom de forêt* before her escape to Arden; Rosalind's criterion is that of her adopted role, as young boy:

| *Cel.* | What shall I call thee when thou art a man? |
| *Ros.* | I'll have no worse a name than Jove's own page, |
| | And therefore look you call me Ganymede. (1. 3. 119–21) |

Celia's choice, instead, is governed equally explicitly by another form of fittingness, that is, according to her social and psychological condition as exile:

| *Ros.* | But what will you be call'd? |
| *Cel.* | Something that hath a reference to my state. |
| | No longer Celia, but Aliena. (122–4) |

The principle expounded by Celia is the same as that ruling a set of more crudely indexical names whose significance is directly related to *characterial and behavioural traits*: Touchstone, Dull, Simple, Sir Toby Belch, Malvolio, Feste, Froth, Parolles. Having imposed these meaningful denominations, Shakespeare fails occasionally (but less frequently than many of his contemporaries) to resist the temptation to exploit their sense for a quick laugh – Holofernes's 'Most dull, honest Dull' (5. 1. 146), or the following exchange in *AWW*, with reference to the metalinguistic 'Parolles' (= many and empty words):

| *Par.* | I beseech your honour to hear me one single word. |
| *Laf.* | You beg a single penny more. Come, you shall ha't; save your word. |
| *Par.* | My name, my good lord, is Parolles. |
| *Laf.* | You beg more than 'word' then. (5. 2. 35–9) |

Close relatives of these behavioural indices, and still within the socio-psychological sphere of aptness, are those surnames evoking professional status, or more particularly, malpractice: Sir Oliver Martext, Mistress Quickly, Mistress Overdone.

But if there are any true candidates for a direct and 'natural' name/owner bond in Shakespeare's nomenclature, then they are surely to be found in those cases where the body of the name is semantically equivalent with the body of the named, or at least some part of it. *MM* has two examples of such corporeal fitness, both of which produce inevitable easy quips – Constable Elbow:

| *Ang.* | Elbow is your name? Why dost thou not speak, Elbow? |
| *Pom.* | He cannot, sir: he's out at elbow (2. 1. 58–60); |

and (a 'mixed', historical-physical instance) the tapster Pompey Bum:

| *Esc.* | What's your name, master tapster? |
| *Pom.* | Pompey. |
| *Esc.* | What else? |
| *Pom.* | Bum, sir. |
| *Esc.* | Troth, and your bum is the greatest thing about you; so that, in the beastliest sense, you are Pompey the Great. (2. 1. 209–16). |

One suspects that the real motivation for Christian (or rather pagan) name and surname here is the passing joke itself. This is certainly the case in *CE*, where the maid Luce is temporarily re-baptized so as to create the occasion for a brief piece of homonymic slapstick; here the lexeme-name is found *in*adequate to show forth the full and impressive dimensions of the denoted body:

| | |
|---|---|
| *Syr. Ant.* | What's her name? |
| *Syr. Dro.* | Nell, sir; but her name and three quarters, that's an ell and three quarters, will not measure her from hip to hip. (3. 2. 106–9) |

Each of these types of indexical label, then, breaks in one way or another the two basic semantic rules governing proper names in general: first, that they carry no sense (or at most an etymological sense – 'Smith', 'Gardener', 'Fish', etc. – which in practice is conventionally and politely ignored); and second that since they bear a merely accidental or baptismal relationship with the nominee, they tell us nothing about his actual characteristics: 'Proper names ... identify their referents, not by describing them in terms of some relevant property or properties which the name denotes, but by utilizing the unique and arbitrary association which holds between a name and its bearer' (Lyons 1977: 214). Shakespeare's significant christening, on the contrary, has precisely the effect of describing or indicating salient properties.

Even so, of course, the indexical name remains a rather weak and notional version of the 'natural' sign relationship, operating as it does strictly within the bounds of the worldly and more often than not having a risible rather than mystical force. Closer to an immediate physical engagement with nature, within a super-mundane context that warrants the more-than-human capacity of the sign, is the nomination ritual in Bottom's first encounter with the fairies (*MND* 3. 1). Each name-noun in Bottom's fairyland roll-call has at once a personal and a substantive value, appertaining to the fairy bearer and at the same time standing for the part of nature that the creature embodies. The model is predominantly – if ironically – Paracelsan (Paracelsus's medical magus and semiologue being 'the wise man to whom Nature has taught her secrets' and who 'knows the "signs" which reveal her powers', Pachter 1951: 79). Quite improbably, Bottom finds himself in the privileged position aspired to by many a Renaissance Hermetist, namely that of an unmediated communion with the natural essences underlying the lexicon. Perfectly unmoved by his initiation into the mysteries of nature, he greets each elemental spirit (or decodes, as it were, each natural sign) with the ease of one already quite familiar with the worldly denotations of the names – including, it might be noted, their medicinal uses – and now simply adding to his stock of knowledge an acquaintance with their supernatural equivalents:

*Bot.*    I cry your worship's mercy, heartily. I beseech your worship's name?
*Cob.*    Cobweb.
*Bot.*    I shall desire you of more acquaintance, good Master Cobweb: if I cut my finger, I shall make bold with you. Your name, honest gentleman?
*Peas.*    Peaseblossom.
*Bot.*    I pray you, commend me to Mistress Squash, your mother, and to Master Peascod, your father. Good Master Peaseblossom, I shall desire you of more acquaintance too. Your name I beseech you sir?
*Mus.*    Mustardseed.
*Bot.*    Good Master Mustardseed, I know your patience well. That same cowardly giant-like ox-beef hath devoured many a gentleman of your house: I promise you, your kindred hath made my eyes water ere now. I desire you of more acquaintance, good Master Mustardseed. (3. 1. 172–89)

In the fairy realm of Bottom's bottomless dream, each *nomen* is also immediately and magically a *numen*. The forest is revealed to the vision of the 'transformed' weaver as a secret 'text' – the Book of Nature that the Hermetists strove to read – now so readily decipherable that he is not even aware of the change. Bottom's return to a kind of adamic perception of nature and its signs is, precisely, natural.

### (III) 'SO SWEET A STYLE': PASTORALISM AND THE 'LINGUA ADAMICA'

Bottom's effortless engagement with the occult semiosis of the forest amounts, of course, not only to a 'naturalizing' of language but equally to a 'linguisticizing' of the natural scene. The notion that nature manifests itself to the initiated observer as a language belongs not only to the philosophical Platonism of Ficino, Pico or Paracelsus but equally to a literary tradition closely associated in origin with that philosophical movement, namely the pastoral drama of Politian, Tasso, Ariosto, Guarini and their continental and English imitators. Tasso's *Aminta* – directly related, as Richard Cody has shown (1969), to Italian Platonic syncretism – establishes the model for an intimate communion between the 'natural' poetry of the Arcadian shepherd and the poetry of nature in Arcadia itself.

This topic is expounded at the beginning of the most explicitly pastoral scene in Shakespeare, Act 2 scene 1 of *AYLI*, in which we are introduced to the quasi-Arcadian Arden. Duke Senior's celebrated opening oration – together with the eulogistic commentary by Amiens that accompanies it – rehearses the two moments of the landscape–language relationship in pastoral. First an equation is drawn between the natural scene and human discourse ('tongues in trees, books in the running brooks / Sermons in stones'), a discourse and indeed a rhetoric of which the Duke, as adoptive Arcadian, is direct receiver: 'These are counsellors / That feelingly persuade me what I am.' And second, these linguistic metaphors are in turn praised by Amiens as a felicitous verbal rendering of the foresters' present circumstances:

> Happy is your Grace,
> That can translate the stubbornness of fortune
> Into so quiet and so sweet a style.

The 'translation' of the landscape and its language – its 'lexical' items (the scenic components) with their harmonious 'syntactic' relations manifested in a kind of speech ('sermons') or in texts ('books') – into a suitably figural poetic equivalent is the daily business of the Arcadian shepherd-poet. Orlando, the self-elected poet of Arden, acts out the Duke's conventional figures, particularly his 'bibliographical' trope, in the most literal fashion, further textualizing the forest through his amorous verses:

> O Rosalind, these trees shall be my books,
> And in their barks my thoughts I'll character. (3. 2. 5–6)

The trees become doubly 'readable', books containing books.

But Orlando's romantic gesture is another game of good Ariostan and Tassonian stock, and specifically an allusion to the Angelica and Medoro episode in *Orlando Furioso* ('Among so many pleasures, whenever a straight tree was seen shading a fountain or clear stream, she had a pin or knife ready at once', trans. Lee 1977: 29–30), duly varied in Tasso's *Aminta* (1. 1: the reference to Thyrsis in love writing on trees – 'Lo scrisse in mille piante'). This 'already-overworked topos in European literature' (Lee 1977: 7) is pregnant, moreover, with more or less automatic iconographic associations relating to a long and eminent series of sixteenth-century illustrations of the *Orlando* episode (see Figure 2). Orlando's semi-serious conceit becomes an oblique mode of the pseudo-painterly 'iconism' that is, as we shall see, essential to the pastoral style.

It is tempting to see in Shakespeare's debts to Ariosto, Tasso and their imitators some allegiance also to the syncretist (Platonic–Orphic–Hermetic) matrix from which the language of *Orlando Furioso* and *Aminta* springs. Richard Cody is quite unhesitating in asserting the

2       'Angelica and Medoro', engraving by Giorgio Ghisi
after Teodoro Ghisi.

'poetic identity of Platonism and pastoral' in the comedies of Tasso and
Shakespeare alike, although for him the 'token and preferred instance of
Elizabethan aesthetic Platonism under its pastoral-comical aspect' is
not so much *AYLI* as *LLL* (1969: 13). It is always difficult, naturally, to
judge the extent to which well-established literary commonplaces bear
with them the traces of their origins, philosophical or otherwise. But a
partial pastoralism–Platonism association is not implausible with
respect to plays in which, as we have seen, the possibility of a motivated
linguistic sign is definitely present, even if comically.

Amiens's praise of Duke Senior's 'quiet' and 'sweet' translation raises
the related issue of the stylistic options open to pastoral comedy,
particularly under its 'Platonic' aspects. What Tasso, Guarini and their
followers lead us to expect is a sensual and sentimental version of *serio
ludere*, that earnest playfulness which Ficino and Pico upheld as the
characteristically Socratic dialogic mode (see Wind 1967: 236ff.; Cody
1969: 76ff.; see also pp. 156–9 below). In a sense, the sharply ironical play
of the Arden foresters, designed to 'fleet' the time 'carelessly as they did in
the golden world' (1. 1. 118–19) – like the still more acerbic games in
Navarre's park – is a good deal closer in tone and force to Socratic

dialogue than the somewhat saccharine and verbosely voluptuous exchanges that take place in Tasso's Arcadia, not least because the idyllic *ludere* repeatedly surprises with its disenchanted philosophical conclusions (Rosalind's 'men have died from time to time and worms have eaten them', etc.).

Shakespeare's park and greenwood comedies capture less ambiguously the language of the pastoral *favole boschereccie*, however, in the representation of the landscape by means of what we might term the bucolic icon. Pastoral drama – even when its tone is more consistently ludic than *serio* – aspires not only to the vivid evocation of the Arcadian scene, but also and above all to some approximation of a pristine *lingua adamica*, marking off speech in the edenic golden world from the post-Babelian decadence of our own verbal commerce. And of course, the language of Eden is necessarily iconic, springing as it does fresh and direct from newly moulded nature. The Tassonian model for the iconic bucolic mode is a somewhat floridly pictorial description, within a passage of narration, at once detailed and playful:

> A l'ombra d'un bel faggio Silvia e Filli
> sedean un giorno, ed io con loro insieme,
> quando un'ape ingegnosa, che cogliendo
> sen' giva il mel per que' prati fioriti . . .
> forse un fior le credette. (Tasso, *Aminta*, 1573, 1. 2. 441ff.)

('Under the shade of a lovely beech Silvia and Phyllis / Sat one day, and I along with them, / When an industrious bee, which buzzed around / Collecting honey from the flowery meadows / . . . Perhaps mistook [Phyllis] for a flower.') Echoes of this luxurious painterly style and the setting itself – both of which have their (arboreal) roots in Virgil's eclogues – are not far to seek either in *AYLI* ('Under an oak, whose antique root peeps out', 2. 1. 31ff., 'Under an old oak, whose boughs were moss'd with age', 4. 3. 104ff.) or in *LLL* ('Under the cool shade of a sycamore', 5. 2. 89ff.). And indeed, both comedies pay their debts more or less openly to the pastoral tradition and its rhetoric, *AYLI* with its direct comparison of Arden to the golden world and its introduction of Petrarchan shepherds and the like, and *LLL* – which, admittedly, presents at best a brazen world – in Holofernes's elegy for the lost language of the eclogue: 'old Mantuan! old Mantuan! who understandeth thee not, loves thee not' (4. 2. 95–6).

Unquestionably, however, the purest and most convincing version of a greenworld *lingua pristina* – with the possible exception of Armado's seasonal dialogue at the close of *LLL*, the one moment in which the comedy aspires to an authentically Orphic bucolism – is found in the evocation of the wood by the fairy speakers in *MND*. Here it is uncorrupted nature herself putatively speaking, the forest presenting or representing itself, as it were, through the discourse of what in effect are its secret parts:

*Fairy.*  The cowslips tall her pensioners be,
In their gold coats spots you see;
Those be rubies, fairy favours,
In those freckles live their savours.
I must go seek some dew-drop here,
And hang a pearl in every cowslip's ear. (2. 1. 10–15)

The illusion created by the delicately suggestive style of the fairies' descriptions is that of an unmediated experience of that very language of nature perceived by Duke Senior in Arden. Here there is no call for the interpretative intervention or 'translation' of a human agent, although it might be noted that Bottom is able immediately to adopt the fairies' depictive mode after *he* has been, precisely, 'translated': 'Mounsieur Cobweb . . . kill me a red-hipped humble-bee on the top of a thistle; and good mounsieur, bring me the honey-bag', 4. 1. 10ff.). It is, as it were, the 'tongues in trees' themselves that show forth the forest of which they are part.

This powerful double fiction, involving first the creation of the natural scene itself and second the self-definition of an innocent and unmediated language expressing it, is undoubtedly one of the more notable stylistic achievements of the comic canon. It is the closest Shakespeare comes to a serious commitment to the 'edenic' implications of the pastoral tradition.

### (IV) 'THE SONGS OF APOLLO': ORPHIC EFFECTS

The association of the pastoral aspects of certain comedies with the mystical conception of language espoused by the syncretizing Platonists may appear less arbitrary if considered under the aegis of what, in the Renaissance, was held to be one of the profoundest and most ancient of religious cults, namely the Orphic. The revival of the myth of Orpheus as wonder-working poet and prophet was inaugurated, at the end of the fifteenth century, in Neo-Platonic philosophy and on the stage contemporarily: i.e. in the writings of Ficino and Pico, notably the latter's *Conclusiones de modo intelligendi hymnos Orphei*, and in what is generally classified as the first pastoral drama (its author himself being a member of Ficino's Florentine Academy), Politian's *Orfeo*.

For the academic Platonists, Orpheus's claim to reverence lay principally in his position within a long line of so-called *prisci theologi* –

ancient teachers of divine mysteries – that began with Adam and included Moses, Zoroaster, Hermes Trismegistus, Pythagoras, Plato and, finally, Christ himself (see Walker 1953: 105). The particularly elevated status attributed to Orpheus was due in part to his supposed role as teacher of Pythagoras, who in turn passed the secret doctrines on to the divine Plato. The Orphic didactic method, termed by Pico the *poetica theologia*, consisted in encoding the mysteries in apparently trivial hymns and love poems, in order to render them comprehensible to initiates alone: 'In the manner of the ancient theologians, Orpheus interwove the mysteries of his doctrines with the texture of fables, and covered them with a poetic veil, in order that anyone reading his hymns would think them to contain nothing but the sheerest tales and trifles' (Pico, 'Of the Dignity of Man'; see Wind 1967: 18). It was from this immanence within Orphic poetry of divine verities, allegorically disguised, that, according to Pico's commentary on the *Orphica*, its legendary miraculous powers derived. And more specifically, it was the presence of poetically occulted but transcendentally significant names that guaranteed the hymns' sway over nature and supernature: 'The names of those Gods of whom Orpheus doth sing are not of deceiving devils . . . but they are the names of natural and divine virtues' (Pico, Third Orphic Conclusion, quoted by Sir Walter Raleigh, *The History of the World*; see Walker 1953: 12).

The *Orphica* – like the *Hermetica* and the Cabala, to which it was married by the syncretists – appeared to endorse not merely a mystical but a directly magical conception of language, or of a language duly adapted to music and imbued with appropriate spiritual and theological force: 'In natural magic', claims Pico in another Orphic Conclusion, 'nothing is more efficacious than the Hymns of Orpheus, if there be applied to them suitable music, and disposition of the soul, and the other circumstances known to the wise' (quoted in Yates 1964: 78). The prospect offered is that of a triumphant *vis verborum* of the kind which Politian's Orpheus – like Ovid's before him – is shown exercising both over terrestrial nature and over the inhabitants of Hades. And the temptation to carry this doctrine to its logical 'practical' conclusion, i.e. the lyre-accompanied incantation of Orphic hymns designed to secure marvellous 'effects', was not resisted by Ficino, Pico and their followers, so much so that French Platonic academies such as Baïf's Académie de Poésie et de Musique were officially dedicated to the Orphic project of an effect-producing marriage of words and music (see Yates 1947; Pagnini 1974: 88ff.).

Orpheus's parallel literary and dramatic career confirms this mystical revival. Politian's Orpheus is the archetype of those shepherd-poets –

gifted with a passionate eloquence that moves nature, human and otherwise – who people the pastoral drama. 'I have seen the rocks and the waves reply to my complaints from pity', announces Tasso's Aminta. And at the same time, the Orphic 'effects' are upheld by poetic and rhetorical legislators throughout the sixteenth century as the highest and most glorious ideal to which the verbal arts can aspire: 'the Oratour may leade his hearers which way he list, and draw them to what affection he will' (Peacham 1577: Aiii<sup>r</sup>; see also, among English commentators, Wilson, Sidney and Puttenham on the Orphic model).

The Orphic revival, then, brought together a literary-dramatic, a musical-poetic and a philosophical-mystical component under the all-comprehending auspices of a magical conception of the sign. Each of the three direct references to the Orphic myth in Shakespeare's comedies takes up one of these aspects. The dramatic and theatrical potential of Orpheus's violent death – as dramatized, for example, in Politian's play – is considered and dismissed by Theseus in *MND*, on the grounds that the topic is already outworn (thus indicating the extent of the existing dramatic heritage):

> The.    (*Reads*) 'The riot of the tipsy Bacchanals,
> Tearing the Thracian singer in their rage'?
> That is an old device, and it was play'd
> When I from Thebes came last a conqueror. (5. 1. 48–51)

On the other hand, the still fresh potency of Orphic poetry, *sub specie musicae*, is eagerly recommended to the Duke of Verona in *TG*:

> Pro.                    . . . and frame some feeling line
> That may discover such integrity.
> For Orpheus' lute was strung with poets' sinews,
> Whose golden touch could soften steel and stones,
> Make tigers tame, and huge Leviathan
> Forsake unsounded deeps, to dance on sands. (3. 2. 75–80)

Proteus's advice – however bizarrely baroque its central musical metaphor – is in effect the stock rhapsody on the heady powers awaiting the suitably passionate poet-lover. A good deal more sober in tone, but richer in its doctrinal implications, is Lorenzo's reflection on the powers of music in the final scene of *MV*:

> Lor.                    . . . therefore the poet
> Did feign that Orpheus drew trees, stones and floods,
> Since naught so stockish, hard and full of rage,
> But music for the time doth change his nature. (5. 1. 79ff.)

What is suggestive about Lorenzo's otherwise unsurprising allusion is the quasi-philosophical context in which it occurs, the lunary meditation on universal harmony and the music of the spheres that represents the most unambiguously Platonic essay in Shakespeare:

> There's not the smallest orb which thou behold'st
> But in his motion like an angel sings,
> Still quiring to the young-ey'd cherubins;
> Such harmony is in immortal souls. (5. 1. 6off.)

Now, apart from Plato's *Republic* itself, the most authoritative antecedent to Lorenzo's universal system of harmonious correspondences (rendered thoroughly familiar in the sixteenth century through innumerable rehashes) is Pico's *Heptaplus*, with its doctrine of sympathetic 'vertical' relations between worlds: 'Everything which is in the totality of worlds is also in each of them and none of them contains anything which is not to be found in each of the others ... whatever exists in the inferior world will also be found in the superior world, but in a more elevated form' (1489: 188; quoted in Gombrich 1948: 168). And it is this doctrine which lies, as Gombrich has shown, behind the Neo-Platonic conception of the sign: 'It is by virtue of this interrelated harmony that one object can signify another and that by contemplating a visible thing we can gain insight into the invisible world' (1948: 167–8). More specifically, it is such a 'paradigmatic' system of sympathies that explains the Orphic effects, the music of the hymns being in harmony with that of the heavenly bodies, and their poetry containing the disguised names of celestial virtues. The principle of trans-world harmony thus incorporates

> a theory of language according to which the word is considered as a magical symbol that not only denotes objects but also exerts powers connected with those objects, because it contains their substance or essence. As in any kind of magic, all things are sympathetically linked, in vertical series through many levels from god to material things, and in horizontal ones on any given level. (Walker 1954: 231)

In the light of this only too familiar dogmatic heritage, Lorenzo's exposition takes on a pleasingly self-referential complexity. His reflection on the 'effects' of Orphic music within a system of *harmonia universalis* is itself accompanied, in best Orphic fashion, by harmonious music. It might thus be seen to imply an optimism regarding its own potential sway – the 'enchanting' power of the very scene in progress – over the present theatrical auditors, however 'stockish, hard and full of rage' they may prove. Of course, this disguised declaration of dramaturgical self-confidence is not without its dangers, especially that of a painfully ironic distance between Orphic dogma and theatrical practice, or between the striving after magical effects and the humiliating failure to work them. But happily, the history of the comedy's theatrical fortunes confirms Lorenzo's optimism.

Neither in its musical nor in its linguistic guise is the myth (evidently enchanting in itself) of a nature-taming efficacy restricted to these direct Orphic allusions in the plays. While the doctrine of the sway of music over the passions receives its classic statement in the opening speech of *TN*, and a more burlesque expression in Jaques's exaggerated melancholic *furore* at the first suspicion of a note in *AYLI*, it is the complementary possibility of a poetic or simply verbal form of persuasive *vis* that is posed in *LLL* and *AWW*.

The chimera of an irresistible verbal magnetism is constantly present and fatally alluring to the academicians in *LLL*. The motif first appears in the ladies' initial eulogies to the scholars, prior to the latter's precipitous fall from grace. Rosaline's awe at Berowne's discursive charisma is particularly striking.

> Which his fair tongue (conceit's expositor)
> Delivers in such apt and gracious words
> That aged ears play truant at his tales,
> And younger hearings are quite ravished;
> So sweet and voluble is his discourse (2. 1. 72–6)

It might be noted that the hyperbolic terms of Rosaline's praise are almost exactly those adopted by Sidney in his account of the poet's supreme and quasi-musical gift for persuasion through delight (where the Orphic, as well as the Horatian, paradigm is implicit): 'hee commeth to you with words set in delightfull proportion, either accompanied with, or prepared for the well inchaunting skill of music; and with a tale forsooth he commeth unto you: with a tale which holdeth children from play, and old men from the chimney corner' (1595: Eiv[r]).

Berowne himself adapts the topic to characterize Boyet's charm with the ladies, attributing to him, somewhat sardonically, a curious form of flirtatious and infallible *lingua adamica* (musical to boot):

> This gallant pins the wenches on his sleeve;
> Had he been Adam, he had tempted Eve.
> A' can carve too, and lisp: . . .
>               nay, he can sing
> A mean most meanly, and, in ushering,
> Mend him who can: the ladies call him sweet. (5. 2. 321–9)

As for Armado – who is always promising marvellous locutionary feats ('I will tell thee wonders', etc.) – Navarre's metadiscursive sketch of him adjusts the model still further; here we have Orpheus as Narcissus, at

once divine source and transported receiver of his own harmonious
verbal flow:

> A man in all the world's new fashion planted,
> That hath a mint of phrases in his brain;
> One who the music of his own vain tongue
> Doth ravish like enchanting harmony. (1. 1. 163–6)

If such notional 'effects' seem to take us far from the supposed
'theological' import of Orphic magic, nonetheless the more solemn
mythological and semantic underpinnings of the cult do emerge in the
comedy, namely in Berowne's spectacular metaphysical manifesto in
4.3. In the course of his impassioned and elaborate exhortation to his
fellow-scholars in favour of Eros, Berowne produces a remarkably
authoritative excursus on the inspirational sources of 'divine' poetic
eloquence:

> Love's tongue proves dainty Bacchus gross in taste.
> For valour, is not Love a Hercules,
> Still climbing trees in the Hesperides?
> Subtle as Sphinx, as sweet and musical
> As bright Apollo's lute, strung with his hair;
> And when Love speaks, the voice of all the gods
> Make heaven drowsy with the harmony.
> Never durst poet touch a pen to write
> Until his ink were temper'd with Love's sighs;
> O! then his lines would ravish savage ears,
> And plant in tyrants mild humility. (4. 3. 335–45)

Berowne's equating of the poetic with the erotic in the production –
under the auspices of Apollonian music – of heaven-moving effects, has
a firm enough basis in the tenets of the *prisca theologia*. Orpheus was
upheld as the recipient of the divine Apollonian lyre, and indeed, in one
tradition, as the son of Apollo himself (see Guthrie 1935: 27). The high
standing among the theologians that Ficino attributed to him depended
in part on his supposed embodiment of all four of the Platonic *furori* –
the poetic, the Bacchic, the erotic (all present in Berowne's exposition),
together with the prophetic (see Walker 1953: 100). As Berowne
suggests, however, it is Eros that rules over Orphic poetry, dedicated as
it is to this the oldest of gods. Berowne's erotic poetics are thus
doctrinally impeccable: 'love', as Ficino states in his commentary on
the *Symposium*, 'is the Ruler of the Arts. Artists seek after and care for
nothing but love' (1944 ed.: 150). What Berowne is proposing, therefore,
is a cultivation of language under Eros that is at once an Orphic cult and
a Herculean task, the very 'love's labour' of the title; and this further
allusion in his mythological mélange is perfectly coherent with the rest,

one of Hercules's most memorable achievements having been precisely the Orpheus-like linking of his hearers 'together by the eares in a chaine, to draw them and leade them euen as he listed. For his witte was so greate, his tongue so eloquente, and his experience suche, that . . . euerye one was . . . driuen to do that whiche he woulde' (Wilson 1553: Aii[r]).

In the wake of Berowne's eruditely mystical, or at least mystifying, performance ('Berowne would like', as Richard Cody puts it, 'to be taken for an adept in poetic theology', 1969: 116), Eros is officially sanctified as patron of the scholars' poetic and rhetorical labours ('*King*. Saint Cupid then!', a war-cry which is ironically echoed later by the Princess: 'Saint Denis to Saint Cupid!', 5. 2. 87). And as Berowne's earlier 'erotic' monologue suggests, the most salient characteristic of Cupid as ruler over poetic language is his legendary blindness:

> This wimpled, whining, purblind, wayward boy,
> This signor junior, giant-dwarf, dan Cupid;
> Regent of love rhymes, lord of folded arms. (3. 1. 174ff.)

This again is perfectly in keeping with Berowne's ostentatiously advertised Orphic programme. The 'mystery' of the Blind Cupid was central to Neo-Platonic Orphism, and indeed represented one of the most widely canvassed objects of the Platonists' more ardent philosophical speculations: 'Love united the intelligible intellect to the first and secret beauty by a certain life which is better than intelligence. The theologian of the Greeks [Orpheus] himself therefore calls this love blind' (Ficino, quoting Proclus; see Wind 1967: 57). The putative profundity of the mystery lies in the paradox whereby the very blindness of Cupid assists the Platonic lover in reaching a more intense vision or insight: 'It adds a precious seeing', as Berowne puts it (4. 3. 329). Erotic blindness, in going 'beyond' the intellect, permits the Orphic initiate by 'closing the eyes of the soul, after this manner to become established in the unknown and occult unity of beings' (Proclus, trans. Taylor 1787, 1: 79). As Edgar Wind has pointed out (1967: 58), 'a mocking echo of the mystic phraseology' of this dogma is found in *MND*:

> Love looks not with the eyes, but with the mind;
> And therefore is wing'd Cupid painted blind. (1. 1. 234–5)

In brief, Berowne's thesis is that the scholars' surrender to Eros amounts to anything but a renunciation of their original 'occult' academic aims; on the contrary, it represents a far profounder commitment to the cultivation of power-enhancing philosophy, in the form of the mystery of Blind Love. What changes is the linguistic field of the labours: no longer Navarre's abstruse texts but the ardent poetry and *amour courtois* of the Platonic lover, with, as their prize, a god-like eloquential efficacy. So much for the theory. The problem is, of course, that the amorous blindness governing the lords and their language is anything but the insight-bestowing and super-intellectual force recommended by Ficino, just as in practice their version of Orphism is banal sentimental compliment. And the result is the inevitable and humiliating defeat of their effect-seeking, the 'loss' of their amorous labours which the play's title announces. As an ironical underlining of the debacle, the men are forced to recognize that any 'effects' being wrought are those produced by the unravished ladies themselves and their ready wit:

> *Ber.* Here stand I, lady, dart thy skill at me,
> Bruise me with scorn, confound me with a flout,
> Thrust thy sharp wit quite through my ignorance,
> Cut me to pieces with thy keen conceit. (5. 2. 396–9.)

But then Orpheus's own end was scarcely more enviable.

In *AWW* the topic of the wonderfully gifted speaker able, in Samuel Daniel's words, to 'moove, delight and sway the affections of men in what Scythian sorte soever [his speech] be disposed or uttered' (1603: 11–12) is closely related to the comedy's central thematic opposition between the old age and the new. Bertram's father, representative *par excellence* of the previous and glorious generation, is characterized in the King of France's reminiscence as, above all, a coercively imposing talker:

> Such a man
> Might be a copy to these younger times;
> Which, followed well, would demonstrate them now
> But goers backward. . . .
> Would I were with him! He would always say –
> Methinks I hear him now; his plausive words
> He scatter'd not in ears, but grafted them
> To grow there and to bear. (1. 2. 45–55)

The implication is that this 'grafting' power of persuasion has been lost along with the moral and cultural attributes of a past which, like all mythical golden ages, is recalled as an era of miraculous happenings. Lafew complains at the repudiation by the degenerate present of this old magic: 'They say miracles are past; and we have our philosophical persons to make modern and familiar things supernatural and causeless' (2. 3. 1ff.). It is, however, the very combination of magical powers with a startlingly 'plausive' eloquence that survives in Helena, embodiment of the older values. And that these two aspects of Helena's inheritance are intimately linked is suggested in her first encounter with the King; it is, indeed, her attempt to convince him that she is the authentic recipient of her father's magical knowledge ('On's bed of death / Many receipts he gave me') that first reveals her similarly quasi-supernatural verbal potency:

> King. Methinks in thee some blessed spirit doth speak
> His powerful sound within an organ weak;
> And what impossibility would slay
> In common sense, sense saves another way. (2. 1. 174–7)

Thereafter, the twin effects of Helena's magic – the medicinal and the rhetorical – unfold in parallel fashion. If her inherited healing powers are triumphantly affirmed in the King's immediate recovery, her old-world speaking powers are repeatedly confirmed by the auditors she compels to attend and respond:

> Count. Ah, what sharp stings are in her mildest words! (3. 4. 18)

> Laf.                    He lost a wife
> . . . whose words all ears took captive;
> Whose dear perfection hearts that scorn'd to serve
> Humbly call'd mistress. (5. 3. 15–19)

And while the comedy's magical *dea ex machina* dénouement is perceived immediately as a piece of visual conjuring ('*King*. Is there no exorcist / Beguiles the truer office of mine eyes?', 5. 3. 298–9), it is at the same time the victorious culmination of Helena's entire verbal campaign, the final effect of her persuasiveness:

> Hel. Will you be mine now you are doubly won?
> Ber. . . . I'll love her dearly, ever, ever dearly. (5. 3. 307–10)

In Shakespearean comedy, the miraculous word is wielded by Eurydice.

(v) 'THE WORDS OF MERCURY': HERMETIC MYSTERIES

The text of *LLL*, as is only too well-known, bears an enigmatic tag which in the 1598 Quarto appears to be a post-dramatic suffix, while in the 1623 Folio it is attributed to Armado as the play's closing statement: 'The words of Mercury are harsh after the songs of Apollo.' Whatever its textual status, the motto has attracted a deal of attention over the years. It is usual, and probably logical, to read it as a comment on what has gone before, perhaps a summary of the play's metalinguistic moral (see, for example, Evans 1975). It can hardly be said, however, that any very precise *object*-language or languages have been identified, giving more than a vague sense to the Apollonian 'songs' or the harsh Mercurial 'words' of the tag, whether the two terms be in opposition or in conjunction.

Now, 'the songs of Apollo' seems a perfectly appertinent title or congruent epitheton for that optimistic Orphism which, as we have seen, runs, albeit in parodic form, throughout the comedy as it ran throughout the Renaissance, since incantation accompanied by the Apollonian lyre was its purest and most literal expression. In this sense the second term in the motto might be understood as referring not to any actual songs in the comedy (there is only one, and that by way of a closing ceremony), but rather to all the would-be enchanting linguistic productions with which the play is replete.

As for the other presumably presiding linguistic deity and his harsh words, E. K. Chambers confidently denies his pertinence to the text proper: 'Mercury has nothing to do with what precedes' (1930, 1: 338). This judgment has been contested more recently by Anne Barton (1978) and J. M. Nosworthy (1979), both of whom, surely correctly, identify Mercury with the messenger Marcade, who reports the death of the King of France, thereby interrupting the reigning 'Apollonian' festivities. Nevertheless, it might be objected that this does not fully answer Chambers's dismissal of the god and his relevance to the work, since his 'what precedes' is presumably intended to refer to the play as a whole, and not merely to its ending. The issue, then, is whether it is possible to trace any more consistent or persistent aspects of the play and its language attributable to the patronage of Mercury, lending weight to Marcade's brief appearance and preciser significance to the metalanguage of the tag.

It is the comedy's 'academic' exordium – as with many of the semantic questions at issue – which provides the first hint of a definite Mercurial strain in the rhetorical proceedings. King Ferdinand, in inaugurating his Platonical garden, issues a hyperbolic pledge of ambiguous referentiality:

Navarre shall be the wonder of the world. (1. 1. 12)

The grammatical subject of the King's brag may be understood either topographically, i.e. referring to the court that is about to gain international fame, or personally, referring narcissistically to the speaker himself, by means of the self-nomination device found frequently in Shakespeare (and baptized by S. Viswanathan 'illeism with a difference', 1969). This second and apparently less plausible reading is reinforced by a passage from Henry Helmes's Gray's Inn masque *Gesta Grayorum* (1594) – probable source of the play's Muscovite episode (see Bullough 1957, 1: 431–2) – which Navarre's boast and its context echo quite distinctly. In the passage in question the protagonist Prince Henry of Purpoole is advised by a counsellor to set up 'a spacious, wonderful Garden' in which he can devote himself entirely to the study of philosophy: 'Then when your Excellency shall have added depth of knowledge to the fierceness of spirits, and greatness of your Power, then indeed you shall lay a *Trismegistus*; and then, when all other Miracles and Wonders shall cease, by reason that you shall have discovered their natural Causes, you shall be left the only Miracle and *Wonder of the World*' (1688 ed.: 35, my italics).

The parallels between the two situations of discourse are quite extensive and highly suggestive, despite the fact that in *LLL* it is the King himself who has to exhort his followers to subscribe to his project. The two academic programmes as such, comprising an austere devotion to 'living philosophy' in an enclosed garden context, are all but identical. And the end in view would also appear to be the same; Purpoole's counsellor advises the Prince to search out the hidden 'natural Causes' of things, while Navarre proposes a course of study into matters 'which else we should not know', the 'things hid and barr'd . . . from common sense' of Berowne's sarcastic gloss. In both cases what is promised to the academic devotees is not mere intellectual glory but prodigious powers, or indeed, in the case of *LLL*, outright apotheosis ('study's god-like recompense').

Where the two texts differ is in the explicitness with which the miracle-achieving 'philosophy' is described. Helmes's counsellor assures the Prince that he 'shall lay a *Trismegistus*', a patent indication that the deep-cause-unearthing texts to which he should dedicate himself are the books of the *Hermetica*, the mystical and magical doctrines attributed in the Renaissance to Hermes Trismegistus (the 'thrice greatest'), putative Egyptian divinity (cognate with Thoth) and *priscus theologus*. The specification is, in any case, almost superfluous, since the profound and miraculous philosophy of which the counsellor speaks was automatically identifiable by Helmes's academic audience with the notorious 'deep' cult of Hermetism. Helmes, indeed – and after him, Shakespeare – is clearly alluding to one of the most prestigious Platonizing texts of the period, Pico della Mirandola's oration 'Of the Dignity of Man', in which the figure of the miraculous *homo hermeticus* is invoked in the form of a quotation from the *Asclepius* (the most directly 'magical' of the Hermetic texts): 'A great Miracle, Asclepius, is Man' (1942 ed.: 347). In his oration, Pico recommends Hermetic magic as a means to the releasing of marvellous forces divinely concealed in the world, things hid and barred from common sense: '[*Mageia*], in calling forth into the light as if from their hiding-places the powers scattered and sown in the world by the loving kindness of God, does not so much work wonders as diligently serve a wonder-working nature' (353).

In short, there is good reason to suppose a direct line of descent from Pico's Great Miracle to Navarre's wonder of the world, via Helmes's Purpoole, and that what is strongly implied in the King's invitation to discover those arcana 'I am forbid to know' (Berowne) is an incitement to 'lay a *Trismegistus*'. And this is no more nor less than one would expect of even the most precarious and notional of *académies françaises*, in whose curricula the *Hermetica* were but daily staple (see Yates 1947). Neither does such a conclusion presuppose on Shakespeare's part any very profound learning in the occult arts. The figure and works of Hermes had long since passed, if in name only, into English literary culture, as a speech in Nashe's *Summer's Last Will and Testament* further testifies:

*Winter.* Till Hermes, secretary to the gods,
Or Hermes Trismegistus, as some will,
Weary with graving in blind characters,
And figures of familiar beasts and plants,
Invented letters to write withal.
In them he penn'd the fables of the gods,
The giants' war, and thousand tales besides. (1972 ed.: 185–6)

Nashe's description indicates that the step from the Egyptian Trismegistus to the Roman Mercury, by way of the Greek Hermes, is really no step at all: the three deities were regularly conjoined or simply confused in the Renaissance (Mercurius Trismegistus is the Latin form of the name used by Ficino and others). The composite figure produced by this conjunction is a copiously linguistic or semiotic divinity: messenger of the gods, patron of eloquence, of tidings, of commerce and of alchemical and magical signs, while, as Nashe's account illustrates, the main specific attribute that Trismegistus brings to the list, apart from his supposed authorship of the *Hermetica*, is a claim to the invention of writing itself. God of the literal sign, deity of texts and their interpretation (or hermeneutics, the science named after him): it is this graphic bias that made Hermes the ideal figurehead for the bookish academicism initiated by Ficino, his first translator, and aspired to by Navarre, who sees as its end an appropriately epigraphic form of immortality: 'Let fame . . . live register'd upon our brazen tombs.'

The conception of the linguistic sign espoused in the Hermetic books amply confirms that of the misread Plato, of the *Orphica* and of the *prisca theologia* in general: the *Pimander*, in particular, has as one of its metaphysical and theological underpinnings the notion of the Luminous Word and its universal powers. In this respect, Orphism and Hermetism, the songs of Apollo and the words of Mercury, are perfectly compatible in their mystical semantic premises, as indeed academic syncretism demanded. The difference, of course, is that while Orphism is essentially oral, bound to the efficacy of incantation, Hermetic magic is necessarily graphic, drawing on the privileged relationship between the inscribed sign and its supramundane referent. Here the 'national' character of the Egyptian Hermes does bear a precise significance. For the original script that he devised in which to pen the fables of the gods was not only generically hierographic but specifically hieroglyphic. And the hieroglyph was the paradigm for the semantic naturalists of a supra-conventional sign – halfway between the linguistic and the visual – able to capture in its ideographical iconicity the full force of its denotation (see Gombrich 1948).

The extraordinary burgeoning of pious hieroglyphology that went hand in hand with Hermetism in sixteenth-century Europe, especially the cult of Horapollo and of Valeriano's *Hieroglyphica*, bears witness to the sway that the nostalgia for a natural and uncorrupted linguistic *icon symbolica* held over the times (see Giehlow 1915; Boas 1950). Even the vulgarized version of the cult, the profusion of emblems, imprese and devices during the second half of the century, still bore the traces of the hieratic semantics from which it issued, as such works as Bruno's *Degli eroici furori* and Abraham Fraunce's tract *Insignium, armorum, emblematum, hieroglyphicorum . . . explicatio* (1588a) testify (on the mystical pretensions of emblems, see Boas 1950; Praz 1964).

An ardent conviction that pseudo-hieroglyphical *icones symbolicae* and emblems might encode the profoundest of Hermetic mysteries was commonplace (Gombrich 1948). Of all the possible objects of such encoding, nothing attracted greater admiration than the time-tested oxymoronic adage *festina lente* ('make haste slowly'), singled out on account of its ancientness – the Emperor Augustus adopted it as his motto – and because of its paradoxical form, in keeping with the mystagogic style. Even Erasmus, not given to pagan enthusiasms, found the maxim steeped 'in the mysteries of ancient philosophy' (quoted in Wind 1967: 107). The iconographic variations on the maxim, beyond the famous Aldine emblem of the dolphin and anchor, were virtually innumerable. A further index to the presence, however fragmentary and travestied, of the pagan mysteries in *LLL* is the maltreatment to which this most sacred of apophthegms is subjected in the play. It is, indeed, iconized in the encounters between the ingenious Moth and the slow Armado, the Butterfly and Crab of Augustus's device (Figure 3; see Deonna 1954) and varied in Moth's exchanges with the rustic Costard:

3    'Festina lente', emblem from Gabriele Symeone, *Le sententiose imprese.*

Butterfly and Crab-apple. Armado provides a patent signal to the allusion, as Edgar Wind has observed (1967: 108ff.) with his command to Moth to fetch Costard: 'bring him *festinately* hither' (3. 1. 4–5). This heralds an elaborate travesty of a somewhat more *recherché* impresa for the same paradoxical topic, Alfonso D'Este's soldierly device (Figure 4) described by Paolo Giovio (in Samuel Daniel's 1585 translation, Eii[r]:

> *Alphonso* Duke of *Ferara*, a Captaine of resolute Prowesse and admirable constancie, when he went to the Batell of *Rauenna*, did beare a Globe or round boule of mettle, full within of artificiall fire, which powred forth flames by certaine creueis, and it was so cunningly contriued, that at due time and place would issue forth, making great confusion of those, which were within the daunger thereof. The inuention wanted a Posie which was afterwardes added by the famous *Aristo* [*sic*], and it was *Loco & tempore.* (see Wind 1967: 108)

The conceit of slow and heavy metal becoming rapid and explosive 'at due time and place' provides Moth with a suitably mystifying device or trick of his own at his master's expense ('making great confusion'):

Arm.    The way is but short: away!
Moth.   As swift as lead, sir.
Arm.    The meaning, pretty ingenious?
        Is not lead a metal heavy, dull, and slow?
Moth.   *Minime*, honest master; or rather, master, no.

153

*Arm.*        I say lead is slow.

*Moth.*                        You are too swift, sir, to say so:

                Is that lead slow which is fir'd from a gun?

*Arm.*        Sweet smoke of rhetoric!

                He reputes me a cannon, and the bullet, that's he –

                I shoot thee at the swain.

*Moth.*                              Thump then, and I flee. (3. 1. 53–62)

4        'Loco et tempore', emblem from Paolo Giovio, *Dialogo dell'imprese militari et amorose* (also in Symeone, p. 68)

While Symeone's verse moral – 'Like a ball, in which fire is kept closed for a time / To deceive the incautious minds of others / So the man who attacks his enemy in the right time and place / Shows himself at that moment to be wise and prudent' (my translation) – might attract the vainglorious and armipotent Armado, it is in fact an accurate enough description of Moth's well-timed verbal explosions. The lepidopteral flutterings of Moth's swift invention are similarly held back by the crustacean denseness of the crabby Spaniard in an earlier debate on the same subject of festination:

*Arm.*        And therefore apt, because quick.

*Moth.*       Speak you this in my praise, master?

*Arm.*        In thy condign praise.

*Moth.*       I will praise an eel with the same praise.

*Arm.*        What! that an eel is ingenious?

*Moth.*       That an eel is quick. (1. 2. 23–8)

The joke here – apart from the obvious bawdy connotations of Moth's image – appears to lie in a further burlesque allusion to the slow-haste iconography, that is to the emblem devised by Erasmus himself for the 'mystery', showing an eel or echeneis entwined about an arrow (the device was borrowed by Alciati (Figure 5), whose emblem was in turn Englished by Whitney, 1586: 188). In the device, of course, the eel (one of Horapollo's hieroglyphic beasts (Horapollo, II: 103; Boas 1950: 108), or remora, represents *lentitudo*, restraining the swiftness of the arrow (see Whitney's moral: 'Aboute the arrowe swifte ECHENEIS slowe doth foulde: / which, biddes us in our actions haste, no more then reason woulde'; the motto is 'Maturandum'). Moth's reversal of the Erasmian symbolism is clearly intended as an oblique dig at his master's intellectual retardation.

5      'Maturandum', emblem from Andrea Alciati,
*Emblemata*.

The association of the oxymoronic and the enigmatic with the Hermetic is not accidental. One of the chief corollaries of Hermetism on the Ficinian–Piconian model is a poetics of obscure stylistic encoding corresponding to the occultation of the mysteries themselves in the sacred texts: the slogan coined by Pico in the oration is *editos ... et non editos*, published and not published, indicating the simultaneous disclosure of the verities to the initiated and concealment from the profane. A notorious apology for such a mystifying stylistics is found in the preface to George Chapman's genuinely obscure Hermetic poem *Ovids Banquet of Sence*: 'with that darknes [obscuritie] wil I still labour to be shaddowed: rich minerals are digd out of the bowels of the earth, not found in the superficies and dust of it' (1595: A2ʳ). The rhetorical means to the achievement of this strategic darkness was precisely the cultivation of the enigma and the paradox, bringing together unresolvable contrarieties in antithetical form. One of the great models here was the *serio ludere* of Nicolaus Cusanus (after Socrates): those quasi-magical 'serious games' which 'consisted in finding within common experience an unusual object endowed with the kind of contradictory attributes which are difficult to imagine united in the deity' (Wind 1967: 222; see pp. 138–9 above).

The pursuit of obscurity, of the enigma and of the paradox is conducted by most of Navarre's courtiers and hangers-on. Admiration for the *non editus,* expressed everywhere by the pedants (by Holofernes, for example, in his mockery of the profane Dull, 4. 2. 13ff.), has its most emblematic and ridiculous issue in the clash between the mystifying Armado and the uninitiated Costard, in which it is the concept of the enigma itself that proves too unpublished for the rustic:

Moth. A wonder, master! here's a costard broken in a shin.
Arm. Some enigma, some riddle: come, thy l'envoy; begin.
Cost. No egma, no riddle, no l'envoy; no salve in the mail, sir. O, sir, plantain, a plain plantain! (3. 1. 67–70)

And yet even the dull Dull manages a somewhat half-hearted essay in the enigmatic mode:

Dull. You two are book-men: can you tell me by your wit
What was a month old at Cain's birth, that's not five weeks old as yet? (4. 2. 33–4)

Naturally, the most serious exercises in *serio ludere* are reserved for the academicians proper, notably in the 'overspying' episode (4.3), the play's central 'doctrinal' moment. In the first part of the scene, Berowne hides in a tree to spy on his erring fellows, a situation which provokes from him an auto-ironical comment on his achievement of the promised apotheosis:

Ber. All hid, all hid; an old infant play
Like a demi-god here sit I in the sky. (4. 3. 75–6)

Berowne's position parodies, as his own observation underlines, the doctrine of the Concealed God, central to Cusanus's theory and practice of *serio ludere*, whose purpose, indeed, was to reflect the theological paradox of the deity's simultaneous presence and absence (Cusanus's thought, it might be noted, had been introduced into England by the arch Hermetist Giordano Bruno). Once revealed to his shame-faced companions, Berowne maintains his moral superiority in mocking the King's infantile behaviour:

To see a King transformed to a gnat;
To see great Hercules whipping a gig. (163–4)

Berowne's antithetical image is in perfect accord with the 'serious games' framework, since the whipping of a top is one of Cusanus's main paradigms in *De possest* of the *vis mystical ludi*, the power of childish play (the top with its rotation and apparent stasis) to mirror the deepest of mystical contradictions.

The episode develops, after Berowne's abrupt fall from the godhead, into a display on his part of his adeptness in the paradox game, in attempting to express the divinity of his mistress through the yoking of outrageously contradictory propositions, as Navarre is quick to note:

*Ber.*     Is ebony like her? O wood divine! . . .
          No face is fair that is not full so black.
*King.*    O paradox! Black is the badge of hell,
          The hue of dungeons and the school of night. (243ff.)

It is in this context, then, that we find the probable allusion to the Raleigh–Chapman Platonic–Hermetic circle, the School of Night, that once troubled and intrigued commentators with its tantalizing hint of some doctrinal intent on Shakespeare's part (see Yates 1936).

In any event, the serious games lead triumphantly to Berowne's long oration in favour of female beauty as the true mystery, the authentic object of 'academic' devotion, proposing as his symbol of female divinity the eyes (the conceit is found in Bruno's *Degli eroici furori*, while Bruno in turn probably borrowed it from Cusanus or from Horapollo's *Hieroglyphica*, in both of which exemplary sources the eyes similarly symbolize the divine; see Figure 6):

Quo modo Deum.

6     Divine eye, from Horapollo, *Hieroglyphica*.

*Ber.*    From women's eyes this doctrine I derive:
          They are the ground, the books, the academes,
          From whence doth spring the true Promethean fire ...
          For where is any author in the world
          Teaches such beauty as a woman's eye?
          Learning is but an adjunct to ourself
          And where we are learning likewise is:
          Then when ourselves we see in ladies' eyes,
          Do we not likewise see our learning there? (4. 3. 299ff.)

Berowne's final paradox is that he draws upon the 'adjuncts' of bookish philosophy in order to argue against it ('How well he's read, to reason against reading!' as Navarre puts it in the opening scene, 1. 1. 94). His plea in favour of Eros is explicitly pitched against Navarre's aspiration to Wonderhood through the secrets revealed in 'forbidden' texts (i.e. the 'leaden contemplation' and 'slow arts' he scorns, 317, 320). But it is the repudiation itself, with its allusions to the Bacchic Erotic and Orphic mysteries and, not least, to the 'Egyptian' riddling mode beloved to the Platonists ('Subtle as Sphinx', 338), that constitutes the culmination of the quasi-mystagogic vein in the comedy's language.

In the event, the frustration of the ex-academicians' erotic strategy is signalled by the sudden appearance of Hermes–Mercury himself, the thrice greatest (or 'thrice-worthy gentleman' as Moth wittily baptizes the three-role-playing Holofernes of the pageant, 5. 1. 34), bringing news from the gods. The message he brings is of death, the final mystery, reminding us, as Nosworthy notes (1979: 109), that he is also the Psychopomp, leader of souls. Marcade's entry – cutting short the series of stage emblems that Jonson would have termed 'court hieroglyphs' (for example, the young Hercules with snakes in either hand, 5. 2. 583ff.; see Freeman 1948: 94) – is made all the more dramatic by the briefness of his message, curtailed even further by the Princess's anticipation:

*Mar.*    The King your father –
*Prin.*   Dead, for my life!
*Mar.*    Even so: my tale is told. (5. 2. 712ff.)

There is clearly nothing *non editus* in the Mercurial style here, but Marcade's extreme laconicism is altogether appropriate to the doctrinal and iconographic tradition which represented Mercurius Trismegistus as eloquent but silent (in Achille Bocchi's *Symbolicae quaestiones* (1555, emblem lxiv) he is shown putting a forefinger to his lips (Figure 7)). Silence represents the furthest expression of the enigmatic. 'Apollo inspires by his music', as Edgar Wind remarks, 'poetic frenzy as well as poetic measure; Hermes, the god of eloquence, advises silence' (1967: 196). And silence, the restraining of their eloquence, is precisely what

7       Hermes Trismegistus, from Achille Bocchi,
*Symbolicae quaestiones.*

the ladies advise the scholars to maintain for one year in order to demonstrate (*festina lente*) their maturity (5. 2. 78off.).

If the tone of events after Marcade's mission grows, under the sign of Mercury, dark and austere (Berowne: 'The scene begins to cloud', 714), to the cost of the Apollonian gaiety the scholars have endeavoured to establish, it is surely another of the multiple ironies of the finale that the negative force which defeats them is the force that was to guarantee their glorification. In the end, the serious games become more serious than they had intended.

### (VI) 'M.O.A.I.': ON MALVOLIO'S TETRAGRAMMATON (WITH A GLANCE AT MISTRESS QUICKLY'S GARTER)

Where the change of tone that marks the ending of *LLL* is dramatically unexpected, the transformation of style and atmosphere in the final scene of *MWW* is perfectly vertiginous. Five acts of the unremittingly mundane are resolved in a masque-like fairy spectacle of ritual cleansing, led by a poetically pastoralizing Mistress Quickly as the unlikeliest of Fairy Queens. The fairies' task is to remind Falstaff of the moral responsibilities of the knighthood, a message which they emblematize or emblazon in a garland figuring the Garter and its ancient motto:

> *Quick.*  Each fair instalment, coat, and sev'ral crest,
> With loyal blazon, evermore be blest;
> And nightly, meadow-fairies, look you sing,
> Like to the Garter's compass, in a ring:
> Th' expressure that it bears, green let it be,
> More fertile-fresh than all the field to see;
> And *Honi soit qui mal y pense* write
> In em'rald tufts, flowers purple, blue and white,
> Like sapphire, pearl, and rich embroidery
> Buckled below fair knighthood's bending knee:
> Fairies use flowers for their charactery. (5. 5. 64–74)

In spite of the normally gross worldliness of the Mistress of ceremonies, the fairies' natural-supernatural floral 'charactery' – an authentic theatrical court hieroglyph serving as the 'expressure' of a serious ethical precept – is the gravest and least ironical manifestation in the canon of that 'mystical' graphism hinted at throughout *LLL* and occasionally in other comedies: in Julia's hypostasizing of the 'wounded' written name in *TG*; in Orlando's passionate tree-inscribing in *AYLI*; and, an episode that could scarcely be further removed in manner and function from the finale of *MWW*, the epistolary practical joke played against Malvolio in *TN*.

Malvolio, in what is in effect the central event of the comic subplot and the most memorable scene of the play, discovers a riddle-ridden billet-doux written and planted by the servant Maria. And in deciphering the letters of the letter he searches first for clues as to the sender's identity (falling inevitably into the well-laid trap of the unwitting obscenity) – 'By my life, this is my lady's hand: these be her very C's, her U's, and her T's, and thus she makes her great P's' (2. 5. 87–90) – and then for some indication of the fortunate addressee of his lady's declarations of love:

> 'M.O.A.I. doth sway my life.' – Nay, but first let me see, let me see ... what should that alphabetical position portend? If I could make that resemble something in me! Softly! 'M.O.A.I.' – ... 'M' – Malvolio! Why, that begins my name! ... 'M' – But then there is no consonancy in the sequel; that suffers under probation: 'A' should follow, but 'O' does. ... And then 'I' comes behind. ... 'M.O.A.I.' This simulation is not as the former: and yet, to crush this a little, it would bow to me, for every one of those letters are in my name. (2. 5. 112ff.)

Malvolio's decoding of the puzzle is carried out strictly according to the practical jokers' plan, and as such simply demonstrates, as it is designed to, his monstrous narcissism. But the episode takes on a potential semantic thickness if seen in the light of certain contemporary theories and practices connected with the graphic sign, and in particular regarding the transcendent character of the character.

Graphomania, a sanguine faith in the calligraphic or, better still, typographic sign and its time-defeating fixity, was one of the acuter forms of semiotic credulity manifested in esoteric circles: 'According to the principles of the most secret philosophy', runs Pico's twenty-fourth Magical Conclusion, 'it has to be acknowledged that characters and figures have more power in magical operations than any other material qualities' (1486a: 147, my translation). Agrippa is equally emphatic:

> *Of the Virtue of Writing* . . . The use of words and speech is to express the inwards of the mind, and from thence to draw forth the secrets of the thoughts, and to declare the will of the speaker. Now, writing is the last expression of the mind, and is the number of speech and voice, as, also, the collection, state, end, continuing, and interaction, making a habit, which is not perfected with the act of one's voice. And whatsoever is in the mind, in voice, in operation, and in speech, the whole and all of this is in writing. (1533: 215)

Such literal-mindedness, while generalized (Agrippa, for example, insists upon the superior powers of writing *per se*), was not indiscriminate: it took as its privileged objects the Egyptian hieroglyph, naturally, and above all the characters of the *lingua sacratissima*, Hebrew. The doctrinal basis for the promotion of Hebrew above other languages in terms of its antiqueness and expressive purity was in the first instance, of course, the biblical account of Adam's original naming. But the more enthusiastic forms of Renaissance Hebraicism emphasized not so much the nominative intervention of Adam as the unmediated divine origins of the Hebrew alphabet, whose very formal and diacritical properties represent the forms of the created universe:

> But before all notes of languages, the writing of the Hebrews is, of all, the most sacred in the figures of the characters, points of vowels, and tops of accents; or consisting in matter, form and spirit. The position of the stars being first made in the seat of God, which is Heaven, after the figure of them (as the masters of the Hebrews testify) are most fully formed the letters of the Celestial Mysteries, as by their figure, form and signification, so by the numbers signified by them, and also by the various harmonies of their conjunction. (Agrippa 1533: 216)

Nor were such wild re-elaborations of Genesis restricted to occult dogmatists. A particularly rich and 'scientific' expression of the same alphabetical fancy is found in Alexander Top's grammatological tract

*The Oliue Leafe* (1603), in which 'all Abces' are made to derive from the 'hieroglyphs of our first fathers' (note the 'Egyptian' contamination), the Hebrew symbols, the number and form of which correspond to the first created phenomena, 'Seeing that all thinges which the Lord wrought or commaunded in the first weeke, exceeded not the number of two and twentie. And . . . every one of these severall *Hebrew* letters, should signifie or importe some speciall workmanshyp of the Lordes Creation' (Sig. B2). In what amounts to an extraordinarily suggestive myth of the origin and infinity of semiosis, Top describes how God 'signed off' each of his works by inscribing upon it the Hebrew sign which in turn signifies 'sign':

> The Lord concluded every one of his actions or creatures, with this proper demonstration, *Eth*, which is taken for a Signe, Figure, Letter, Forme, or Marke; . . . God created the figure, signe or letter, of the Heavens &c. Or the very hieroglyphs of them, this worde beeing the singular of *Othoth*, which signifies Figures, Letters, Causes, Signes, or Tokens, of all sortes. (Sig. A4)

The sacred letter becomes the model and condition of all signification in the world.

The real appeal of this abecedarian piety to the syncretizing Platonists of the age was neither scientific nor theological, however. What fired their imaginations was rather the possibility of translating mystical Hebraic alphabetism into efficacious magical operations: 'No names inasmuch as they are meaningful, and insofar as they are names, can, taken singly by themselves, have power in magical operations, unless they be Hebrew names, or names originally derived therefrom' (Pico 1486a: 147). The form of magic Pico is referring to, of course, is Cabalistic, the vulgarized 'practical' version of the mystical tradition inherited from medieval Spanish Jews (and perhaps hinted at, in still more vulgar form, in the reference in *MWW* to the Witch of Brainford's working 'by charms, by spells, by th'*figure*', 4. 2. 162–3).

In practice, Cabalistic magic amounted to little more than the abusing of certain Rabbinical exegetical tools designed to decipher the texts of the Old Testament and the Torah: operations such as *gematria* (interchanging words), *notarikon* (acrostic reading) and, most appealing of all, *themurah* (anagrammatical transposition). In their 'marginal' application, such textual manipulations became means to invoke supernatural forces, and the greatest faith was invested in them, as the German magus Johannes Reuchlin testifies: 'By means of the mixing by the revolving alphabet, so much is hidden from uncultivated persons, and revealed through Jeremiah to the holy leaders of the contemplative life . . . From [the Jews] this alphabetical Cabala, i.e. "Reception", through which the greatest secrets of the divines are made known, passed down to posterity' (1494: 3150, my translation).

Behind the anagrams, acrostics and *ars combinatoria* lay the hope of divining sacred names occulted in the holy texts and thereby of releasing the powers connected, for example, with the named angels ruling over celestial bodies. From the medieval Cabalists the magi inherited seventy-two names for such angels, together with ten names for the Sephiroth or emanations of divine power, names for the Son and, holier still, the miraculous and ineffable *tetragrammaton* (*YHWH*), the name of God Himself. To this *verbum mirificum* was delegated the omnipotence of its divine bearer, diffused into its four characters: 'Thus God is alive, and the *name* of the living God is alive also, and the letters of the living Name are alive also: God is alive on His own account, the name is alive on His account, the Letters are alive on account of the Name' (Oswald Croll 1608: 87, my translation). It might be noted, as a passing curiosity, that *Finnegans Wake*, a work rich in occulted references to the occult – to the 'heroicized furibouts of the Nolanus theory' (163: Bruno the Nolan's *Eroici Furori*), to the Emerald Tables of Hermes Trismegistus (misquoted in 'as broad above as he is below', 444), to the 'juggle-monkysh agripment' of the Cabalist Agrippa, etc. – associates the name of God and the emanations of the Sephiroth with Shakespearean comedy, and specifically with *LLL* ('mild's vapour moist'), perhaps with an eye to Berowne's great 'Hermetic' speech: 'the heavenly one with his constellatria and his emanations stood between, and she tried all she tried to make the Mookse look up at her (but *he* was fore too adiaptotously farseeing) and to make the Gripes hear how coy she could be (though he was too schysmatically auricular about his *ens* to heed her) but it was all mild's vapour moist' (157; see McHugh's *Annotations*, 1980). There may be, as we will see, a more direct, if parodic, link between the comedies and Cabalistic operations.

In England, where the earliest news of Cabalism is probably Thomas More's reference to Pico's immersion in 'the secret misteries of the hebrieus' (Preface to Pico's Letters; Pico 1510: Aiii$^r$), the 'practical' Cabala gained relatively little open following, although Henry Howard commends it in his *Defensative* (see Blau 1944: 63) and Everard Digby and John Dee appear to have subscribed to it (see Secret 1969: 229–30). Yet the notoriety of the sacred-name-divining transpositions of Hebrew letters was considerable in the latter part of the sixteenth century. Reginald Scot's *Discoverie of Witchcraft* (1584, probable partial source for *MND*), for instance, in deploring 'the prophanation of God's name', forbidden in the Commandments, takes as a peculiarly diabolical example thereof 'the Cabalists [who] tooke upon them, by the ten names of God, and his angels, expressed in the Scriptures, to worke woonders' (40). A more detailed and less polemical account is given by William Camden, who in his *Remaines* traces the history of the Cabala from the 'litterall law' received by Moses and describes Cabalistic *modi operandi* employing 'the sacred names of God . . . consisting of Alphabetary revolution, which they will have to be Anagrammatisme, by which they say *Marie* resolved made, *Our holie Mistris*' (1605: 169).

Camden's Anagrammatism leads us back to Malvolio and his letter. The anagrammatical procedure he hits upon in his decoding – 'to crush this a little' – is, as Maria's antic demands, an absurd form of name-divination ('To whom should this be?'). And there is a hint in the 'fustian riddle', as Fabian terms it – 'M.O.A.I. doth sway my life' – that the name to be divined is indeed divine, or at least of supraterrestrial influence: the verb 'sway' has precise astrological connotations, used 'technically' to refer to the celestial bodies and their ascendancy over the earth.

Malvolio's transfiguration or 'crushing' of the 'alphabetical position' thus becomes a grotesque species of *themurah*, conducted, what is more, on an albeit debased tetragrammaton, complete with occult reference. The fact that the exegesis is successfully bent on identifying the hidden referent of the four-character 'simulation' with the would-be all-swaying exegete himself emphatically confirms the premise of Maria's ploy, namely Malvolio's prodigious *amour propre*: 'the best persuaded of himself, so crammed (as he thinks) with excellencies, that it is his grounds of faith that all that look on him love him: and on that vice in him will my revenge find notable cause to work' (2. 3. 149–53).

## (VII) SYNCRETIC MAGIC, OR THE IDEA OF THE THEATRE

In a late sixteenth-century tract by Giulio Camillo, the various ingredients of that extraordinary doctrinal stew that went under the name of Neo-Platonic syncretism – a dash of Orpheus, a splash of Hermes, a sprinkling of the Cabala, mixed in with the meatier dogmata of a Christianized Plato, of Plotinus and the rest – are brought together once more in roughly the usual quantities. What the *pasticcio* produces, however, is not the familiar philosophical hash but an idea for or rather the idea of a theatre. The intuition underlying Camillo's *L'idea del teatro* (1550) is that the theatre, as playhouse and as stage display, represents a potentially ideal artistic expression of the mystical Platonic semantics and semiotics to which he subscribes, bringing together as it does iconic and linguistic signs in an unrivalled complementarity. Invoking the precepts of the 'secretissimi theologi', the Cabalists, regarding the supercelestial spheres whose forces his magical theatre aspires to embody, Camillo fills the hypothetical playhouse with statues and icons of Apollo, Hermes Trismegistus, Orpheus, Hercules and other divine patrons. He compares to the power of such images that of well-proportioned poetic expression, which has a similarly important place in his imaginary creation:

> I have read, I believe in Hermes Trismegistus, that in Egypt there were once certain sculptors of statues, so excellent that when they had brought some statues to perfect proportion these were found to be animated by angelic spirits, because such perfection could not exist without a soul. Similar to such statues I find words, for the power of composition, the aim of which is to maintain in proportions pleasing to the ear all the words that can dress human thought, proposing, postponing, interpreting. Such words, as soon as they are placed in proportion, become when uttered animated with harmony. (33–4, my translation)

For all its esoteric trappings, Camillo's idea of a magically 'animated' theatrical art founded on the harmonious marriage of the visual and the verbal is no more than the motivating principle of every endeavour in the dramatic theatre. The fullest expression of the idea is found in *The Tempest* with its central metatheatrical trope of the magus as *metteur-en-scène* (and vice versa).

In this perspective, a certain semiotic animism, or faith in the sign and its capacity to be animated by its referent, may be equivalent to an optimism regarding the expressive plentitude of the dramatic representation itself. The supernatural wood and its natural names in *MND*; the magically iconic finales of *AYLI*, *AWW* and *MWW*; the anagrammatic name-divination of *TN*; the unwitting enchantments of *CE* ('How can she thus call us by our names? / Unless it be by inspiration'; 'I'll stop mine ears against the mermaid's song', etc.); the Orphic and Hermetic traces in *LLL*: ironical or in earnest, these versions of the transcendent sign in the comedies are also vivid metaphors for a dramaturgical commitment (itself at once earnest and ironically self-deflating) to the transformational powers of theatre itself, namely its ability to persuade the spectator that the set of bodies and other worldly signs presented to him do indeed embody, for the duration of the spectacle, the properties of another sphere.

It is scarcely surprising that, among these images of transcendence, it is the notion of *vis verborum*, of a triumphantly animate language, that emerges most frequently. For a dramaturgy dedicated principally to the word, the appeal of such a prospect is evident, as, indeed, is the significance of the graphic or textual bias of much of the semantic credulity in the plays. Navarre's belief in a world-conquering textuality is the hope that the dramatist, at his most optimistic, invests in his art. Even though it is more often than not accompanied by failure and humiliation in the comedies, faith in the word is implicit in their creation.

## (VIII) FOUL WORDS, FOUL WIND

Comedy cannot, however, live by faith alone. It depends also and above all on a set of dramaturgic and rhetorical *conventions* (*fabula* and character types, plot complications, codified modes of exposition, etc.) which, however much they may have become 'naturalized' over the ages, remain cognizable or recognizable as such. And these generic norms are in turn part of the global conventionality of dramatic theatre as a rule-bound cultural institution. A sober and agnostic Idea of the Theatre accepts that all of its constituent signs are necessarily subject to the mediation of this-worldly convention. In dialectical opposition to all the manifold forms of cultivation, reification, deification or simple adoration of the word, there emerges in a number of comedies a pronounced vein of linguistic scepticism which has its own authoritative doctrinal backing in the contemporary debate on the sign. A brief overview of this alternative theoretical tradition will help to define better the precise force of those moments of metalinguistic doubt, disgust or happy disrespect in the plays.

Semiotic, and especially linguistic, conventionalism found patronage in the sixteenth century in a number of intellectual movements opposed for academic, ideological or gnoseological motives to the sanctification of the sign: Aristotelian scholasticism (or what was left of it); Protestant iconoclasm; the Catholic campaign against the occult arts; philosophical scepticism; and, at the end of the period, Baconian empiricism. For all these quite distinct schools of thought or polemic the classic source and weightiest authority for the conventionalist theory of language is Aristotle's '*ad placitum*' definition of meaning in the *De interpretatione*, usually and misleadingly read as a 'reply' to the *Cratylus*: 'By a noun [or name] we mean a sound significant by convention, which has no reference to time, and of which no part is significant apart from the rest . . . The limitation "by convention" was introduced because nothing is by nature noun or name – it is only so when it becomes a symbol' (1941 ed.: 40). Aristotle's discussion of the name furnishes the basis for an authentically analytical semantics, however limited in scope: beyond the affirming of the 'convention' principle, he insists on the mediating presence between name and object of a conceptual third term ('spoken words are the symbols of mental experience') and further distinguishes meaning from truth, word meaning from propositional content, etc. Here, unmistakably, the question of signification is separated from the problem of reference, a divorce which is unthinkable in naturalistic notions of the name. Language may be studied, empirically and independently of what it represents, as an autonomous system of rules.

Non-mystical doctrines of the sign in the latter part of the sixteenth century gained another prestigious point of reference, Sextus Empiricus's *Pyrrhoniarum hypotypwsewm libri tres*, translated into Latin in 1562 and which, in addition to subscribing resolutely to the conventionalist view of signification – 'the significance of names is based on conventions and not on nature (for otherwise all men, barbarians as well as Greeks, would understand all the things signified by the terms, besides the fact that it is in our power at any time to point out and signify the objects by any other names we may choose)' (II: xviii) – provides precious information regarding Stoic theory. The Stoics' semiotic model – applied, that is, to the sign in general – adds to the triangular Aristotelian scheme (in their terms comprising the *semàinon*, or sign vehicle, *semainòmenon*, or signified concept, and *pragma*, the object) a fourth element, the *lekton*, or, roughly, sense as distinct from mental concept. This move further affirms the autonomy of symbolic systems, especially language, from the represented extra-semiotic universe, since the *lekton* resides in the relations among the sign vehicles themselves (Sextus Empiricus: *ibid.*). The conjunction of so sophisticated an attitude towards signification with Sextus's sceptical Pyrrhonian metaphysics was of considerable importance to the development of linguistic scepticism in the later Renaissance.

Of the more recent philosophical schools espousing a rigorously analytical semantics, nominalism – against which, indeed, the Neo-Platonists were in part reacting – survived in a somewhat etiolated form in the sixteenth-century universities (see Ashworth 1974: 4ff.). The medieval nominalists, notably Abelard, Petrus Hispanus and, in the fourteenth century, William of Ockham, elaborated a complex and wide-based framework for the classification of *modi signandi*, employing a notable range of operative distinctions (those, for example, between absolute and connotative terms, univocal and equivocal terms, conventional and indexical signs, signs of the first and second intention, etc.). In an extreme form, as represented for instance by Roscelin, the nominalistic theory of universal terms wished to reduce them to empty signs, or mere *vox* or *flatus vocis*, or so much idle breath. This gesture, inevitably, entered into circulation more readily than the intricate conceptual machinery of Ockham.

167

One of the direct heirs to this medieval philosophical tradition was Martin Luther, who had been taught by nominalist logicians at Erfurt. Something of the *via moderna* of nominalistic analysis is discernible in Luther's formidable demystification of sacramental symbols in his *De captivitate babylonica ecclesiae* (1520). Luther's theological standard is the this-worldly allegiance of signs supposedly invested with incarnational powers when employed in liturgical rites: 'in every sacrament the sign as such is incomparably less than the thing signified ... along with the divine promises signs have also been given to picture that which the words signify, or as they now say, that which the sacrament "effectively signifies". We shall see how much truth there is in this' (trans. Steinhauser 1959: 23, 64).

Luther's iconoclasm served as a model for all later Protestant diatribes against idolatrous sign-worship in Catholic and other superstitious rituals. Elizabethan England provided a fair number, among them Reginald Scot's deriding of the 'thousand consecrated or rather execrated things' of the Mass, together with the sundry 'charmes, voices, images, charactres, stones, plants, metals, herbes' etc. ('There is', he complains, 'great varietie hereof') (1584: 175). Scot's prime paradigm of the idolatrized sign is the word, whose sphere of operation, he insists, is limited to human intercourse and whose substantive presence is purely phonetic: 'New qualities may be added by humane art, but no new substance can be made or created by man. ... For by the sound of words nothing cometh, nothing goeth, otherwise than God in nature hath ordained to be doone by ordinarie speech, or else by his speciall ordinance' (*ibid.*). Scot's target here, namely the idea that any verbal formula, sacramental or esoteric, may exercise plastic power or executive influence over the physical world, is shared by the Puritan William Perkins, who, in a similarly generalized onslaught against the image ('A thing fained in the mind by imagination is an idol'), elaborates a more articulate lexiclasm. Perkins assails the lexical idol on two fronts, that of its merely vocal constitution (all speech is reduced to *flatus vocis*): 'All words made and uttered by men, are in their owne nature but sounds framed by the tongue, of the breath that commeth from the lungs. And that which is only a bare sound, in all reason can have no virtue in it to cause a reall worke, muche less to produce a wonder' (1600, III: 631); and that of the 'at pleasure' human origins of meaning:

> That which is in nature nothing but a bare signification, cannot serve to worke a wonder, and this is in the nature of all words; for as they be framed of mans breath they are naturall, but yet in regard of frame and articulation they are artificiall and significant, and the

> use of them in every language is, to signifie that which the author
> there of intended; for the first signification of words, depended upon
> the will and pleasure of man that framed and invented them. (*ibid.*)

Ironically, much the same arguments are rehearsed by Catholic
writers in the Church's campaign against occult practices. Indeed the
vociferousness of the polemic (which contributed, among other
achievements, to the condemnation and execution of Giordano Bruno
in 1603) reflects in part the force of the Protestant accusation of idolatry.
Among the early anti-magical polemicists was Pico's nephew Gian-
franco, but the most sustained and lucidly argued case is offered by the
Jesuit Martin Del Rio in his *Disquisitiorum magicorum libri sex*. Del
Rio systematically dismantles the Neo-Platonists' Hebraicism and
Hermetism, opposing to the principle of the propriety of names that of
the arbitrary status of the sign:

> But indeed, the names that signify the nature of things (the names of
> the creatures that Adam, as it is believed, imposed) cannot have
> received any influx from nature: because corporeal things cannot
> by nature bring about any effect in that which is without body, as
> names are . . . Therefore, the first influx of celestial energy assigned
> nothing to them. What influence imposed and merely arbitrary
> denomination might have, not even Argus, who is reputed to be
> many-eyed, could see. (1633: 52, my translation)

Idolatry of linguistic forms is likewise the original sin that the science
of signs proposed by Francis Bacon in *The Aduancement of Learning*
('This portion of knowledge, touching the *Notes of thinges*, and
Cogitations in generall [that] I finde not enquired, but deficient') has to
purge, since it constitutes the single most intractable impediment to
any serious empirical enquiry into symbolic systems of representation:
'Here, therefore, is the first distemper of learning, when men study
words and not matter; . . . for words are but the images of matter; and
except they have life of reason and invention, to fall in love with them is
all one as to fall in love with a picture' (1605: 24–5). The inaugurating
gesture of Bacon's scientific enterprise, logically, is the classification of
the varieties of such Pygmalion-like errors, whereby certain empty
lexical units are automatically taken to denote actual slices of the
extra-linguistic domain: in particular, the 'idols of the tribe' or abstract
universals, and the 'idols of the market place', popularly current terms
(like 'primum mobile') signifying false concepts that, once lexically
labelled, prove all but impossible to eradicate: 'words are but the current
tokens or marks of popular notions of things; which notions, if they be
grossly and variably collected out of particulars, it is not the laborious
examination either of consequence of arguments, or the truth of

propositions, that can ever correct that error, being, as the physicians speak, in the first digestion' (1605: 126).

Bacon's preoccupation, then, is less with any credulous pretension to bestow executive capacity upon verbal forms than with the very real power of linguistic representation to establish its own order of things and then seduce the soberest enquirer into accepting this universe of discourse as the actual economy of perceptible *prima materia*: 'and though we think we govern our words and prescribe it well *loquendum ut vulgus sentiendum ut sapientes*, yet certain it is that words, as a tartar's bow, do shoot back upon the understanding of the wisest and mightily entangle and pervert the judgment' (1605: 134). Bacon's unequivocal subscribing to the Aristotelian doctrine of the sign – with a degree of polite scorn for pseudo-philological searchers after the phonetic rightness of names – is thus instrumental to his critique of language as a cognitive tool, a critique which leads him to propose the invention of other symbols 'competent to expresse cogitations', i.e. something akin to the notation of modern symbolic logic: '*Ad placitum* are the characters real before mentioned [ciphers, etc.] and words: although some have been willing by various enquiry, or rather by apt feigning to have derived imposition of names from reason and intendment; a speculation elegant, and, by reason it searcheth into antiquity, reverent; but sparingly mixed with truth and of small fruit' (137–8).

Although it has quite a different end in view, the Baconian critique of the sign shares certain positions with the two main currents of philosophical scepticism in the period. The major achievement of the 'academic' sceptical mode (i.e. modelled on Cicero's *Academica*), Francesco Sanchez's impressively austere *Quod nihil scitur* (1581), takes Socrates's anti-epistemological maxim, 'Nec unum hoc scio, me nihil scire', as the starting-point for an uncompromising deconstruction of man's gnoseological pretensions, by means of a radical questioning of the linguistic bases of knowledge. All sciences are founded on definitions, which, instead of pointing outwards to the supposedly represented *res*, lead merely to other definitions, and so on in an infinite interpretative *regressus* that produces nothing but a closed infra-referential circuit:

> I do not know even this, that I know nothing: yet I deduce, neither me, nor others. Let the proposition be a standard to me, then the sequel follows, that nothing is known. Sharpen your wits. I will proceed. From the name let us come to the thing. For to me every definition is nominal, and virtually every question. . . . And if we do not know, by what means can we demonstrate? By none at all. You

nonetheless claim the definition to be what the nature of the thing demonstrates. Give me one demonstration. You do not have one. Thus I conclude. (1581: 14, my translation).

'There's more adoe', as Sanchez's cousin Montaigne puts the matter in John Florio's translation (1603), 'to interpret interpretations than to interpret things. . . . We doe but inter-glos ourselves' (636). Montaigne's 'Pyrrhonian' mode of scepticism – closer to Sextus Empiricus in its anecdotal and aphoristic manner of argument – embraces a thorough mistrust of language, not as a form of epistemological nihilism but, as likewise with Sanchez, by way of a fideistic plea for the leap of faith which alone, unlike our vain pursuit of nomination, brings us to true knowledge:

> There is both the name, and the thing: the name, is a voyce which noteth, and signifieth the thing: the name, is neither part of the thing nor of substance: it is a stranger-piece ioyned to the thing, and from it. God who in and by himself is all fulnesse, and the tipe of all perfection, cannot inwardly be augmented, or encreased: yet by his name be encreased and augmented, by the blessing and praise which we give unto exteriour workes. . . . We are all hollow and emptie, and it is not with breath and words that we should fill our selves. We have neede of a more solide substance to repaire our selves. (359)

Montaigne's exemplum of the treachery of language – apart from the self-perpetuating definitional chain, for which he shares Sanchez's distrust ('one word is changed for another word') – is the instance of linguistic 'propriety' *par excellence*, the personal name. Appearing to promise a unique and intimate bond with the nominee, the proper name instead proves an exemplary case of lexical promiscuity, yoking as it does a potentially limitless series of individuals under a single nominal unit:

> Is it *Peter* or *William*. And what is that but a word for all mouths? or three or four dashes of a pen, first so easie to be varied, as I could willingly aske those, whom the honour of so many victories concerneth. . . . they are dashes, and tricks of the pen common unto a thousand men. How many are there in all races of families both of one name and surname? And how many in divers families, races, ages, and countries? History has known three Socrates, five Platos, eight Aristotles. . . . Who letteth my horse boy to call himself Pompey the Great? (150–1)

(Note, in the light of this view of the proper name and its abusability, the irony of the possible pun on Florio's *Montaigne* in *LLL* (see Richard David, Introduction to Arden ed.: xxxiii): '*Arm.* [to Hol.] Do you not educate youth at the charge-house on the top of the mountain?', 5. 1. 74–5.)

The particular disparagement reserved by Montaigne for dashes and tricks of the pen is not casual. What for the linguistic mystics is the supreme vehicle of semiotic embodiment, the graphic sign, is for Montaigne the epitome of the detachment of language from the world. He is correspondingly contemptuous of texts and of the debilitating scholarship directed towards them: 'The studie and plodding on bookes, is a languishing & weak kinde of motion, and which heateth or earnesteth nothing; wheareas conference doth both learne, teach and exercise at once' (553).

Montaigne's virile dismissal of name and book leads us back directly to the comedies, and specifically to Berowne's oration in the first scene of *LLL* opposing Navarre's Academe. Berowne's reply begins precisely, *verbatim et literatim*, with exclamatory derision towards the weak and languishing 'studie and plodding on bookes', capable only of deviating the seeker from the truth:

> Ber.    Why! all delights are vain, but that most vain
> Which with pain purchas'd doth inherit pain:
> As, painfully to pore upon a book
> To seek the light of truth; while truth the while
> Doth falsely blind the eyesight of his look: . . .
> Small have continual plodders ever won,
> Save base authority from others' books. (I. I. 72ff.)

Berowne's rational anti-rationalist stand develops into the second most conspicuous avowal of linguistic scepticism in Shakespearean drama (after Juliet's 'rose'), in the guise of an aphoristic 'Pyrrhonian' scoffing at the idle proliferation of names bestowed *ad placitum* by the erudite:

> Ber.    These earthly godfathers of heaven's lights,
> That give a name to every fixed star,
> Have no more profit of their shining nights
> Than those that walk and wot not what they are.
> Too much to know is to know nought but fame;
> And every godfather can give a name. (88ff.)

As with all of Berowne's 'doctrinal' positions, the tone here is ambiguous and the argument is immediately retracted as 'barbarism'. And yet the move itself of disavowing Navarre's incipient Platonism through the demystification of the text and the name is acute and philosophically sound, and adds considerably to the play's metalinguistic dialectic (the more so since, as we shall see, his passing scepticism corresponds to the treatment that the word receives from the ladies).

An analogous polarity arises in *AWW*, in which, however, just as Helena's natural locutionary magic is presented without irony, so the counterposed deflation of the word – enacted by the King, chief beneficiary and admirer of Helena's powers – is unequivocally proposed in earnest. The King's fiercely nominalistic harangue arises by way of a moral rebuke to Bertram and his overvaluation of titular forms:

King.     'Tis only title thou disdain'st in her, the which
          I can build up. Strange is it that our bloods,
          Of colour, weight, and heat, pour'd all together,
          Would quite confound distinction, yet stands off
          In differences so mighty. If she be
          All that is virtuous, save what thou dislik'st –
          A poor physician's daughter – thou dislik'st
          Of virtue for the name. But do not so. . . .
                              Good alone
          Is good, without a name; vileness is so:
          The property by what it is should go,
          Not by the title. . . .
                              The mere word's a slave,
          Debosh'd on every tomb, on every grave
          A lying trophy, and as oft is dumb,
          Where dust and damn'd oblivion is the tomb
          Of honour'd bones indeed. (2. 3. 117ff.)

The King's depreciation of the deboshed name (again the paradigm is graphic) is in a sense borne out by Bertram's own later behaviour, when his overprizing of social titles gives way to a devaluation of his marriage vows (an attitude that is figured metonymically in his association with Parolles, nominal and behavioural representative of empty verbal forms). The point is underlined in the finale, when Helena, in response to the King's amazement at her magical reappearance, echoes his oration (and, by the way, Montaigne's essay 'On Glory': 'There is both the name and the thing'):

King.                     Is there no exorcist
          Beguiles the truer office of mine eyes?
          Is't real that I see?
Hel.                      No, my good lord;
          'Tis but the shadow of a wife you see;
          The name and not the thing. (5. 3. 298–302)

Elsewhere, the *nomen est vox* disclaimer is good for a spirited quip, as in Jaques's affectation in *AYLI* of aristocratic disregard for the *termini technici* of prosody:

Jaques.   Come, more, another stanzo. Call you 'em stanzos?
Amiens.   What you will, Monsieur Jaques.
Jaques.   Nay, I care not for their names, they owe me nothing (2. 5. 16–20);

the jibe is later turned against him when he takes capricious exception to 'Rosalind' ('at pleasure', as Orlando points out, does not necessarily mean at *his* pleasure):

| | |
|---|---|
| *Jaques.* | Rosalind is your love's name? |
| *Orl.* | Yes, just. |
| *Jaques.* | I do not like her name. |
| *Orl.* | There was no thought of pleasing you when she was christened. |

(3. 2. 259–63)

In its proverbial 'words are but wind' form, the gesture provides an irresistible occasion, not resisted in *CE*, for a resounding *turpis locutio* or, as Puttenham would have termed it ('every godfather') 'foule speeche'. The breath of the vowels – 'All words [are] made . . . of the breath that commeth of the lungs' (Perkins, see above, p. 168 – is readily transformable into the wind of the bowels, base *flatus vocis* into baser *flatus viscerarum*:

| | |
|---|---|
| *Eph. Dro.* | A man may break a word with you, sir, and words are but wind; |
| | Ay, and break it in your face, so he break it not behind. |

(3. 1. 74–6)

For Beatrice in her somewhat politer version of the jest in *MA*, what 'commeth of the lungs' is mere halitosis:

| | |
|---|---|
| *Beatr.* | . . . ere I go, let me go with what I came for, which is, with knowing what hath passed between you and Claudio. |
| *Ben.* | Only foul words – and thereupon I will kiss thee. |
| *Beatr.* | Foul words is but foul wind, and foul wind is but foul breath, and foul breath is noisome – therefore I will part unkissed. |
| *Ben.* | Thou hast frighted the word out of his right sense, so forcible is thy wit. (5. 2. 46–52) |

Benedick's complaint at the wilful misinterpretation of his foul word 'foul' draws attention to one of the predominant semantic principles of Shakespearean (and in general, Elizabethan) comedy: the frighting of the word out of its sense, on the basis of the contingency of the relationship between the two. That is to say, the conventional and arbitrary character of the sign is institutionalized in comic discourse, particularly in those forms of equivocation that exploit, as Benedick objects, the divergent senses of a single lexeme or the discordant senses of two or more homonymic or phonetically similar lexemes. The official vehicles of this 'convention' convention are, naturally, the clowns, some of whom are perfectly articulate on their fulfilment of this function. Thus Feste in *TN* prefaces a definition of his deviating professional activity with a moral and sociolinguistic meditation on the constitutional semantic and ethical instability of the word that makes his licensed 'corruption' possible:

| | |
|---|---|
| *Clown.* | You have said, sir. To see this age! A sentence is but a chev'ril glove to a good wit – how quickly the wrong side may be turned outward! |
| *Viola.* | Nay, that's certain: they that dally nicely with words may quickly make them wanton. |
| *Clown.* | I would therefore my sister had had no name, sir. |
| *Viola.* | Why, man? |
| *Clown.* | Why, sir, her name's a word, and to dally with that word might make my sister wanton. But indeed, words are very rascals, since bonds disgraced them. |
| *Viola.* | Thy reason, man? |
| *Clown.* | Troth, sir, I can yield you none without words, and words are grown so false, I am loath to prove reason with them. . . . |
| *Viola.* | Art thou not the Lady Olivia's fool? |
| *Clown.* | No indeed sir, the Lady Olivia has no folly . . . I am indeed not her fool, but her corrupter of words. (3. 1. 11–37) |

In practice, Feste is very sparing in the word-corrupting and sentence-turning to which he lays claim (belonging, like Touchstone and Lavatch, to the class of 'logical' or dialectical later clowns). The true practitioners of the mode of wordplay that turns phonetic coincidence into semantic mutilation are the early clowns, particularly Launce and Speed in *TG*, who are also capable of a certain 'professional' awareness of what they are about:

| | |
|---|---|
| *Spe.* | How now, Signor Launce! What news with your mastership? |
| *Lau.* | With my master's ship? Why, it is at sea. |
| *Spe.* | Well, your old vice still: mistake the word. (3. 1. 277–80) |

And yet the undisputed past masters or mistresses of linguistic contingency, of the accidental and arbitrary word-meaning bond, are not the official clowns but the aristocratic ladies in *LLL*, whose knowing pursuit of the homonymic pun and whose unrelenting juggling *ad extremum* with sense relations provide the most effective of responses to the multiform semantic naïveté affected by the scholars and pedants:

| | |
|---|---|
| *Boy.* | I was as willing to grapple as he was to board. |
| *Kath.* | Two hot sheeps, marry! |
| *Boy.* | And wherefore not ships? No sheep, sweet lamb, unless we feed on your lips. |
| *Kath.* | You sheep, and I pasture: shall that finish the jest? |
| *Boy.* | So you grant pasture for me. (2. 1. 217ff.) |

| | |
|---|---|
| *Kath.* | . . . a light heart lives long. |
| *Ros.* | What's your dark meaning, mouse, of this light word? |
| *Kath.* | A light condition in a beauty dark. |
| *Ros.* | We need more light to find your meaning out. |
| *Kath.* | You'll mar the light by taking it in snuff. Therefore I'll darkly end the argument. |

| | |
|---|---|
| *Ros.* | Look what you do, you do it still i' the dark. |
| *Kath.* | So do not you, for you are a light wench. |
| *Ros.* | Indeed I weigh not you, and therefore light. . . . |
| *Prin.* | Well bandied both; a set of wit well play'd (5. 2. 18ff.) |

The meanings of light words may indeed be dark, but in the sets of semantic tennis so essential to Shakespearean comedy, they too are light enough to be tossed endlessly back and forth or simply carried off on the (*flatus vocis* or perhaps *spiritus comoediae*) wind.

# 4　Acts

Signs relate not only to each other and to the world they stand for but to the human subjects who put them *into* the world. The relationship between signs, their users and the circumstances of their use is the territory of pragmatics, as defined by Charles Morris: 'pragmatics . . . deals with the origin, uses and effects of signs within the behaviour in which they occur' (1946: 219). Where the last chapter explored the make-up and signifying powers of linguistic signs, the following pages have to do precisely with their 'practical' origin, uses and effects.

The drama is an especially inviting terrain for a pragmatics of fictional discourse. Etymology alone suggests as much. 'Drama', as any introductory manual on the subject will begin by pointing out, derives from Greek *dran* ('to do'). 'Pragmatics' also derives from Greek, from *pragma* ('act') which in turn comes from the verb *prattein* (likewise 'to do'). The art of doing is an irresistible object for the science of doing, especially in that sphere of *pragma* (the dominant sphere in Shakespearean drama) that Pirandello calls 'spoken action'.

Now the pragmatic character of dramatic language – its very definition as a series of doings – is founded on what is here baptized as the 'conversational fiction' (see Introduction, p. 15). It is only the convention whereby characters *talk* themselves and their world into existence that allows us to explore the dialogic exchange as a form of *praxis*. The conversational fiction itself, at least in Shakespearean comedy, involves five main elements, each of which is examined in one of the following five sections:

(a)　The configuration of speakers and circumstances (section (ii)).

(b)　The 'managing' of the talk, and particularly of turn-taking, through signals which present the dialogue *as* a conversation (section (iii)).

(c)　The performance of speech acts (illocutionary acts) within the speech exchange (section (iv)).

(d)　The relationship of the speaker to his acts: thus his

177

intentions, his expressive purposes, and his commitment or otherwise to what he says, together with his success or failure in communicating his intentions, purposes and commitment to his listeners (section (v)).

(e)     The effects of the acts performed upon the listener (section (vi)).

Since the aim of the chapter is to reveal not only the pragmatics of Shakespearean comedy but, as it were, the Shakespearean pragmatics of comedy – i.e. the self-consciousness or self-dramatization of the represented doings – it necessarily marries contemporary pragmatic models (speech-act theory, conversation analysis, etc.) with Renaissance notions of speaking-as-doing. Reference is made to rhetorical and ethical principles of conversational decorum (ii), of expression and intention (iv) and of effect (v), in the conviction that an explicit corpus of 'speech-act' theories was readily accessible to Shakespeare and his audience.

## (II) CONVERSATIONS, SITUATIONS

In one of her characteristic moral meditations, Portia in *MV* reflects on the roots of the intimate friendship between Bassanio and Antonio:

> for in companions
> That do converse and waste the time together,
> Whose souls do bear an egall yoke of love,
> There must be needs a like proportion
> Of lineaments, of manners, and of spirit. (3. 4. 11–15)

Portia identifies in time-whiling intimate talk both the index and the ground of the profound bond between the two men. Such an evaluation of the 'wasting' of time in familiar conversation – namely as an essential token and ingredient of interpersonal equality and harmony – is fully confirmed by the licence and positive dramatic weight allowed to informal talk exchanges within the play itself (Antonio with Bassanio; Portia with Nerissa; Portia with Bassanio; Lorenzo with Jessica, etc.).

Talk about talk, or conversation about conversation, is so ubiquitous in the comedies as to become virtually transparent:

> We have convers'd and spent our hours together

> Did you converse, sir, with this gentlewoman?

> I did converse this quondam day with a companion

> We had an hour's talk of that wart

Look you who comes here / A young man and an old in solemn talk.
(etc.)

This suggests, of course, that conversational business is itself omni-present and transparent. In a sense this is true, since the dialogue is institutionally, if not constitutionally, nothing but *conversatio*: the co-operation of dramatic persons through verbal intercourse. But as Portia's reflection suggests, conversing is at the same time a specific activity or interactivity calling for a particular commitment and attention, especially in the kind of conversation she has in mind, the familiar 'time-wasting' talk between interlocutors who, in terms of their status as participants in the event, bear a more or less 'egall yoke' and 'like proportion'.

The comedies are able to explore talk, talkers and talking situations more freely than the other genres, in part because of the relative looseness of narrative constraints. The familiar, intimate and appar-ently free-ranging conversation of which Portia speaks is far more frequent in these plays than in the tragedies or history plays (an extreme case in point being the dramatization of 'civil conversation' in *TG*, in which almost every scene involves a one-to-one give and take of personal confidences). What this means is that in Shakespeare's comic dramaturgy the conversational situation and its characteristic elements assume more weight and attract more direct notice than elsewhere. Indeed, it is fair to say that the dramatic 'scene' in the comedies is defined or perceived in the first instance precisely as a conversational *situation of utterance* (see Lyons 1977): i.e. as a configuration of speaker(s), addressee(s), together with other possible listener(s), discus-sing a given conversational topic in a particular set of spatial and temporal circumstances. And it is the very variation and transformation of these speaking situations which give much of the momentum to Shakespeare's comic plot – so much so, that it is worth reflecting briefly on the 'repertory' of conversational situations, considered as dynamic transformational elements in the structure of the plays.

### (1) Degree zero

The canonical situation of utterance, point of definition and departure for all transformations or complications, might be formulated as *I–you–it* – i.e. the one-to-one speaker–addressee exchange on some shared topic. It is this 'transparent' configuration that, logically enough, most frequently opens the plays: Lucentio and Tranio converse on the former's plan to study philosophy in Padua (*TS*); Valentine and Proteus on love (*TG*); Theseus and Hippolyta on their wedding festivities (*MND*); the Duke of Ephesus and Egeon on the latter's background and fate (*CE*: a relatively 'public' opening); Orlando and Adam on Oliver's unjust behaviour (*AYLI*); Orsino and Curio on the former's love for Olivia (*TN*); Duke Senior and Escalus on Angelo (*MM*).

Naturally, this rudimentary triangular scheme is transformational in itself, to the extent that the speaker–addressee (I–you) roles are by definition interchangeable, while the governing conversational topic, far from being fixed, is subject to continual evolution, digression and contradiction.

### (2) Much noting of the ado

The addressee is a privileged class of listener. His presence and attention are presupposed by the talk and indexically marked throughout ('Hear'st thou, Biondello?'). Non-addressed and unmarked secondary listeners, instead – unless they be future addressees, as in multi-person exchanges – are normally negligible presences whose listening is of no dramatic weight (attendants, for example, whose attending is not, as it were, attended to).

A substantial shift in the conversational configuration is brought about, paradoxically, only by the addition of *unauthorized* listeners. Clandestine participation in the exchange, whether unwitting (over-hearing) or strategic (eavesdropping), usually has the effect of fore-grounding the very act of listening. Throughout *MA*, the auditory 'noting' of the punning title represents the chief generative principle of the plot, which can be broken down into a chain of ten dramatically decisive acts of hearing, and above all, of overhearing, actual, invented or staged conversations:

(1)     A servant of Antonio's overhears Don Pedro's confession to Claudio of his supposed love for Hero. The event is reported to Antonio who in turn relates it to Leonato ('were thus overheard by a man of mine'). The latter decides to prepare his daughter for the Prince's courtship (1. 2. 6ff.).

(2)     Borachio overhears Don Pedro's offer to woo Hero on Claudio's behalf, and reports the exchange to Don John ('comes me the prince and Claudio, hand in hand in sad conference. I whipped me behind the arras, and there heard it agreed upon', 1. 3. 54ff.).

(3)     Don John, on hearing of the 'sad conference', decides to impede the planned match ('this may prove food to my displeasure', 1. 3. 61–2).

(4)    Benedick, in disguise, at the masque, hears himself insulted
       by Beatrice, also in disguise, and reports the maltreatment to
       his friends ('she speaks poniards, and every word stabs', 2. 1.
       231–2).

(5)    Benedick's friends stage-manage a scene in which, hidden in
       the arbour, he overhears the false revelation of Beatrice's love
       for him, together with disparagement of his qualities.
       Convinced by the acted exchange, he decides to requite
       Beatrice's love ('This can be no trick: the conference was
       sadly borne; . . . happy are they that can hear their detractors,
       and can put them to mending', 2. 3. 211f., 220f.).

(6)    Beatrice's friends arrange a parallel conversational trap for
       her, with identical results ('*Beatr.* What fire is in mine ears?
       Can this be true?/Stand I condemned for pride and scorn so
       much?', 3. 1. 107ff.).

(7)    Borachio sets up an amorous colloquy with Margaret before
       the eavesdropping Claudio and Don Pedro, thereby convinc-
       ing them of Hero's disloyalty ('*Don P.* Myself, my brother,
       and this grieved count, / Did see her, hear her . . . / Talk with a
       ruffian at her chamber-window', 4. 1. 88–91).

(8)    Borachio's account of his stratagem to Conrade is in turn over-
       heard by the Nightwatchmen ('Some treason, masters, yet
       stand close') who consequently arrest the two interlocutors.

(9)    Hero, on hearing the accusation against her, faints, and is
       pronounced dead ('Thy slander hath gone through and
       through her heart', 5. 1. 68).

(10)   Claudio and Don Pedro hear Borachio's confession and repent
       of their error ('*Don P.* Runs not this speech like iron through
       your blood?/*Claudio.* I have drunk poison whiles he uttered
       it', 5. 1. 239–40).

As the quoted metacommunicational comments suggest, the bias
throughout *MA* is towards the reception of speech. Indeed, what is
*theatrically* notable about the noting in the play is that the overhearer
or unauthorized listener is in the foreground not only figuratively
within the drama but also, in all likelihood, *physically* on stage (see (5),
(6) and (8)). The result is that the dramatic priority of audition is
strikingly iconized. Just as it is strikingly lexicalized throughout the
text: 'hear' and its derivatives occur no less than fifty-eight times; 'ear'
and 'ears' ten times; 'note', in its auditory sense, five times; 'mark', in
the same sense, four; 'overhear' three, together with single instances of
'listen', 'hearken', and a rare use of 'hearsay' (found elsewhere in

Shakespeare only in Sonnet xxi). (On the functions of eavesdropping and the orientation towards the listener in *MA*, see Mullini 1979).

### (3) Turn'd into tongue

In terms of the triangular conversational model, *MA* is characterized by a kind of structural imbalance. The consistent orientation towards the listener in the comedy is in direct opposition with the extreme volubility of its two main characters, who are figured synecdochically as Tongues: Benedick disdains Beatrice as 'my Lady tongue', while Beatrice in turn complains that Benedick has been 'turn'd into tongue'. And it is, of course, a central irony that the play's two Tongues are fatally tricked in the very act of listening.

If the auricular comes to dominate over the lingual in *MA*, the reverse is true in *TS*, which is in a sense a dramatization of the condition of logorrhea. The play's bias towards the speaker, to the virtual exclusion of listener and listening, is apparent rhetorically in Petruchio's conspicuous monologues (rare in the comic canon) and lexically in the obsessive lingual or metalingual figure (synecdoche for the speaker and metonymy for speech itself) applied to the Shrew: Gremio, in the opening scene, remarks on Bianca's having to 'bear the penance of her tongue' (1. 1. 89); Hortensio, in the following scene, couples her name with her prime attribute: 'Her name is Katherina Minola/Renown'd in Padua for her scolding tongue' (1. 2. 98–9); and in the same scene Tranio confirms the notoriety of the organ, contrasting it with Bianca's decorous restraint: 'The one as famous for a scolding tongue / As is the other for beauteous modesty' (1. 2. 25 2–3), and so on. The full weight of the all-tongue-no-ears imbalance in the play emerges in Petruchio's design to 'charm her chattering tongue' by refusing to receive or perceive Katherina's verbal assaults (a deliberate self-deafening), opposing to them instead a still more determined loquacity:

> Say that she rail, why then I'll tell her plain
> She sings as sweetly as a nightingale. (2. 1. 171–2)

On the vocal pandemonium that inevitably results, the comedy's marginal and intimidated internal auditors can only comment with bemused irony from the sidelines:

*Bap.*     Nay, let them go, a couple of quiet ones. (3. 2. 238)

### (4) Doubling

A particularly potent species of situational (or 'dramatic') irony arises in the comedies from the following variation on the I–you–it scheme: one participant, unbeknown to his interlocutor, occupies simultaneously the 'it' position of topic. A conspicuous instance of such 'doubling', in this case of addressee as topic, appears in Lucio's insulting of the disguised Duke in *MM* (3. 2). Significantly, Lucio opens the conversation by distinguishing between addressee ('Friar Lodowick') and proposed conversational topic, the Duke: 'What news, friar, of the Duke?', before launching into his disastrous tirade against, in effect, both. The point is insistently underlined by his interlocutor's mild signals on the inappropriateness of his talk ('You are pleasant, sir, and speak apace'; 'I have never heard the absent Duke much detected for women; he was not indeed that way'; 'You do him wrong, surely' until the 'Friar' steps up the irony by threatening to refer Lucio's harangue to the 'absent' topical Duke himself ('He shall know you better, sir, if I may live to report you'), without in the least impressing his co-conversationalist.

The opposite variation, with speaker doubling as topic unbeknown to the addressee, is presented in *MWW* in Falstaff's encounter with the disguised Ford, who invites his interlocutor first to render him cuckold ('lay an amiable siege to the honesty of this Ford's wife') and then to discourse on him. Ford gets in exchange the very name of his potential condition:

Ford.   Do you know Ford, sir?
Fal.    Hang him, poor cuckoldly knave! I know him not. (2. 2. 284–6)

### (5) Reports

The doubling game involving Lucio and the Duke in *MM* is considerably extended and complicated when their conversation (in 3. 2) is later reported, twice (in 5. 1). On both occasions the original situation of utterance between Lucio and 'Friar Lodowick' is ironically embedded or *mise en abyme* within another exchange involving the same interlocutors. On the first occasion Lucio, before the Duke, attempts to outmove the 'absent' friar by turning the latter's anticipated accusation (namely that Lucio had insulted the Duke) against *him*:

Lucio.   My lord, I know him. 'Tis a meddling friar;
         I do not like the man; had he been lay, my lord,
         For certain words he spake against your Grace
         In your retirement, I had swing'd him soundly. (130–3)

Lucio's lie creates knotty situational complications which can best be unravelled with the help of Roman Jakobson's famous distinctions (1957) between the current speech event (E$^s$) and the narrated or reported event ($E^n$), and between participants in the current speech event ($P^s$) (here a distinction must be drawn between speaker $P^{s1}$ and addressee $P^{s2}$) and participants in the narrated event (speaker $P^{n1}$ and addressee $P^{n2}$). A further distinction might be added for our purposes, namely between the topic of the current speech event ($T^s$) (the topic being, naturally, the narrated event itself) and the topic of the narrated event ($T^n$). Using Jakobson's symbols, Lucio's version of the original conversation can be represented diagrammatically as follows:

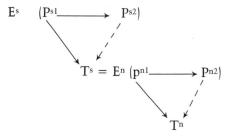

where $P^{n2} = P^{s1}$ and $T^n = P^{s2}$.

In other words: in current situation $E^s$ speaker Lucio ($P^{s1}$) recounts to addressee Duke Vincentio ($P^{s2}$) an exchange $E^n$ in which, in the presence of Lucio himself ($P^{n2} = P^{s1}$), Friar Lodowick ($P^{n1}$) had insulted the Duke ($T^n = P^{s2}$). But unbeknown to Lucio – and it is this that renders the complications lively – the Duke, as participant in both $E^s$ and $E^n$, is well aware of the true overlappings involved, whereby Lucio's diagram is in itself accurate, but with the following variations in the code: $P^{s2}$ is indeed equal to $T^n$ (i.e. the Duke *was* the topic of the original exchange), while $P^{s1}$ (Lucio) does not correspond to $P^{n2}$ (addressee in the narrated event) as claimed, but to $P^{n1}$ (the insulting speaker in $E^n$).

Later in the same scene, when the Duke temporarily resumes his friar's habit, Lucio again forestalls Lodowick's threatened report by promptly turning the accusation directly against him:

> And do you remember what you said of the Duke? . . .
> And was the Duke a fleshmonger, a fool and a coward,
> As you then reported him to be? (5. 1. 328ff.)

In Lucio's reconstruction – diagrammatically identical to his earlier false report – the participants in the current speech event are found to coincide with those of the narrated event as follows: $P^{s1}$ (speaker Lucio) = $P^{n2}$ (addressee in narrated event); $P^{s2}$ (addressee Friar) = $P^{n1}$ (speaker in narrated event); $T^n$ = the 'absent' Duke. For the theatrical audience, however, the correspondences are otherwise disposed, with the Duke occupying as many as three of the agentical roles within the double situation:

$P^{s1}$ (speaker Lucio) = $P^{n1}$ (speaker in narrated event);
$P^{s2}$ (addressee Duke) = $P^{n2}$ (addressee in narrated event);
$T^n$ is also the both-times-present (and doubly offended) Duke.

It is not the elementary algebra – nor the rudimentary geometry – that matters here, but the *poetics* that it illustrates. From the elements of the simple 'pragmatic' scheme, Shakespeare is able to create a dynamic series of reversals and transformations, culminating in the dramatically and ethically weighty moment of Lucio's self-trapping prior to the Duke's unmasking (and thus the play's dénouement). In *MM* the interplay between *énonciation* and *énoncé*, between dramatic situation of utterance and reported event, is not only theatrically effective – playing as it does on physical disguise and unmasking, on the Duke's double performance, on the contrast between the dramatic here and now and conflicting 'narrative' pasts – but also thematically functional, being loaded with the comedy's central ethical issue of insincerity or 'infelicity' (see (v) below).

### (6) Possibilities

Like the rest of us, Shakespeare's dramatic speakers – particularly when alone – commonly construct their own 'possible' speech events, in projecting or hypothesizing what they will say, would say, would have said or could have said in some future, past or imaginary situation. As with embedded reports, these projections take on interest when they coincide or, still more, conflict with the 'actual' speaking configuration. The tormenting of Malvolio in *TN* is an exemplary case. After reading the false love-letter, Malvolio predicts his future verbal behaviour, especially towards his inamorata's uncle:

> I will be proud, I will read politic authors, I will baffle Sir Toby, I will wash off gross acquaintance, I will be point-device the very man. (2. 5. 161–4)

The highly improbable world in which Malvolio is licensed to 'baffle' or humiliate Sir Toby to his face is in poignant contrast with the simultaneous act of eavesdropping by Sir Toby and his fellow conspirators, an event that represents nothing if not the cruel baffling of Malvolio himself, the very converse of his imagined conversing.

### (III) 'THANKFUL FOR GOOD TURNS': FIGHTING FOR THE FLOOR

Among the more formidable problems facing Carpenter Quince in *MND* in his efforts as theatre director is his actors' absolute inability to speak on cue, in the right order and within the textually defined limits:

| | |
|---|---|
| *Quin.* | Speak, Pyramus; Thisbe, stand forth; . . . |
| *Flu.* | Must I speak now? |
| *Quin.* | Ay, marry must you; for you must understand he goes but to see a noise that he heard, and is to come again . . . Why you must not speak that yet; that you answer to Pyramus. You speak all your part at once, cues and all. (3. 1. 77–95) |

Quince's single directorial principle, on which all his theatrical authority is based, is that characters and actors alike speak in turn, and not beyond the bounds of that turn. An elementary rule, no doubt, but he is not altogether mistaken in giving it such weight, since the decorum of every dramatic representation – with its rehearsed dialogic and scenic alternations, its carefully managed entrances and exits, its programmed apportionment of stage space, etc. – does indeed depend essentially on the category of the turn.

Quince's modest one-at-a-time yardstick resembles somewhat the most important pragmatic rules for conversation, as formulated by Renaissance moral legislators on 'civil conversation' and, in a descriptive rather than prescriptive spirit, by ethnologists and sociologists in our own day. The duty to await, and to remain within, one's turn is the all-founding 'civilized' tenet of etiquette guides such as Giovanni della Casa's *Galateo* (or 'Treatise . . . on the Modes of Behaviour that should be Observed or Avoided in Common Conversation', 1559). Della Casa prohibits, among other social sins, conversational floor-holding or -hogging ('There are many that are not able to stop speaking and, like a ship driven by the force of the first launch, keep on going', 115), turn-stealing ('others have such a greed for talking . . . that they take the words out of the mouth of him who has begun talking', *ibid.*), speech-breaking ('to interrupt or prevent another from speaking is an annoying habit, and displeases no less than when a man is on the point of running and someone restrains him', 116), impatient prompting ('if someone is slow in speaking, one should not anticipate or suggest the words to him, as if one had a sufficiency of them and he a deficiency', 117) and, on the contrary, excessive silence ('But just as speaking too much is annoying, so keeping too quiet provokes displeasure: because remaining silent while others converse, appears a desire not to play one's part', 118), all on the sacred principle that 'the most pleasing custom is for each person to talk, or to stay silent, *when his turn comes*' (118, my translation and italics). In comparison, the first four conversational rules given by the sociologists Sacks, Schegloff and Jefferson in their modern and scientific 'systematics' for turn-taking in talk (1974) read as follows:

|       |                                                                  |
|-------|------------------------------------------------------------------|
| (1)   | speaker-change recurs, or at least occurs;                       |
| (2)   | overwhelmingly, one party talks at a time;                       |
| (3)   | occurrences of more than one speaker at a time are common, but brief; |
| (4)   | transitions (from one turn to a next) with no gap and no overlap are common. |

In his attempted management of the dramatic talk, Quince is justly anxious to ensure not only that speaker-change recurs, or at least occurs (rule 1) and that one party (exclusively, not overwhelmingly) talks at a time (rule 2), but that there should be no gaps or overlaps between speeches (rule 4), or, worse still, anticipations of future speeches.

The parallel here is not particularly fanciful: 'natural' conversation and dramatic dialogue are both members of the class designated by Sacks *et al.* as 'speech exchange systems', and as such have economies founded on the principle of alternation. The constraints involved are unquestionably more powerful in the case of the drama, since on stage the exchange has to be rendered both audible and, as it were, followable for the auditor, whereby smooth transitions become the norm and the gap and overlap are all but eliminated. For similar reasons, another of the ethnologists' conversational rules (Sacks *et al.*, rule 13) – 'Various "turn-constructional units" are employed; e.g. turns can be projectedly "one word long" or they can be sentential in length' – requires modification in the case of dramatic dialogue, especially Shake-spearean. Turns or speeches may indeed be of any length, but are normally syntactically and semantically self-sufficient and rhetorically well-ordered. Here the requirement of repeatability, in addition to that of followability, imposes greater textual coherence: the same dialogue must be re-utterable in a potentially unlimited number of perform-ances, a factor that serves to distinguish the dramatic exchange from the often hesitant, inconclusive, reiterative and disordered progress of our 'natural' talk, with all its false starts, fillers, re-thinks, non-sentences and the like.

Up to this point, with the suggested qualifications, the comparison between the conversational and dramatic exchange systems is tenable. Where the analogy fails to hold at all, however, is in the actual organization and purpose of the turns. Consider rules 5 to 11 in the Sacks–Schegloff–Jefferson system:

|       |                                                  |
|-------|--------------------------------------------------|
| (5)   | turn order is not fixed, but varies;             |
| (6)   | turn size is not fixed, but varies;              |
| (7)   | length of conversation is not specified in advance; |
| (8)   | what parties say is not specified in advance;    |

(9)     relative distribution of turns is not specified in advance;
(10)    number of parties can vary;
(11)    talk can be continuous or discontinuous.

Clearly enough, non-premeditation is the groundrule of our non-fictional speech activities. To determine the size, order and above all the content of turns in advance would normally amount to falsification or fabrication (of the kind represented in the contrived exchanges in *MA*). And the 'textual' coherence of our natural talk is generally limited to the requirements of relevance and comprehensibility. In the drama, on the contrary, despite the supposed 'spontaneity' of the dialogue on the part of the dramatic speakers, and while for the *audience* nothing is in fact specified in advance, the succession, content and sheer length of contributions are at all times determined by the laws of textuality and narrativity. Not only is each turn, in other words, bound to the unfolding of information, to the semantic and rhetorical organization of the discourse and to the progress of the plot, but it is in itself an event within the surface narrative structure of the play.

What the textual and narrative status of the dramatic turn means is the effective elimination of the most characteristic feature of the management of natural talk: namely, the strategic negotiating of the conversational floor. Sacks and colleagues identify two such negotiational strategies, together with a class of measures for patching up infringements:

(12)    turn-allocation techniques are obviously used. A current speaker may select a next speaker (as when he addresses a question to another party); or parties may self-select in starting to talk;
(14)    repair mechanisms exist for dealing with turn-taking errors and violations.

Turn-allocation and repair techniques derive from what we might term the *ceteris paribus* democratic premise on which natural talk is founded: all other things being equal (we are not, for example, conversing with a monarch, a president or an armed terrorist), every participant has an equal right to the floor, so that speaking turns, rather than being predetermined, have to be booked, assigned or fought for.

Rhetorical equality of this kind is quite alien to the drama, in which, obviously, the distribution of discourse is not democratic but dramaturgic. Dramatic speakers clearly do *not* have the same rights to the floor. The chief dramatic agents may be allowed a virtually unlimited locutionary licence, and indeed the relative importance of their roles is in part indicated by the very size and frequency of their contributions: the rule here, is not so much speaker self-selects as protagonist self-defines. In tragedy and the history play, in particular, the pride-of-lions' share of the dialogic goods is frequently seized by a single character (Henry V, Macbeth). In these genres the question of floor-apportionment scarcely arises, in any case, since the economy of discourse usually corresponds to the social hierarchy it represents: the rhetorical protagonist is also at the apex of the dramatic realm, whereby the democratic all-things-being-equal principle is waived *a priori*.

In Shakespearean comedy, instead, turn-allocation and repair signals do play a significant part in maintaining the conversational fiction. This may be linked to the relative weakness of hierarchical factors (clowns, servants, petty officials, criminals and all manner of social riff-raff may be permitted more say than their evident betters) and to the relative looseness of narrative ties, permitting the dialogue to assume more readily the guise of the negotiated free-for-all. At their most automatic, these fictional strategies tend to authenticate the dialogue as non-premeditated give and take (on authentication see Burns 1972), while at their most elaborate they come to dramatize the verbal interaction in progress, bringing into the foreground, as it were, the very floor. The typology that follows, designed to identify the most recurrent kinds of signal, draws liberally on the categories furnished by analysts of natural talk.

### (1) I pray you tell it

The conversational move 'in which next turn is allocated by current speaker's selecting next speaker' is an all-purpose means of motivating dialogic transition and in particular of encoding the eliciting of narrative information. Such 'you-next' allocation is implicit, of course, in every question or in every utterance entailing some kind of sequel (accusations, challenges, refutations of some earlier utterance by the interlocutor, etc.). It becomes explicit, instead, in the form of a request to the addressee to take the floor, an invitation to tell the tellable:

Bass.                                 Ere I ope this letter
        I pray you tell me how my good friend doth. (*MV* 3. 2. 233–4)

Val.        When would you use it? Pray, sir, tell me that. (*TG* 3. 1. 124)

Cel.        I pray you tell it. (*AYLI* 4. 3. 97)

Codified instances of this kind are, or course, legion. But the turn invitation takes on particular dramatic weight in heavily expository exchanges, especially at their beginnings, as in the first encounter between Bassanio and Antonio in *MV*, where the take-the-floor signal serves also to define, somewhat laboriously, the main topic:

| | |
|---|---|
| *Ant.* | Well, tell me now what lady is the same |
| | To whom you swore a secret pilgrimage – |
| | That you to-day promised to tell me of? |
| *Bass.* | 'Tis not unknown to you, Antonio. (1. 1. 119ff.) |

The fullest and most imposing case of a striking turn signal serving to frame an urgently dramatic speaking situation appears in the confrontation between Isabella and Angelo before the Duke in the last scene of *MM*. The Duke's ironical invitation to Isabella to take the floor by disclosing her wrongs to the very man she intends to accuse is not refused but strategically deflected:

| | |
|---|---|
| *Duke.* | Relate your wrongs. In what? By whom? Be brief. |
| | Here is Lord Angelo shall give you justice, |
| | Reveal yourself to him. |
| *Isab.* | O worthy Duke, |
| | You bid me seek redemption of the devil. |
| | Hear me yourself. (5. 1. 27ff.) |

Outright refusal of the entreaty to hold forth inevitably foregrounds the *non*-turn itself as an event of a kind (i.e. as a tactical act of withholding). In one instance, namely Petruchio's silence on the subject of his late arrival for his wedding, it simply masks an informational void – Petruchio has nothing to relate except the deliberate causing of the delay itself, so that his conventional disclaimer (the event is not 'tellable') is in fact accurate enough:

| | |
|---|---|
| *Tra.* | And tell us what occasion of import |
| | Hath all so long detain'd you from your wife |
| | And sent you hither so unlike yourself? |
| *Pet.* | Tedious were it to tell, and harsh to hear. (3. 2. 100ff.) |

But on another occasion, Bottom's tormenting of his colleagues on the mysteries of his transformation, the refusal places the internal would-be auditors in a decidedly underprivileged position compared with the theatrical spectators, who have been ocular witnesses to the happening in question and so happily forgo the withheld narrative exposition:

| | |
|---|---|
| *Bot.* | Masters, I am to discourse wonders: but ask me not what; for if I tell you, I am no true Athenian. I will tell you everything, right as it fell out. |
| *Quin.* | Let us hear, sweet Bottom. |
| *Bot.* | Not a word of me. (4. 2. 28–31) |

At a certain degree of elaborateness and explicitness, of course, the invitation to speak ceases to 'conversationalize' the dialogue and comes, on the contrary, to frame the following contribution as a requested rhetorical display, a party turn rather than talking turn. Petruchio, for example, commissions directorially a demonstration by Katherina of her new tameness:

Pet.  Katherine, I charge thee, tell these headstrong women
    What duty they do owe their lords and husbands. (5. 2. 131–2)

But the clear theatrical connotations of Petruchio's directing and Katherina's performance merely bring us back to the effective coincidence in the drama between the fictional conversational turn and the actual dialogic (and potential acting) turn, a dramaturgic ambivalence that is nicely played upon by Beatrice in her impatient nudging of Claudio to accept Hero's hand:

Beatr.  Speak, Count, 'tis your cue. (2. 1. 287)

### (2) Nay forward

Goffman (1975: 12) distinguishes from other signals, and from the turn proper, 'booster-like encouragements' designed to maintain the status quo of the exchange and get the current speaker to complete or continue his contribution. In the comedies, keep-going cues of this kind have the primary effect of dramatizing the speaker's difficulties, or reluctance, and thus of foregrounding the actual 'production' of the speech or utterance. The opening of CE, the most directly expository and thus least 'theatrical' beginning in the comic canon, provides an exemplary instance: the long background-setting narrative is broken up and enlivened by the Duke's having to drag the desired dramatic information out of Egeon, whose tiredness and despair leave him ill-disposed and ill-equipped to play the conventional role of the scene setter:

Duke.  Nay forward, old man, do not break off so. (1. 1. 96)

More directly dramatizing, or at least more intensely dramatic, is the 'booster-like' support offered from the sidelines to Isabella in her attempted persuasion of Angelo in MM, signals that again bring attention to bear on the discomfort experienced by the speaker:

Lucio.  Give't not o'er so. – To him again, entreat him. (2. 2. 43ff.)

### (3) Peace your tattlings

Among the commoner features of natural dialogue that are inevitably purged from its dramatic equivalent are the gestural and vocal (but non-verbal) 'back-channel signals' which inform the speaker of the reception of his discourse (see Yngve 1971; Duncan 1973). Such paralinguistic feedback is entirely the province of the actor and his mimetic powers. Texts can only furnish lexicalized responses: ay or nay or their more elaborate equivalents. In the comedies, the most popular listener response would appear to be the emphatic nay, a rudely direct signal designed to bring to a rapid end a turn that is being badly received, or has gone on too long, or is nonsensical, pointless or offensive – a violent means of securing 'transition', no doubt, but also and above all a way of highlighting some species of verbal abortion:

*Cel.*    Cry holla to thy tongue, I prithee (*AYLI* 3. 2. 240)

*Ros.*    Not one word more, my maids, break off, break off (*LLL* 5. 2. 262)

*Leon.*                    I pray thee, cease thy counsel,
Which falls into mine ears as profitless
As water in a sieve (*MA* 5. 1. 3ff.)

*Maria.*    Peace, you rogue, no more o' that (*TN* 1. 5. 28)

*Feste.*    ... leave thy vain bibble babble. (*TN* 4. 2.100)

An entire scene in *MWW* is underscored by attempts to staunch the flow of uninvited observations from Mistress Quickly:

*Evans.*    Peace your tattlings! (4. 1. 21)

        Leave your prabbles, 'oman (42)

        'Oman forbear (47)

        For shame, 'oman (55)

*Mrs P.*    Prithee hold thy peace. (66)

### (4) 'Pauca verba'

Quantitative constraints on both natural and dramatic talk are never absolute: 'turn size', as Sacks and colleagues put it, 'is not fixed, but varies' (1974: 709). But this is not to say that considerations of economy play no part in the decorum of social intercourse. On the contrary, the very possibility of conversational co-operation, and thus of dialogic alternation, depends on each participant's due sense of limit. Indeed, of the maxims on which the philosopher H. P. Grice founds his proposed logic of conversation (1967), three have to do precisely with turn length – two so-called maxims of quantity:

(1)    make your contribution as informative as is required (for the current purposes of the exchange)

(2)      do not make your contribution more informative than is required

and one of manner:

Be brief (avoid unnecessary prolixity).

Grice's (descriptive) principles, particularly the latter two, resemble quite closely the (prescriptive) axioms for discursive decorum stated by ethical commentators in the Renaissance: 'And there is a measure to be used in mans speech or tale, so as it be neither for shortnesse too darke, not for length too tedious' (Puttenham 1589: Ggi^v); 'let our Discourse then be sober and sparing ... To talk much, and to talk well, are Qualities that seldom or never go together' (Charron 1601: 1529); 'it is one of the blessings of nature, speech; but to ride still upon the top of it is too vehement' (Cornwallis, 'Of Silence and Secrecie', 1601: 222). This simply suggests, naturally, the universality or *longue durée* of the value of succinctness in social exchange.

The 'informational' criterion for judging the suitable length of turns proposed by Grice and his Renaissance predecessors ('as informative as is required (for the current purposes of the exchange)') is by and large applicable, in the drama, to expository dialogue and thus, generally, to the more 'serious' scenes in Shakespearean comedy. The presence of such a quantitative constraint is particularly evident in *MV*, a play in which words are consistently weighed, most emblematically in the case of Shylock's bond and its wording. A good deal is made, in the play's opening scene, of Gratiano's careless prolixity, contrasting conspicuously as it does with the sombre reticence maintained by Antonio. Gratiano's vaunted loquacity, within a context or co-text of grave exposition, is deemed by his fellows both selfish (overriding their speaking rights) and vacuous, bereft of propositional (i.e. narrative) content sufficient to justify his exhibitionistic floor-holding:

Gra.                    Let me play the fool ...
         O my Antonio, I do know of these
         That therefore only are reputed wise
         For saying nothing; when I am very sure
         If they should speak, would almost damn those ears
         Which (hearing them) would call their brothers fools, –
         I'll tell thee more of this another time. ...
         I'll end my exhortation after dinner.
Lor.     Well, we will leave you then till dinner-time.
         I must be one of these same dumb wise men,
         For Gratiano never lets me speak.
Gra.     Well keep me company but two years more
         Thou shalt not know the sound of thine own tongue.

| | |
|---|---|
| *Ant.* | Fare you well, I'll grow a talker for this gear. |
| *Gra.* | Thanks i'faith, for silence is only commendable |
| | In a neat's tongue dried, and a maid not vendible. |

*(Exeunt Gratiano and Lorenzo)*

| | |
|---|---|
| *Ant.* | It is that anything now. |
| *Bass.* | Gratiano speaks an infinite deal of nothing (more than any man in Venice), his reasons are as two grains of wheat hid in two bushels of chaff: you shall seek all day ere you find them, and when you have them, they are not worth the search. (1. 1. 79–118) |

There is, perhaps, a certain irony in so much talk about too much talk. And Gratiano's verbal indecorum might also be viewed more positively, as a mode of generous excess quite alien to the calculating and puritanical linguistic commercialism upheld by Shylock, who, indeed, morally upbraids the Venetian in the court scene, not so much for his insults as for his irresponsible wasting of breath:

| | |
|---|---|
| *Shy.* | Till thou canst rail the seal from off my bond |
| | Thou but offend'st thy lungs to speak so loud: |
| | Repair thy wit good youth, or it will fall |
| | To cureless ruin. (4. 1. 139–42) |

But in the main it is self-limitation that prevails in Venice and Belmont, as the play's unusual richness in 'size' markers would suggest. Salerio, for example, is prompted to check the undue long-windedness with which Solanio – his fellow and near-homonymous standard-bearer for the cause of Exposition within the comedy – struggles, despite his (rather loquacious) denial, to get out the bad but simple news of Antonio's losses:

| | |
|---|---|
| *Sol.* | Now what news on the Rialto? |
| *Sal.* | Why yet it lives there uncheck'd, that Antonio hath a ship of rich lading wrack'd on the narrow seas . . . |
| *Sol.* | I would she were as lying a gossip in that, as ever knapp'd ginger . . . but it is true, without any slips of prolixity, or crossing the plain highway of talk, that the good Antonio, the honest Antonio; – O that I had a title good enough to keep his name company! – |
| *Sal.* | Come, the full stop. |
| *Sol.* | Ha! what sayest thou? – why the end is, he hath lost a ship. (3. 1. 1–17) |

And Portia hastens to justify her lengthy declaration of love for Bassanio (scarcely a case of untoward conversational egocentrism) by presenting it as a strategic spinning-out of discourse and time in order to delay the fatal choosing of the casket:

| | |
|---|---|
| *Por.* | I speak too long, but 'tis to peise the time, |
| | To eche it, and to draw it out in length, |
| | To stay you from election. (3. 2. 22ff.) |

All of this anxiety over the expenditure of words and of speaking time is
duly parodied by the play's licensed breath-waster, Launcelot Gobbo, in
the mystifying nonsense he produces for his father, prefaced by the
routine 'brevity' tag:

*Laun.*     To be brief, the very truth is, that the Jew having done me wrong,
            doth cause me as my father (being I hope an old man) shall frutify
            unto you. (2. 2. 125ff.)

Burlesque size signals of this kind, not surprisingly, are the only species
in evidence in *MWW*, a play hardly dominated by the puritanical value
of breath-saving. Calls for succinctness are either ludicrously over-
extended in themselves:

*Host.*     Speak, breathe, discuss; brief, short, quick, snap (4. 5. 2.);

or dismissed with disdain (particularly by Falstaff, the incarnation of
discursive excess):

*Evans.*    *Pauca verba;* Sir John, good worts.
*Fal.*      Good worts? Good cabbage. (1. 1. 112ff.)


### (5) You are i' the wrong

'Repair mechanisms exist for dealing with turn-taking errors and
violations' (Sacks *et al.*, rule 14: see p. 188 above). The ethical and
practical consequences of things going wrong are highly variable.
Interruptions, misunderstandings and inappropriate contributions in
familiar talk between friends may be patched up unceremonially or
even ignored. But in more formal circumstances, when the social points
to be won or lost are high, the perils of mistiming and misjudgment may
be as great and as grave in talk as they are on stage (missed cues,
mistimed entrances and exits, obvious anticipations, etc.).

   The species of transgression that gives rise in the plays to most
trouble – and to consequent repairs and reprimands – is precisely a
misapprehension of the social terms of the exchange: the taking or
mistaking of what is, from the interlocutor's viewpoint, serious and
decorous intercourse for a familiar free-for-all. These are the terms in
which Antipholus of Syracuse views his servant's otherwise inexplicable
utterances in *CE* (referential opaqueness is interpreted as pragmatic
misjudgment):

*Syr. Ant.*  I am not in a sportive humour now (1. 2. 58)

             Come Dromio, come, these jests are out of season,
             Reserve them till a merrier hour than this (1. 2. 68f.);

and the same terms provide the frame within which Lucio's persistent infringement of formal turn constraints is judged by Duke Vincentio in the last scene of *MM* (Lucio defies the speak-when-spoken-to rule in force in the presence of the Duke, applying instead the free-speech principle he adapts to all circumstances):

| | |
|---|---|
| Isab. | one Lucio |
| | As then the messenger. |
| Lucio. | That's I, and't like your Grace . . . |
| Duke. | (*to Lucio*) You were not bid to speak. |
| Lucio. | No, my good lord, |
| | Nor wish'd to hold my peace. |
| Duke. | I wish you now, then; |
| | Pray take note of it; |
| | And when you have a business for yourself, |
| | Pray heaven you then be perfect. |
| Lucio. | I warrant your honour. |
| Duke. | The warrant's for yourself: take heed to't. |
| Isab. | This gentleman told somewhat of my tale. |
| Lucio. | Right. |
| Duke. | It may be right, but you are i' the wrong |
| | To speak before your time. (5. 1. 74–89) |

### (6) Ha! ha! what sayest thou?

Not all troubles in talk are suffered by speakers. The act of listening carries not only its responsibilities but also its hazards, first among which is the failure to receive or decode the semantic or referential content of the message. Non-fictional listeners are frequently forced to make uncomfortable resort to what Goffman baptizes as 'rerun signals', verbal or paralinguistic requests for a (preferably clearer) replay of a turn. 'He who sends such a signal', as Goffman comments, 'can be demonstrating that he is, in fact, oriented to the talk, but that he has not grasped the semantic meanings the speaker attempted to convey. He thus addresses himself to the *process* of communication, not to *what* was communicated – for, after all, he professes not to have understood that' (1975: 15).

Rerun requests often mark in the comedies the *distance* that arises between speakers and listeners due to a lack of shared knowledge, particularly as a result of the vicissitudes of plot. Where keep-going boosters tend to dramatize the speaker's 'production' difficulties, these signals emphasize the toils of reception, the hearer's apprehension at his misapprehension. In *CE*, inevitably, they appear after every dark reference to recent (and unshared) events ('What mean you, sir?'; 'What answer, sir?'; 'What means this jest?', etc.), just as in *TN* similar bemusement is expressed by Olivia at Malvolio's cryptic quotations from the love-letter ('Why, how dost thou, man? What is the matter with thee?'; 'What mean'st thou by that, Malvolio?'; 'What say'st thou?', etc.).

Alternatively, the need for a replay may be an index to genuine *incapacity*, linguistic or intellectual, on the part of the listener. Armado's inability to perceive his page's obliquely encoded meanings, for example, is betrayed in precisely this fashion ('How meanest thou?'; 'Ha? ha? what sayest thou?'; 'The meaning, pretty ingenious?'), as is Dr Caius's precarious hold on English lexis:

| | |
|---|---|
| Host. | A word, Monseur Mockwater. |
| Caius. | Mock-water? Vat is dat? |
| Host. | Mock-vater, in our English tongue, is valour, bully. (2. 3. 53ff.) |
| Host. | He will clapper-claw thee tightly, bully. |
| Caius. | Clapper-de-claw? Vat is dat? |
| Host. | That is, he will make thee amends. (2. 3. 61ff.) |

This simple request-gloss pattern becomes a form of mutual violence in the finale of *TS*, where the very business of clarifying meaning is offered and received as an act of aggression:

| | |
|---|---|
| Widow. | He that is giddy thinks the world turns round. . . . |
| Kath. | 'He that is giddy thinks the world turns round' – |
| | I pray you tell me what you meant by that. |
| Widow. | Your husband, being troubled with a shrew, |
| | Measures my husband's sorrow by his woe. |
| | And now you know my meaning. |
| Kath. | A very mean meaning. |
| Widow. | Right, I mean you. |
| Kath. | And I am mean, indeed, respecting you. (5. 2. 20–32) |

### (7) Shall I have audience?

The 'speaker self-selects' strategy is canonical in the drama inasmuch as whoever holds or takes the floor is assumed, by the audience, to have the *right* to it, unless indications (repair signals, etc.) are given to the contrary. Explicit turn claims of the 'let me speak' or 'lend me your ears' varieties, superfluous in fact, may serve within the conversational fiction to introduce significant and substantial contributions, particularly if they come from relatively insignificant and insubstantial speakers: the 'Good madam, hear me speak' which precedes Fabian's confession of his and his fellows' misdeed in *TN* (5. 1. 354ff.), for example, or the 'Signior Bassanio, hear me' with which Gratiano prefaces his promise to reform his behaviour in *MV* (2. 2. 180ff.).

But the request to get a word in, edgewise or otherwise, appears more frequently as another pointer to the pains of audition, and more specifically to the frustration of enforced silence: Fenton's abortive efforts to obtain a hearing from Page in *MWW* ('Sir, will you hear me?/No, good Master Fenton', 3. 4. 72); or Katherina's desperate endeavour to break Petruchio's monologic monopoly in *TS* ('Why, sir, I trust I may have leave to speak,/And speak I will. I am no child, no babe./Your betters have endur'd me say my mind', 4. 3. 73–5); or Holofernes's emphatic demand for performing rights in the midst of his rhetorical rivals ('Shall I have audience?', *LLL* 5. 1. 125).

### (8) Battles

Holofernes's call for an audience is matched a few lines later by a counter-request from Armado ('Shall I tell you a thing?'), and indeed the entire encounter between the pedants unfolds in this fashion as a struggle for dominion, characterized by interruptions ('*Hol.* . . . the page, Hercules –/*Arm.* Pardon, sir, error') and exhibitionistic up-stagings. 'Battles for the floor are a normal and significant part of conversation, and . . . we speakers possess some very specific verbal weaponry with which we wage such battles,' affirms Mary Louise Pratt (1977: 101), somewhat hyperbolically perhaps, but the statement is true at least of speaking situations (heated discussions, contests between raconteurs, and so on) where the locutionary floor is especially highly prized.

Sustained fights over turns are correspondingly limited, within the comic canon, to those plays in which the opportunity to hold forth is seen to promise power or glory: in *TS*, for instance, most obviously in the Petruchio–Katherina competitions but also in the squabbles over the right to address Bianca:

| | |
|---|---|
| *Luc.* | Fiddler, forbear. You grow too forward, sir . . . |
| *Hor.* | But, wrangling pedant . . . |
| | Then give me leave to have prerogative, . . . |
| *Luc.* | Preposterous ass . . . |
| | Then give me leave to read philosophy, |
| | And while I pause, serve in your harmony. |
| *Hor.* | Sirrah, I will not bear these braves of thine (3. 1. 1.ff.); |

and above all in *LLL*, in which the privilege of partaking actively of the great feast of languages has to be arduously earned, given the general voraciousness of appetite. The dispute over the right to narrate the banal breaking of Costard's costard is a representative instance:

| | |
|---|---|
| *Arm.* | But tell me; how was there a costard broken in a shin? |
| *Moth.* | I will tell you sensibly. |

*Cost.*      Thou hast no feeling of it, Moth: I will speak that l'envoy.
             I, Costard . . . (3. 1. 112ff.)

In the play's metatheatrical finale, such competitiveness over speaking space becomes a more literal striving to 'have audience', a conflict as to who is 'on', waged between official performers and uncooperative auditors (see also p. 45 above).

*Arm.*      The armipotent Mars, of lances the almighty,
             Gave Hector a gift, –
*Dum.*    A gilt nutmeg.
*Ber.*     A lemon.
*Long.*    Stuck with cloves.
*Dum.*    No, cloven.
*Arm.*     Peace!
             The armipotent Mars, of lances the almighty,
             Gave Hector a gift, the heir of Ilion;
             A man so breath'd . . .
             I am that flower, –
*Dum.*                 That mint.
*Long.*                   That columbine.
*Arm.*     Sweet Lord Longaville, rein thy tongue.
*Long.*    I must rather give it rein, for it runs against Hector.
*Arm.*     The sweet war-man is dead and rotten; sweet chucks, beat not the bones of the buried; . . . But I will forward with my device. Sweet royalty, bestow on me the sense of hearing.
*Prin.*     Speak, brave Hector; we are much delighted. (5. 2. 637ff.)

Here the relationship between theatrical and talking turns ceases to be a limited analogy and becomes instead direct: as Hector's painful defeat suggests, the floor, whether conversational or stage, needs always to be strategically conquered.


(IV) 'LAWFUL MEANING IN A LAWFUL ACT':
ILLOCUTIONARY FORCES AND INTERLOCUTORY
FARCES

If the mechanics of natural talk are founded on alternation, its actual *motor*-force derives from a somewhat different 'pragmatic' source, namely the alternated utterances themselves as interpersonal events. The drama – Shakespearean in particular – has come to represent an attractive, if somewhat eccentric, zone of application for the theory and analysis of such linguistic events or speech acts, despite J. L. Austin's passing comment, in formulating his original notion of 'performative', on the institutional emptiness of speech acts performed on stage: 'performative utterance will . . . be *in a peculiar way* hollow if said by an actor on the stage' (1962: 22). Austin's concern, of course, is with the particular non-practical (or 'unserious') status of dramatic discourse, which never entails the personal intentions and responsibilities of the material speakers on stage: '[the actors], as opposed to the fictional characters they portray', as R. M. Gale has put the matter, 'do not command, question and assert by their use of imperatival, interrogative and declarative sentences respectively. E.g. they, as opposed to the characters they portray, cannot be charged with having asserted something false, having issued an unwise command, etc., for they only pretend to assert and command these things' (1971: 337). In Austin's terms, the actors merely perform the locutionary (phonetic-syntactic) act 'of saying something', i.e. the act of uttering the words of their speeches; it is to the *dramatis personae*, instead, that the full illocutionary act performed 'in saying something' – the act, e.g. of commanding or advising or requesting – is attributed.

Within the bounds of the dramatic fiction – as opposed to the theatrical representation – speech acts retain their integral and 'serious' status. And indeed, one of the characteristics of much dramatic dialogue, compared with other forms of conversational or literary discourse, is, as a series of commentators after Austin have observed, a marked heightening of the illocutionary intensity or purity of the utterances, due to the intimate bond between verbal and narrative action: 'Illocutions', says Richard Ohmann, 'are the vehicle of the play's action . . .; conflict is enacted, not in an idealized clash of positions or beliefs, whatever that would be. Illocutionary acts move the play along' (1973: 87); a claim confirmed in 'performative' terms by Alessandro Serpieri: 'since all utterances in the theatre, apart from performative utterances in the strict sense, are of a *non*-constative kind, the drama as a whole is performative' (1978a: 25; for similar positions see Chambers 1980; Savona 1980; Short 1981). Thus from Austin's cursory remarking of the *non*-performative nature of the dramatic utterance, we have arrived, on altogether different grounds, at the assertion of its *absolute* performativity. And the fullest embodiment of such illocutionary or performative purity would appear to be Shakespearean tragedy: Ohmann cites *Hamlet* and Serpieri *Macbeth* as exemplary instances.

When applied to Shakespearean comedy, instead, this notion of illocutionary or performative intensity is qualified by the very rhetorical multiformity of the verbal activities on show (see Introduction, pp. 8–12), whereby the speech act or sequence of acts ceases to be uniformly and automatically the principal linguistic currency. In the comedies, the illocution, like other genres of language-game, achieves prominence when it comes to fulfil the major strategic and thematic functions of a given scene or exchange, and any investigation into the pragmatic aspects of discourse in these plays will have to determine where and by what means the foregrounding of the speech act comes about.

One measure both of the types of speech act performed and of their relative dramatic and thematic weight within a text is the presence of those lexical illocutionary indicators baptized by Austin as 'performative verbs', i.e. 'those verbs which make explicit . . . the illocutionary force of an utterance, or what illocutionary act it is that we are performing in issuing that utterance' (1962: 149). The canonical form of these verbs is the first person singular present indicative active ('I state/order/promise', etc.). Austin constructs on this basis a preliminary typology of illocutionary forces or acts, a typology deemed unsatisfactory, and so revised, by a number of later theorists, notably John Searle (1975b), who, like Austin, distinguishes five classes of act according to their purpose or the kind of commitment they entail: *representatives*, acts which commit the speaker in varying degrees to the truth of the proposition expressed ('I affirm/state/assert/swear/ suggest (that x)'); *directives*, attempts to induce the listener to do something ('I command/order/ask/request/implore/beg/invite/ permit (you to do x)'); *commissives*, which 'commit the speaker to a certain course of action' (Austin 1962: 157) ('I promise/undertake/vow/ give my word/guarantee (to do x)'); *expressives*, whose purpose is to express the specified psychological state of the speaker, especially with regard to the listener ('I thank/congratulate/apologize to/offer my condolences to/welcome (you)'), and *declarations*, acts whose successful execution brings about the state of affairs proposed by the utterance ('I resign,' 'I sentence (you to x)', 'I name (this ship y)', I declare (this meeting open)').

If one applies Austin's 'simple test' of 'going through the dictionary (a concise one should do) in a liberal spirit' (1962: 150), but substituting or supplementing the dictionary with a Shakespeare concordance (the Harvard one should do), one is able to chart the range and frequency of performative verbs in the comic canon, thereby providing a preliminary map of the dominant types of act and of the relative illocutionary intensity of single plays ('say', 'speak' and other *locutionary* indicators are, of course, excluded). The first and perhaps most striking datum that emerges is that by far the most recurrent type of illocution performed (or at least lexicalized) in the comedies, and with a particularly high rate of frequency in comparison with the rest of the canon, is the 'transitive' class of the directive. In first position one finds 'bid' (with 109 occurrences out of 353), followed by 'beseech' (61 out of 230) and 'ask'

(61 out of 179), then 'entreat' (44 out of 120), 'command' (42 out of 183), 'beg' (26 out of 103), 'plead' (19 out of 50) and 'demand' (18 out of 62). Of the other classes, the representative is conspicuously represented only by 'confess' (55 out of 129) and 'deny' (52 out of 137), the commissive by 'promise' (verb and substantive: 43 out of 108) and 'vow' (likewise verb and substantive: 27 out of 89), and the expressive by 'scorn' (40 out of 109) and 'protest' (26 out of 56). Declarations are rare, the most frequent being 'sentence' (17 out of 42, but all in substantive form).

The prevalence of the directive, especially in the form of the urgent request or entreaty ('bid', 'beseech', 'ask', 'entreat', 'plead', etc.), plainly reflects the narrative pattern and configuration of roles (or in A. J. Greimas's terms (1966, 1970), the *actantial* scheme) that characterize *fabula* and plot in many of the comedies, whereby a leading character or group of characters (Egeon, Navarre and his followers, the rejected lovers in *MND*, Katherina, Isabella, Bassanio and friends, etc.) is forced by the vicissitudes of plot into a position of supplication towards whichever figure, be he antagonist or object of devotion, temporarily or permanently wields the power (thus the Duke of Ephesus, the Princess of France and her followers, the rejecting lovers, Petruchio, Angelo and Shylock respectively).

For similar reasons – namely the strict relationship between illocutionary and narrative patterns – the plays which, according to this adapted version of Austin's performative verb test, manifest the greatest and most consistent degree of illocutionary density are the later and 'darker' comedies, *MA*, *MV*, *AWW* and *MM*: those comedies, in other words, that are governed by powerful and intricate plot mechanisms founded on interpersonal and ethical strife. And it is particularly in the climactic scenes of moral confrontation and resolution that illocutionary force and narrative and thematic structure come to coincide through the insistent lexical labelling of the speech acts being, about to be or recently performed. In the case of *MV*, for example – a comedy explicitly marked by the ethical and practical implications of word-giving ('oath' occurs twelve times, 'promise' seven, etc.) and by the dialectic of offer or supplication and resistance thereto ('offer' appears ten times, 'bid' eighteen, 'beg' eight, 'beseech' seven, 'entreat' five and 'deny' thirteen) – the great 'performative' climax arises in the decisive encounter between Shylock and his debtors in the trial of 4. 1. The court hearing unfolds in three phases, with corresponding shifts in discursive emphasis. In the first phase, prior to the arrival of Portia, attention is insistently drawn to the dynamic of request and refusal between the Christians and Shylock:

Duke.    We all expect *a gentle answer*, Jew!

| | |
|---|---|
| *Shy.* | *I have possess'd* your grace of what I purpose, |
| | And by our holy Sabbath *have I sworn* |
| | To have the due and forfeit of my bond, – |
| | If *you deny* it, let the danger light |
| | Upon your charter and your city's freedom! |
| | *You'll ask me* why I rather choose to have |
| | A weight of carrion flesh, than to receive |
| | Three thousand ducats: *I'll not answer* that! |
| | But say it is my humour, – *is it answer'd?* |
| | . . . what, *are you answer'd* yet? |
| | . . . now for *your answer:* |
| | . . . *are you answered?* |
| *Bass.* | This is *no answer* thou unfeeling man, |
| | *To excuse* the current of thy cruelty. |
| *Shy.* | I am not bound to please thee with *my answers!* . . . |
| *Ant.* | *I pray you think you question* with the Jew, – |
| | You may as well go stand upon the beach |
| | And *bid* the main flood bate his usual height, |
| | You may as well *use question* with the wolf, |
| | Why he hath made the the ewe bleat for the lamb: |
| | You may as well *forbid* the mountain pines |
| | To wag their high tops, and to make no noise . . . |
| | Therefore (*I do beseech you*) |
| | *Make no more offers*, use no farther means . . . |
| *Shy.* | . . . *shall I say* to you, |
| | Let them be free . . . |
| | *you will answer* |
| | 'The slaves are ours' – so *do I answer* you: |
| | The pound of flesh which *I demand* of him |
| | Is dearly bought, 'tis mine and I will have it: |
| | If *you deny* me, fie upon your law! |
| | There is no force in *the decrees* of Venice: |
| | I stand for judgment, – *answer*, shall I have it? (4. 1. 34–103) |

(Italics in the extracts in this section are mine.) Shylock's obduracy here, marked by his scornful toying with different versions of the same performative verb phrase ('is it answer'd?', etc.), brings about an effective reversal of illocutionary roles: the passage begins with the Duke's demand for an answer from Shylock and concludes with Shylock's demand for an answer from the Duke. This reversal is in turn emblematic of the apparent ideological force of each directive: the first a seemingly powerless invitation to exercise Christian charity, the second a seemingly irresistible demand for literal justice. The impossibility of an authentic exchange between these two positions is suggested by the singular fact that, despite the notable density of illocutionary markers in the passage (indicated by the italics), only one of the many performative verb phrases – Shylock's 'I demand of him' –

actually refers to a direct speech act being simultaneously performed; the others all have to do with past ('I have possess'd'; 'have I sworn') or with hypothetical ('If you deny it'; 'You'll ask me'; 'You may as well . . . bid . . . use question . . . forbid'; 'shall I say'; 'you will answer'; 'If you deny') or with refused illocutions ('I'll not answer'; 'no answer'). And particularly significant in this respect are the meta-illocutions, or better, anti-directives (pleas not to plea) issued by Antony – '(I do beseech you)/Make no more offers' and the strange 'I pray you think you [or according to Keightley's plausible emendation, 'I pray you stint your'] question with the Jew' – since they render explicit the perlocutionary impotence of the Christians' would-be persuasion (on perlocutions, see section (v) of this chapter).

The scene's second interactional phase (lines 104–66) is concerned primarily with affirming the absolute performative power invested in the Venetian court. The Duke, by way of a counter to Shylock's uncomfortable demand (line 103 above), asserts the decisive executive or 'declarative' authority of his pronouncements – including that of adjourning the proceedings – and his delegation of this authority to the appointed judge:

Duke.    Upon my power *I may dismiss* this court,
         Unless Bellario (a learned doctor,
         Whom I have sent for *to determine* this)
         Comes here today.

The Duke's move serves as a signal for the entry of Nerissa, bearing a letter from the same nominated judge ('*Ner.* Bellario *greets* your grace'), who – after a parenthesis confirming Shylock's imperviousness to supplication ('*Gra.* . . . can no prayers pierce thee? *Shy.* No, none that thou hast wit enough to make') – delegates in turn the power of sentence to Portia:

Duke.    This letter from Bellario *doth commend*
         A young and learned doctor to our court: . . .
         (*Reads*). . . he is furnished with my opinion, which (better'd with his
         own learning, the greatness whereof *I cannot enough commend*),
         comes with him at my importunity, to fill up *your grace's request*
         in my stead. *I beseech you* let his lack of years be no impediment . . .
         I leave him to *your gracious acceptance*, whose trial shall better
         publish *his commendation*

a power which is immediately and unceremoniously granted to Portia on her entry:

Duke.    You are welcome, take your place.

The initial stage of the trial proper (lines 169–300) confirms and amplifies the scene's opening pattern, with Shylock in the ascendant.

Her deliberative authority having been established, Portia proceeds to
reflect on the legitimacy and efficacy of Shylock's bond and on the
sentence she in turn is bound to make in its regard:

| | |
|---|---|
| *Por.* | Of a strange nature is the suit you follow |
| | Yet in such rule, that the Venetian law |
| | *Cannot impugn* you as you *proceed* . . . |
| | Do you *confess* the bond? |
| *Ant.* | I do. . . . |
| *Por.* | . . . if thou follow, this strict court of Venice |
| | Must needs *give sentence* 'gainst the merchant there. |
| *Bass.* | . . . And *I beseech* you |
| | Wrest once the law to your authority, – |
| | To do a great right, do a little wrong, – |
| | And curb this cruel devil of his will. |
| *Por.* | It must not be, there is no power in Venice |
| | Can alter a decree established. |

At this, Shylock, finding himself in so favourable a position, consoli-
dates it by assuming decisively his legitimate role as protagonist not
only of the legal but of the verbal action. With a further hyperbolical
dramatization of his intransigency towards all acts of persuasion –

| | |
|---|---|
| *Por.* | . . . be merciful, |
| | Take thrice thy money, *bid me* tear the bond. |
| *Shy.* | When it is paid, according to the tenour. |
| | . . . by my soul I swear, |
| | There is no power in the tongue of man |
| | To alter me, – I stay here on my bond – |

he redoubles the already more than explicit 'directive' force of the bond
itself in his insistent call for immediate sentence (being supported in
this direction by the self-immolating Antonio):

| | |
|---|---|
| *Shy.* | *I charge you* by the law |
| | Whereof you are a well-deserving pillar, |
| | *Proceed to judgment*: . . . |
| *Ant.* | Most heartily *I do beseech* the court |
| | *To give the judgment.* |

And after an ironical little 'doubling' episode in which Portia and
Nerissa (as opposed to judge and clerk) appear as speakers or receivers of
a series of 'possible' speech acts –

| | |
|---|---|
| *Ant.* | (*To Bass.*) *Commend me* to your honourable wife, |
| | *Tell her* the process of Antonio's end, |
| | *Say how* I lov'd you, *speak me fair* in death: |
| | And when the tale is told, *bid her* be judge |
| | Whether Bassanio had not once a love: . . . |
| *Bass.* | Antonio, I am married to a wife |
| | Which is as dear to me as life itself, |

> But life itself, my wife, and all the world,
> Are not with me esteem'd above thy life. . . .

Por.    Your wife would give you little thanks for that
> If she were by to hear you *make the offer.*

Gra.    I have a wife whom, *I protest,* I love, –
> I wish she were in heaven, so she *could*
> *Entreat* some power to change this currish Jew.

Ner.    'Tis well *you offer* it behind her back,
> *The wish* would make else an unquiet house. –

Portia brings the exchange to a first and false climax with her provocatively figural (chiastic) sentence in Shylock's favour (on chiasmus, see pp. 253–7 below):

Shy.    We trifle time, *I pray thee pursue sentence.*
Por.    A pound of that same merchant's flesh is thine,
> *The court awards it,* and *the law doth give it.*
Shy.    Most rightful judge!
Por.    And you must cut this flesh from off his breast,
> *The law allows it,* and *the court awards it.*
Shy.    Most learned judge! *a sentence,* come prepare.

The rest of the hearing (301–96) enacts a vertiginous withdrawal from this seemingly definitive endorsement of Shylock's claim, so much so that within a mere fourteen lines he is forced by Portia's legalistic punctiliousness into accepting the Christians' proposal:

Shy.    I take *this offer* then – pay the bond thrice
> And let the Christian go. . . .
> Why then let the devil give him good of it:
> I'll stay no longer *question*

and thereafter into the position of receiver of – if not direct supplicator for – the Duke's grace:

Por.    Down therefore, and *beg mercy* of the duke.
Gra.    *Beg* that thou may'st have leave to hang thyself . . .
Duke.    That thou shalt see the difference of our spirit
> *I pardon thee thy life* before thou *ask it:* . . .
Shy.    Nay, take my life and all; *pardon not* that, – . . .
Duke.    He shall do this, or else *I do recant*
> *The pardon* that *I* late *pronounced* here.
Por.    Art thou contented Jew? what dost thou say?
Shy.    I am content. . . .
> *I pray you* give me leave to go from hence,
> I am not well.

The scene ends with an extra-tribunal postscript or post-act (397–453) that can be seen as a lighter-toned, but for all that pungent, variation on the supplication-refusal-reversal movement of the court exchange

proper. Like the hearing itself, it begins with a directive from the Duke
(an invitation to Portia) again declined:

Duke. Sir, *I entreat you* home with me to dinner.
Por. *I humbly do desire* your grace of *pardon*,
   I must away.

Bassanio, again as in the trial, intervenes with a bold offer, which is at
first politely refused but then accepted in embarrassingly modified form
and immediately reneged:

Bass. Three thousand ducats due unto the Jew
   We freely cope your courteous pains withal.
Por. ... He is well paid that is well satisfied ...
Bass. Dear sir, of force *I must attempt you* further,
   Take some remembrance of us as a tribute,
   Not as a fee: *grant me* two things *I pray you,* –
   *Not to deny me*, and *to pardon me.*
Por. You press me far, and therefore I will yield, –
   Give me your gloves, I'll wear them for your sake,
   And (for your love) I'll take this ring from you, –
   Do not draw back your hand, I'll take no more,
   And *you* in love *shall not deny me* this! ...
Bass. There's more depends on this than on the value, –
   The dearest ring in Venice will I give you,
   And find it out by proclamation,
   Only for this *I pray you pardon me!*
Por. I see, sir, you are liberal in *offers,* –
   You taught me first *to beg,* and now methinks
   You teach me how a beggar *should be answer'd.*
Bass. Good sir, this ring was given me by my wife,
   And when she put it on, she *made me vow*
   That I should neither sell, nor give, nor lose it.
Por. *That scuse* serves many men to save their gifts.

In this way Bassanio's position is transformed from that of noble subject
of a fine-sounding offer to that of ignoble object of a humiliating
accusation, and he is morally bound ('*Ant.* Let his deservings and my
love withal/Be valu'd gainst your wife's *commandment*') to accept
Portia's acceptance. And in this episode as well, of course, the logic at
work is that of locutionary 'doubling', since the conflicting speech acts
that give rise to Bassanio's moral dilemma – his wife's 'commandment'
and the judge's act of acceptance – come in fact from a single (if doubled)
speaker. And what is uttered obviously takes on added 'action' force
from the institutional nature of the proceedings (the ducal hearing;
compare the finale of *MM*). But the special lexical and structural
prominence of speech acts in this scene is likewise due, as we have seen,
to their strategically indirect and tortuous performance: the continual

postponing, suspending and protracting of illocutions bring into question their very definition, thus lending critical weight to the labelling (accurate or otherwise) of what is going on.

In the same play and elsewhere, these twin factors, protracted or interrupted performance and the labours of definition, are also responsible for some of the more grotesquely farcical moments in those comic scenes which reflect in burlesque form the patterns and issues of the main verbal action. Thus the dominant type of act in *MV*, the directive, reappears (and in its two preferred forms, the supplication and the invitation or 'bidding') as a source of humorous business in the Launcelot Gobbo episodes. The progress of the Christians' appeals to Shylock – broken off and taken up again in the give and take of the hearing – is anticipated in the combined but hardly co-ordinated efforts of Old and Young Gobbo to persuade Bassanio (himself, of course, one of the pleading Christians) to employ young Launcelot; with the difference, of course, that the Gobbos, despite their prevarications and mutual interruptions, immediately succeed:

| | |
|---|---|
| *Laun.* | To him, father. |
| *Gob.* | God bless your worship. |
| *Bass.* | Gramercy, wouldst thou aught with me? |
| *Gob.* | Here's my son sir, a poor boy. |
| *Laun.* | Not a poor boy, sir, but the rich Jew's man that would sir as my father *shall specify.* |
| *Gob.* | He hath a great infection sir, (as one would say) to serve. |
| *Laun.* | Indeed the short and the long is, I serve the Jew, and have a desire as my father shall specify. . . . |
| *Gob.* | I have here a dish of doves that I would bestow upon your worship, and *my suit* is – |
| *Laun.* | In very brief, *the suit* is impertinent to myself, as your worship shall know by this honest old man, and though I say it, though old man, yet (poor man) my father. |
| *Bass.* | One speak for both, what would you? |
| *Laun.* | That is the very defect of the matter, sir. |
| *Bass.* | I know thee well, thou hast obtain'd *thy suit.* (2. 2. 113–37) |

And if the Christians' linguistic commerce with Shylock is recurrently underscored by the performative verb 'bid' (see above), it is the same verb that signals the trouble into which Launcelot's verbal doings lead him with the Jew:

| | |
|---|---|
| *Shy.* | Why Jessica I say! |
| *Laun.* | Why Jessica! |
| *Shy.* | Who *bids* thee call? I do not *bid* thee call. |
| *Laun.* | Your worship was wont to tell me, I could do nothing without *bidding.* |
| *Jes.* | Call you? what is your will? |

*Shy.* I am *bid* forth to supper Jessica. (2. 5. 6–11)

This jest bears more than a family resemblance to a piece of master–servant cross-talk in *TG*:

*Val.* Ah, Silvia, Silvia!
*Spe.* Madam Silvia! Madam Silvia!
*Val.* How now, sirrah?
*Spe.* She is not within hearing, sir.
*Val.* Why, sir, who *bade* you call her?
*Spe.* Your worship, sir, or else I mistook.
*Val.* Well, you'll still be too forward.
*Spe.* And yet I was last *chidden* for being too slow. (2. 1. 6–13)

As the exchange with Shylock continues, Launcelot, in bidding his ex-master to leave for the appointment with Bassanio, manages to transform this purely physical action ('approach') into a species of illocution, again with strong moral connotations – an error which Shylock picks up with a certain restraint:

*Laun.* I beseech you, sir, go, my young master doth expect your *reproach*.
*Shy.* So do I his.

This particular variety of linguistic incompetence, whereby illocutionary forces give rise to malapropistic farces, is shared by other clowns and fools in the later comedies, among them Sir Andrew Aguecheek in *TN*, who stumbles over an invitation from Sir Toby to address Maria:

*Sir And.* Bless you, fair shrew.
*Maria.* And you too, sir.
*Sir To.* *Accost*, Sir Andrew, *accost*.
*Sir And.* What's that?
*Sir To.* My niece's chambermaid.
*Sir And.* Good Mistress Accost, I desire better acquaintance.
*Maria.* My name is Mary, sir.
*Sir And.* Good Mistress Mary Accost –
*Sir To.* You mistake, knight. 'Accost' is front her, board her, woo her, assail her.
*Sir And.* By my troth, I would not undertake her in this company. Is that the meaning of 'accost'? (1. 3. 46–58);

and Constable Elbow in *MM*, who, in his efforts to provide before his betters a full-fledged and fine-sounding performative phrase ('I protest') succeeds instead in producing a piece of uxorial abuse:

*Elbow.* My wife, sir, whom I *detest* before heaven and your honour –
*Esc.* How? Thy wife?
*Elbow.* Ay, sir: whom I thank heaven is an honest woman –
*Esc.* Dost thou detest her therefore?
*Elbow.* I say, sir, I will detest myself also, as well as she. (2. 1. 68–72)

Like the verbal pratt-falls and *lazzi* of Launcelot Gobbo, the misnomers and misapprehensions created by Elbow are thematically close to the all too serious *querelles* engaged in by his social superiors. In a reversal of his own unwitting misogamy, for example, he interprets another reference to his wife, in itself complimentary enough, as an outrageous calumny, a misconstruction that parodies the pattern of slanderous accusation and report dominating the play's last scene:

Pom.   By this hand, sir, his wife is a more respected person than any of us all.
Elbow.  Varlet, thou liest! Thou liest, wicked varlet! ... Prove this, thou wicked Hannibal, or I'll have mine action of battery on thee.
Esc.    If he took you a box o' th' ear, you might have your action of slander too. (2. 1. 162–78)

Apart from his lexical agonies, Elbow's difficulties with the acts of others have to do with an essential aspect of the performance and reception of illocutions, baptized by Austin as 'uptake':

> Unless a certain effect is achieved, the illocutionary act will not have been happily, successfully performed. This is not to say that the illocutionary act is the achieving of a certain effect. I cannot be said to have warned an audience unless it hears what I say and takes what I say in a certain sense. ... Generally the effect amounts to bringing about the understanding of the meaning and of the force of the locution. So the performance of an illocutionary act involves the securing of *uptake*. (1962: 116–17)

A deal of Shakespearean foolery – of which the Elbow episode is an involuntary instance – derives from the *failure* to secure uptake or make the force of the speech act understood ('*Luc.* You understand me? / *Bion.* I, sir? Ne'er a whit', *TS* 1. 1. 234). The result is an abyss between the (more or less evident) illocutionary intentions of the speaker and the (more or less aberrant) decoding on the part of the listener. An extended exercise in playfully deliberate non-uptake is provided in *AYLI*, in Rosalind's dealings with the amorous Phebe. The shepherdess, fatally impressed by Rosalind–Ganymede's reprimands ('Sweet youth, I pray you *chide* a year together', 3. 5. 64), undertakes before her admirer Silvio to reply in kind ('I'll write to him a very *taunting* letter', 3. 5. 134), using Silvio himself as messenger. On reading the letter in Silvio's presence, Rosalind duly plays on the distance between this declared intent and the hyperbolically complimentary love poem that Phebe has actually addressed to her, pretending to interpret the Petrarchan eulogy as 'very taunting' vituperation. What she produces is an ironical version of Searle's 'indirect' speech act, in which 'the speaker may utter a sentence ... and also mean another illocution with a different propositional content'

(1975a: 59–60); compare Valentine in *TG*: 'For "get you gone" she does not mean "away!"' (3. 1. 101):

| Ros. | She Phebes me. Mark how the tyrant writes. |
| | *(Reads) Art thou god to shepherd turn'd* |
| | *That a maiden's heart hath burn'd?* |
| | Can a woman rail thus? |
| Sil. | Call you this railing? |
| Ros. | *(Reads) Why, thy godhead laid apart,* |
| | *Warr'st thou with a woman's heart?* |
| | Did you ever hear such railing? |
| | *Whiles the eye of man did woo me,* |
| | *That could do no vengeance to me.* |
| | Meaning me a beast. . . . |
| Sil. | Call you this chiding? (4. 3. 39–64) |

The effect is not so much illocutionary as dislocationary, a fracturing of that perfect specularity between intention and effect that is the necessary condition of successful or 'happy' communication: 'In the case of illocutionary acts we succeed in doing what we are trying to do by getting our audience to recognize what we are trying to do. . . . the speaker *S* intends to produce an illocutionary effect *IE* in the hearer *H* by means of getting *H* to recognize *S*'s intention to produce *IE*' (Searle 1969: 47). A more radical breach in this ideal intentional circularity is caused (and eventually healed) in *MND* by Puck's magic, which mixes relationships and crosses purposes amongst the protesting lovers, leaving the previously spurned Helena justifiably slow on the illocutionary uptake:

| Lys. | Content with Hermia? No. *I do repent* |
| | The tedious minutes I with her have spent. |
| | Not Hermia, but Helena I love. . . . |
| Hel. | Wherefore was I to this keen *mockery* born? |
| | When at your hands did I deserve this *scorn?* . . . |
| | But you must *flout* my insufficiency? |
| | Good troth, you do me wrong, good sooth, you do, |
| | In such disdainful manner me *to woo.* . . . |
| Lys. | Why should you think that I should *woo* in *scorn?* |
| | *Scorn* and *derision* never come in tears. |
| | Look when I *vow,* I weep; and *vows* so born, |
| | In their nativity all truth appears. . . . |
| Hel. | You do advance your cunning more and more. |
| | When truth kills truth, O devilish-holy fray! |
| | These *vows* are Hermia's: will you give her o'er? . . . |
| Lys. | I had no judgment when to her I *swore.* |
| Her. | Nor none, in my mind, now you give her o'er. |
| Lys. | Demetrius loves her, and he loves not you. |
| Dem. | *(Waking)* O Helen, goddess, nymph, perfect, divine! . . . |

*Hel.*    O spite! O hell! I see you all are bent
           To set against me for your merriment. (2. 2. 110ff.; 3. 2. 122ff.)

Getting our audience to recognize what we are trying to do presupposes that we ourselves are in perfect control of what we *are* doing, a condition that does not always correspond with the laws of comedy.

### (v) 'MY WORDS EXPRESS MY PURPOSE': INTENTION, EXPRESSION, 'ETHOS'

One of the points where contemporary speech-act theory coincides with Renaissance rhetorical models is in this very question of the intentionality of language, and more particularly in the declared faith in its perfect expressive adequacy with respect to the speaker's communicative intentions. John Searle's 'principle of expressibility', according to which 'whatever can be meant can be said', so that 'for any meaning X and any speaker S whenever S means (intends to convey, wishes to communicate in an utterance, etc.) X then it is possible that there is some expression E such that E is an exact expression of or formulation of X' (1969: 19–20), is close in its rationalistic optimism to what we might baptize as the 'principle of expressivity' espoused by sixteenth- and early seventeenth-century rhetoricians and moralists, such as Thomas Wilson: 'The tongue is ordained to expresse the mynde, that one might understand anothers meanynge' (1553: Aiiʳ) and William Camden: '*Locutio* is defined, *Animi sensus per vocem expressio*. On which ground I build these consequences, that the first and principall point sought in every language, is that we may expresse the meaning of our mindes aptly to each other' (1605: 34).

The peculiar bias of this principle of expressivity is often (doubly) mentalistic, the mind figuring both as point of origin and as point of arrival for the utterance: 'tongues were devised by men, that they might communicate amongst themselves, and expresse one to another their conceits' (Huarte 1594: 103–4); 'the uttering sweetly and properly the conceits of the minde . . . is the end of speech' (Sidney 1595: Liʳ). Such an emphasis undoubtedly reflects Cicero's insistence, in the *De oratore*, on the unity of *res* and *verba*, conceptual matter and discourse, and the correspondingly rational mould that his rhetorical machinery adopts. And a direct ideological corollary of this tenet is a Christianized version of Isocrates's defence of rhetoric, whose first article of faith is the affirmation of the *logos* as the foundation and instrument of human civilization, raising man above the unreasoning beasts: 'and to the end that this soveraign rule of reason, might spread abroade her bewtifull branches, and that wisdome might bring forth most plentifully her sweete and pleasaunt fruites, for the common use and utility of mankind, the lord God hath ioyned to the mind of man speech, which he hath made the instrument of our understanding, and key of conceptions, . . . and herein is it that we do so far passe and excell all other creatures, and not they, in that we have the gifte of speech and reason, and not they' (Peacham 1577: Aiiʳ).

There are broadly two ways in which the mind–verbal expression relationship is characterized by Renaissance commentators: as *indexical contiguity* or as *iconic identity*. The sober topographical analogy elaborated by William Cornwallis suggests a metonymic vicinity between mind and speech which, ideally at least, enriches the rational faculties themselves: 'I confesse speech is to the minde as convenient Havens to Townes, by whose currents they grow rich and mighty' (1601: 115). But a stronger claim is made for verbal expression by those humanist *letterati*, like Puttenham or Jonson, who depict the intellect–speech bond not as a form of adjacency but as a mode of reproduction. Language, in this conception, is nothing less than a simulacrum of the speaker's mental disposition: '[speech is] the image of man (*mentis character*) for man is but his minde, and as his minde is tempered and qualified, so are his speeches and language at large, and his manner of utterance the very warpe and woofe of his conceits' (Puttenham 1589: 124); 'It springs out of the most retired and inmost parts of us, and is the image of the present of it, the mind' (Jonson 1641: 46).

A similar identification of discourse with its mental source (or 'conceit') is the most recurrent aspect of a general faith in the expressive capacities of language in *LLL*. The austere intellectualism vaunted by the scholars ('The mind shall banquet, though the body pine') finds at first a complimentary echo in the ladies' admiration of their speech (and Berowne's in particular) as a resplendent 'key of conceptions':

Ros.      His eye begets occasion for his wit;
            For every object that the one doth catch
            The other turns to a mirth-moving jest,
            Which his fair tongue (conceit's expositor)
            Delivers in such apt and gracious words. (2. 1. 69ff.)

And the pedants, naturally, invest all their efforts in the elaboration of *verba* as a hopeful sign of intellectual *res*, or to cite Sidney's appropriately pedantic pun, *oratio* as an index of *ratio* ('it argues facility'; 'a good lustre of conceit', etc.). In this respect as in others, however, masculine glory is short-lived, and it is in the end the ladies' language that comes to be identified with the sharp minds which it shows forth:

*Boy.*      The tongues of mocking wenches are as keen
            As is the razor's edge invisible,
            Cutting a smaller hair than may be seen;
            Above the sense of sense; so sensible
            Seemeth their conference; their conceits have wings
            Fleeter than arrows, bullets, wind, thought, swifter things.

                                         (5. 2. 256ff.)

*Ber.*      Here stand I, lady; dart thy skill at me; . . .
            Cut me to pieces with thy keen conceit. (5. 2. 396–9)

There is an evident appeal – to would-be humanist scholars especially – in restricting the allegiances of discourse to the intellect, a restriction which generally figured as a strategic move in the defence of the dignity of speech and the speech arts. But the most sanguine version of the expressivity principle extends the representational or indeed reproductive capacities of language to the entire psychological and spiritual make-up of its user. Speech is no longer *mentis character*, sign of the mind, but *characteris mensio*, measure of personality as a whole. Thomas Wright's psychology of the passions, for example, is founded on just such an extended (and still iconic) conception of linguistic expression: 'wordes represent most exactly the very image of the minde and soule: wherefore *Democritus* called speech *eidwlon to Bion*, the image of life; for in woordes, as in a glass may be seene, a mans life and indications . . . Whereupon grew that old prouerbe, frequented of *Socrates*, and approued of antient Philosophers *loquere ut te videam*, speake that I may knowe thee' (1601: 162–3). In this more ambitious account of the speaker–speech bond the privileged organ is no longer, of course, the brain but the heart (alone or coupled with the soul), which finds in language a faithful delegate or duplicate: '[Speech] is the Image and Interpreter of the Soul; the Messenger of the Heart, the Door by which all that lies within comes out, & shews itself abroad' (Charron 1601: 117).

This cardiac metonymy for personal expression recurs in the comedies, appropriately enough, in the context of discourse on or of the passions, whether of the choleric kind that seizes Katherina in her frustration at having to keep quiet ('Thus you may coniecture by words, the passions of the mind, when the speech manifestly carieth the coate of . . . choller', Wright 1601: 164):

*Kath.*    My tongue will tell the anger of my heart,
          Or else my heart conceialing it will break,
          And rather than it shall, I will be free
          Even to the uttermost, as I please, in words (*TS* 4. 3. 77–80);

or, more commonly, of the romantic-erotic variety, expounded ingenuously, for example, by Proteus before his fall from innocence in *TG*:

Pro.  (*Aside*) Sweet love, sweet lines, sweet life!
      Here is her hand, the agent of her heart;
      Here is her oath for love, her honour's pawn (1. 3. 45ff.);

rather less ingenuously by Bertram in *AWW*:

King.                 You remember
      The daughter of this lord?
Ber.  Admiringly, my liege. At first
      I struck my choice upon her, ere my heart
      Durst make too bold a herald of my tongue (5. 3. 42–6);

and somewhat sarcastically in *MA* after Benedick's loss of the organ in question to Beatrice:

D. Pedro.  He hath twice or thrice cut Cupid's bowstring, and the little
           hangman dare not shoot at him. He hath a heart as sound as a bell,
           and his tongue is the clapper; for what his heart thinks his tongue
           speaks. (3. 2. 9–13)

Implicit in the 'heart's messenger' commonplace are powerful presuppositions of integrity and direction: sender and message are one because the messenger moves directly and without deviation from its source. The metaphor lends itself readily to moral prescription rather than 'scientific' description, and indeed it is omnipresent in those appeals for unswerving sincerity that were common to all moralists of the age, whether austerely Puritan like William Perkins: 'The tongue is the messenger of the heart, and therefore as oft as we speake without meditation going before, so oft the messenger runneth without his arrand . . . It is made a note of a righteous man, to speake the truth from the heart: they that deale truely are Gods delight' (1600: 440–1); philosophically erudite, like Primaudaye: 'A good man alwaies draweth good things out of the treasures of his hart . . . let all vaine speech be banished from us, and let us take great heed, that we never speake, either in sport or earnest, any word that is not true' (1586: 119, 128); or literarily humanistic, like Ben Jonson: 'a wise tongue should not be licentious and wandering, but moved, and, as it were, governed with certain reins from the heart and bottom of the breast' (1641: 27).

Of course, the call for heartfelt sincerity introduces at the same time the possibility of its opposite, namely of a breach in the heart–speech integrity. In this moral application of the metaphor, allegiance to the heart is not a necessary constituent of *all* utterances but rather a necessary condition for ethically sound (and hearty) speech. A somewhat analogous – although less rigidly prescriptive – principle is present in contemporary speech-act models, in the notion of the 'sincerity condition' that determines the performance of 'happy' acts: 'where, as often, the procedure [for happy acts] is designed for use by persons having certain thoughts, feelings, or intentions, . . . then a person participating in and so invoking the procedure must in fact have those thoughts, feelings, or intentions' (Austin 1962: 39).

Apologies for the sincerity constraint are commonplace in Shakespeare, but in two cases the appeal for heart-bound directness appears more than a passing literary topic. The Princess of France in *LLL* consistently advocates, and duly rewards, unflattering honesty, as in her treatment of the gauche forester:

> Here, good my glass, take this for telling true:
> Fair payment for foul words is more than due (4. 1. 18–19);

a gesture recalled in Theseus's generous reception of the 'simple' (i.e. sincere) Mechanicals and their artistic offering in *MND*:

> For never anything can be amiss
> When simpleness and duty tender it. (5. 1. 82–3)

When immediately afterwards, however, Theseus elaborates such praise of simplicity in a celebrated reflective *exemplum*, what he upholds is not so much heartfelt verbal expression as artless *non-expression*, opposing it to facile oratorical fluency:

> Where I have come, great clerks have purposed
> To greet me with premeditated welcomes;
> Where I have seen them shiver and look pale,
> Make periods in the midst of sentences,
> Throttle their practis'd accents in their fears,
> And, in conclusion, dumbly have broke off,
> Not paying me a welcome. Trust me, sweet,
> Out of this silence yet I pick'd a welcome,
> And in the modesty of fearful duty
> I read as much as from the rattling tongue
> Of saucy and audacious eloquence.
> Love, therefore, and tongue-tied simplicity
> In least speak most, to my capacity. (5. 1. 93–105)

Theseus's valorization of stammering ineloquence as an index of sincerity effectively reverses the ideological force of the expressivity principle as expounded by the rhetorical enthusiasts of the age, for whom eloquence represented an absolute moral and social, indeed quasi-religious, value: 'For he that is emonge the reasonable, of all the most reasonable, and emonge the wittye, of all moste wittye, and emonge the eloquente, of all mooste eloquente: him thincke I emonge all menne, not onelye to be taken for a singuler manne, but rather to be counted for halfe a God. For in sekynge the excellencye hereof, the soner he draweth to perfection, the nygher he commeth to GOD who is the chiefe wisedome' (Wilson 1553: Aiii^v). Wilson and other Renaissance rhetoricians happily endorse that optimistic equation of eloquential power with ethical integrity that has its most succinct expression in Cato's slogan *vir bonus dicendi peritus* ('a good man skilled in speaking'), and that is carried to its furthest extreme in Quintilian's *Institutio oratoria*, where moral righteousness actually becomes the chief requisite for rhetorical success: 'I do not merely assert that the ideal orator should be a good man, but I affirm that no man can be an orator unless he is a good man' (XII. i. 3; see Dixon 1971: 18). This claim is impatiently repudiated, in Shakespeare's day, not only by ferociously anti-rhetorical Puritans but also by the severer moralists like Montaigne, distrustful, with Theseus, of 'saucy and audacious eloquence', and still more so of the 'false' speech arts that elected it as their end: 'A Rhetorician of ancient times, said, that his trade was, to make small things appeare great . . . Had hee lived in Sparta, he had doubtlesse beene well whipped, for professing a false, a cozening and deceitfull arte. . . . It is an instrument devised, to busie, to manage, and to agitate a vulgar and disordered multitude' (1603: 165–6).

The dispute over the morality of eloquent speech and its cultivation is at least as old as Plato's *Gorgias*. But it is Aristotle's *Rhetoric* that best exemplifies the radical ethical ambiguity which characterizes the principle of expressivity encoded in the classical rhetorical tradition. Indeed, it is Aristotle who, in his attempt to refound rhetoric on scientific investigative principles, first proposes *ethos* (the moral character of the speaker) as a strictly rhetorical rather than extra- or pre-discursive factor. It is classified (I. ii. 3) as one of the three 'artificial' proofs, i.e. 'furnished by the speech' itself rather than by external ('inartificial') means. The orator's ethical status (including the degree of his moral commitment to what he says) is the single most influential factor in determining his rhetorical success: 'The orator persuades by moral character when his speech is delivered in such a manner as to render him worthy of confidence; for we feel confident in a greater degree more readily in persons of worth in regard to everything in general, but where there is certainty and there is no room for doubt, our confidence is absolute.' But this decisively weighty factor is itself a *product* of, rather than a determinant of, the oration: 'But this confidence must be due to the speech itself, not to any preconceived idea of the speaker's character' (I. ii. 4).

The founding move in the Aristotelian system is thus the election of heart and soul not as internal cause for external expressive effect but as one effect (among others) of rhetorical *heuresis* or invention. The ideological consequences of this are very extensive and are indeed perfectly explicit within the *Rhetoric* itself. The successful speaker will be capable of discovering or inventing any proof, and so of constructing the appropriate *ethos*, necessary to his cause, and it is the business of rhetorical science to facilitate his task: 'The orator should be able to prove opposites . . . Rhetoric and Dialectic alone of all the arts prove opposites' (I. i. 12). Moral character becomes not so much a question of authenticity as of authority or power (imposition, persuasion), and ethics itself, of which rhetoric is a product, is synonymous with the science of power, or politics: 'Thus it appears that Rhetoric is as it were an offshoot of Dialectic and of the science of Ethics, which may reasonably be called Politics' (I. ii. 4).

In a word, the sober Aristotelian account of the speaker–discourse relationship is at an extreme remove in substance and tone from the ardent moralism of Cicero and Quintilian. In the *Rhetoric*, it is true, the moral integrity of the orator is somewhat pallidly and perfunctorily recommended on account of its social desirability ('one ought not persuade people to do what is wrong', I. ii. 12), but as such it has nothing to do with that self that the audience perceives at the receiving end of the oration and still less with the actual efficacy of the speaker's rhetorical efforts. If the most conspicuous Renaissance heir to such an unsentimental political philosophy of speech and ethics is obviously Machiavelli, its influence is felt far more widely and indeed contributed considerably to the suspicion reserved by austerer moralists of the age towards human discourse and the art of rhetoric: an art which in this period aspired to combine Ciceronian eloquential piety with Aristotelian investigative objectivity.

And this vexed question has a more than marginal pertinence to the drama. *Ethos* reappears within the Aristotelian corpus as a key term in the *Poetics*, where it denotes the dramatic person and where it constitutes one of the six essential components of dramatic structure. In this context, as in the *Rhetoric*, character is represented as a factor constructed or inferred by the audience, which attributes personal and moral integrity to the fictional individuals on the basis of their acts (*praxis*) and verbal expression (*lexis*): 'by the "characters" [I mean] that in accordance with which we say that the persons who are acting have a defined moral character' (50a. 5–6). The character that appears to lie behind – but is instead the creation of – the speech, acts (or speech acts) of the stage speakers has much the same status as the product of the speech and acts of Aristotle's orator (who is, in this sense, a kind of actor-dramatist). The difference is, of course, that the dramatic *persona* is an explicit fiction (see the prologue to Richard Edward's *Damon and Pithias* (1564), which extends the fictional character-inferred-from-speech principle to (Elizabethan) comedy and its decorum:

> In comedies the greatest skill is this, rightly to touch
> All things to the quick and eke to frame each person so,
> That by his common talk you may his nature rightly know.
> (see Bradbrook 1955: 49).

Nor was the creation of the dramatic *ethos* without its own practical (ethical) consequences in Shakespeare's age. It was the very assumption of a false or fictional identity in speech and acts (or in Edward Dering's words, the use of 'fluant terms, and imbossed words to varnish out their lies and fables', quoted in Fraser 1970: 4) that condemned Elizabethan actors to eternal damnation in the eyes of the simpler puritanical souls of the day (the same souls, naturally, that held the arts of speech in such odium). Jonas Barish rehearses the accusation succinctly: 'Players are evil because they try to substitute a self of their own contriving for the one given them by God' (1966: 333; the charge is parodied by Berowne: '*Cost.* I Pompey am – *Ber.* You lie, you are not he'). One of the earliest of the Elizabethan anti-theatrical pamphlets, the *Second and Third Blast of Retreat* by sometime playwright Anthony Munday (1586), places in direct opposition the heartfelt language of the sermon with the impious and dishonest (but evidently more appealing) speech of the stage representation:

> But when I see the word of truth proceeding from the hart, and uttered by the mouth of the reuerend preachers, to be receaued of the most parte into the eare, and but of a fewe rooted in the hart: I cannot by anie means beleeue that the wordes proceeding from a prophane plaier, and uttered in scorning sort, interlaced with filthie, lewde, and ungodlie speeches, haue greater force to mooue men unto virtue, than the wordes of truth uttered by the godlie Preacher. (114)

The direct political result of this attitude towards the language of the 'prophane' player arrived some sixty years later with the Puritan victory of the sermon over the stage (see chapter five).

The moral of all this is expressed well in Touchstone's touchstone: the truest poetry is the most feigning. The ethical principles of dramatic discourse are the laws of fiction, and the essential condition of speech acts on stage is their constitutional insincerity. The actor utters a (locutionary) act to which he has absolutely no (illocutionary) commitment, a fact that has scandalized the righteous from Tertullian down. And yet it is perhaps this very *dictio-fictio* identity that makes the ethical duties of speech so powerful and recurrent a thematic force in the drama, Renaissance drama in particular. The integrity of dramatic agents and actions is so much tied to the plastic capacities of discourse (*lexis* as a form of *praxis*) that the question of linguistic ethics comes to imply the very ontogenesis of the character, of his local habitation, name and the rest.

Not surprisingly, then, ethical 'authenticity' – in a word, sincerity – is an all but obsessive concern of Shakespeare's comic dramaturgy. The creation of fictional *personae* by the very fictional *personae* is one of the major sources of trouble – and thus of lying fables and plots – in the canon, most insistently so in *MM*, a play which relentlessly dramatizes the moral and rhetorical ambiguities of the *ethos*. Duke Vincentio's choice of Angelo as his substitute (after his opening refusal of an ethical-political-rhetorical exposition on the Aristotelian model: 'Of government the properties to unfold / Would seem in me t'affect speech and discourse') is presented as a delegating of public image ('figure') together with the political authority necessary to sustain it:

> I say, bid come before us Angelo.
> What figure of us, think you, he will bear?
> For you must know, we have with special soul
> Elected him our absence to supply;
> Lent him our terror, drest him with our love,
> And given his deputation all the organs
> Of our own power. (I. I. 15–21)

And the election itself is motivated in similar terms, namely on the grounds of the 'character' (*ethos* / image) that Angelo's past behaviour has created. In his eulogy, Vincentio explicitly reads this behaviour as a form of discourse, specifically a narrative, that transparently shows forth the deputy's interior life:

> Angelo:
> There is a kind of character in thy life
> That to th'observer doth thy history
> Fully unfold. (27ff.)

The Duke's apparent tranquillity in his choice of Angelo as his public double or simulacrum ('at full ourself') and in transferring to him his arbitrary powers is founded on the presumed (iconic) fidelity of this external discourse to Angelo's inner self (NB the 'heart' again):

> But I do bend my speech
> To one that can my part in him advertise:
> Hold therefore, Angelo.
> In our remove, be thou at full ourself.
> Mortality and mercy in Vienna
> Live in thy tongue, and heart. (40–5)

Now the situation stage-managed by Vincentio is unmistakably *experimental*: a political and moral laboratory test, as it were, in which the Duke himself, present as observer and ready to intervene in case of disaster, is able to note the effects of power on the exerciser and on the community upon which it is exercised. The elements of the experiment are necessarily pure: absolute authority, an immaculate image on the part of the main agent, an unappealable death sentence, an encounter with a spotlessly chaste and flawlessly beautiful virgin by way of crucial test. And what is put to the test is precisely the advertised 'character'–'heart' bond, infrangibly welded in Angelo's behaviour until Isabella's appeal. The progressive fracturing of this bond, and the consequent duplicity of Angelo's verbal behaviour, is commented on by the deputy himself with perfect candour (from the theatrical audience's viewpoint there is never any risk of a confusion of *ethé*). The first indication of such an ethical split, in the aftermath of Isabella's supplication, is the divorce that arises between Angelo's prayers (the most inward and private of acts) and his intellectual and emotional commitment, which lies elsewhere:

> When I would pray and think, I think and pray
> To several subjects: Heaven hath my empty words,
> Whilst my invention, hearing not my tongue,
> Anchors on Isabel: Heaven in my mouth,
> As if I did but only chew his name,
> And in my heart the strong and swelling evil
> Of my conception (2. 4. 1–7)

The striking parallel here with Claudius's devotional incapacity in *Hamlet* ('My words fly up, my thoughts remain below') is more than casual. The term 'invention' employed by Angelo to denote his thought processes, but powerfully associated also with the rhetorical faculty of *inventio* (or *heuresis*, the faculty, that is, that comprehends *ethos*), is something of a clue: hereafter Angelo's outward behaviour (like Claudius's throughout *Hamlet*) is indeed the product of oratorical invention rather than personal commitment. His monologue concludes – immediately prior to Isabella's reappearance – with a declaration of transformed intent, i.e. the knowing exploitation of 'forms' (or 'figure') in the construction of a false public self. The chosen metaphor for this construction is again that of inscribed discourse:

> O place, O form,
> How often dost thou with thy case, thy habit,
> Wrench awe from fools, and tie the wiser souls
> To thy false seeming! Blood, thou art blood.
> Let's write good angel on the devil's horn –
> 'Tis not the devil's crest. (2. 4. 12–17)

Angelo's disclosure to Isabella of this new passional character is in turn experimental at first, a tentative sounding of his audience and object of desire through interrogation, insinuation and open self-contradiction:

| | |
|---|---|
| *Ang.* | I shall pose you quickly. |
| | Which had you rather, that the most just law |
| | Now took your brother's life; or, to redeem him, |
| | Give up your body to such sweet uncleanness |
| | As she that he hath stain'd? |
| *Isab.* | Sir, believe this: |
| | I had rather give my body than my soul. |
| *Ang.* | I talk not of your soul: our compelled sins |
| | Stand more for number than for accompt. |
| *Isab.* | How say you? |
| *Ang.* | Nay, I'll not warrant that: for I can speak |
| | Against the thing I say. (2. 4. 51–60) |

The deputy's declared self-gainsaying here is not simply a matter of his 'withdrawing for the moment a suggestion too crudely phrased' (J. W. Lever, note to Arden ed.). It amounts also to a bald manifesto: Angelo has the licence to impose and assert whatever he desires, to adopt positions *pro* or *con* in any practical or moral issue ('the orator should be able to prove opposites'), and may thus proceed to recant his former moral rigidity without risk.

In abandoning such circumspection and declaring openly his lust, Angelo claims a renewed expressive integrity and directness:

> Believe me, on my honour,
> My words express my purpose (2. 4. 147–8),

a claim which is accurate enough with respect to his dealings with Isabella but which has become a fiction with respect to his public 'form'. The point immediately emerges when Isabella threatens to publicize his duplicity ('Seeming, seeming!/I will proclaim thee, Angelo, look for't'). Angelo responds with an unexceptionable statement of the political mechanisms of the *ethos* in its oratorical guise, vaunting that unmatchably persuasive 'history' which his past and future behaviour will continue to unfold in public, and the weight of which will crush all ethical credibility from Isabella's revelations:

> Who will believe thee, Isabel?
> My unsoil'd name, th'austereness of my life,
> My vouch against you, and my place i'th'state
> Will so your accusation overweigh,
> That you shall stifle in your own report,
> And smell of calumny. . . .

> As for you,
> Say what you can: my false o'erweighs your true. (2. 4. 153ff.)

Nor is the lesson lost on Isabella herself, who soliloquizes with equal lucidity on the social dangers born of a marriage brought about in accordance with the best Machiavellian model of the exercise of power – a marriage, that is, between absolute verbal authority and absolute (but disguised) dedication to self :

> To whom should I complain? Did I tell this,
> Who would believe me? O perilous mouths,
> That bear in them one and the self-same tongue
> Either of condemnation or approof,
> Bidding the law make curtsey to their will,
> Hooking both right and wrong to th'appetite,
> To follow as it draw! (2. 4. 170–6)

The violent clash of proofs – the artificial (Angelo's 'figure') versus the inartificial (the women's testimonies against him) – that occurs in the finale seems to vindicate Angelo's confidence in his public self, to which the Duke at first gives official credence ('his worth and credit/That's seal'd in approbation', 5. 1. 243–4). But it is resolved in a two-stage process of de-masking and (presumed) moral re-integration whereby Angelo's words are indeed made to express his purpose, or vice versa: he is obliged, that is, to fulfil his marriage pledge to Mariana, and then counselled to match his heart to the word and the deed ('Look that you love your wife').

The same pattern of exposed duplicity and ethical re-soldering is present in the still more precipitous resolution of *TG*, a play whose motor force derives from the moral tergiversations and verbal dissimulations of the protean Proteus. The ethical aporia in which Proteus indulges over the choice of love objects is analogous to the agonies of Angelo after his first meeting with Isabella:

> To leave my Julia, shall I be forsworn;
> To love fair Silvia, shall I be forsworn;
> To wrong my friend, I shall be much forsworn.
> And ev'n that power which gave me first my oath
> Provokes me to this threefold perjury.
> Love bade me swear, and Love bids me forswear. (2. 6. 1ff.)

But what is significant about Proteus's dubiety – and this is one measure of the ideological and rhetorical distance between the two comedies – is that the act of apostasy he contemplates is prompted not by any actual encounter with Silvia but merely by Valentine's description of her: a description that the rhetoricians would have classed as *ethopoeia*, that degenerate figural version of the Aristotelian *ethos* that consists in a vivid verbal painting of the characterial virtues and vices (in Silvia's case, only the former) of a given individual:

| | |
|---|---|
| Pro. | I know you joy not in a love-discourse. |
| Val. | Ay, Proteus, but that life is alter'd now: |
| | I have done penance for contemning Love, . . . |
| Pro. | Enough: I read your fortune in your eye. |
| | Was this the idol that you worship so? |
| Val. | Even she; and is she not a heavenly saint? |
| Pro. | No; but she is an earthly paragon. |
| Val. | Call her divine. |
| Pro. | I will not flatter her. |
| Val. | O flatter me; for love delights in praises . . . |
| | Then speak the truth by her: if not divine, |
| | Yet let her be a principality, |
| | Sovereign to all the creatures of the earth. (2. 4. 122ff.) |

As he admits in his first soliloquy, Proteus's love is supplanted by a love-discourse, and its object by a verbal icon or image:

> Even as one heat another heat expels,
> Or as one nail by strength drives out another,
> So the remembrance of my former love
> Is by a newer object quite forgotten.
> Is it mine eye, or Valentius' praise,
> Her true perfection, or my false transgression,
> That makes me thus reasonless, to reason thus? . . .
> 'Tis but her picture I have yet beheld,
> And that hath dazzled my reason's light. (2. 4. 188ff.)

Nor is Proteus's seduction by Valentine's discursive 'picture' a casual indication of emotional superficiality, as his successive behaviour reveals. He proceeds discursively to eliminate his former inamorata ('I will forget that Julia is alive, / Rememb'ring that my love to her is dead', 2. 6. 27–8); discursively he convinces himself of the necessity of his own cause ('I cannot now prove constant to myself, / Without some treachery us'd to Valentine', 2. 6. 31–2); and correspondingly prepares his own campaign of revelations ('I'll give her father notice'), insinuations ('some sly trick') and seduction to win Silvia and remove his rivals. The question of ethical coherence in all this scarcely arises, since Proteus is able fully to re-integrate his own sense of self ('constant to myself') through his auto-persuasions, while he acknowledges the inauthenticity of his adopted 'colour' and the calculated illocutionary transgressions that go with it simply as necessary and sufficient persuasive means:

Already have I been false to Valentine,
And now I must be as unjust to Thurio:
Under the colour of commending him,
I have access my own love to prefer. (4. 2. 1–4)

What eventually breaks the (ethically vicious) linguistic circle in which Proteus is caught is the response of Silvia herself, who accurately and incisively identifies the governing principles of his attempted seduction. Resisting his protestations of passion and fidelity on the grounds of their vacuity ('Thou subtle, perjur'd, false, disloyal man,/ Think'st thou I am shallow, so conseitless,/To be seduced by thy flattery/That hast deceiv'd so many with thy vows?', 4. 2. 92–5), Silvia grants him only what – as her unforgivingly acute commentary underlines – has been all along the object of his passion, her picture:

Pro.      Madam: if your heart be so obdurate,
            Vouchsafe me yet your picture for my love,
            The picture that is hanging in your chamber:
            To that I'll speak, to that I'll sigh and weep . . .
Sil.       I am very loath to be your idol, sir;
            But, since your falsehood shall become you well
            To worship shadows, and adore false shapes,
            Send to me in the morning, and I'll send it. (4. 2. 116ff.)

It is the lucidity and severity of Silvia's judgment – her equation of Proteus's infatuation with her image (first verbal, then visual) with the 'false shapes' of his own verbal deeds – that eventually provoke him out of his rhetorical self-sufficiency and into a threatened form of physical persuasion ('Nay, if the gentle spirit of moving words/Can no way change you to a milder form,/I'll woo you like a soldier, at arm's end', 5. 4. 55ff.). At which point, Proteus's constructed *persona* having effectively disintegrated, he is persuaded – by Valentine's cursory curse (5. 4. 60ff.) – to abandon it as readily as he was seduced into it, promptly rediscovering his former self and his original passion:

O heaven, were man
But constant, he were perfect. That one error
Fills him with faults; makes him run through all th'sins;
Inconstancy falls off, ere it begins.
What is in Silvia's face but I may spy
More fresh in Julia's, with a constant eye? (5. 4. 109–14)

The extreme facility of Proteus's redemption has frequently prompted the charge of inverisimilitude; but his own pious recantation suggests that the *volte-face* (the turning or returning, i.e. of his ethical 'face') is to be taken not in psychological but in moral terms, attributable to the inconstancy or instability of the *ethos* itself in its oratorical conception.

And in effect, since Proteus's threatened rape is immediately thwarted, the events never depart from that circumscribed zone of rhetorical operations (descriptions, persuasions, revelations, refusals, recantations) in which Proteus moves, whereby he is fully redeemable by and into discourse, being restored to those undertakings ('all thy oaths', 5. 4. 100) that he has not, in fact, succeeded in betraying definitively.

In *TG*, as in *MM*, ethical integrity is salvaged *in extremis* and *ab extra* through a more or less enforced return to the original word-bond that prevents a fatal act of forswearing. The risks involved are refracted – as so often in Shakespearean comedy – in less solemn form in the language of the clowns, here not only in Launce's passing comments on his master's inconstancy ('I am but a fool, look you, and yet I have the wit to think my master is kind of a knave', 3. 1. 261–3), but more decisively in his banter with Speed, notably his refusal of the latter's greeting:

| | |
|---|---|
| *Spe.* | Launce, by mine honesty, welcome to Padua. |
| *Lau.* | Forswear not thyself, sweet youth, for I am not welcome. I reckon this always, that a man is never undone till he be hanged, nor never welcome to a place till certain shot be paid, and the hostess say 'welcome'. (2. 5. 1–6) |

Speed's supposed violation of the rules of welcoming is a somewhat spurious version of the species of illocutionary emptiness that Austin baptizes as 'infelicity', and that regards not the legitimacy of the act (a greeting is always and in any case a greeting) but its actual correspondence to the speaker's mental or emotional state:

> The last type of case is that of . . . insincerities and infractions or breaches. Here, we say, the performance is *not* void, although it is still unhappy. . . . where, as often the [illocutionary] procedure is designed for use by persons having certain thoughts, feelings or intentions . . . then a person participating in and so invoking the procedure must in fact have those thoughts, feelings, or intentions. (1962: 39)

Speed's breach is not so much ethical – the sincerity of his feelings is not in doubt – as substantial, since Launce's version of the illocutionary procedure for welcoming includes a non-verbal (and specifically liquid) token of those feelings. A parallel episode in *LLL*, however, represents a more serious case of 'unhappiness'; it is again the welcome that causes the trouble:

| | |
|---|---|
| *King.* | Fair princess, welcome to the court of Navarre. |
| *Prin.* | Fair I give you back again; and welcome I have not yet: the roof of this court is too high to be yours, and welcome to the wide fields too base to be mine. |
| *King.* | You shall be welcome, madam, to my court. |
| *Prin.* | I will be welcome then: conduct me thither. (2. 1. 90–5) |

The Princess's pitiless anatomy of the unhappy Navarre and his emptily conventional gesture points out a double non-correspondence: between illocutionary act and illocutionary sequel (the King's welcome is not accompanied by the hospitality it entails or at least implies), and thus between act and illocutionary commitment ('those thoughts, feelings or intentions'). These two sources of infelicity – crucial to the comedy and its moral agonies – are, of course, complementary. The lack of the requisite feelings (a defect emblematically if ludicrously illustrated by Costard's veto against Moth as narrator of an event that only Costard himself has the necessary and painful experiential authority to report: 'Arm. But tell me; how was there a costard broken in a shin? / Moth. I will tell you sensibly. Cost. Thou hast no feeling of it, Moth: I will speak that l'envoy', 3. 1. 110ff.) is inevitably translated into a lack of engagement in the consequences of the act. This is clearest in the case of the lords' various vows, and indeed the Princess's rejection of Navarre's welcome is immediately followed by an equally demystifying and equally accurate disparagement of his vaunted academic oath, again associating its (predicted) non-fulfilment with the shallowness of the vower's intent ('will'):

| | |
|---|---|
| King. | Hear me, dear lady; I have sworn an oath. |
| Prin. | Our Lady help my lord! he'll be forsworn. |
| King. | Not for the world, fair madam, by my will. |
| Prin. | Why, will shall break it will, and nothing else. (2. 1. 96–9) |

This form of unhappiness is of considerably more thematic and dramatic import in LLL than any kind of illocutionary success. The (as it were anti-performative) verb 'forswear' and its derivatives occur, it might be noted, twenty-two times – far more often than in any other Shakespearean work – and 'perjure' and its derivatives thirteen, again a clear record. And as always, the verbal pattern lexicalizes the narrative pattern; indeed the chain of the main events can be reduced to the following skeletal scheme: (1) Vow – (2) Forswearing – (3) New Vow – (4) Frustration of second vow. The oath that inaugurates the comedy is itself thrown almost at once into doubt not only by Berowne's reluctant commitment ('By yea and nay, sir, then I swore in jest') but especially by the very political circumstances in which it is undertaken:

| | |
|---|---|
| Ber. | This article, my liege, yourself must break; |
| | For well you know here comes in embassy |
| | The French king's daughter with yourself to speak. (1. 1. 131ff.) |

Predicting from the outset the unhappy fate of the vow, Berowne prepares his self-defence, an 'artificial' argument that will save his face at the moment of the debacle:

> Necessity will make us all forsworn
> Three thousand times within these three years' space; ...
> If I break faith, this word shall speak for me,
> I am forsworn on mere necessity. (1. 1. 148ff.)

Berowne's premeditated proof is a clue to a conception of the verbal undertaking as a particularly effective 'ethical' strategy (*euche* = the vow as oratorical gambit) that, however, can be readily countered and undone by an equally efficacious move under the *ethos* rubric, namely *dicaeologia* or excusing by necessity.

The search for proofs able to erase the oath without loss of personal or moral prestige becomes critcal in the overspying scene (4. 3), first in the *flatus vocis* argument that Longaville tries out in his sonnet ('vows are but breath') and then in the men's desperate choral call for argumentational subterfuges capable of discounting the (inartificial) evidence of their forswearing (note the choice of terms connoting the semantic fields of *ethos* and *inventio*: 'prove', 'authority', 'tricks', 'quillets', etc.):

| | |
|---|---|
| *King.* | But what of this? Are we not all in love? |
| *Ber.* | O! nothing so sure; and thereby all forsworn. |
| *King.* | Then leave this chat; and, good Berowne, now prove |
| | Our loving lawful, and our faith not torn. |
| *Dum.* | Ay, marry, there; some flattery for this evil. |
| *Long.* | O! some authority how to proceed; |
| | Some tricks, some quillets, how to cheat the devil. |
| *Dum.* | Some salve for perjury. |
| *Ber.* | O! 'tis more than need. (4. 3. 278–85) |

Berowne's response – his great 'erotic' oration – sufficiently restores the men's sense of 'authority' to encourage them to risk their quillets before the women and attempt to seal their second vow (of marriage). But in the event the trick is produced by the women themselves, whose stratagem of exchanging favours traps their suitors into a second act of ethical infelicity, a vow offered to the wrong partner:

| | |
|---|---|
| *Prin.* | Your oath once broke, you force not to forswear. |
| *King.* | Despise me, when I break this oath of mine. |
| *Prin.* | I will; and therefore keep it. Rosaline, |
| | What did the Russian whisper in your ear? |
| *Ros.* | Madam, he swore that he did hold me dear |
| | As precious eyesight ... |
| | adding thereto, moreover, |
| | That he would wed me, or else die my lover. (5. 2. 440ff.) |

It is here that the opposing conception of the verbal undertaking – the sincerity principle – emerges, propounded in the unforgiving moral reprimands that accompany the ladies' resistance to the offered oaths:

| | |
|---|---|
| *Prin.* | This field shall hold me, and so hold your vow: |
| | Nor God, nor I, delights in perjur'd men. . . . |
| | No, no, my lord, your grace is perjur'd much, |
| | Full of dear guiltiness, and therefore this: . . . |
| | Your oath I will not trust; . . . |
| *Ros.* | You must be purged to your sins are rack'd: |
| | You are attaint with faults and perjury. (5. 2. 345ff.; 782ff.) |

'Accuracy and morality alike', observes Austin, citing Hippolytus, 'are on the side of the plain saying that *our word is our bond*' (1962: 10). A promise counts as a promise, a vow as a vow, whatever the actual intentions of the performer and whatever his subsequent behaviour. It is this simple precept that the Princess insists upon, demanding that the King and his followers acknowledge that their undertakings are *ipso facto* social deeds with precise consequences and ungainsayable extra-discursive responsibilities. The issue becomes of critical importance in the context of the international diplomacy in which the two potentates are obliged briefly to engage and in which more than personal happiness (in both senses) is at stake. The Princess, significantly, is quick to seize upon a diplomatic pledge made by Navarre, in order to secure its unrenegable binding force:

| | |
|---|---|
| *King.* | I do protest I never heard of it; |
| | And if you prove it I'll repay it back, |
| | Or yield up Aquitaine. |
| *Prin.* | We arrest your word. (2. 1. 157–9) |

Rhetoric, ethics and politics, as Aristotle affirms, belong to the same family.

### (VI) 'MAKE PASSIONATE MY SENSE OF HEARING': PERSUASIONS, PERLOCUTIONS, 'PATHOS'

Bassanio, having chosen the right casket and having subsequently received Portia's eloquent self-offer, endeavours to describe the almost uncontrollable passions that her words have moved in him. The allegory he elaborates to represent so intensely personal an experience is curiously 'public':

> Madam, you have bereft me of all words,
> Only my blood speaks to you in my veins,
> And there is such confusion in my powers,
> As after some oration fairly spoke
> By a beloved prince, there doth appear
> Among the buzzing pleased multitude,
> Where every something being blent together,
> Turns to a wild of nothing, save of joy
> Express'd, and not express'd. (3. 2. 175–83)

But Bassanio's comparison of his (somewhat wordy) speechlessness with the dumb transport of an orator's audience is not as incongruous as it may seem. The topic is found in Elizabethan psychological treatises precisely as a privileged illustration of the potency of human passion: 'I remember a Preacher in Italy, who had such power over his auditors' affections, that when it pleased him he could cause them shed abundance of teares' (Wright 1601: 5). Elizabethan psychology, like Elizabethan social models of language, derived very largely from classical rhetoric. Wright's (and with it Bassanio's) sanguine description of the effects of oratory can be traced back – via Cicero's Crassus ('there is to my mind no more excellent thing than the power, by means of oratory, to get hold on assemblies of men, win their good will, or divert them from wherever he wishes' (De oratore I. viii. 30) – to Aristotle's Rhetoric, and specifically to the definition of the artificial proof of pathos: 'The orator persuades by means of his hearers, when they are roused to emotion by his speech; for the judgments we deliver are not the same when we are influenced by joy or sorrow, love or hate' (1. ii. 4).

Pathos, in Aristotle's system of proofs, fully reciprocates ethos, being at once an effect of it (listeners are moved only if they give credence to the speaker) and an aid to it (working on the audience's emotions is the surest way to affirm one's authority). This bilateral model of the communicational circuit was extended by Renaissance commentators to speech at large. Primaudaye, for example, accounts for linguistic reception as a direct translation of the ethical ('credit') into the pathetical ('pricketh forward'): '[Speech is] of great efficacie and force, and wonderfully pricketh forward those that hear us, causing them to give credit to our saiengs, and working in them a desire to resemble us' (1586: 120–1). Here again the transformational process at work is strictly iconic, complementing perfectly the supposed iconicity of expression: speech, itself a simulacrum for the speaker, drives the listener to become his double in turn ('to resemble us').

Now the image of the pathetic or passionate reception of speech is commonplace in the plays: the 'fire' experienced by Beatrice (MA 3. 1.104ff.); Angelo's agitation at Isabella's pleas ('She speaks, and 'tis such sense/That my sense breeds with it', MM 2. 2. 142f.); the 'plague' caught by Olivia at Viola's embassy (TN 1. 5. 299); Orlando's inarticulate rapture at Rosalind's compliments (confirming Bassanio's claim that true pathos is 'express'd, and not express'd'):

> Can I not say, 'I thank you'? My better parts
> Are all thrown down, and that which here stands up
> Is but a quintain, a mere lifeless block . . .

ACTS

> What passion hangs these weights upon my tongue?
> I cannot speak to her, yet she urg'd conference. (*AYLI* 1. 2. 239–47)

We are once more, of course, in the realm of Orpheus, although here from the viewpoint of the swayed listener and with reference, in this 'conversational' context, to an Orphism *sub specie pragmatica*.

The prospect of an ecstatically pathetical listening experience is evoked repeatedly by Armado in *LLL*, both in response to his own linguistic productions ('O! with – but with this I passion to say wherewith –', 1. 1. 254–5), and more especially with respect to the party pieces he commissions from his page ('make passionate my sense of hearing', 3. 1. 1). It is Moth, indeed, who attracts two of only three explicit attributions of the pathetic in Shakespeare (the third being reserved for Orlando by Rosalind–Ganymede: 'I will think you the most pathetical break-promise', *AYLI* 4. 1. 181–2); Armado eulogizes one of Moth's briefer exhibitions in these terms:

Moth.   My father's wit and my mother's tongue assist me!
Arm.   Sweet invocation of a child; most pretty and pathetical (1. 2. 89–91);

and the judgment is later confirmed by Costard:

> And his page o't'other side, that handful of wit!
> Ah! heavens, it is a most pathetical nit. (4. 1. 148–9)

Modern speech-act jargon translates *pathos* into 'perlocutionary effect'. The terms of Austin's definition are not altogether dissimilar to those of the rhetoricians: 'Saying something will often, or even normally, produce certain consequential effects upon the feelings, thoughts, or actions of the audience . . . and it may be done with the design, intention, or purpose of producing them' (1962: 101). Perlocutionary acts – 'what we bring about or achieve *by* saying something, such as convincing, persuading, deterring, and even, say, surprising or misleading' (109) – have to do, then, precisely with pricking forward those that hear us, effecting some change in their attitudes or emotions. The orientation of classical rhetoric is in this sense eminently perlocutionary, the act of persuasion being its unquestioned end.

Perlocutionary success is not, generally speaking, a fruitful source of comic plotting in Shakespeare. Only one of the comedies has a principal plot structured on the apparent achievement of 'consequential effects': *TS*. Petruchio (that pure Perlocutio) is, at least on a literal reading, the most spectacularly fortunate of Shakespeare's persuaders, since, unlike, say, Iago or Richard III, he not only achieves his 'perlocutionary object' (the taming) but also, presumably, what Austin calls the 'perlocutionary sequel' to which it leads (a calm and affluent marriage). Petruchio himself comments generously on his goals (the verb 'woo' and derivatives occur twenty-five times, 'tame' twelve), on his determination to achieve them in full ('And 'tis my hope to end successfully', 4. 1. 176), on the means to this achievement and on the supposed success itself, demonstrated in the meta-perlocutionary show in which Katherina is persuaded to conquer the other wives in the cause of uxorial obedience:

> See where she comes, and brings your froward wives
> As prisoners to her womanly persuasion. (5. 2. 120–1)

(For an 'ironical' reading of this speech, placing in doubt Petruchio's success, see Kahn 1977.)

Petruchio's vaunted triumph is prefigured in the ease with which another improbable perlocutionary effort, the convincing of Sly to change not only mind and heart but identity ('Persuade him that he hath been lunatic') is accomplished in the induction. Correspondingly, the two examples of 'anti-perlocutionary' openings (the 'cease to persuade' of TG and the 'persuade me not' of MWW) herald plots based on overall perlocutionary failure: Proteus's and Falstaff's respectively. This is the more familiar narrative pattern: consider the failures of Angelo and Bertram, for instance, or the doubly lost perlocutionary labours of Navarre and followers, first to convince the ladies of their worth (object) and subsequently to achieve the expected marriage (sequel). This miscarriage is marked, interestingly, by the women's prescription of a course of therapy, designed specifically to remedy the affective inadequacies of the men's speech. Berowne, in particular, is sentenced by Rosaline to a spell in hospital, an appropriate context in which to test the pathetic powers of his language over the all too authentic agonies of his audience:

> Oft have I heard of you, my Lord Berowne,
> Before I saw you, and the world's large tongue
> Proclaims you for a man replete with mocks;
> Full of comparisons and wounding flouts,
> Which you on all estates will execute
> That lie within the mercy of your wit:
> To weed this wormwood from your fruitful brain,
> And there withal to win me, if you please,
> Without the which I am not to be won,
> You shall this twelve month term from day to day,
> Visit the speechless sick, and still converse
> With groaning wretches; and your task shall be
> With all the fierce endeavour of your wit
> To enforce the pained impotent to smile. (5. 2. 833–46)

The tone of severe moral censure and the negative vegetal imagery
employed by Rosaline suggest a conviction that *pathos*, the orientation
of speech towards the listener and its allegiance to his feelings, is not
only a desirable oratorical end but a social (and religious) duty, a view
which Rosaline proceeds immediately to propound in what amounts to
an accusation of communicational narcissism on the part of Berowne
and his complacently self-directed wit:

> A jest's prosperity lies in the ear
> Of him that hears it, never in the tongue
> Of him that makes it. (5. 2. 853–5)

Rosaline's stand on behalf of the hetero-communicational goals of
discourse is a common enough Renaissance *locus*. 'Especially', insists
Primaudaye, 'we must strive to make it known, that we love and
reverence those with whom we speake' (1586: 125); and 'Especially',
writes his compatriot Charron with equal emphasis, 'we should be
careful not to transgress this rule of profiting others' (1601: 1532). The
gesture is cursorily made in various of the Elizabethan rhetoric books:
'that all may understande it, the beste were first and foremost to tell
every thyng in order so muche as is nedeful' (Wilson 1553: 1532); 'And
there is a decencie, that euery speech should be to the appetite and
delight, or dignitie, of the hearer & not for any respect arrogant or
undutifull' (Puttenham 1589: Ggiᵛ).

And yet there is more than a codified social piety in Rosaline's
homily. The particular (post-theatrical) circumstances, together with
Berowne's comments on the nonfulfilment of comic canons (see p. 71)
recall a second Aristotelian tradition to which the moving of an
audience is central. The *Poetics* reserves the accomplishment of a full
(i.e. pitiful and fearful) *pathos* for tragedy, a goal which is invoked in
*MND* in the performance ('that will ask some tears' 1. 2. 121) and
reception ('This passion, and the death of a dear friend; would go near to
make a man look sad', 5. 1. 277–8) of the tragic 'Pyramus and Thisbe'.
But the 'passion of loud laughter' which this particular tragedy
inadvertently provokes in at least one auditor (5. 1. 64) is also accounted
for by Aristotle, if less extensively, in the case of comedy. Moving the
audience to such delight is, according to Sidney's paraphrase of
Aristotle, the specifically pragmatic (rather than cognitive) end of the
drama: 'For, as *Aristotle* sayth, it is not *Gnosis* but *Praxis* must be the
fruit. And howe *Praxis* cannot be, without being mooued to practise, it is
no hard matter to consider' (1595: Eiiiʳ). Comedy, like all drama, being,
as Franco Fornari puts it (1979), a series of effects designed to create
affects, aspires always to pathetic or perlocutionary success: moving,

persuading, convincing or delighting being its object, and the gratification and (for Sidney at least) edification of the auditor its sequel.

Now Aristotle identifies as the main source of comic delight the double plot ('this particular pleasure is not the one that springs from tragedy, but is more characteristic of comedy', 53a. 36f.), a feature of most Shakespearean comedies but effectively absent from *LLL*, like the lamented comic conclusion ('doth not end like an old play'), and with it, in theory, the 'particular pleasure' that the traditional structure of comedy supposedly affords. The strictures that Rosaline directs against Berowne's non-communicative wit might amount, in this prospect, to a presentiment of affective impotence on the part of the play itself and its witty verbal structure. This is indeed the verdict of a number of critics, among them J. L. Calderwood, whose metadramatic reading of the comedy takes its conclusion as an admission of dramaturgic failure: 'despite the mirth it has begotten, the intercourse of wit and words has laboured in vain to give birth to drama' (1969: 79). But whether the labours of the play's wit, like the lords', are really lost is for the auditors themselves to decide as part of their own receptional labours: labours that are, as Sidney observes, not *gnosis* but *praxis*.

# 5 Figures

## (I) FIGURATIONS, CONFIGURATIONS, DISFIGURATIONS

'What is the figure? What is the figure?': Holofernes's anxiously insistent rhetorical question (*LLL* 5. 1. 58) serves at least to raise the genuine issue of the liaison between drama and rhetoric, a liaison that is anything but exhausted in those ideological and moral affinities of theatre with oratory that were briefly traced in the last chapter. It is true that the most immediate, or at least the most evident, point of contact between the stage and the classical rhetorical system lies in the histrionic-oratorical moment of the delivery – the *actio* or *hypocrisis* that Demosthenes (reported by Thomas Wilson and Francis Bacon, among other sixteenth-century commentators) claimed disparagingly to be 'the chiefe parte of an orator' but more properly 'the vertue of a player' (Bacon 1625: 518; compare Wilson 1553: 117), and that Thomas Heywood, reversing the terms of Demosthenes's comparison, defends as an indispensable guide to decorous stage action:

> [Rhetoric] instructs [the actor] to fit his phrases to his action and his action to his phrase, and his pronunciation to them both. . . . without a comely and elegant gesture, a gratious and a bewitching kinde of action, a naturall and a familiar motion of the head, the hand, the body, and a moderate and fit countenace sutable to all the rest, I hold all the rest as nothing. (1612: 13–14; compare Hamlet's advice to the players)

Actors and orators alike are good (or bad) hypocrites. The comparison is pertinent to Holofernes himself – would-be actor, director and dramatist as well as eminent rhetorician – who does indeed uphold delivery as the last triumphant act in his own creative rhetorical (and later dramatic) productions:

> This is a gift that I have, simple, simple; a foolish extravagant spirit, full of forms, figures, shapes, objects, ideas, apprehensions, motions, revolutions: these are begot in the womb of *pia mater*, and delivered upon the mellowing of occasion. (4. 2. 64–9)

But it might be noted, however, that Holofernes's self-encomium (like its negative image, Antony's unconvincing disclaimer at the end of his great oration in *Julius Caesar*: 'For I have neither wit, nor words, nor worth,/Action, nor utterance, nor the power of speech/To stir men's blood', 3. 2. 223ff.) is not limited to *actio* ('delivered upon the mellowing of occasion'), running as it does the whole gamut of the five traditional parts of rhetoric, each of which has an equally plausible relationship with one of the phases of dramatic production. *Inventio* ('objects, ideas, apprehensions') and *dispositio* or arrangement ('begot in the womb of *pia mater*') are pertinent not only to the compositional labours of the playwright in elaborating story and plot (the lives of the Worthies, for example), but likewise to the work of the actor in 'inventing' his own histrionic resources and in 'arranging' his stage actions; *memoria* ('the ventricle of memory') is if anything dearer to the theatrical than to the oratorical performer. But it is to Holofernes's idolatrized *elocutio* – or *lexis* or *phrasis* or simple 'style' ('forms, figures, shapes') – that both the language of the drama and the languages of the stage owe their most powerful allegiance.

Both the language of the drama and the languages of the stage: this is an essential coupling here, since if the style or *elocutio* with which this chapter is concerned is in the first instance verbal, it is nonetheless impossible – as we will repeatedly see – to appreciate the structural and thematic weight of verbal figures in the comedies outside the framework of theatrical display as a whole. This figurality is founded in part on the ontology of fiction, whereby the dramatic representation and its propositions are allowed the non-literal status of all poetic discourse – 'What Childe is there, that Comming to a Play, and seeing *Thebes* written in great Letters upon an olde doore, doth beleeve that it is Thebes?' (Sidney 1595: Hl[r]) – and in part on the analogy, irresistible to Renaissance humanist commentators, between the figures of speech and the elaborations of the non-verbal languages that contributed to the actor's art. This is especially the case with gesture, whose semiotic articulateness as the 'speache of the body' (Wilson, following Cicero, 1553: 118[v]) removes it from its merely parasitic or, better, paralinguistic role within the delivery (*actio*) and brings it instead under the rubric of style, with all its expressive resources: 'the Countenance, the Hands, the whole Body, the every Part and Gesture speak as well as the Mouth, and follow the Movements of the Soul, and give a lively Image of the Affections within' (Charron 1601: 1537). And the privileged example of an autonomously articulate gestural language is, of course, the body-movement of the actor: 'The internall conceites and affections of our mind, are not onely expressed with wordes, but also declared with actions: as it appeareth in Comedies, where dumb showes often expresse the whole matter' (Wright 1601: 195).

Now the logical consequence of the notion of a corporeal figurality is the search for ordered gestural patterns corresponding more or less directly to the movements of the rhetorical tropes and schemes, a search that brings us clearly into the territory of the dance, another prominent component of Elizabethan theatrical performance (and not least of Shakespearean comedy). The rhetoric of the dance has an impressive sixteenth-century pedigree, comprehending, not least, Sir Thomas Elyot's apology for dancing, particularly the French 'bace dance', as a mode of allegory (each of the eight movements of the base dance corresponding metaphorically to some virtue: honour, maturity, providence, industry, circumspection, election, experience, modesty, Elyot 1531; see Bindella 1971), and culminating in the extended and explicit parallelism of Thoinot Arbeau's *Orchesography* (1588):

> But practically all the *savants* hold that dancing is a kind of dumb rhetoric by which the author, without speaking a single word, can, by virtue of his movements, make the spectators understand that he is gay, worthy to be praised, loved, and adored. Is it not your opinion that dancing is a manner of speech, expressed in terms of the movements of the dancer's feet? Does he not say tacitly to his mistress . . . 'Dost thou not love me? Dost thou not desire me?' (1925 ed.: 23)

In Thomas Wright the parallel already appears as an established commonplace: 'by gestures in dancing some can give to understand most mechanical arts and trades. The rhetoricians likewise . . . prescribe many rules of action' (1601: 196).

It is no doubt to this tradition concerning the eloquent (and in Arbeau's case erotic) Terpsichorean twists and turns of the body that Moth refers in his brilliantly vivid evocation of the base French *bransle* as a means of amorous persuasion:

> Master, will you win your love with a French brawl? . . . jig off a tune at the tongue's end, canary to it with your feet, humour it with turning up your eyelids, sigh a note and sing a note, something through the throat as if you swallowed love with singing love, sometime through the nose, as if you snuffed up love by smelling love; with your hat penthouse-like o'er the shop of your eyes; with your arms crossed on your thin-belly doublet like a rabbit on a spit; or your hands in your pocket, like a man after the old painting . . . These are complements, these are humours, these betray nice wenches. (3. 1. 6ff.)

Moth's detailed verbal mimesis of the dancer's nonchalant movements, or *actio* – recommended, however, as a form of modish gestural *elocutio* – is of course perfectly appropriate to a comedy that unites throughout elaborately ordered bodily configurations with conspicuously advertised verbal patterns. Furthermore, the very issue of linguistic and bodily figurality is unmistakably central to the play, finding its main metaphors in the dressing-up, making-up and masquerading ('And when masquerades are added she has it in her power to move her lover sometimes to anger, sometimes to pity and commisseration, sometimes to hatred, sometimes to love' (Arbeau 1588: 23) that are the chief insignias of the dramatic actor's trade, at least on the Elizabethan stage (see section (iv) below).

It is in this sense that the acute figural self-consciousness of *LLL* goes beyond the limits of its own verbal patterns to include the rhetoric of the dramatic representation as a whole. This is further suggested by other possible figures for figures in the play, involving the dramatic place (the King's 'curious-knotted garden', see p. 94 above) and events within it, notably the shoot and its accompanying references: the talk of 'pricks' ('The preyful princess pierc'd and prick'd'; 'let the mark have a prick on it'; 'She's too hard for you at pricks'), apart from its obvious double sense, recalls Ascham's *Toxophilus* ('Three or foure that went to shote at the pryckes', 1545: Ai$^r$), a treatise that explores, as K. J. Wilson has shown (1976), the art of shooting precisely as an allegory for the art of rhetoric, and for *elocutio* in particular. The ladies' 'hard' verbal pricks are indeed instances of stylish rhetorical archery. The pan-semiotic character of the play's rhetorical commentary is more directly evident in its four explicit references to the art, of which only one (Armado's enthusiastic 'sweet smoke of rhetoric', 3. 1. 60) has to do specifically or at least positively with verbal operations: the others regard the 'still' or dumb rhetoric of the heart (2. 1. 228), the 'heavenly' and equally silent rhetoric of the beloved's eye (4. 3. 57) and the rejected 'painted' rhetoric in all its forms (4. 3. 235).

Consequently, style in *LLL*, as one of its running puns would suggest, is a perceptible and (if only phonetically) physical dramatic presence, a step on which the play's speakers and auditors may raise themselves:

Ber.  Well, sir, be it as the style shall give us cause to climb in the merriness (1. 1. 197–8)

and over which they are bound either to go or to fall:

Boy.   I am much deceiv'd but I remember the style.
Prin.  Else your memory is bad, going o'er it erewhile. (4. 1. 97–8)

And as such it becomes object not only of *micro*-rhetorical consciousness and anatomy (the 'most fine figure' or 'forms, figures, shapes', or 'figures pedantical' variously discovered), but of *macro*-descriptions at the level of personal styles or *idiolects* (which are indeed highly distinctive in the play). Reciprocal rhetorical portraits take the place of character sketches; thus Navarre on Armado:

> ... A refined traveller of Spain;
> A man in all the world's new fashion planted,
> That hath a mint of phrases in his brain;
> One who the music of his own vain tongue
> Doth ravish like enchanting harmony;
> A man of complements (1. 1. 162ff.);

Holofernes again on Armado (verbal and behavioural *elocutio*):

> His humour is lofty, his discourse peremptory, his tongue filed, his eye ambitious, his gait majestical, and his general behaviour vain, ridiculous, and thrasonical (5. 1. 9ff.);

Berowne on Boyet (again verbal and gestural style):

> This fellow picks up wit, as pigeons pease,
> And utters it again when God doth please.
> He is wit's pedlar, and retails his wares
> At wakes, and wassails, meetings, markets, fairs; ...
> This gallant pins the wenches on his sleeve;
> Had he been Adam, he had tempted Eve.
> A' can carve too, and lisp: why, this is he
> That kiss'd his hand away in courtesy;
> This is the ape of form, monsieur the nice,
> That, when he plays at tables, chides the dice
> In honourable terms. (5. 2. 315ff.)

Similar idiolectal frames are present in all of those comedies in which *elocutio* and its devices perform a well-defined narrative and theatrical function. In *MA*, for example, the style of ironical diatribe is inevitably and consistently brought to attention within the secondary plot, and produces, in addition to more 'local' figural commentary, a precise metadiscursive sketch of Beatrice, mistress of the game:

> *Hero.*                    I never yet saw man,
> How wise, how noble, young, how rarely featur'd
> But she would spell him backward: if fair-fac'd,
> She would swear the gentleman should be her sister;
> If black, why, Nature, drawing of an antic,
> Made a foul blot; ...
> So turns she every man the wrong side out,
> And never gives to truth and virtue that
> Which simpleness and merit purchaseth. (3. 1. 59–70)

In *TS*, likewise, the greatest dramatic importance attaches to the ironical simile, as Petruchio reveals in a generous prospective self-portrait:

> I'll attend her here,
> And woo her with some spirit when she comes.
> Say that she rail, why then I'll tell her plain
> She sings as sweetly as a nightingale.
> Say that she frown, I'll say she looks as clear
> As morning roses newly wash'd with dew.
> Say she be mute and will not speak a word,
> Then I'll commend her volubility. (2. 1. 168ff.)

*TS* is at times close to *LLL* in the detailed concern it manifests with its own stylistic constitution. Petruchio's similitudinous swashbuckling is analysed even by his servant, who promises 'and he begin once he'll rail in his rope-tricks. I'll tell you what, sir, and she stand him but a little, he will throw a figure in her face, and so disfigure her with it' (1. 2. 110ff.). Petruchio's 'rope-tricks', or rhetorics, or rhetorical tropes, or trope-tricks, or any-old-rope-rhetoric have, in any case, as considerable a presence in the action ('he will throw a figure') as the old rhetorical rope on offer in *LLL*. And as in *LLL*, the cultivation of the verbal arts is in keeping with the explicitly 'humanistic' setting – Padua, the 'nursery of the arts' (1. 1. 2) – and is programmatically announced from the outset:

> Let's be no stoics nor no stocks, I pray,
> Or so devote to Aristotle's checks
> As Ovid be an outcast quite abjur'd.
> Balk logic with acquaintance that you have,
> And practice rhetoric in your common talk (1. 1. 31–5)

As in *LLL*, moreover, the rope-tricks of *elocutio* are extended in *TS* beyond language to the body and its discourse (specifically to significant costume: Petruchio's 'mad attire' with its metaphorical 'meaning', etc.).

Like its component styles themselves, the stylistic objects of *AYLI* are more various and are not limited to any one speaker or narrative stratum: the 'sweet' bucolic style of the Duke, the supposedly 'cruel and boisterous style' of Phebe, the 'tedious' homiletic mode of Orlando's verses and the 'pretty' sentiments of his romantic discourse, etc. And if the most accurate description in the play is prompted by the virtuoso fooling of Touchstone, that Toxophilus of wit – 'He uses his folly like a stalking-horse, and under the presentation of that he shoots his wit' (5. 4. 105–6) – it is the clown himself who affects, as part of that very fooling, an ostentatious 'technical' figural knowledge. Indeed, the same cunning clowning that wins the Duke's admiration is an elaborate pseudo-rhetorical typology, a treatise on the modes of verbal defence modelled on a hybrid between the manual of etiquette and the manual of fencing (like shooting, a ready allegory for *elocutio*):

I did dislike the cut of a certain courtier's beard; he sent me word, if I said his beard was not well cut, he was in the mind it was; this is called the Retort Courteous. If I sent him word again, it was not well cut, he would send me word he cut it to please himself; this is called the Quip Modest. If again it was not well cut, he disabled my judgement: this is call'd the Reply Churlish. If again it was not well cut, he would answer I spake not true; this is called the Reproof Valiant. If again it was not well cut, he would say, I lie; this is called the Countercheck Quarrelsome. And so to the Lie Circumstantial and the Lie Direct. (5. 4. 68ff.)

Touchstone's anatomy of the 'lie seven times removed' is almost certainly contaminated by Puttenham's Englishing of the terms of classical rhetoric (the 'dry mock' (irony), the 'civil jest' (*asteismus*), the 'bitter taunt' (sarcasm), the 'broad flout' (antiphrasis), etc.). In his own mystifying stylistic fencing with his rustic rival William, he wields the category of the figure as a form of cultural one-upmanship, the epitome of the courtly urbanity (of the kind embodied in Puttenham's *Arte*) he claims to represent:

Touch.   Give me your hand. Art thou learned?
Will.    No sir.
Touch.   Then learn this of me. To have is to have: for it is a figure in rhetoric that drink, being poured out of a cup into a glass, by filling the one doth empty the other. For all your writers do consent that *ipse* is he. Now you are not *ipse*, for I am he. (5. 1. 37–43)

Touchstone's is only one of a number of abuses to which the figure of the figure is inevitably subjected in the comedies. The term lends itself to a range of more or less obvious puns, among them Speed's calligraphic-epistolary *antanaclasis* in *TG* (a play in which *antanaclasis* itself is a dominant figure):

Spe.   Why, she woos you by a figure.
Val.   What figure?
Spe.   By a letter, I should say.
Val.   Why, she hath not writ to me.
Spe.   What need she, when she hath made you write to yourself? (2. 1. 140–4);

or Moth's numerical *asteismus* in *LLL*:

Arm.   A most fine figure!
Moth.  To prove you a cipher (1. 1. 51–2);

or, most irresistible of all, Grumio's 'figure'/'disfigure' quibble on Petruchio's rope-tricks (see above), evoking the dramatic-theatrical encounter between rhetorical figure and human figure (Katherina's face). It is this very encounter in its different (figurative) forms, and with its attendant configurations and disfigurations of the figures as essential components of the comic and thematic structures of the plays, that will be examined in this chapter, organized according to three broad figural groupings (schemes, proverbs, tropes). Throughout it is the *theatricality* of figural acts that is at issue, rather than the simple identification and labelling of devices. The what-is-the-figure game has an undoubted appeal (and not to Holofernes alone), but Richard Sherry's warning – which might well be directed towards Shakespeare's pedant himself – is sacrosanct: 'The common scholemasters be want in readynge, to saye unto their scholers: *Hic est figura*: and sometyme to axe them, *Per quam figuram*? But what profit is herein if they go no further?' (1550: Aiv^v). Going further, in this context, means taking the figure seriously as a dynamic and generative element of the drama at all its levels.

(II) 'OUT OF HIS FIVE SENTENCES': SCHEMES AND THEMES

There is a received notion in Shakespearean criticism that what marks and limits the 'early' Shakespeare is a devotion to conspicuous verbal forms designed to foreground the linguistic signifier: 'Characteristic of the early style . . . is Shakespeare's eagerness to exploit the sound of words as well as their meaning. The word as word takes on a life of its own' (Turner 1974: 11). The terms of this critical tradition are effectively set by Coleridge, who, in his remarks on *LLL*, takes the play's profusion of verbal patterns as sign and product of professional inexperience (see Introduction, p. 4): 'Sometimes you see this youthful god of poetry connecting disparate thoughts purely by means of resemblances in the words expressing them' (1960, I: 86). Much the same terms, and unmistakably the same tone, reappear in Swinburne: 'in *LLL* the fancy for the most part runs wild as the wind, and the structure of the story is that of a house of cards which the wind builds and unbuilds at pleasure. Here we find a very riot of rhymes, wild and wanton in their half-grown grace' (1880: 47); are slightly varied by Granville-Barker: 'The early plays abound . . . in elaborate embroidery of language done for its own sake' (1927: 8); and are accepted by any number of more recent commentators, among them A. C. Hamilton: '*LLL* complements the other plays: the diction of melody and words is all that we do remember' (1967: 130).

Now although the objects of this somewhat embarrassed critical patronization remain at best generic, there can be little doubt that the patterns responsible for the 'elaborate embroidery', 'resemblances in the words', 'riot of rhymes', 'diction of melody' and 'sound of words' are those phonetic, morphological and syntactic devices – indeed plentiful in the earlier plays – classified in classical rhetoric as the 'schemes'. In effect, Coleridge and his followers are heirs to a figural tradition which similarly regarded schematic patterns with a certain suspicion. While the sophistic founders of the art, notably Gorgias, had unashamedly pursued phonetic and syntactic play as the highest expression of mental dexterity, the rationalistic Ciceronian reform of rhetoric inevitably came to privilege more 'substantial' figural forms. Quintilian's division of the *figurae verborum* into tropes and schemes is not merely technical but evaluative. The trope is an intellectually demanding device, *ornatus difficilis*, capable of the most considerable conceptual depth. The scheme, her easier and emptier-headed sister, *ornatus facilis*, is by definition deprived of any semantic co-ordinates ('in the Trope there is a chaunge of signifycation, but not in the Scheme', Peacham 1577: Ei^v). Being limited in its functions to the superstructure of speech and writing (Greek *skhēma*, 'form'), the scheme will penetrate the ear but never – or at most only dimly and subliminally – the mind: 'And that first sort of figure [the scheme] dothe serue th'eare onely and may be therefore called Auricular' (Puttenham 1589: 159–60).

Implicit in the 'facility' attributed to schematic figures is the same shallowness or callowness with which the young Shakespeare and his language are charged. The danger is that of degeneration into infantile ostentation, a danger which is evident in the kinship, and in some cases perfect coincidence, of the schemes with the so-called 'vices of language' with which the speaker wins the ridicule of his listeners (*conciliatio* or euphemism, for example, is given as a scheme by Quintilian and as a vice by Peacham; *bomphiologia* or bombastic speech appears as a scheme in Sherry, as a vice in Puttenham; Puttenham gives *tapinosis* or the 'abbaser' first as a scheme and later as a vice, etc.). A consequent reluctance to take these figures seriously, and to afford them anything like the same critical weight or space as the tropological 'changes of signification' endures still. Metaphor, metonymy, synecdoche and irony have achieved a general academic respectability that one can scarcely imagine being accorded to epistrophe or chiasmus or hendiadys. Nowhere is this more apparent than in Shakespearean stylistic criticism: 'imagery' – i.e. tropical language, and especially metaphor – has been the staple of a critical industry that has given only token acknowledgment to 'sound patterns' as potential objects of analysis. And the poetic or dramaturgic principle behind this choice is not far to seek: the trope is deemed capable of participating fully in the thematic development of the drama (see, e.g., Clemen 1951; Charney 1961), while the scheme remains a more or less inert mode of verbal *appliqué*, able at best to provide an attractive formal framework to the drama proper.

Much of the ideological force of this confident preference, however, is in practice undermined by the difficulty of upholding any absolute two-branch division of the 'figures of words'. So many demarcation disputes have arisen over the centuries that the stability of Quintilian's system is thrown seriously into question. One rhetorician's trope will often prove, given time, another's scheme: *epitheton*, the qualifier, given by Quintilian as a trope, becomes in Susenbrotus and other Renaissance manuals a scheme (Puttenham hedges and gives it as both); *hyperbaton*, departure from normal word order, the schematic class *par excellence*, is curiously considered as a trope by Quintilian, who in other cases, such as *prosopopeia*, fails to decide and opts for a tropical-schematic hybrid. The moral is, of course, that no discursive move can be semantically neutral or neuter in context. In operation, the most elementary schematic pattern will be seen to effect some conceptual or semantic shift. Those simple devices of clausal symmetry and parallelism that have won such scorn for *TG* (figures such as isocolon, epimone, etc.) in reality enact essential equivalences or antitheses of thought:

> Pro. He after honour hunts, I after love;
> He leaves his friends to dignify them more;
> I leave myself, my friends, and all, for love. (1. 1. 63ff.)

The equally rudimentary devices of lexical and morphemic repetition on show in *LLL* in fact create relations of semantic tension as well as of formal correspondence between the various occurrences of the reiterated lexeme or morpheme, a factor that is explicitly codified in the case of *ploce* (a 'speedy iteration of one word' involving variation in sense):

> And then grace us in the disgrace of death . . .
> The grosser manners of these world's delights
> He throws upon the gross world's baser slaves . . .
> Your oath is pass'd to pass away from these. (1. 1. 3; 29f.; 49)

And the most 'facile' ornaments of all, patterns of phonemic iteration (alliteration, assonance, consonance, rhyme, etc.) act not only to materialize the form of the expression, or speech continuum – crucial in an oral art like theatre – but also to order and segment the very form of the content, accentuating its continuities and disjunctions:

> Prin. The effect of my intent is to cross theirs:
> They do it but in mockery merriment;
> And mock for mock is only my intent. . . .
> There's no such sport as sport by sport o'erthrown,
> To make theirs ours and ours none but our own:

So shall we stay, mocking intended game,
And they, well mock'd, depart away with shame. (5. 2. 138ff.)

Much the same lesson appears to emerge from contemporary semantics, with its increasing tendency (Lyons 1977; Kempson 1977) to englobe the territories of phonology, morphology and syntax, i.e. those very areas within which these devices operate. The temptation might be to abandon the scheme altogether as a working and workable category, but in effect – precisely in marking off these 'structural' levels of analysis – it does correspond intuitively to a group of rhetorical games in some degree distinct from tropological operations and the so-called figures of thought. What need not be accepted uncritically, however, are the conceptual and dramaturgic limitations imposed on the scheme in the rhetorical-critical tradition. Indeed, the attempt will be made here to reverse this tradition and to explore the roles of these 'surface' forms within the narrative and potential stage make-up of the very group of plays under accusation.

## (1) (Syn)tactics

Perhaps nothing excites greater indifference, if not outright impatience, in contemporary audiences than those intra- and transphrastic patterns that ostend the syntactic organization of discourse. Not only are we no longer accustomed to processing aesthetic information over lengthy stretches of talk, but our conception of syntax is, on the whole, far more severely functional than that of our Renaissance forebears: we do not expect to have to pay active attention to it as a plastic medium in itself. And yet there is an authentic functionality in many of the syntactic schemes which our resistance leads us to overlook: in a word, the role of foregrounded syntax *in* the dramatic dialogue in translating, as it were, the syntax *of* the dramatic narrative.

In one of the very rare modern attempts to re-evaluate the dramatic – and indeed theatrical – importance of syntactic structures in Shakespeare (specifically in *Hamlet*), Alessandro Serpieri (1980b) elaborates a general rhetorical-dramaturgic principle that is certainly extendible to the comic canon:

> Of the various levels of the text, the syntactic, the semantic, the phonic-rhythmic-metrical . . . the syntactic level appears to be the most decisive in the stage transcodification of the peculiar modes of speech marking the various characters. . . . The syntactic level is the one at which the dramatis personae are most clearly distinguished since it is there that the grammatical and stylistic competence, the figures of thought and thus the ideological positions that characterize them are expressed. (13, my translation)

245

The centrality of syntax in the rhetoric of the dramatic representation is emphatically upheld by Thomas Heywood, whose *Apology for Actors* recommends rhetoric – still under the aegis of *actio*, but likewise under that of *elocutio* – above all for the 'punctuational' control it allows the orator and actor over the flow of discourse: 'To come to Rhetoricke, it not only emboldens a scholler to speake, but instructs him to speake well, and with iudgement, to obserue his commas, colons, & full poynts, his parentheses, his breathing spaces and distinctions' (1612: 13).

Now among the syntactic schemes whose decided 'easiness' is most likely to irritate today (as the critical history of *TG* suggests) is the insistent iteration of words or phrases at the beginning or end of verses and clauses (*anaphora*: $\frac{Axxxx}{Axxxx}$; *epistrophe*: $\frac{xxxxA}{xxxxA}$). Virtually all the speakers in *TG* employ the anaphoric mode in at least one speech, and over the widest possible range of topics, so that it comes to represent part of an overall rather than individual stylistic idiolect in the play. Thus Julia on her faith in Proteus:

> His words are bonds, his oaths are oracles,
> His love sincere, his thoughts immaculate,
> His tears pure messengers sent from his heart,
> His heart as far from fraud as heaven from earth (2. 7. 75–8);

Valentine on the scourges inflicted by love:

> Whose high imperious thoughts have punish'd me
> With bitter fasts, with penitential groans,
> With nightly tears, and daily heart-sore sighs (2. 4. 125ff.);

Panthino on sons leaving home:

> Some to the wars, to try their fortune there;
> Some, to discover islands far away;
> Some, to the studious universities. (1. 3. 8ff.)

In each of these cases the repetition appears perfectly in earnest, and in each instance serves to express coincidence and integration (*all* Proteus's qualities, *all* possible punishments of love, *all* sons, etc.). This is plainly the automatized function of the figure, the reiteration and accumulation of corresponding grammatical subjects and predicates by way of *conjunction*, and as such it represents faithfully enough the harmonious dramatic situation in the comedy's early scenes (conjunction of the two friends and of the lovers within the two couples etc.).

Quite distinct in its effect is Proteus's heavily patterned monologue debating the choice of mistresses, i.e. that fulcral moment in the play when its initial conjunctions begin to fracture. What Proteus accumu-

246

lates are no longer correspondences but alternatives, so that the role of lexical repetition becomes *dis*junctive. The stepping-up of schematic intensity here (both anaphora and epistrophe (the combined form *symploce*: $^{AxxxB}_{AxxxB}$) together with perfect isocolon) is an evident index of the sophistry of Proteus's reasoning:

> To leave my Julia, shall I be forsworn;
> To love fair Silvia, shall I be forsworn;
> To wrong my friend, I shall be much forsworn. (2. 6. 1ff.)

Disjunction becomes thereafter the dominant anaphoric function, as in Julia's parading of the ironical conflicts in her role:

> Alas, poor Proteus, thou hast entertain'd
> A fox . . .
> Alas, poor fool, why do I pity him . . .?
> Because he loves her, he despiseth me,
> Because I love him, I must pity him. . . .
> To plead for that which I would not obtain;
> To carry that which I would have refused;
> To praise his faith which I would have disprais'd. (4. 4. 91ff.)

It is this *dialectical* version of the initial repetition that represents one of the more powerful stylistic features of *TG* and that acts, in particular, as a highly effective pivot for dialogic takeover. What we might baptize as the disjunctive echo provides an endlessly variable mode of two-handed repartee in the play:

*Pro.*   So, by your circumstance, you call me fool.
*Val.*   So, by your circumstance, I fear you'll prove (1. 1. 36–7)

*Spe.*   What an ass art thou, I understand thee not.
*Lau.*   What a block art thou, that thou canst not! (2. 5. 23–4) (etc.)

Instant reverberation of this kind is already fairly close to travesty, and what saves the plentiful patterning of *TG* from absurdity is just this knowing testing of the limits of feasibility, to the point of caricature. A test-case is the play's most obsessively reiterated disjunction, the modest 'and yet' ('And yet I would I had o'erlook'd the letter'; 'And yet a thousand times it answers "no"'; 'And yet I was last chidden for being too slow', etc.). Launce loads the connector with an impossible heap of antitheses in his self-contradictory iffing-and-butting over his beloved:

> I am but a fool, look you, and yet I have the wit to think my master is a kind of knave; . . . yet I am in love, but a team of horse shall not pluck that from me; nor who 'tis I love; and yet 'tis a woman; but what woman I will not tell myself; and yet 'tis a milk-maid; yet 'tis not a maid, for she hath had gossips; yet 'tis a maid, for she is her master's maid, and serves for wages (3. 1. 261–9);

a feat that is denied to Valentine, defeated by the predictability of the device and so doubly forestalled in his iterative prime:

| | |
|---|---|
| *Val.* | And yet – |
| *Sil.* | A pretty period. Well, I guess the sequel; |
| | And yet I will not name it; and yet I care not. |
| | And yet take this again; and yet I thank you, |
| | Meaning henceforth to trouble you no more. |
| *Spe.* | (*Aside*) And yet you will; and yet another 'yet'. (2. 1. 108ff.) |

   This 'figure of report', as Puttenham re-christens it, is an exemplary instance of the *facilis* put to fairly arduous dramatic and comic service. And it would be idle, above all, to attempt to assess the figure and its conjuctive/disjunctive functionality in *TG* separately from the underlying structural configurations of the comedy, which are manifestly binary: the two titular gentlemen; their two ladies; the two specular servant-clowns; the two main geographical locations (Verona and Milan); and most important, the two-phase principal action (the apostasy of Proteus causing the disintegration of these couplings; the repentance of the same bringing about re-integration), within which the 'reporting' scheme finds its matrix and which it in turn brings, as it were, to the surface (on the binary or specular model in Shakespeare, see Pagnini 1976).

   It would be mistaken, also, to suppose that anaphoric repetition of this massy kind has no place in the rhetorically more sober later comedies. On the contrary, some of the most celebrated and dignified of Shakespeare's 'later' orations are structured on it (not least Portia's trial speech, in which rhetorical anaphora coincides with grammatical anaphora to lend the oration its structural and semantic coherence: 'It droppeth . . . It blesseth . . . It is enthroned . . . It is an attribute'). But the characteristic use of the scheme is not only conjunctive or associative but indeed *choral*: it is the figure of the harmonious dénouement, the point of final syntactic concord that translates, for example, the *harmonia universalis* of the last scene of *MV* ('In such a night'), or that enacts the all-yoking resolutions of the magical masque in *AYLI*:

| | |
|---|---|
| *Ros.* | (*To the Duke*) To you I give myself, for I am yours. |
| | (*To Orl.*) To you I give myself, for I am yours. |
| *Duke S.* | If there be truth in sight, you are my daughter. |
| *Orl.* | If there be truth in sight, you are my Rosalind. |
| *Phebe.* | If sight and shape be true, |
| | Why then my love adieu . . . |
| *Hymen.* | . . . You and you no cross shall part. |
| | You and you are heart in heart. |
| | You to his love must accord. (5. 4. 115ff.) |

248

The mode even seduces the professedly anti-rhetorical Jaques, who, prior to his departure for the hermitage, issues (how much in earnest is a matter of judgment) his own resolutive Hymenal dispensations:

| | |
|---|---|
| (To Duke | You to your former honour I bequeath, |
| S.) | Your patience and your virtue well deserve it. |
| (To Orl.) | You to a love that your true faith doth merit: |
| (To Oli.) | You to your land and love and great allies: |
| (To Sil.) | You to a long and well-deserved bed. (5. 4. 185ff.) |

Perhaps equally unpromising as candidates for theatricality are the cluster of schemes operating varieties of syntactic *inversion* and *progression*. Unpromising, since again these figures appear autonomously formal and elaborately literary, often to the point of preciosity. Indeed, the most 'transgressive' class of these devices, known generically as *hyperbaton* (i.e. a 'going beyond' or 'overstepping' (the limit)), licenses deviations or aberrations in word and clause order that are by definition excessive. The risk is explicit, the intent implicit: the limit is overstepped by way of a baroque flourish designed to gratify the indulgently aristocratic *cognoscente* (if only the speaker himself). And of course the court in *LLL* provides the right environment of leisurely tolerance towards decorative trespasses, of which Berowne, in particular, produces a veritable (rogue's) gallery in the opening scene (inversion of adverb/verb, object/relative clause, verb/object order: all forms of *anastrophe*):

> When I to feast expressly am forbid (1. 1. 62);
> Or, having sworn too hard a keeping oath (1. 1. 65);
> The French king's daughter with yourself to speak. (1. 1. 134) (etc.)

While the Princess permits herself the occasional decorously restrained touch of sinful syntax ('Here, good my glass', etc.), and Holofernes does not so much invert as simply revert (namely to Latin order: 'A soul feminine saluteth us'), Berowne's true rival in the delicate art of going beyond is the honey-tongued Boyet, equally adept in the nonchalant anastrophe ('Proud of employment, willingly I go', 2. 1. 35), and prepared to take the business of clause transposition to an entropic extreme that brings him close to the condition quaintly labelled (and recommended) by Susenbrotus (1540) as *confusio*, i.e. syntactic chaos (note, for example, the past participle phrase left daintily dangling in Boyet's narrative):

> If my observation, which very seldom lies,
> By the heart's still rhetoric disclosed with eyes
> Deceive me not now, Navarre is infected. (2. 1. 227–9)

Yet the deviations of Boyet or Berowne represent merely a knowing and patrician flirtation with the danger of grotesquerie. Where the overstepping steps over into the authentically grotesque, the zone of the ingenuously rather than ingeniously precious, is in those schematic *cornucopiae verborum*, the literary productions of Armado. Armado's brand of inversion is of a more radical nature, namely that form of syntactic-temporal-logical upheaval that bears the dignifying title of *hysteron proteron* ('the latter (in place of) the former'):

> I shall be forsworn, which is a great argument of falsehood, if I love.
> (I. 2. 159–60)

The consequences of the overturning are especially marked in the Spaniard's epistolary account of his sniffing-out (*in fragrante delicto*, as it were) of Costard's sexual offence; the letter's relentless juggling with subjects and predicates, agents and patients, main and subordinate clauses, renders the actual narrative sequence brilliantly opaque:

> Him, I, as my ever-esteemed duty pricks me on, have sent to thee, to receive the meed of punishment, by thy sweet grace's officer, Anthony Dull, a man of good repute. (I. 1. 259ff.)

Into this transgression (grammatical) concerning transgression (erotical) there enters an intriguing note of rhetorical reflexivity. In his horrified description, earlier in the same letter, of Costard's misdeed – 'that obscure and most preposterous event' – Armado chooses what is in effect a synonym for his own figural practice: 'preposterous' (literally 'before after') being precisely Puttenham's alternative coinage for cart-before-horse inversion: 'Ye haue another manner of disordered speach, when ye misplace your words or clauses and set that before which should be behind ... the Greeks call it *Histeron proteron*, we name it the preposterous' (1589: 170).

But there is perhaps a further and further-reaching implication to be drawn from Armado's oblique self-glossing. His fantastically figured epistle – and here we arrive at the question of the particular *theatrical* status of these inversion schemes – becomes in the event a kind of dramatic script in miniature: a narrative (or *apologia*, of which the drama is one species, see Sonnino 1968: 226) delegated to another speaker (Navarre) to perform for the gratification of an attentive public (among them Berowne: 'This is ... the best that ever I heard'). And in practice the obscure logical-syntactic deviations of the letter are kin to the statutory transformations that *all* dramatic narrative undergoes in its passage from the underlying *fabula* to the actual plot. At the level of the *fabula*, such as it is, the events that Armado attempts (or better, attempts not) to represent can be reconstructed in the following logico-temporal order: Navarre's decree against intercourse of all kinds with women (A); Costard's offence (some form of intercourse) (B); Armado's discovery of the crime during his walk (C); Dull's consignment of the offender to the King, with letter (D); Navarre's sentence (E). At the level of plot, such as *it* is, this modest series unfolds in the following transformed order: Navarre's decree (A); the arrival of Dull with Costard and the letter (D); the account of Armado's walk (C); the description of the offence (B); Navarre's sentence (E). An inversion that is simply preposterous.

In the case of *LLL*, the logical and chronological order of things is so exiguous anyway that the effects of any narrative *hysteron proteron* remain strictly limited. This is obviously not true of a comedy like *MA*, whose narrative interest depends very considerably on the displacements that arise between *fabula* and plot: the postponement, for example, of the news of Hero's non-death, or the strategic juxtaposition of bits of the Don John conspiracy with phases in the Beatrice–Benedick clash. For this reason a deal of emblematic significance attaches to the syntactic aberrations of the comic go-between responsible for resolving the different strands of the plot, Constable Dogberry. Dogberry's derangements of time and logic, unlike Armado's, are evidently to be attributed not to excess but to deficiency:

> If you meet a thief, you may suspect him, by virtue of your office, to be no true man; . . . The most peaceable way for you, if you do take a thief, is to let him show himself what he is, and steal out of your company. (3. 3. 49–59)

And yet Dogberry, like Armado, has to narrate a crime (precisely the Don John conspiracy), and in doing so achieves a sequential disorder (compare his instructions to his men: 'Write down that they hope they serve God: and write "God" first, for God defend but God should go before such villains', 4. 2. 17–19) that is no less preposterous and no less open to parody:

Dog.   Marry, sir, they have committed false report, moreover they have spoken untruths, secondarily they are slanders, sixthly and lastly they have belied a lady, thirdly they have verified unjust things, and to conclude, they are lying knaves.

D. Pedro.  First I ask thee what they have done, thirdly I ask thee what's their offence, sixth and lastly why they are committed, and to conclude, what lay you to their charge. (5. 1. 210–18)

But then the *dispositio* of the comedy itself follows just this secondarily-sixthly-thirdly (dis)articulation.

Armado's letter, then, as a kind of digest of dramaturgic devices, reduced to absurdity: this albeit improbable reading does find confirmation in other figural follies on display. A notable instance is the form of apostrophe that Armado tries out in his passing attempt at narrative *pathos*:

> which with – O! with – but with this I passion to say wherewith.
> (1. 1. 253ff.)

Now apostrophe – scheme of *di*version rather than inversion – is a monologic figure inherited from classical drama (orientation towards the gods, the muses, etc.), and is brought out occasionally in *LLL* in order to (over)-dramatize the toils of the play's internal authors: Armado himself ('Assist me, some extemporal god of rhyme', 1. 2. 172f.), Berowne ('O my little heart! . . . Well I will love, write, sigh, pray', 3. 1. 181ff) and the rest. But the specific and somewhat degenerate species of apostrophe deployed in the letter is *parenthesis*, a brand of syntactic overstepping that 'setteth a sentence asunder by the interposition of another' (Peacham 1577; compare Heywood: 'his parantheses, his breathing spaces', see above, p. 246). And parenthesis is the *modus operandi* of another ubiquitous and intimately related dramaturgic convention, namely the aside, a convention that is used most effectively in this play against Armado himself (he fails, ironically, to perceive or recognize it) by his page:

| Moth. | . . . the hobby-horse is but a colt, – and your love perhaps a hackney. (*Aside*) . . . |
| Arm. | Fetch hither the swain: he must carry me a letter. |
| Moth. | A message well sympathized: a horse to be ambassador for an ass. |
| Arm. | Ha? ha? what sayest thou? (3. 1. 29–50) |

For all its inward, outward and backward turns along the way, however, Armado's letter *is* intended to arrive somewhere: at the highest possible final pitch. Its structural principle is that of *increase* or *crescendo*, whereby even the epithets describing poor Dull have to be arranged in reverse order of importance: 'good repute, carriage, bearing and estimation' (1. 1. 262–3). This is, as Puttenham would have it, the 'climbing' figure of *climax* (literally, the 'ladder'), a scheme that presents a mounting 'by divers degrees and steps' (Fraunce 1588b: Cvii$^v$) over a series of words, clauses or sentences, and that is representable diagrammatically as follows:

In the case of Armado, the investment of linguistic libido is such that the attempted climax becomes not merely schematic but virtually erotic (in accordance with the topic he usually applies it to, as it were mimetically):

> I do affect the very ground, which is base, where her shoe, which is
> baser, guided by her foot, which is basest, doth tread. . . . Love is a
> familiar; Love is a devil: there is no evil angel but Love. (1. 2. 156–63)

The rhetorical ladder is evidently an irresistible means of advancement
in the comedy; Holofernes clambers up a long and latinate one, again on
the inexhaustible theme of Dull and his qualities ('after his undressed,
unpolished, uneducated, unpruned, untrained, or rather unlettered, or
ratherest unconfirmed fashion', 4. 2. 16–18); Berowne reaches his
climax – optimistically – with Rosaline ('the clown bore it, the fool sent
it, and the lady hath it: sweet clown, sweeter fool, sweetest lady', 4. 3.
15–16); while the other lords play at the dialogic climbing over the
topical body of Berowne himself, until the latter intervenes to ruin the
sequence:

| | |
|---|---|
| King. | How well he's read, to reason against reading! |
| Dum. | Proceeded well, to stop all good proceeding! |
| Long. | He weeds the corn, and still lets grow the weeding. |
| Ber. | The spring is near, when green geese are a-breeding. |
| Dum. | How follows that? (1. 1. 94–8) |

Berowne's anticlimactic sport-spoiling here emphasizes the risk run in
attempting the figure, i.e. the *failure* of the verbal swelling to achieve
the promised (orgasmic) conclusion. Such terminal impotence is in
some degree shared by all the examples cited. And it is this failure which
suggests the larger dramatic resonances of the scheme. Climax, the
indispensable end (in more senses than one) of classical dramaturgy, is
in some measure attained in all the comedies, with the single and
notorious exception of *LLL* itself. The narrative and erotic non-
consummation of the comedy's finale ('Jack hath not Jill') is the perfect
structural equivalent to these local figural flops. Labours, up ladders, lost.

Another scheme, another theme: in one of his habitual satirical
asides, Armado's page produces a stock pun on his master's penury:

| | |
|---|---|
| Arm. | I love not to be crossed. |
| Moth. | He speaks the mere contrary: crosses love not him (*Aside*) (1. 2. 32–3) |

The main joke here is monetary ('crosses' as metonymy for the coins
that bear them and that Armado does not possess). It is not, perhaps,
among Moth's best. But the line does take on a dose of extra wit if read
simultaneously as a piece of canny self-glossing. For with Armado's
reproach it creates a perfect example of that specular relationship
A⟍  ⟋B
—  ⤬  — that goes under the name of *chiasmus* (literally,
B⟋  ⟍A 'crossing'):

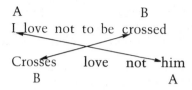

And the accompanying gloss ('he speaks the mere contrary') explains quite exactly the very 'crossing' procedure at work: mere or absolute reversal of the preceding syntagm. Nor is the exercise an isolated one, syntactic mirroring being one of Moth's preferred ploys in the relentless parodic guying of his master – either in the form of the full chiastic cross:

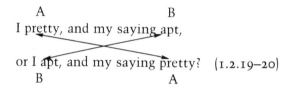

or in that of its sister-scheme, *antimetabole* (literally, the 'about-turn', confused with chiasmus by Puttenham and others), which limits the 'mere contrary' mirroring to a single verse or sentence, but which is procedurally identical (ABBA):

A⟶B ⟶C⟶ ⟵C⟵ B⟵
these betray nice wenches, that would be betrayed

⟵ A E⟶ F⟶
without these; and make them men of note

⟵ F⟵ E
(do you note, men?) (3.1.20–3)

Now where the specular turn-abouts of antimetabole tend to be restricted to self-satisfying self-reflection (as in Berowne's confessional series 'they have pitched a toil; I am toiling in a pitch, – pitch that defiles; defile! a foul word', 4. 3. 2–3), X (i.e. the *chi* of chiasmus) typically marks those spots in *LLL* where a critical – or more properly, crucial – choice has to be made between antithetical possibilities (A *versus* B). Thus it appears repeatedly in the opening scene to signal the men's Hercules-at-the-crossroads option between the active and the contemplative life; the opposing terms of the choice are held in perfect syntagmatic-paradigmatic balance through the sovraposition:

FIGURES

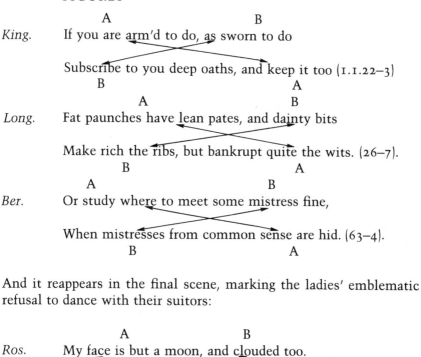

```
               A                    B
King.    If you are arm'd to do, as sworn to do

         Subscribe to you deep oaths, and keep it too  (1.1.22–3)
               B                    A
                    A                    B
Long.    Fat paunches have lean pates, and dainty bits

         Make rich the ribs, but bankrupt quite the wits.  (26–7).
               B                    A
               A                    B
Ber.     Or study where to meet some mistress fine,

         When mistresses from common sense are hid.  (63–4).
               B                    A
```

And it reappears in the final scene, marking the ladies' emblematic refusal to dance with their suitors:

```
               A                B
Ros.     My face is but a moon, and clouded too.

King.    Blessed are clouds, to do as such clouds do . . .
               B                A
               A                                B
Ros.     You took the moon at full, but now she's changed.

King.    Yet still she is the moon, and I the man.
               B                A
               A                                B
         The music plays; vouchsafe some motion to it.

Ros.     Our ears vouchsafe it.
               B
King.                              But your legs should do it. (5.2.203–217)
                                             A
```

The narrative correlative to this dialogic cruciform is quite precise and quite unmistakable. Navarre's invitation to dance, intended for the Princess, is in fact addressed to the masked Rosaline, and is part of the unwitting four-way exchange of partners that sets up a double actantial chiasmus among the eight characters involved (the initials below stand

255

for Navarre, Berowne, the Princess and Rosaline; Dumain, Longaville, Katherine and Maria; the dotted arrows represent the supposed courtship relations, the continuous arrows the actual couplings effected):

An analogous – although clearly more radical and structurally indispensable – interchange provides the main fun in *CE*. Here the actantial mix-up is of course the expression of the perfect double mirroring between the two sets of twins, but the resulting cross-over pattern is much the same ($A^1$ = Antipholus of Ephesus, $A^2$ = Antipholus of Syracuse, $D^1$ = Dromio of Ephesus, $D^2$ = Dromio of Syracuse):

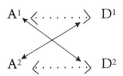

And significantly, *CE* is the other Shakespearean comedy rich in chiastic schemes, involving monologically and dialogically the exchanged *dramatis personae* themselves:

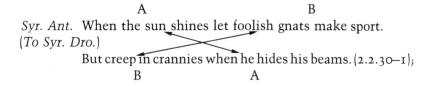

Syr. Dro. Well, sir, I thank you.
Syr. Ant.                                        Thank me, sir, for what?

                                A                                        B
Syr. Dro. Marry, sir, for this something that you gave me for nothing.

Syr. Ant. I'll make amends next to give you nothing for something. (49–54).
                                        B                        A

A                    B
*Adr.*       Thou art an elm, my husband, I a vine,
*(To Syr. Ant.)*
         Whose weakness married to thy stronger state . . .
         B                    A
                              (2.2.175–6).

If these dramatic-figural transections in *CE* necessarily have an immediate visual counterpart in the facial and costumic puns created amongst the actors, and in the confusing succession of their entrances and exits, those in *LLL* lend themselves to any number of possible scenic translations in terms of the arrangement of the players and their cross-stage movements ('You that way: we this way', as Armado is made to say at the end of the Folio text). Four-way – and occasionally eight-way – intercrossing patterns are a likely feature of any stage production of the comedy, which presents repeated quadrilateral configuration of speakers. The irony here is that the ladies decline the very dance formation, traditional to comic endings (compare *MND*, *AYLI, MA*), that would most directly transcode their rhetorical play into the kinesic and proxemic schemes of intersecting movements and partner-exchange (chiasmus is in this sense the purest embodiment of the supposedly Terpsichorean origins of the scheme in general: 'Scheme is a Greke worde, and signifyeth properlye the maner of gesture that daunsers use to make', Sherry 1550: Bvʳ). In *LLL* the dancing remains figurative, or at least figural.

### (2) The devices (and the vices) of the word

In one of his more literally schoolboyish jokes, Moth reduces the specular game at which he is so adept (ABBA) to the letter:

| | |
|---|---|
| *Arm.* | *(To Hol.)* Monsieur, are you not lettered? |
| *Moth.* | Yes, yes, he teaches boys the horn-book. |
| | What is a, b, spelt backward with the horn on his head? |
| *Hol.* | Ba, *pueritia*, with a horn added. |
| *Moth.* | Ba! most silly sheep with a horn. You hear his learning. (5. 1. 43–8) |

The schoolmaster's justified fear of being the double target for Moth's alphabetical mirroring (implying both his sheep-like ignorance and his be-horned ('wit-old') state) simply provokes another bout of anti-pedagogical letter-torturing that heavily underlines the point:

| | |
|---|---|
| *Hol.* | *Quis, quis*, thou consonant? |
| *Moth.* | The last of the five vowels, if you repeat them, or the fifth, if I. |

257

| Hol. | I will repeat them; a, e, i, – |
| Moth. | The sheep: the other two concludes it; o,u. . . . |
| Hol. | What is the figure? what is the figure? |
| Moth. | Horns. (5. 1. 49–58) |

*Per quam figuram?*: the bemused pedagogue himself can only respond (sheepishly) with his stock didactic interrogation. But Holofernes's suspicion that he has been out-figured is not mistaken, even if he fails to identify the actual winning move. For Moth's conundrums are in effect playful varieties of *metaplasm* (or 'new moulding'), the genre of schemes 'that alter the phonic or graphic continuity of the message, i.e. the form of the expression in its phonic or graphic manifestation' (Groupe μ 1970: II. 0. 1, my translation).

Metaplastic play, the mutation or mutilation of the normal structure of words or smaller units, is what is chiefly responsible for the extraordinary theatricalization in *LLL* of the material (or precisely, *plastic*) qualities of language, the 'form of the expression' as such. Such theatricalization finds its main thematic expression in the equation between the phonemic-morphemic features of speech and the human body and its alimentary functions. Thus if the cuckoldly Holofernes is identified as a horned vowel ('u', 'you', 'ewe'), the diminutive Moth is in turn dismissed as a 'consonant', i.e. a unit or body unable to stand alone (consonants are always attached to vowels). Immediately prior to his skirmish with the schoolmaster, however, Moth is allowed a full 'lexical' status as a little word, which, in keeping with his own gastronomic metaphor for the pedants' morphological follies, is swallowable-whole:

| Moth. | They have been at a great feast of languages, and stolen the scraps. |
| Cost. | O, they have lived long on the alms-basket of words. I marvel thy master hath not eaten thee for a word; for thou art not so long by the head as *honorificabilitudinitatibus*: thou art easier swallowed than a flap-dragon. (5. 1. 35–41) |

The word-structure-as-body trope recurs frequently in the other extensively metaplastic comedy, *MWW*, in which the operated-on corpus (or at times corpse) is that of the vernacular itself, the play's protagonist together with that other large-bodied victim, Falstaff. The specific metaphor, applied principally to the play's 'foreign' speakers and their inadvertent aberrations, is that of violent assault on the body in question: 'Here will be' predicts Mistress Quickly of her master Caius's speech, 'an old abusing of God's patience and the King's English' (1. 4. 4–5); the vulgar and its parts substitute the organs of the would-be duellers Caius and Evans: '*Host.* Disarm them both, and let them

258

question; let them keep their limbs whole, and hack our English' (3. 1. 71–2); Evans's phonation 'makes fritters of English' (5. 5. 144), and so on. The mother tongue is even psychologically victimized, for example by Nym's obsessively modish word-choice – 'Page. Here's a fellow frights English out of his wits' (2. 1. 134–5) – or, according to Bardolph's brilliant malapropism, by Slender's inebriation: 'Why, sir, for my part, I say the gentleman had drunk himself out of his five sentences' (1. 1. 157–8).

Now of the different kinds and levels of verbal 'hacking', that which most directly materializes the speech continuum – in rendering it decoratively or comically opaque – is the phonetic variety. Obviously there are distinctions to be made, in terms of attributed intentionality, between the figural mutation and the erroneous mutilation of phonetic structure. The pronunciational violations of Caius and Evans or of the rustics in *LLL* can scarcely be considered as rhetorical moves proper. And yet these deviations are unquestionably part of the rhetoric *of* the comedies, functioning, that is, as comic devices rather than as mere 'dialectal' variations designed to lend sociolinguistic breadth to the dramatic worlds in question. In this sense the most appropriate general framework for the analysis of decoration and error alike is precisely the grammatical-rhetorical class – itself poised between device and error – of the phonetic metaplasm, the more so since the *modi operandi* of the different forms of frittering, 'intentional' or otherwise, are much the same. The principles at work in the phonetic schemes are broadly three (see Groupe μ 1970: 11): *addition; omission* or *suppression; transformation* (suppression-addition).

### (a) Addition

Holofernes's poem on the death of the deer is – as it is intended to be – a model demonstration of the two main kinds of phonetic addition: the simple and the repetitive or accumulative. The latter is represented by the pedant's promised letter-affecting ('The preyful princess pierc'd and prick'd a pretty pleasing pricket'), which recalls Thomas Wilson's example of manic *parimion* (as opposed to more restrained alliteration); Wilson's burlesque draws on the same repeated consonant with its emphatic plosive force: 'some use overmuche repetition of some one letter, as pitiful pouertie praieth for a penye, but puffed presumpcio, passeth not a poynct, pompeying his pouche, wit pestilent pleasure' (1553: 87ʳ). But what Shakespeare's pedant is evidently proudest of is the simple additional operation that follows, an exemplification-cum-analysis of the power of *paragoge*, the addition of letter or phoneme to the end of a word. The poem itself hastens to point out the witty ambiguities of the addition, which transforms the deer's hurt ('sore') into a hurt deer ('sorel') and at the same time plays on the mathematical symbolism of the added letter:

> Some say a sore; but not a sore, till now made sore with shooting.
> The dogs did yell; put 'ell to sore, then sorel jumps from thicket;
> Or pricket sore, or else sore'll the people fall a-hooting.
> If sore be sore, then 'ell to sore makes fifty sores – O – sorel!
> Of one sore I an hundred make, by adding but one more l. (4. 2.56–60)

In its degenerate form as an involuntary phonetic redundancy, the added end-sound becomes the /a:/ that Caius suffixes to every final consonant and that characterizes him as a Frenchman: 'a green-a box'; 'take-a you rapier', 'contact-a'; 'peace-a your tongue', etc. And yet the same superfluous vowel, prefixed to the word (prosthesis), can serve as a prosodic nicety and index of aristocratic leisureliness (redundancy as discursive ease):

Ber.     Still a-repairing, ever out of frame (3. 1. 186)

(imitated in Holofernes's 'fall a-hooting'). A similar double rule applies to the addition of phoneme or syllable within the word (epenthesis), interpretable as an 'archaistic' refinement (Boyet's 'peeping thorough desire', 2. 1. 234) or as simple lexical incompetence (Armado's 'infamonize me among potentates', 5. 2. 670).

### (b) Suppression
Sir Nathaniel, after his public reading of Berowne's sonnet, is upbraided for spoiling the poem's rhythm:

Hol.     You find not the apostrophus, and so miss the accent. (4. 2. 115–16)

The accusation is that of having unwittingly restored a sound omitted for prosodic reasons (presumably the /e/ missing from 'vow'd' and 'bow'd' in the poem). Apostrophus, 'the rejecting of a vowel from the beginning or end of a word' (Ben Jonson, quoted by Richard David, Arden ed., note to 4. 2. 115), and related modes of omission are affected by rustics and aristocrats alike in the play, for reasons of 'dialectal' necessity or stylistic choice: 'O't'other side' (Costard) and 'out o' th' way' (Berowne); 'an't shall please you' (Dull) and 'to's seemeth it' (Boyet) or 'let me do't' (Princess), etc. A less automatized shared example is the /a/ for 'he' that is adopted innocently by Dull ('a' must fast three days a week', 1. 2. 121) and affected by his social superiors ('Prin. A' speaks not like a man', 5. 2. 522; 'Ber. A' can carve too', 5. 2. 323); 'Boy. . . . and that a' wears next his heart', 5. 2. 705–6), giving rise to an apostrophic orgy in one of the Princess's more contrived witticisms:

FIGURES

Whoe'er a' was, a' show'd a mounting mind. (4. 1. 4.)

It might be noted, in passing, that the reverse process, a *deliberate* missing or rather filling-in of the *apostrophus*, is part of the archaizing style that the comedy's aristocrats on occasion affect. Both Berowne (in the Second Folio text) and the Princess (in the First Quarto text) restore the possessive "'s" to an (etymologically dubious) adjectival dignity:

Ber.    To show his teeth as white as whale his bone (5. 2. 332)

Prin.    A' speaks not like a man of God his making (5. 2. 522)

Phonetic suppression in *MWW*, the inadvertent *apostrophus*, is one of Evans's more striking achievements; it is always the initial phoneme, and usually the semivowel /w/ (as in "elshman') to go: 'for all the 'orld'; "ork upon the case'; 'can you affection the 'oman?', etc.

### (c) Transformation (suppression-addition)

'Master Person, *quasi* pierce-one': the process of phonetic transformation almost always depends on Holofernes's *quasi*, i.e. on the closeness of the substituted and substituting sounds, since it is this that permits the immediate recognition of the witty or unwitting operation being carried out. And this vicinity is obviously more recognizable when the sounds in the transformational relationship are actually juxtaposed: the canonical principle of *paronomasia* (as distinct from the homonymic pun, where the transformation is purely semantic). Puttenham proudly quotes an example from his own now lost interlude, *The Wooer*, which plays on the kinship of two labial consonants: 'They be lubbers not lovers that so use to say' (Ziii^r). It duly shows up in *TG*:

Spe.    . . . my master is become a notable lover . . .
Lau.    A notable lubber, as thou reportest him to be. (2. 5. 37–40)

More fruitful, perhaps, at least in *LLL*, is punning vowel transformation: ship/sheep (2. 1. 218); in/on/one (4. 1. 78); tittles/titles (4. 1. 83); etc.

Still in its 'rhetorical' guise, phonetic substitution – like addition and suppression – can produce on occasion an elegantly archaic touch ('*Boy*. With libbard's head on knee', 5. 2. 542). But for the rest it is the prerogative of those who aspire beyond the limits of their phonological competence: Costard with his 'demsel', 'gardon', 'parfect' and 'God dig-you-den' (for 'God give you good even'), or Armado with his strange 'Chirrah', picked up by Holofernes ('*Quare* chirrah, not sirrah?', 5. 1. 31–2), which may echo the odd mode of address mocked by Wilson in his recollection of an affected Cambridge man: 'he made humbly his thre curtesies and sayd in this maner. Cha good even my good lorde' (1553: 87^r).

261

A rather more consistent system of substitutions is attempted in *MWW*, as part of its mimesis of the 'strange'. Evans un-voices virtually all consonants: voiced/b/becomes voiceless/p/('petter' 'prains');/v/ becomes/f/('fery');/d/becomes/t/('goot'), etc. The exception is the voiceless/k/, which is turned instead into voiced/g/('knog', 'stog'). Caius in turn reduces both/w/and/f/to/v/('vill', 'vetch'),/ð/to/d/ ('Dat', 'des') and/θ/to/t/('trot'), but in referring to Evans, is evidently contaminated by the Welshman's own voicelessness:

> he has pray his Pible well. (2. 3. 7)

In theatrical performance, all of these operations register as fully 'auricular' events within the spoken utterance, so that the appropriate terms in which to define them are undoubtedly phonetic. In the rhetoric books, on the contrary, metaplasms are in the first instance 'ortho-graphical' figures, changes not of sounds but of letters. And so, in a sense, they appear in the play-texts: as graphic devices *destined* for phonetic realization. Figures which remain prevalently graphic or orthographic in function are of course very few, their theatricality being necessarily limited – the occasional 'anagrammatical' re-mix, more perceptible to eye than ear (the Duke's 'perversely she persevers so' in *TG*, for example, 3. 2. 28), and the odd literal game, like the added 'e' of the on/one puns in *LLL* and *TG*.

But the issue of graphic-phonetic (and so, by implication, textual-oral) priority is very much alive in the grammatical and rhetorical universe of the late Tudor period. And it enters directly into the metalanguage of *LLL*, adding a certain topical and controversial colour to the comedy's dramatization of language as material event. Holofernes complains loudly of Armado's (metaplastic) violation of what he takes to be correct pronunciation:

> He draweth out the thread of his verbosity finer than the staple of his argument. I abhor such fanatical phantasimes, such insociable and point-devise companions; such rackers of orthography, as to speak dout, fine, when he should say doubt; det, when he should pronounce debt, – d, e, b, t, not d, e, t; he clepeth a calf, cauf; half, hauf; neighbour *vocatur* nebour; neigh abbreviated ne. This is abhominable, which he would call abominable. (5. 1. 17ff.)

Holofernes's critique is intended to be stylistic ('the thread of his verbosity'), but his objections, and most of his examples, come from the spelling reform debate of the day, particularly from Bullokar's tract *The Booke at Large* (1580), dedicated to the same topic of the non-correspondence between written and spoken English: 'Also as touching

... superfluous letters, I finde, that :b: in doubt :l: in shoulder, and that :g: generally before :h: ... in one sillable, and also :g: before :n: in one sillable, are unsounded' (16). The irony of Holofernes's borrowing is that he perfectly reverses the principles of Bullokar and the other spelling reformers, who demanded a phonetically faithful 'true writing ... to make us certayne wyth what letters euery member of our speach ought to be written' (Hart 1569, Epistle). This *absolute authority of sound* becomes for Holofernes the *absolute tyranny of writing*, especially in the case of latinate words: it is speech that has to obey the dictates of spelling. Thus where Bullokar sees superflous letters, Holofernes hears omitted phonemes, orthography put on the rack in the cause of 'point-devise' rhetorical preciosity.

The schoolmaster's philographic delirium is plainly a symptom of his fetishistic bookishness: 'the text', as he puts it, 'most infallibly concludes it' (4. 2. 156). Grammar – i.e. Latin grammar ('Priscian a little scratched') – retains for him its original sense of the science of letters, and not least in the 'grammatical' figures he puts so abundantly on show. But, as one might expect of a set of *dramatis personae* themselves arranged schematically over a span of the alphabet – A: Adriano de Armado; B: Berowne, Boyet; C: Costard; D: Dumain, Dull; F: Forester; H: Holofernes; J: Jaquenetta; K: Katherine; L: Longaville; M: Maria, Marcade; N: Navarre, Nathaniel; (O: Rowe's 'Officers and Others'); P: Princess of France (sometimes given in the First Quarto as Q: Queen); R: Rosaline – there is a broader consciousness in the comedy of the graphic and thus textual allegiances of its rhetorical schemes, expressed most tellingly in the mocking reception given to Berowne's letter (and its letters):

| | |
|---|---|
| *Ros.* | O! he hath drawn my picture in his letter. |
| *Prin.* | Any thing like? |
| *Ros.* | Much in the letters, nothing in the praise. |
| *Prin.* | Beauteous as ink; a good conclusion. |
| *Kath.* | Fair as text B in a copy-book. |
| *Ros.* | Ware pencils, ho! let me not die your debtor, |
| | My red domenical, my golden letter: |
| | O! that your face were not so full of O's. (5. 2. 38–45) |

The black B (for Berowne)/black Rosaline association begins and ends with what is in effect the play's most recurrent scheme (so recurrent, in fact, that Dover Wilson wished to eliminate it as a typographical impurity): the exclamatory 'O!' that the rhetoricians elevated with the name of *ecphonesis* ('outcry'). The purest of phonic figures, therefore, of which Berowne is the play's most obsessive exponent ('O my good knave Costard ... O what is remuneration ... O! why then, three-farthing worth of silk . . . O stay slave . . .', etc., 3. 1. 139ff.). It is clearly to be supposed that the letter in question, like Berowne's earlier sonnet ('O! pardon love this wrong', 4. 2. 113), and like all his speeches and texts, draws upon the device, whereby Rosaline's sarcastic wish that Katherine's face 'were not so full of O's' is to be taken also as a further stab at her suitor's style of pathos. The phonic 'O!' is exposed as a graphic 'O'; Berowne's pathetical outcries as calculated textual tactics. There is an ambiguity here that is essential to a play that strategically explores the boundaries between text and performance and that continuously declares – through the copious letters, poems, readings and declamations of which it is composed – the inescapable textuality of its own rhetoric – a textuality and a rhetoric that are in the (theatrical) event, however, genuine (rather than phoney) *phoné*.

Up or down a step in the hierarchy of linguistic structure is the level of greatest stylistic peril: the zone of morphological variation and production. No area of cultural endeavour aroused intenser passions in Tudor England than the pursuit of the 'lexical' brand of eloquence that derived from word-hunting, word-borrowing, word-coining, word-joining, word-reviving or simple word-spinning (see Jones 1953). The passions, and the perils, regarded not so much the cultivation of eloquence itself as what it did to the vernacular. For the question, debated throughout the sixteenth century, as to the lexical adequacy of the English language was long considered a stylistic rather than a structural problem, a matter of the expressive potentialities of the vulgar, especially in its literary application. John Skelton's rhetorical disclaimer in 'Philip Sparrow' – 'My stile as yet direct / with englyshe wordes elect / our natural tonge is rude / And harde to be ennyede / with Pollysshed tearmes lustye / Our language is so rustye' – is an invitation to augment the lexical stock of the language for reasons of style. And the English rhetoricians themselves were particularly sensitive to the issue, both as direct importers of classical 'terms of art' (Wilson, Peacham, etc.) or coiners of English equivalents (Lever, Puttenham), and as upholders of the ideal of eloquence: there are 'moe things', complains Ralph Lever, 'then there are words to express things by' (1573, 'Forespeache'); and Richard Sherry, recalling that 'oure language for the barbarousness and lacke of eloquence hathe bene complayned of', justifies the use of lexical variation and innovation for the ends of *elocutio*: 'But yet an unused worde or poetical, hath also somtyme in the oracion hys dignitie, and beyng put in place (as Cicero sayth) oftentymes the oracyon may seem greater' (1550: Aii$^v$, Bii$^v$). In the end it is the *figural* capacity of English that is placed in doubt by the supposedly primitive state of the lexicon: 'the art of figures of speech seemed so restricted to classical rhetoric and classical authors that it was not until the last quarter of the century, when numerous rhetorics in English appeared . . . that the English language was thought fully capable of employing them' (Jones 1953: 9–10).

It is important to stress the terms of the debate on the vernacular, since the inclusion of morphological minting and tinkering within the territory of *elocutio* has considerable consequences for Elizabethan rhetoric itself. Much of the violent hostility excited by lexical innovation – the century-long campaign against inkhorn terms and related novelties – took on a directly anti-rhetorical aspect, as in the tirade of Sir Thomas Chaloner, translator of Erasmus: '[the Rethoriciens] plainely thynke theim selfes demygods, if lyke horsleches thei can shew two tongues, I mean to mingle their writings with words sought out of strange langages, as if it were alonely thyng for theim to poudre theyr bokes with ynkehorne termes' (quoted in Baugh 1970: 261). The response of the rhetoricians is an even severer odium towards the very lexical excesses they are accused of fostering. No one is more emphatic in his repudiation of the hunt-the-novel-word mode of *elocutio* than Thomas Wilson: 'I know them that thynke Rhethorique to stande wholye upon darke woordes, and hee that can catche an ynke horne terme by the taile, hym thei coumpt to be a fine Englishe man, and a good Rhetorician' (1553: 86ᵛ). Not by chance, the greater part of those much-advertised rhetorical scarecrows, the vices of language, have to do with just these adventures and misadventures in the lexicon: the 'forrein speech', 'foule affectation', 'mingle-mangle', 'uncouthe', 'long language' and related sins of the intemperate word on which Puttenham exercises his Englishing resources.

Now the problem with the rhetoricians' worthy caveats in this morphological minefield is that the virtue (eloquence and the stocking of the vulgar)/vice (foul affectation) relationship is at best dialectical, and the criteria for distinguishing the two at most contextual: 'a good figure', admits Puttenham, 'may become a vice, and by [the poet's] good discretion, a vicious speech go for a vertue in the Poeticall science' (1589: Eeiiᵛ). There can be no *a priori* guarantees as to which side of the moral divide any single coinage or borrowing or adaptation will fall on. *All* lexical operations, inhabiting the shifting boundaries between the *ars recte loquendi* of grammar and the *ars bene dicendi* of rhetoric, invite a disastrous incompatibility between the striking and the acceptable: 'the *virtus* of the *recte*', as Heinrich Lausberg puts it, 'may come into conflict with the *virtus* of the *bene*' (1967: 93, my translation). It is on this dangerous virtuous/vicious ambivalence of schemes of the lexicon that Shakespeare – the most considerable lexical experimenter and satirist of lexical experimentation in the Elizabethan age – draws for a rich stock of rhetorical-comic play.

The hectic lexical spinning, borrowing, coining and joining that goes on in *LLL* re-enacts the whole history of the grammatical-rhetorical Tudor debate on the subject. On the one hand the pedants seek out their latinisms not only as elocutionary ornaments but also as expressions of an anachronistic disdain towards the mother tongue. Armado's passing condemnation of the vernacular – 'which to annothanize in the vulgar (O base and obscure vulgar!)' (4. 1. 69–70) – and Holofernes's scornful dismissal of Dull's illatinity – 'Most barbarous intimation' (4. 2. 13; 'barbarous' used in the sense given in Thomas Thomas's *Dictionarium* (1588): 'rude in doing or speaking . . . ignorant, rustical, churlish; without eloquence') – reflect an attitude that Richard Eden was already able, in 1562, to view with retrospective relief: 'the Latin toonge be accompted ryche, and the Englysshe indigent and barbarous, as it hathe byn in tyme past, muche more than it nowe is, before it was enriched and amplified by sundry bookes in manner of all artes' (quoted in Jones 1953: 18). As a consequence they earn the usual contempt reserved for the inkhornizing 'rhetorician': the 'mint of phrases', 'high-born words', 'plume of feathers', etc. attracted by Armado, together with the more ponderous critique attempted, ironically, by Holofernes ('He draweth out the thread': the precise accusation is that of using a 'high' style of word-choice for a subject that merits a humble style – the *genus attenuato*, literally 'drawn out' – and is anticipated in Berowne's 'How low soever the matter, I hope in God for high words', 1. 1. 190–1). On the other hand, the morphological productivity of the aristocrats suggests a perfect rhetorical ease with a vernacular that has already amply demonstrated its capacity for accommodating newcomers and all-comers. Watching from the margins are the 'barbarous' rustics, bemused or astounded by the entire feast ('Remuneration!') – 'some people', as the lexicographer Edward Phillips observes, 'if they spy but a hard word are as much amazed as if they had met with a hobgoblin' (quoted in Baugh 1970: 260) – but provoked on occasion into producing morphological monstrosities or hobgoblins of their own ('*honorifica*').

For all of these activities, at whatever social level and with whatever end in view, the modalities are those of the phonetic metaplasm, namely addition, suppression and transformation.

*(a) Addition*

That manic form of 'repetitive' addition that is represented on the phonetic plane by alliterative *parimion* has its lexical counterpart in the multiple verbal pile-up, *congeries* (Puttenham's 'heaping figure').

Behind the massing of lexical items lies an optimistic and simple-minded version of Erasmus's *copia verborum*, or, in Elyot's translation, 'plenty of words', a plenty that it is hoped will automatically be *ac rerum* ('and of matter'). This is the conception of amplification as accumulation: 'garnished by the pleasant and sweet sound of words ioyned together' (Fenner 1584: D3ʳ). Used with sufficient irony, the word-heap is the figure of the exuberant descriptive overflow:

Ber.        This wimpled, whining, purblind, wayward boy,
           This signor junior, giant-dwarf, dan Cupid (*LLL* 3. 1. 174–5)

and used with sufficient restraint, the figure of solemn emphasis:

Dum.      To love, to wealth, to pomp, I pine and die. (1. 1. 31)

Erasmus himself, however, warns 'that the aspiration to copia is dangerous . . . it is, assuredly, such a thing as may be striven for at no slight risk, because, according to the proverb, "Not every man has the luck to go to Corinth"' (1513: 11). *Copia*, observes Francis Bacon in his retrospective critique of the English Ciceronians, may remain merely and catastrophically *verborum*: 'for men began to hunt more after words, than matter, and more after the choiseness of the Phrase . . . then after the weight of the matter' (1605: 18ᵛ). And the failure to get to Corinth, or to marry matter with verbiage, is nowhere more evident than in the over-extended congeries, one of the most easily caricatured of excesses:

Pyr.                the fairest dame
          That liv'd, that lov'd, that look'd with cheer. (*MND* 5. 1. 282–3)

The limiting of copiousness to the heaped-up lexical items alone becomes explicit and indeed obligatory in that form of accumulation in which the denotation is supposed to remain unvaried (*synonymia*). Erasmus admits warily that the synonymizing scheme is good 'for plenitude of words. When we use different words to express the same thought' (quoted in Sonnino 1968: 110); in contrast, the enthusiasm of Quintilian is unequivocal: 'it serves to make the sense stronger and more obvious' (IX. iii. 45f.). The trouble is that making the sense obvious through change-ringing is exactly what produces lexical tautology or pleonasm, prohibited by Quintilian as 'a superfluity of words' (VIII. iii. 53f.). Such redundancy is a classic instance of virtuous/vicious identity, its acceptability depending purely on contextual or co-textual factors: 'sometimes the form of pleonasm', Quintilian is obliged to admit, 'may have a pleasing effect when used for emphasis'. The context and co-text of the synonym syndrome in *LLL* are such as to place the figure unappealably on the tautological side of the divide, both because of the characterial stock its exponents belong to (pedant and braggart) and because of the carefully mingled and mangled lexical stock (or 'store', Puttenham's term for the scheme) they draw on:

(Arm.)    ... which here thou viewest, beholdest, surveyest, or seest (1. 1. 239–40)

some delightful ostentation, or show, or pageant, or antic, or firework (5. 1. 103–4)

Hol.    ... *coelo*, the sky, the welkin, the heaven; ... on the face of *terra*, the soil, the land the earth (4. 2. 5–7)

a kind of insinuation, as it were *in via*, in way of explication; *facere*, as it were replication, or, rather, *ostentare*, to show, as it were, his inclination. (4. 2. 13–16)

In the case of Armado, the search for plentiful variation has a particular intertextual history that furnishes another likely contextual clue. The opening of the Spaniard's first letter appears as a frenzy of paraphrastic titles for the addressee, the King:

Great deputy, the welkin's viceregent, and sole dominator of Navarre, my soul's earth's God, and body's fostering patron. (1. 1. 216ff.)

This mode of address resembles very strikingly that of the resolutely inkhornizing physician Andrew Boorde in the dedications to the first two editions of his well-known *Dyetary of Health*. The first edition (1542) has 'To the armypotent Prynce and valyent Lorde Thomas Duke of Norfolke. Andrew Boorde of physicke doctor: doth humlye commendacyon with immortale thankes. ... the message done, I with festinacyon and dylygence did not prolonge the time.' Here the lexical kinship with Armado is quite specific: 'armypotent' appears in the titles Armado bestows on his Worthy – 'The armipotent Mars, of lances the almighty' (5. 2. 637); 'festinacyon' becomes the Spaniard's 'bring him festinately hither' (3. 1. 4–5); 'commendacyon' is transformed into the 'I did commend the black oppressing humour' of the letter itself, with reference to the very Boordean topic of 'the most wholesome physic of thy health-giving air' (1. 1. 228–9), etc. The second edition has instead 'Egregious doctours and maysters of the Eximiouse and Archane Science of Physicke, of your Urbanite Exaspere not your selfe agaynste me for makynge of this lytle volume.' Boorde's second epistle is quoted by Angel Day, in his rhetorical letter-writing treatise, as an example of the very kind of pleonastic logorrhoea to be avoided by the tyro correspondent: 'was there ever seene from a learned man a more preposterous [NB] and confused kind of writing, forced with so many

268

and such odde coyned tearmes in so little uttering?' (1586: 5). It was presumably Day's highly popular manual that drew Shakespeare's attention to this model of 'a ridiculous maner of writing' letters, although it is interesting to note that Shakespeare himself appears to have drawn more directly on the first (unquoted) edition. The tautological and latinizing epistolary opening became something of a rhetorical *topos*; Thomas Wilson quotes what he claims to be another authentic, although anonymous, instance: 'Ponderying, expendyng, and reuoluting with my self, your ingent affabilitee, and ingenious capacitee, for mundane affaires: I cannot but celebrate and extolle your magnificall dexteritee . . . I obtestate your clemencie, to invigilate thus muche for me, accordyng to my confidence, and as you know my condigne merites' (1553: 86ᵛ–87ʳ). The titular permutations of the magnifical or magnificent Armado begin to look almost like economy itself (although compare his 'in thy condign praise', 1. 2. 25).

'Simple' morphological addition in the play – and in the Elizabethan rhetorical universe at large – takes the form of compounding, the yoking of two existing lexical forms into one. Word-joining was viewed by some as a 'native' alternative to neologistic word-coining in the improvement of the eloquence of English; its loudest patron and most spectacular practitioner is Thomas Nashe, who in his preface to *Christ's Tears over Jerusalem* defends the compound as the only salvation from the monosyllabic rusticity of the mother tongue: 'For the compounding of my wordes, therein I imitate rich men, who, having gathered store of white single money together convert a number of those small little scutes into great peeces of gold . . . Our English tongue, of all languages, most swarmeth with the single money of monosillables, which are the only scandal of it' (1593). In the pamphlet itself, Nashe is perfectly faithful to this manifesto: 'Awake your wits, graue authorized Lawe-distributers, and shew your selues as insinuatiue-subtile in smoaking this Citty-sodoming trade out of his starting-holes as the professors of it are vnderpropping it.'

*LLL'S* great compounder is Berowne, whose lexeme-yoking, phrase-heaping, epithet-leaping mode of personal description is indeed Nashean in its almost asyntactic breathlessness (compare the exuberant name-calling in *Pierce Penniless* – the 'pinch-fart penny-father', 'Lady Swine-snout, his yellow-faced mistress . . . like a fore-horse', 'any shame-swollen toad [with a] spit-proof face'; the 'all-to-be-frenchified' courtier, etc.):

Ber.    Some carry-tale, some please-man, some slight zany,
        Some mumble-news, some trencher-knight, some Dick. (5. 2.
            463ff.)

The point is to show the joint.

### (b) Suppression

This is necessarily a somewhat impoverished category in the lexical field. Morphemic absence is not easily measurable, or even registrable, as a 'positive' figural factor, although the scheme *ellipsis* – omission of a word or phrase readily understood from the co-text – does have its own dignity as a standard means to rapid dialogic up-take:

Prin. Our Lady help my lord! he'll be forsworn.
King. Not for the world, fair madam, by my will (*LLL* 2. 1. 97–8)

Pet. Nay, come, Kate, come; you must not look so sour.
Kath. It is my fashion when I see a crab (*TS* 2. 1.226–7)

while the related figure *zeugma* (literally 'yoking' – one verb governing two or more clauses) produces an often comic syntagmatic economy:

Ber. This is the liver vein, which makes flesh a deity;
  A green goose a goddess. (*LLL* 4. 3. 71–2)

More immediately felt are operations of *direct* morphemic undoing, like Moth's affix-suppression (compare Dogberry's '[in]tolerable', *MA* 3. 3. 36) in insulting reference to his master's beloved:

Arm. My love is most immaculate white and red.
Moth. Most maculate thoughts, master, are masked under such colours (1. 2. 85–7)

or the spectators' anatomizing of the Worthies' names into their constituent pseudo-morphemes, duly removed (to equally insulting effect):

Boy. And so adieu, sweet Jude! nay why dost thou stay?
Dum. For the latter end of his name.
Ber. For the ass to the Jude? give it to him: – Jud-as, away! (5. 2. 620–2)

### (c) Transformation (suppression-addition)

The *Oxford English Dictionary* attributes an extraordinary number (over sixty) 'first recorded uses', and first uses in particular senses, to *LLL*. By no means all the supposed novelties are inkhornisms: among them are innocent-looking 'native' forms like 'o'er-eye', 'eye-beam', 'loggerhead', 'push-pin', 'well-liking', 'unsullied', etc. Which suggests, of course, that the attributed wealth of newly minted forms should be viewed with extreme circumspection, not least because of the *OED*'s unacceptably early dating of the play (1588; on the unreliability of the *Dictionary* as a means of determining 'newness', see McKie 1936). It is,

270

nevertheless, obvious that various modes of lexical *productivity* – connoted if not by absolute novelty then at least by improbable applications or, more reliably, by internal reactions to the words in question – are essential to the verbal feast in progress.

The status of neologism proper can be safely accorded only to the play's nonce-words, like Armado's 'annothanize', invented – and this is the point of the pedants' lexical finds – as an eloquent redundancy, a virgin synonym for such established (and thus tarnished) terms as 'translate' or 'interpret': it is not, that is, a case of the 'necessary' minting of a term of art. The similar stylistic motives for Holofernes's coining of the adjectival 'peregrinate' (for 'foreign-sounding', the only instance cited in the *OED*) are unequivocally underlined by Nathaniel's congratulations: 'A most singular and choice epithet' 5. 1. 15).

Hunted treasures of this kind – whose impact is, precisely, 'peregrinate' – need to be distinguished from latinisms frightened out of their already well-established senses. Here the *bene/recte* clash assumes its most farcical aspect. Emblematic is Armado's speech on the King's entertainment, ornamented with two of his more carefully culled lexical blossoms:

> Sir, it is the king's most sweet pleasure and affection to congratulate the princess at her pavilion in the posteriors of the day, which the rude multitude call the afternoon . . . for I must tell thee, it will please his grace, by the world, sometime to lean upon my poor shoulder, and with his royal finger, thus, dally with my excrement, with my mustachio. (5. 1. 79ff.)

'Posteriors' for afternoon; 'excrement' for moustache (the accompanying glosses stress the tautology of the choices): Armado's striving for the *bene* through lexical substitution founders not so much on the *recte* as in the rectum. The result for the 'rude multitude' (the audience) is rude *double entendre*. The pedants are 'more aware of "a most singular and choice epithet",' observes William Matthews 'than of the vulgar (and usually unseemly) connotations of words that they themselves use' (1964: 5). Connotational insensitivity of this kind is analysed by Thomas More in his resistance, on democratic or demotic principles, to Tyndale's use of the imported latinism 'congregation' in his translation of the Bible:

> And I sayed and yet I say, that this is trew of the usuall synifycacyon of these wordes tham selfe in the englyshe tonge, by the comen custome of us englyshe peple, that eyther now do use these wordes in our langage, or that have used byfore oure dayes. And I saye that this comen custome and usage of speche is the onely thynge, by whyche we knowe the ryght and proper synificacyon of any worde

... Then say I now that in England this worde congregacyon dyd never sygnyfye the number of crysten people as cristen people, wyth a connotacyon or consyderacyon of theyr fayth or crystendome. (1532: 167)

The same sociolinguistic moral (founded on unmistakably conventionalistic semantic principles) emerges somewhat more subtly from an encounter between one of the play's rustics and one of its lexical hobgoblins. Armado promises freedom to the imprisoned Costard in return for acting as his go-between, and seizes the occasion for a further display of neologizing *synonymia*:

*Arm.* Sirrah Costard, I will enfranchise thee.
*Cost.* O! marry me to one Frances – I smell some l'envoy, some goose in this.
*Arm.* By my sweet soul, I mean setting thee at liberty, enfreedoming thy person: thou wert immured, restrained, captivated, bound. (3. 1. 118–22)

The awesome verb in question represents another of the comedy's moments of rhetorical self-revelation, it being Richard Mulcaster's term for the very process of 'enfreedoming' foreign lexical forms: 'Enfranchisement, which directeth the right writing [i.e. adapting] of all incorporate foren words' (1582: 60). The moral sting for Armado lies in the tail of Mulcaster's discussion of this otherwise valid mode of vocabulary-enrichment, when, espousing principles similar to More's, he warns against the excessively arbitrary (peregrinate) imposition of the borrowed term: 'And tho the learned enfranchiser maie sometime yeild to much to the foren, either for shew of learning, or by persuasion, that it is best so, yet he doth not well, considering that the verie nature of enfranchisement doth enforce obedience to the enfranchisers lawes, not to be measured by his bare person, but by the custom, reason and sound of his cuntries speche' (174). In practice, it is not the liberated word as such that yields too much to the foreign but, as Mulcaster suggests, the *speaker* and what he *does* with it. A matter, in other words, of *ethos*, or of getting away with lexical robbery. Armado's 'festinately' – like Berowne's 'remuneration' and the rest – may in this context be more opaquely connotative (of minting itself) than instrumentally denotative, but as F. P. Wilson notes (1969: 101), Cornwall's 'Advise the Duke ... to a most festinate preparation' in *King Lear* (3. 7. 9–10) and Ulysses's 'Let not virtue seek/Remuneration for the thing it was' in *Troilus and Cressida* (3. 3. 169–70) are soberly functional.

The case is quite different with non-enfranchised borrowings – *guerdon, imitari, haud credo* – which always remain in part interlinguistic citations or mentions, represented ideally (and typographically)

FIGURES

between inverted commas and/or in italics. The rhetorical efficacy of the 'pure' foreign loan lies precisely in its *non*-adaptation, and the vertiginous code-switching that this connotes: not the eloquence of the enriched lexicon but the exotic appeal of boundary-crossing ('The deer was, as you know, *sanguis*, in blood; . . . like a jewel in the ear of *coelo* . . . on the face of *terra*', 4. 2. 3ff.). And if the liberated loan-word appears to the simple as a monstrosity, the still-imprisoned variety remains a mysterious and mystifying phonic body. It is the strategically un-digested quality of the bookmen's *videos* and *quares* that prompts Moth's alimentary metaphors (the pedants have 'stolen the scraps' of other languages) and that provides Costard's own gargantuan and (in comparison with Moth/Mot, little French word) unswallowable Latin body: 'for thou art not so long by the head as *honorificabilitudinitati-bus*' (5. 1. 39–40).

In a sense, the unvulgarized borrowing is the most 'moral' or honest of morphological substitutes; since it necessarily advertises its own origins and thus its user's debt. And yet within the rhetorical criminal code it figures or disfigures among the worst offences: *soriasmus* or mingle mangle, favourite target of the Elizabethan figural vice squad, evidently because it makes no concession at all to the linguistic community into which it strays, so much so that it becomes elected representative of all 'your intollerable vices' in Rosaline's rejection of rhetoric at the end of *LLL*:

Ber.     My love to thee is sound, sans crack or flaw.
Ros.     Sans 'sans', I pray you.
Ber.             Yet I have a trick
Of the old rage: bear with me, I am sick;
I'll leave it by degrees. (5. 2. 415–18)

Not that the prevalence of connotation (in particular the connotation 'novelty') over denotation is the privilege of the loan. A freshly created sense or application for a bit of established stock may set it on a brilliant and fashionable new rhetorical career, as in the case of 'fashion' itself, used by both Navarre and Berowne to characterize Armado's fecundity as modish minter ('A man in all the world's new fashion planted', 1. 1. 163; 'A man of fire-new words, fashion's own knight', 1. 1. 177). The word had acquired, in the late sixteenth century, as Gladys Willcock suggests, a kind of self-referential connotative force as a favourite instance of the specifically linguistic modishness it here denotes: 'The critical point to note about Armado is that the mention of *fashion* . . . flashes the message *language* to the Elizabethan mind. We make no such automatic connection' (1934: 10). More familiar, and more

273

frequently satirized as a vogue term, is that Elizabethan psycho-physiological catch-all, 'humour' (as in Armado's 'black oppressing humour', 1. 1. 228), which serves Nym in *MWW* as a substitute for virtually any existing lexeme (noun, verb, modifier and all), or simply as a hopefully prestigious filler in place of nothing at all: 'slice, that's my humour!' (1. 1. 122); 'Be advised, sir, and pass good humours' (1. 1. 150); 'if you run the nuthook's humour on me' (1. 1. 152); 'is not the humour conceited' (1. 3. 21–2); 'Will that humour pass?' (1. 3. 48); 'Humour me the angels' (1. 3. 53); 'I thank thee for that humour' (1. 3. 60), etc., etc.: 'To give these ignorant, well-spoken days', as Jonson's Asper puts it, 'some taste of their abuse of this word "humour"' (*Every Man Out of His Humour* (1599), Induction). The pathology of Nym's oppressing humour is so emphatic that Page's outrage becomes almost super-fluous: 'The "humour" of it quoth'a! . . . I never heard such a drawling, affecting rogue' (2. 1. 134–7).

Now what foregrounds all these substitutions and transformations is the process of *estrangement*, the form of lexical bracketing-off that derives from the sense of the new, if only of the new usage. But one of the more fertile sources of lexical eloquence throughout the Tudor period entailed the reverse procedure, namely the disinterment of verbal bodies supposedly reeking with antiquity. The paradigm for the cult of the archaism is no longer the mint but the archaeological dig, although in the end, perhaps paradoxically, the rhetorical principle at work is very similar: as with all archaeological endeavours it is the *freshness* of the find that excites real interest. The novel antiquity: this is the linguistic patriot's answer to foreign scrap-stealing, and is the great literary innovation – if we are to believe 'E.K.' – introduced by Edmund Spenser:

> for in my opinion it is one special prayse of many whych are dew to this Poete, that he hath laboures to restore, as to theyr rightfull heritage, such good and naturall English words as have ben long time out of use and almost cleane disherited. Which is the onely cause that our Mother tongue . . . hath long time bene counted most bare and barrein . . . Which default when as some endeavoured to salve and recure, they patched up the holes with peces and rags of other languages. (1579, in Smith 1904: 129–30)

In reality, the archaizing fashion went back well beyound Spenser to the early decades of the century, and the 'farre fetched colours of strange antiquitie' duly found their way into Thomas Wilson's blacklist as the most 'courtly' variety of lexical affectation: 'The fine courtier will talke nothyng but *Chaucer*. The misticall wise menne and Poeticall clerkes, . . . [delyte] muche in their awne darkenesse, especially, when none can

tell what thei dooe saie' (1553: 86ᵛ). It is doubtless his aspiration to the
ranks of 'the fine courtier' that leads Armado to mix pseudo-Chaucerian
antiquities liberally with his latinisms – thus making a mockery of
'E.K.''s anti-inkhorn defence of the revival – in his epistolary self-
presentation to the King (*synonymia* crosses temporal as well as
national frontiers): 'the welkin's viceregent . . . it is ycleped thy park . . .
that low-spirited swain . . . which, as I remember, hight Costard' (1. 1.
216ff.); while the King and fine courtiers proper, anticipating the game,
medievalize their introductory description of the antiquarian himself:

King.    This child of fancy, that Armado hight . . .
         I will use him for my minstrelsy.
Ber.     Armado is a most illustrious wight. (1. 1. 169ff.)

'An old cloak', as Falstaff's proverb puts it (*MWW* 1. 3. 15–16) 'makes a
new jerkin.'

### (III) SAID SAWS

Falstaff's proverbial saying is equally applicable to the proverb as such:
hand-me-down wear, endlessly renewable as fresh discursive garb, at
once the most established and the most adaptable of verbal devices.
*MWW* itself demonstrates something of the generative, or regenerative,
rhetorical versatility of the proverb, employable equally as the
climactic moment in Ford's self-flagellation:

If I have horns to make one mad, let the proverb go with me – I'll be
horn-mad (3. 5. 140–2);

as the 'humorous' (comic / modish) means to the debunking of Falstaff's
vanities:

Fal.     Sometimes the beam of her view gilded my foot, sometimes my
         portly belly.
Pist.    Then did the sun on dunghill shine.
Nym.     I thank thee for that humour (1. 3. 55–8);

and as Evans's indispensable guide to righteous behaviour:

Host.    Shall I lose my parson? My priest? My Sir Hugh? No, he gives me
         the proverbs and the no-verbs. (3. 1. 95–7)

Such range and flexibility have in part to do with the extraordinarily
polymorphic character of the proverb, which calls into play in varying
degrees all five of the traditional rhetorical faculties:

*(a) Proverb as 'inventio'*
In its 'ethical' guise (the deontic pro-verbs and no-verbs), it is classed as a

275

kind of inartificial proof applicable to various topics and situations of discourse. Aristotle (*Rhetoric* I. xv. 14) recommends the proverbial saying as persuasive external evidence, the distillation of general experience, and as such it is defined by many Renaissance commentators: 'Whenas Proverbs are concise, witty and wise Speeches grounded upon long experience, conteining for the most part good caveats, and therefore both profitable and delightfull' (Camden 1605: 301). The connotation of 'long experience' is especially powerful in what the Tudor age defined as the 'old said saw', the anonymous or polygenetic expression of a temporally indefinite popular culture. In the plays the connoted antiquity, when it is the main point of the citation, is often overtly signalled:

Mrs Page.  'Tis old, but true: 'Still swine eats all the draff.' (*MWW* 4. 2. 98)

Pro.  But pearls are fair; and the old saying is,
Black men are pearls, in beauteous ladies' eyes. (*TG* 5. I. 11–12)

Feste.  *Primo, secundo, tertio*, is a good play, and the old saying is, 'The third pays for all.' (*TN* 5. I. 34–5) (etc.)

The 'inartificial' or experiential weight of the old saying is of particular importance in showing forth the ethical oppositions of *MV*. The respective positions in the first encounter between Shylock and the Christians are backed up by volley and counter-volley of justificatory saws: Shylock's 'but ships are but boards, sailors but men' (1. 3. 19–20; see Tilley's *Proverbs in England* (1950), M502); 'to smell pork' (29f.; Tilley J50); 'If I can catch him once upon the hip' (41; Tilley H474); 'And all for use of that which is mine own' (108; O99); and Antonio's 'A goodly apple rotten at the heart' (96; A300) or Bassanio's 'I like not fair terms, and a villain's mind' (175; F3). The paroemeological struggle becomes quite open in the opponents' dialogic sharing of the 'usurers are bawds' maxim (Tilley U28):

Ant.  Or is your gold and silver ewes and rams?
Shy.  I cannot tell, I make it breed as fast, –
But note me, signior
Ant.  Mark you this, Bassanio
The devil can cite Scripture for his purpose (1. 3. 90–3)

(Antonio's caveat concerning Shylock's diabolically able ethical self-defence is itself, it might be noted, a biblical proverb, Tilley D230). Shylock's dependence on the received apophthegm becomes an index of the anachronistic rigidity of his ethical system as a whole, an inadequacy underlined in the pathetic incongruity of the trust he expresses in the archaic lock-up-your-goods (-and-daughters) adage at the very moment of Jessica's escape:

| | |
|---|---|
| *Shy.* | Do as I bid you, shut doors after you, |
| | Fast bind, fast find, – |
| | A proverb never stale in thrifty mind. (*Exit*) |
| *Jes.* | Farewell, – and if my fortune be not crost, |
| | I have a father, you a daughter, lost (*Exit* 2. 5. 52–6) |

The place of the 'ancient' proverb within the moral Christian–Jew polarity is decisively marked by Launcelot Gobbo's choice between Shylock and Bassanio, a choice, in the event, between two parts of a familiar maxim (Tilley G393):

| | |
|---|---|
| *Lau.* | The old proverb is very well parted between my master and you, sir, you have 'the grace of God', sir, and he hath 'enough'. (2. 2. 142–4) |

### (b) Proverb as 'dispositio'

In the elaboration of any argument within discourse, the proverb is an invaluable means to copiousness: 'proverbs alleged', declares Wilson, 'helpe Amplification' (1553: 660). The servant and master dialectic in *CE* unfolds through a chain of proverbial axioms:

| | |
|---|---|
| *Syr. Ant.* | Shall I tell you why? |
| *Syr. Dro.* | Ay, sir, and wherefore; for they say, every why hath a wherefore. |
| *Syr. Ant.* | Why, first for flouting me, and then wherefore, for urging it the second time to me. |
| *Syr. Dro.* | Was there ever any man thus beaten out of season, When in the why and wherefore is neither rhyme nor reason. . . |
| *Syr. Ant.* | Well, sir, learn to jest in good time; there's a time for all things. (2. 2. 43ff.) |

### (c) Proverb as 'elocutio'

The rhetorical multiformity of the proverb is reflected in its mixed figural character. It is in part a schematic discourse fragment, a 'sentence' in two senses – as syntactic unit and as established *sententia*, an ambiguity that is present in Portia's praise for Nerissa's maxims: 'Good sentences, and well pronounced' (*MV* 1. 2. 10.). Its material presence as a delimited syntagm within the flow of discourse is registered in the metaphor of the proverb-stick, a verbal arm (the saying in its entirety as imported unit) with which to assail the interlocutor:

| | |
|---|---|
| *Eph. Dro.* | Have at you with a proverb – shall I set in my staff? |
| *Luce.* | Have at you with another, that's – when? can you tell? (*CE* 3. 1. 51–2) |

| | |
|---|---|
| *Ros.* | Shall I come upon thee with an old saying, that was a man, when King Pepin of France was a little boy, as touching the hit it? |

*Boy.*    So I may answer thee with one as old, that was a woman when
          Queen Guinever of Britain was a little wench, as touching
          the hit it.
*Ros.*    Thou canst not hit it, hit, it, hit it,
          Thou canst not hit it, my good man.
*Boy.*    An I cannot, cannot, cannot,
          An I cannot, another can. (*LLL* 4. 1. 120–9)

Elaborate presentational framing of this kind transforms the mere
*adoption* of the proverbial expression into the definite *activity* of
proverb-quoting: or the *proverbium* into *paroemia*, according to the
distinction of the rhetoricians. Attention is drawn to the *saying* of the
saying, a 'pragmatization' of an otherwise rather inert phrasal importa-
tion, that is essential to its efficacy in the drama. The activizing and
de-autonomizing of over-familiar saws produces some of the more
sophisticated fooling in *TN*. Feste subjects the most banally tautological of catch-phrases to such an emphatic pseudo-historical fanfare and
to such a chop-logical chopping-up into used and mentioned bits and
pieces that the said saying itself all but disappears from view:

> *Bonos dies*, Sir Toby: for as the old hermit of Prague, that never saw
> pen and ink, very wittily said to a niece of King Gorboduc, 'That that
> is, is': so I, being master Parson, am Master Parson; for what is 'that'
> but 'that'? and 'is' but 'is'? (4. 2. 13–17)

The revitalizing of the dead or moribund dictum in *TN* depends on a
kind of specious hermeneutics, an interpretative elaboration that
wrenches the saying from its codified sense:

*Clown.*    Lady, *cucullus non facit monachum*: that's as much to say, as I wear
            not motley in my brain (1. 5. 53–5)

or claims to restore it to freshly discovered origins:

*Clown.*    He shall see none to fear.
*Maria.*    A good lenten answer. I can tell thee where that saying was born, of 'I
            fear no colours'.
*Clown.*    Where, good Mistress Mary?
*Maria.*    In the wars, and that you may be bold to say in your foolery. (1. 5.
            8–13)

The squeezing of comic energy out of more or less inanimate
ready-made expressions tends to be directly disproportionate to the
entity of the unit: the more inconspicuous the phrase, the more
determined and inventive its theatrical reanimation. Within the general
figural category of the *proverbium* were grouped not only full-scale
maxims, *sententiae*, adages and apophthegms but also the briefest of
catch-phrases, by-words and idiomatic scraps of all kinds (see Wilson

1969: 146). It is an especially compact and colourless 'proverbial' idiom that generates an entire scene of clowning in *AWW*, fifty-six lines of insistent comic business dedicated to Lavatch's three-word response for all conversational seasons (the catch-phrase as pragmatic catch-all):

| | |
|---|---|
| *Clown.* | . . . but for me, I have an answer that will serve all men. |
| *Count.* | Marry, that's a bountiful answer that fits all questions. |
| *Clown.* | It is like a barber's chair that fits all buttocks: the pin-buttock, the quatch-buttock, the brawn buttock, or any buttock. |
| *Count.* | I pray you, sir, are you a courtier? |
| *Clown.* | O Lord, sir! There's a simple putting off. More, more, a hundred of them. |
| *Count.* | Sir, I am a poor friend of yours that loves you. |
| *Clown.* | O Lord, sir! Thick, thick; spare not me. |
| *Count.* | O Lord, sir! Nay, put me to't, I warrant you. (2. 2. 13ff.) |

The chief point of Lavatch's ironical pride in his stratagem lies in the true sociolinguistic connotations of the simple by-word used in place of a considered answer, connotations that are by no means always courtly. If only by dramaturgic convention, it is the 'rustic' device *par excellence*, able to characterize alone, for example, the dialect of a character like the country wench Jaquenetta (who uses Lavatch's 'simple putting off', it must be said, to notable effect in evading Armado's approaches):

| | |
|---|---|
| *Arm.* | I will visit thee at the lodge. |
| *Jaq.* | That's hereby. |
| *Arm.* | I know where it is situate. |
| *Jaq.* | Lord, how wise you are! |
| *Arm.* | I will tell thee wonders. |
| *Jaq.* | With that face? |
| *Arm.* | I love thee. |
| *Jaq.* | So I heard you say. |
| *Arm.* | And so farewell. |
| *Jaq.* | Fair weather after you! (1. 2. 126–35) |

Now these more or less comic uses of the proverbial expression – battering, expansion, stock responses, etc. – depend essentially on its syntactic *integrity*, on its being perceived as a discrete and entire unit. But one of the more interesting modes of dramatization of the proverb in the comedies involves precisely the *dis*integration of the proverbial syntagm, its reduction to one or two key words dropped, as it were, into the dialogue and acting by way of allusive pointers, without bracketing off a continuous stretch of discourse as in the full citation: 'we must be alert', as Hilda Hulme warns, 'for the briefest reference to proverb usage within the dramatic dialogue. The smallest splinter may be a sharply pointed "quotation" within the charged language of an Elizabethan playwright' (1962: 45). The peculiar associative force of the proverb 'splinter' derives, of course, from what is left *out*, or more exactly from what is left *implicit*. Proverbial key words, especially when applied as predicates, inevitably invite the audience to supply what has been suppressed. Bardolph's angry 'You Banbury cheese!', shouted at the slender Slender in *MWW* (I. I. 118), can only be understood as a metonymy for the missing adjective coupled with it in the full dictum: 'As thin as Banbury cheese' (Tilley C268). Holofernes's 'twice-sod simplicity' (*LLL* 4. 2. 21) implies for the proverbially competent auditor (everyone in Shakespeare's audience) that Constable Dull, to whom it is applied, belongs to the cabbage family: 'Crambe bis posita mars' runs the (Erasmian) adage, or in Lyly's version 'Colewarts twice sodden' (Tilley C5111); while the unsaid simile in Berowne's reference to the 'eagle-sighted eye' daring to look on Rosaline's brow (4. 3. 222–3) is somewhat more complimentary: 'As Eagle's eye', the maxim appears in Spenser, 'can behold the Sun' (Tilley E3). The unspeakably clinging and oppressive quality of Hermia's devotion is expressed with fulminous rapidity in Lysander's 'thou burr' (*MND* 3. 2. 160), the explanatory tag to which is provided by Lucio in *MM*: 'I am a kind of burr, I shall stick' (4. 3. 177).

There is quite a distinct kind of dramatic 'dispersion' of the proverb in its citation form (the codified wording, that is, in which it is normally quoted and collected): the paraphrase containing no specific lexical clues to its own proverbial status. What is retained, rendering the transformed saying recognizable, is no longer the key word but the *kernel proposition*. And the audience's cognitive or re-cognitive task is not so much a 'filling-in' as a 'translating back'. The effect is still, however, that of a de-familiarizing estrangement of the codified proposition as such: Orsino's order to his attendants, 'Some four or five attend him; / All, if you will; for I myself am best/When least in company' (*TN* I. 4. 36–8), recasting the usual 'never less alone than when alone' (in which the double *alone* is the indispensable verbal clue, Tilley A228); or Friar Francis's 'For to strange sores strangely they strain the cure' (*MA* 4. I. 251), which retains the binary structure – virtually amplified into a ternary structure with the near-homonymic 'strain' – of the customary 'extreme (desperate) disease/extreme (desperate) remedy', while transforming its wording (Tilley D357). And at its most functional, the proverbial paraphrase, like the splinter, leaves implicit the central aspect of the allusion, thereby calling on the auditor to provide, as part of his re-paraphrasing toils, his own inference. Bassanio's fumbling excuse for having given away Portia's ring gets him into further trouble on these very implicational grounds:

| Bass. | I swear to thee, even by thine own fair eyes |
| | Wherein I see myself – |
| Por. | Mark you but that! |
| | In both my eyes he doubly sees himself. (5. 1. 242ff.) |

Bassanio's self-defence actually amounts, for the proverbially literate, to a self-accusation of gross (or double) immaturity: 'To look babies [= small reflections of oneself] in another's eyes' being a well-established bit of oral English lore (see Tilley B8). The accusation implied, instead, in Proteus's dismissal of Speed – 'Go, go, be gone, to save your ship from wrack, / Which cannot perish having thee aboard, / Being destin'd to a drier death on shore' (*TG* 1. 1. 142–4) – although more articulate, is more automatically reconstructed (compare *The Tempest*, 1. 1. 71, where the same inference is to be drawn): 'He that's ordained to be hanged', runs Cotgrave's collected version of the saw, 'will never be drowned' (see Tilley B139).

But if these operations have to do with the saw – kept whole, fragmented, or dissolved in the propositional dynamic of the dialogue – in its syntagmatic and thus schematic identity, the proverb is also (for many rhetoricians primarily) a class of trope; 'Proverbs', says Aristotle, 'are metaphors from species to species' (*Rhetoric*, III. xi. 14). This metaphorical shift generally departs from the abstract species (tenor) to arrive at the concrete (vehicle), and the proverb often enters into the tropical characterization of immaterial forces within the drama, notably time and its effects, as in Navarre's 'cormorant devouring Time' (*LLL* 1. 1. 4: 'Time devours all things', Tilley T326), and the range of variations on the 'Take time by the forelock' adage, with its invitingly quaint tail, 'for she is bald behind' (T311). It is reduced to its solemn first part in *MA* ('He meant to take the present time by the top', 1. 2. 12–13) and *AWW* ('Let's take the instant by the forward top', 5. 3. 39) and to its grotesque conclusion within Dromio's philosophical delirium in *CE*:

| Syr. Dro. | . . . by a rule as plain as the plain bald pate of Father Time himself. . . . There's no time for a man to recover his hair that grows bald by nature . . . Time himself is bald, and therefore to the world's end will have bald followers. |
| Syr. Ant. | I knew 'twould be a bald conclusion. (2. 1. 68ff.; 105ff.) |

Where the species-to-species movement is explicit – in proverbial similes of the 'good as gold' or 'hot as toast' variety – it is difficult to avoid the impression of trite rapidity, and indeed the codified comparison is used in the comedies for its very connotations of simple-minded facility. The later acts of *LLL* present a parade of similitudinous commonplaces, all of them mocking or mocked in their conceptual shallowness: Dumain's feebly automatic compliments on the stature and complexion of his lady immediately receive the treatment they deserve:

*Dum.*   As upright as the cedar. [cf. Tilley C207]
*Ber.*                                  Stoop, I say;
         Her shoulder is with child.
*Dum.*                      As fair as day [D56]
*Ber.*   Ay, as some days, but then no sun must shine. (4. 3. 86ff.)

The same amorous superficiality, betrayed in Dumain's mistaken wooing of Maria, is suggested in her own wrily facile similitude on the subject (Tilley B83):

Dumain is mine, as sure as bark on tree. (5. 2. 285)

And this savouring by the ladies of their triumph is closed by the Princess with another knowingly hackneyed (and rapid) simile for their very rapidity (Tilley R158):

Whip to our tents, as roes run o'er the land. (5. 2. 309)

Revenge of a kind arrives with Berowne's choice of clichéd comparisons belittling Boyet's pretences to charm over the ladies and to superiority over the men: the 'teeth as white as whale his bone' (5. 2. 332; Tilley W279), flashed enticingly at the former, and the eye that 'wounds like a leaden sword', directed over-theatrically at the latter (5. 2. 481; S1054; the vehicle, of course, is the harmless stage prop with its associations of purely histrionic gesture). An extra touch of comparative banality, and the similitudinous saw, particularly in its romantic guise, plunges beyond recovery, an obligatory target for dramaturgic caricature:

*Thisbe.*   His eyes were green as leeks. (*MND* 5. 1. 322; Tiley L176)

Comparisons, as Dogberry says in another would-be saw, are odorous.

   Now these more or less contextualized proverbial similes and metaphors require an immediate dramatic referent (or tenor) to acquire sense. But blown up into the full-length and autonomous *sententia*, the metaphorical vehicle becomes outright allegory, a completely transposed or translated proposition, and as such impressively quotable and collectable: 'With the advent of scholars who made collections of proverbs, the so-called paroemiographers, we find the definition of "proverb" fixed as a more or less allegorical figure of speech' (Whiting 1932: 279–80). The very propositional completeness and autonomy of the allegorical maxim render it hard to digest within the flux of dramatic discourse, where it tends to lie precisely like a precious collector's item brought out for the occasion. Its usefulness in the comedies is consequently limited, on the whole, to occasions of pompous or hysterical over-emphasis, as with Adriana's exclamatory agonies over her errant husband (cf. Tilley L68):

> Far from her nest the lapwing cries away;
> My heart prays for him, though my tongue do curse (*CE* 4. 2.
>     27–8);

or Lysander's dramatic announcement of his abandoning of Hermia (where the same pattern of allegorical maxim (Tilley H560) followed by a somewhat redundant translation into the literal here and now is observed):

> For, as a surfeit of the sweetest things
> The deepest loathing to the stomach brings . . .
> So thou, my surfeit. (*MND* 2. 2. 136ff.)

For the rest, if one discounts the formalized and inevitable moral sententiousness of the casket scrolls in *MV* ('All that glisters is not gold . . . Gilded tombs do worms enfold', etc.), the proverbial allegory represents something of a dramaturgic embarrassment, a ready butt, for instance, for the general burlesquing of rhetorical moralism in *AYLI*. Celia parodies the exclamatory sentence in her teasingly oblique news of Orlando's arrival in the forest (cf. Tilley F738):

> O Lord, Lord! It is a hard matter for friends to meet; but mountains may be remov'd with earthquakes, and so encounter. (3. 2. 181–3)

And the redundant allegory-translation pattern becomes so much fuel for Touchstone's jingling and equivocal caricature of Orlando's love verses (cf., in order, Tilley C135, S687, N360, R182):

> If the cat will after kind,
> So be sure will Rosalind. . . .
> They that reap must sheaf and bind,
> Then to cart with Rosalind.
> Sweetest nut hath sourest rind,
> Such a nut is Rosalind.
> He that sweetest rose will find
> Must find love's prick, and Rosalind. (3. 2. 101ff.)

If the proverb-as-allegory has a difficult and at times forced relationship with the immediate dramatic – and still more, stage – context, the reverse is true for those sayings that codify not metaphoric but metonymic relationships. A series of proverbs taking the body, and especially facial features, as indexical pointers to psychological and moral traits appear to issue directly from the dramatic-theatrical configuration of human figures. The most explicit of these is the adage quoted in Jonson's *Cynthia's Revels* as '[they] hold the face to be the index of the mind' (cf. Tilley F1), and varied in perfect earnest both by Viola in her pledging of faith in the well-seeming Captain:

> There is a fair behaviour in thee, Captain;
> And though that nature with a beauteous wall
> Doth oft close in pollution, yet of thee
> I will believe thou hast a mind that suits
> With this thy fair and outward character (*TN* 1. 2. 47–51)

and by Vincentio–Lodowick in his decoding of the trustworthy Provost (cf. also Tilley F6):

> There is written in your brow, Provost, honesty and constancy; if I read it not truly, my ancient skill beguiles me. (*MM* 4. 2. 152–4)

Of the range of significant and signifying gestures of which the face is capable, the event whose indicative power is proverbial is the blush: *rubor est virtutis color*, '[Red is] a token of grace: they blushe for shame' (Heywood 1562: 189). If the interpretation both of the blush and of the proverb itself and its application is placed in passing doubt at the end of *TG* –

Duke.   I think the boy hath grace in him, he blushes.
Val.    I warrant you, my lord, more grace than boy.
Duke.   What mean you by that saying? (5. 4. 163–5) –

the same interpretative uncertainty is anything but passing in the abortive wedding scene of *MA*. Claudio insists that the *rubor* in Hero's face is an empty sign, or worse an index of anything but *virtus* ('though sometimes', warns Bacon of the proverbial blush, 'it comes from vice'):

> She's but the sign and semblance of her honour.
> Behold how like a maid she blushes here!
> O, what authority and show of truth
> Can cunning sin cover itself withal! (4. 1. 32–5);

while the standard proverbial reading of the sign is upheld by Friar Francis:

>               I have mark'd
> A thousand blushing apparitions
> To start in her face . . .
> Trust not my reading nor my observations . . .
> If this sweet lady lie not guiltless here. (4. 1. 158ff.)

In the event, the justice of the play's outcome coincides with the justness of the old saw.

### (d) Proverb as 'memoria'

Transmitted over generations by collective memory (mother of

284

wisdom, as the saw says), the proverb depends on the sharpness of individual recall for its deployment at the rhetorically opportune moment. 'I do now remember a saying', says Touchstone, producing at the right time the right maxim to deflate William and his self-attributed 'pretty wit', '"The fool doth think he is wise, but the wise man knows himself to be a fool"' (*AYLI* 5. 1. 29–31).

### (e) Proverb as 'actio'

Old said saws have indeed to be said and re-said in order to survive, and each re-saying of the saying is a special kind of utterance-act, somewhere between fresh illocution and quotation, subject to rules of competence of its own. The proverbial performance, particularly if the saying is given in its full citation form, will normally be paralinguistically marked off from the discourse into which it is placed, as A. J. Greimas notes:

> In spoken language, proverbs and sayings are clearly distinguished from the rest of the verbal sequence because of the change of intonation with which they are uttered: one has the impression that the speaker voluntarily abandons his own voice and takes on another when he has to utter a segment of speech that does not belong to him and that he merely quotes . . . a proverb or saying represents an element of a *particular code*, inserted within transmitted messages. (1970: 309)

The intonational signalling of the full proverb-performance – possibly accompanied also by kinesic markers – will generally be further emphasized in stage delivery, in correspondence with the overall histrionic heightening of the enunciation. The printed texts of the comedies on occasion indicate typographically this paralinguistic shift – the Folio text of *MWW*, for instance, places between inverted commas Ford's lengthy and formal *sententia* (ceremoniously introduced and marked off, in addition, by textual deixis):

> experience . . . hath taught me to say this:
> 'Love like a shadow flies when substance love pursues;
> 'Pursuing that that flies, and flying what pursues. (2. 2. 198ff.)

In the Elizabethan literary-rhetorical context, in which the proverb enjoyed immense prestige and an unprecedented rate of production, the 'particular code' to which Greimas refers appears in practice as a set of sub-codes, each of which commands its own connotations and calls, perhaps, upon a specific kind or degree of intonational colouring. This is especially true of sayings that bear powerful and recognizable intertextual traces, and whose provenience may be the main motive for the citation. The most unmistakable of these are doubtless biblical expressions that have entered into proverb lore, oral and literary – Dromio of Syracuse's punning and logic-chopping use in *CE* of Corinthians (ix. 14, 'Satan himself is transformed into an angel of light'; cf. Tilley D231): 'And here she comes in the habit of a light wench, and thereof comes that the wenches say "God damn me", that's as much as to say, "God make me a light wench"': It is written, they appear to men like angels of light' (4. 3. 5off.); Shylock's ironical glance at the New Testament (Matthew xx. 15, 'Is it not lawful for me to do what I will with mine own?'; see Tilley O99) in his negotiations with the Christians: 'You call me misbeliever . . . And all for use of that which is mine own' (1. 3. 106–8); Berowne's crowing citation of a sermonly saw, again from Matthew (vii. 3; Tilley M1191; note that the proverbial 'mote' may well be another motivation for the multiply punning name Moth, see Kökeritz 1953: 320): 'You found his mote; the King your mote did see; / But I a beam do find in each of three' (4. 3. 158–9); etc. Such sayings presumably demand a degree of enunciational solemnity, if only of a mock variety.

Certain paroemiographical collections acquired an authority – among ex-grammar school boys especially – such as to mark the gathered sayings themselves permanently, whatever their later careers. The 'puerile' atmosphere of the classroom is re-evoked by Nathaniel in his pedantic allusion to the Elizabethan schoolboy's proverbial *vade mecum*, Leonard Culman's *Sententiae pueriles*: 'for society, saith the text, is the happiness of life' (4. 2. 154–5; see Smith 1963: n. 130). But the most admired and (not least by Shakespeare) most ransacked of these collections was without question Erasmus's *Adagia*, and the peculiar force of the Erasmian adage – thanks to successive generations of pedagogues – survived all mutations and abuses. Its sententious dignity and authority are preserved intact in Isabella's moralizing on the very topic of authority: 'But man, proud man, / Dress'd in a little brief authority' (*MM* 2. 2. 118ff.; *Magistratus virum indicat*; see Tilley A402), and is intended to lend substance and support to Orlando's tedious homily of love: 'how brief the life of man / Runs his erring pilgrimage' (*AYLI* 3. 2. 126–7; *Peregrinatio quaedam est vita*; Tilley L249). It is this same weight that sharpens the irony of Petruchio's praise of Katherina's shyness: 'For she's not froward, but modest as the dove' (*TS* 2. 1. 286: *Columbae . . . nihil mitius*; Tilley D573); gives point to Launcelot Gobbo's tormenting of his blind father: 'Nay, indeed, if you had your eyes you might fail of the knowing me; it is a wise father that knows his own child' (*MV* 2. 2. 72–4, reversing Erasmus's *quo dicunt; sapientem esse filium, qui patrem suum noscit*; Tilley C309); and renders gratingly incongruous Touchstone's thoughts on Audrey's flesh and the uses to which she, and he, put it: 'to cast away honesty upon a foul slut were to put good meat into an unclean dish' (*AYLI* 3. 3. 31–2: *Cibum in matellum ne immittas*; Tilley M834). And if Launcelot Gobbo's flirting with a mythico-geographical catch-phrase collected in the *Adagia* gets him into trouble over the gender of monsters – 'thus when I shun Scylla, your father, I fell into Charybdis, your mother' (*MV* 3. 5. 17–18; Tilley S169), then Costard's attempt to restore an Erasmian adage to its original and glorious Latin comes to grief in arriving only halfway, being contaminated en route not only by the speaker's country references but more specifically by an altogether less prestigious saw (the 'sun on dunghill' proverb used against Falstaff):

*Cost.*     . . . thou hast it *ad dunghill*, at the fingers' ends, as they say.
*Hol.*     O, I smell false Latin: dunghill for *unguem*. (*LLL* 5. 1. 70–2; Tilley F245)

As a literary phenomenon, the proverb owes a great deal of its modish status in the late Elizabethan period to the extraordinarily dense argumentative-decorative accumulation of adages found in romances like Pettie's *Petite Palace* and, far more so, Lyly's *Euphues*. The 'euphuistic' maxim – didactic, allegorical, sententious, often taken from nature, particularly 'unatural' nature – is one of the more readily identifiable and imitable of figural devices (as Falstaff demonstrates in his parody of the pompous regal mode in *1 Henry IV*, 2. 4. 394ff.). Entire paragraphs in *Euphues* are made up, as it were, of saw-chains, sayings strung out in tautological or antithetical amplification of a given topic: 'As therefore the sweetest rose hath his prickle, the finest velvet his brack, the fairest flour his bran, the sharpest wit his wanton will, . . . the finest cloth is soonest eaten with moths, the cambric sooner stained than the coarse canvas . . . whose wit being like wax apt to receive any impression' (1578: 10–11). Echoes of Lyly's proliferating proverbialism are to be found everywhere in Shakespeare, but the one play which approaches *Euphues* not only in the paroemic intensity of its passages and the dialectical use to which the proverb is put (on similar topics of maturation, friendship, passion, fidelity, courtliness, betrayal, etc.), but in direct indebtedness, is *TG*. The comedy's opening debate on the subjects of home-keeping and love-resisting has an all but line-and-page-reference acknowledgment to the textual origins of its own axiomatic style (the cited 'writers' being Pettie: 'For as in the fairest rose is soonest found a canker'; 'The finer wit he was endued withal, the sooner was he made thrall and subject to love'; and Lyly: 'as the canker soonest entreth into the white rose'; 'love easily entreth into the sharp wit without resistance, see Tilley C56, W576):

| | |
|---|---|
| *Pro.* | Yet writers say: as in the sweetest bud<br>The eating canker dwells, so eating love<br>Inhabits in the finest wits of all. |
| *Val.* | And writers say: as the most forward bud<br>Is eaten by the canker ere it blow,<br>Even so by love the young and tender wit<br>Is turn'd to folly. (1. 1. 42ff.) |

This game of antithetical or see-sawing saw-saying is even here, despite the intensity of the love-debate, on the borders of burlesque in the undigested literariness of the material; it moves a step closer when the opponents in the euphuistic proverb-contest are not civilly conversing gentlemen but the bantering Julia and her maid, who exchange jingling maxims, again on the topic of love and its manifestation:

| | |
|---|---|
| *Jul.* | His little speaking shows his love but small. |
| *Luc.* | Fire that's closest kept burns most of all. |
| *Jul.* | They do not love that do not show their love. |
| *Luc.* | O, they love least that let men know their love (1. 2. 29–32) |

(the sources are likewise the same: Pettie: 'and as hidden flames by force kept down are most ardent'; 'those that love most speak least'; and Lyly: 'the fire kept close burneth most furious'; 'True love lacketh a tongue', see Tilley F265, L165) and weightier sentences on Julia's impatient passion:

| | |
|---|---|
| *Jul.* | Thou wouldst as soon go kindle fire with snow<br>As seek to quench the fire of love with words. |
| *Luc.* | I do not seek to quench your love's hot fire,<br>But qualify the fire's extreme rage,<br>Lest it should burn above the bounds of reason. |
| *Jul.* | The more thou damm'st it up, the more it burns:<br>The current that with gentle murmur glides,<br>Thou know'st, being stopp'd, impatiently doth rage (2. 7. 19ff.) |

(Pettie: 'As the swift running stream . . . if there be any dam . . . it rageth and roareth and swelleth above the banks'; Lyly: 'He that stoppeth the stream forceth it to swell higher', S929; on 'kindle fire with snow' proverb, see Tilley F284). Lyly's all-accommodating similitudes provide for Proteus's amorous and moral tergiversations a ready-laid argumentation path (Lyly's 'The fire that burneth, taketh away the heat of the burn', Tilley F277, married with Erasmus's propositionally identical *clavum clavo pellere*; and Pettie's 'who is so foolish that will not be content to change for the better', duly varied by Lyly' B26):

Even as one heat another heat expels,
Or as one nail by strength drives out another,
So the remembrance of my former love
Is by a newer object quite forgotten . . .

And he wants wit that wants resolved will
To learn his wit t'exchange the bad for better. (2. 4. 188–91; 2. 6.
12–13)

And they lend the two original contenders for Silvia's hand some easily
fired ammunition for their competing wit-volleys (Lyly's 'the chameleon though he have most guts draweth least breath' (1580: 24)
together with Erasmus's *Chameleon omnem imitatur colorem praeter-
quam album*):

| | |
|---|---|
| *Sil.* | What, angry, Sir Thurio? Do you change colour? |
| *Val.* | Give him leave, madam, he is a kind of chameleon. |
| *Thu.* | That hath more mind to feed on your blood than live in your air. |
| | (2. 4. 23–6) |

Such ammunition is, naturally, common property in the comedy,
serving equally well even for Speed's simple – though suitably
euphuized – request for a good meal from his master (Valentine's satiety
after feeding on Silvia's beauty is itself, as Warwick Bond points out in
the 1906 edition of the play, a glance at Lyly's 'Euphues fed on one dish
which ever stood before him, the beauty of *Lucilla'*):

| | |
|---|---|
| *Val.* | I have dined. |
| *Spe.* | Ay, but hearken, sir: though the chameleon Love can feed on the air, I am one that am nourished by my victuals; and would fain have meat. (2. 1. 161–4) |

In Shakespearean comedy, it is the proverb itself that is the rhetorical
chameleon, adaptable to all contexts and ends.

(IV) TAFFETA PHRASES, THREE-PIL'D HYPERBOLES:
THE BEYOND-THE-TROPE TROPE

The trope, etymologically and semantically a 'turn', is presented in *TS*
as a turn of quite another sort, a kind of circus act: Grumio's 'rope-
tricks' (1. 2. 111, deciphered by G. R. Hibbard in the 1968 edition of the
play as 'trope-tricks', see above p. 240) suggest that Petruchio's lively
way with figures is really only a showy form of sleight-of-tongue. This
notion of the disreputable trickiness of the tropical turn is recurrent in
the comedies; Benedick's equine equation for Beatrice's loquacity ('I
would my horse had the speed of your tongue, and so good a continuer',
*MA* 1. 1. 130f.) is dismissed by the speedy lady herself as a 'jade's trick' or
horsy number, and is thus presumably more vulgar still than
Petruchio's rope turn; and the fantastical Lucio in *MM* defends himself
as best he can before the Duke by claiming that his past insults were

uttered 'but according to the trick', i.e. they are not to be taken literally (5. 1. 502–3).

Now there is a certain albeit wry justice in this line of commentary. Tropical language – metaphor, metonymy, irony, hyperbole and the rest – does have a decidedly different status on the dramatic stage with respect to the poetic page (see Serpieri 1980a). However familiar an aspect of Elizabethan dramatic language, the semantic figure leads a more difficult life in the drama than in purely literary forms precisely because of its inclusion within a spectacular and 'active' mode of representation. In comedy especially the *tropical* turn has indeed to take on something of the pragmatic character of a *theatrical* turn or act in order to register within the full rhetoric of the performance. So much so that when its presence is directly signalled within the plays, it is a jokily *tangible*, if scarcely wholesome, presence: Parolles's '[I] smell somewhat strong of [Fortune's] strong displeasure' figure, for instance, leads to verbal-gestural business which again puts the trope as such into disrepute:

Clown.   Prithee, allow the wind.
Par.      Nay, you need not to stop your nose, sir. I spake but by a metaphor.
Clown.   Indeed, sir, if your metaphor stink I will stop my nose, or against any
         man's metaphor. (5. 2. 8–13)

The comic principle here (at work likewise in Beatrice's 'jade's trick') is to take the metaphorical vehicle for its tenor, or the figural act as the direct embodiment of the (unsavoury) image it expresses. The same principle bestows canine qualities on a similitude of Tranio's:

Tra.      O sir, Lucentio slipp'd me like his greyhound,
         Which runs himself and catches for his master.
Pet.      A good swift simile, but something currish. (*TS* 5. 2. 52–4)

This is the rule for the perception and reception of the trope in the plays: palpable but suspicious, if not maleficent. Similes snap like lances against bodies ('*Beatr.* . . . he'll but break a comparison or two upon me', *MA* 2. 1. 136f.); or offer false support, in reality cutting ('*Clown.* I do pity his distress in my similes of comfort, and leave him to your lordship', *AWW* 5. 2. 24–5); simile and irony together – ironical similes – hurt doubly ('*Ros.* Full of comparisons and wounding flouts', *LLL* 5. 2. 836); and the full allegory or extended metaphor is no less than an instrument of torture for extorting reluctant information:

Lau.      Thou shalt never get such a secret from me but by a parable.
Spe.      'Tis well that I get it so. (*TG* 2. 5. 34–6)

Malodorous metaphor, skirmishing simile, injurious irony, atrocious allegory: each species of figural turn is able to create an inescapable if uncomfortable dramatic impact. But what leaves its mark as the most persistently (and most troublingly) felt variety of semantic twisting in the comedies is the normally less considered overblowing and overplaying figure of *hyperbole*. In its conventionalized literary or poetic form, hyperbole appears as the quaintly overstated romantic (or 'Petrarchan') conceit, a more or less colourless mode of complimentary colouring with its obligatory references to the lover's unimaginable sufferings:

> *Val.*   I have done penance for contemning Love,
> Whose high imperious thoughts have punish'd me
> With bitter fasts, with penitential groans,
> With nightly tears, and daily heart-sore sighs

and to the mistress's indescribable perfection:

> is she not a heavenly saint? . . .
> if not divine,
> Yet let her be a principality,
> Sovereign to all the creatures of the earth. (*TG* 2. 4. 124ff.)

Such automatic poeticizing exaggeration, with its lengthy literary history and its codified points of reference, lends itself to cool debunking by Rosalind (on the lover's mortal agonies):

> *Orl.*   Then, in mine own person, I die.
> *Ros.*   No, faith, die by attorney. The poor world is almost six thousand years old, and in all this time there was not any man died in his own person, videlicet, in a love-cause. Troilus had his brains dashed out with a Grecian club, yet he did what he could to die before, and he is one of the patterns of love (*AYLI* 4. 1. 88ff.)

to analytic deconstruction by Boyet (on the superlativeness of the mistress's or mistresses' charms):

> *Moth.*   All hail, the richest beauties on the earth!
> *Boy.*   Beauties no richer than rich taffeta (*LLL* 5. 2. 157ff.)

and to satirical alienation by Viola (on the loved-one's uncataloguable qualities):

> Most radiant, exquisite, and unmatchable beauty – I pray you tell me if this be the lady of the house, for I never saw her. I would be loath to cast away my speech. (*TN* 1. 5. 171ff.)

It is the *de-literarized* hyperbole, removed from the polite limits of sclerotic poetic convention and put into direct and emphatic dialogic action, that fills dramatic world and stage to overflowing: the figure of expressive heightening, of grandiose gesture, of amplified volume (literally a 'throwing beyond' normal bounds), hyperbole is *the histrionic trope of tropes*. 'I for his immoderate excess', declares Puttenham in his own rather theatrical name-this-figure performative, 'cal him the ouer reacher' (1589: Yii^r): the chosen name is itself a dramaturgic metaphor, evoking the dramatic type of the hubristic bound-for-a-fall protagonist of many a classical tragedy (and anticipating a long line of hyperbolic overreachers in Elizabethan drama, for whom the model-in-chief is of course Tamburlaine). Within the comic canon, immoderate excess, or shameless rhetorical overacting, is the role assumed by Petruchio, that prince (together with Jonson's Volpone) of comic verbal overdoers (*TS*, it might be noted, is the only Shakespearean play in which the term 'overreach' appears in any form, 3. 2. 143). The magnified volume of Petruchio's language (in terms both of perceived noise and of perceptible style decibels) is evidently what Grumio has in mind in his reference to his master's turns: 'and he begin once, he'll *rail* in his rope-tricks' (1. 2. 110–11). Petruchio puts this vocal-figural amplifying into practice almost immediately in the artfully overblown commonplaces he chooses in order to depict his putatively Othello-like adventurous past ('of most disastrous chances,/Of moving accidents by flood and field;/Of hair-breadth scapes', *Othello* 1. 3. 134ff.; on hyperbole in Othello, see Serpieri 1978b):

> Have I not in my time heard lions roar?
> Have I not heard the sea, puff'd up with winds,
> Rage like an angry bear chafed with sweat?
> Have I not heard great ordnance in the field,
> And heaven's artillery thunder in the skies . . . ? (1. 2. 199ff.)

Petruchio's noisiest hyperboles, as here, are themselves images of noise, especially of the vocal kind emitted by Katherina ('though she chide as loud/As thunder when the clouds in autumn crack' (1. 2. 94–5). 'Rail' (to complain with exaggerated loudness and vehemence) becomes one of the comedy's rhetorical key words, characterizing the clamorous clash of sonic and stylistic titans: 'say that she rail', reflects Petruchio, preparing more ironically hyperbolic similes for Katherina, 'why then I'll tell her plain/She sings as sweetly as a nightingale . . . she looks as clear/As morning roses newly wash'd with dew' (2. 1. 171ff.); and looking forward to marital (or martial) life, promises 'I'll rail and bawl' (4. 1. 193), finding the opportunity to exercise his emphatic rope-trickery in the maltreatment, for his wife's benefit, of the tailor and his gown ('Tis like a demi-cannon . . . carv'd like an apple tart . . . like to a censer in a barber's shop', 4. 3. 88ff.). The tropological structure of the comedy becomes, as it were, an extensive rail network.

Overreaching as a habitual way of speech is inevitably associated with Armado. The dramatic type with which he is identified by Berowne, the 'braggart' (5. 2. 536), institutionalizes the hyperbolic style, which the chief models for the type – the *miles gloriosus*, Capitano Spavento, etc. – employ obsessively as their only verbal resource. Elsewhere in the comic canon the term 'brag' (even Armado's imminent paternity is announced by Costard as 'the child brags in her belly already', 5. 2. 668–9) is synonymous with the figure of exaggeration, as in Rosalind's irreverent reference to 'Caesar's thrasonical brag of I came, saw, and overcame ' (*AYLI* 5. 2. 30–1), a hyperbole that Armado himself cites as a model of the climax: 'he it was that might rightly say, *veni, vidi, vici . . . videlicet*, he came, saw, and overcame: he came, one; saw, two; overcame, three' (4. 1. 68ff.). Rosalind's 'thrasonical' is also applied to Armado by Holofernes in his critique of the Spaniard's verbal and behavioural grandiosity: 'his humour is lofty, his discourse peremptory, his tongue filed, his eye ambitious, his gait majestical, and his general behaviour vain, ridiculous, and thrasonical' (5. 1. 9–12). The adjective is another dramaturgic and stylistic clue, being derived from Thraso, the hyperbolical *miles* in Terence's *Eunuchus*. And it is confirmed by Navarre's 'the magnificent Armado' (1. 1. 189), which connotes not only the vaunted military finery of the magnificent Armada but the grandiloquence implicit in the Latin *magnificus* (great in (verbal) deeds).

And yet what is interesting about Armado's hyperbolic mode is that it very rarely falls into the kind of bellicose swaggering typical of the stock braggart soldier. Closer to the style of the glorious *miles*, on the model of Plautus's Pyrgopolynices ('My shield . . . have it burnished brighter than the bright splendour of the sun, . . . my sword, too, . . . is simply itching to get on an enemy and carve him to little pieces,' etc. (*Miles gloriosus*, trans. Watling 1965) is the passing martial boastfulness of Parolles (who is forced later, 4. 4. 323, 325, to define *himself* as a 'braggart'):

> Noble heroes, my sword and yours are kin. Good sparks and lustrous, a word, good metals. You shall find in the regiment of the Spinii one Captain Spurio, with his cicatrice, an emblem of war, here on his sinister cheek; it was this very sword entrench'd it. (*AWW* 2. 1. 39: the spurious Captain Spurio is doubtless a colleague of the Capitano Spavento of the *commedia* tradition)

Only in his frustrated impersonation of the Worthy Hector does Armado momentarily aspire to the vainglorious soldierly vein, first in the brief epic performance itself:

> A man so breath'd that certain he would fight; yea
> From morn till night, out of his pavilion.
> I am that flower (5. 2. 646ff.);

and then immediately after it under the impulse of rage at his humiliating public 'defeat' by Costard:

> Dost thou infamonize me among potentates? Thou shalt die . . .
> By the north pole I do challenge thee. (67off.)

Armado's rhetorical self-aggrandizement is otherwise of a decidedly more *recherché* nature, presenting him as protagonist of 'the world's debate' not in Navarre's metaphorical sense of war (1. 1. 172), but in the more literal sense of universal discourse or dialogue. Indeed, he is presented as *double* protagonist: (hyperbolically) inexhaustible author of (inexhaustibly) hyperbolic compliments to his lady (of the 'More fairer than fair, beautiful than beauteous, truer than truth itself' variety, 4. 1. 63ff.):

> Devise, wit; write, pen; for I am for whole volumes in folio (1. 2. 174–5),

and at the same time regal subject of literary and oral history, inflating the social differences between himself and Jaquenetta to the heights and depths narrated in the 'ballad . . . of the King and the Beggar' (1. 2. 102–3):

> have commiseration on thy heroical vassal! The magnanimous and
> most illustrate king Cophetua set eye upon the pernicious and
> indubitate beggar Zenelophon, and he it was that might rightly say,
> *veni, vidi, vici* . . . Thus, expecting thy reply, I profane my lips on thy
> foot, my eyes on thy picture, and my heart on thy every part.
> (4. 1. 65ff.)

This discursive protagonism, of time-spanning macrocosmic proportions, is ironically confirmed in the hyperboles which Armado provokes from others, such as Navarre's 'A man of complements, whom right and wrong/Have chose as umpire of their mutiny' (1. 1. 167–8), electing him as arbiter between virtue and vice (presumably of a verbal kind – 'complements' – as indeed hyperbole itself is precariously perched midway between rhetorical vice and virtue; see below); and such as Berowne's 'the best that ever I heard' in response to Armado's first letter (1. 1. 271–2), or the Princess's 'what vane? what weathercock? did you ever hear better?' in response to the second (4. 1. 86–7).

But then exaggeration is in any case the play's most striking general tropical mode. Navarre, from his exordium with its (Armadian) martial inflation of the scholars' campaign –

> Therefore, brave conquerors – for so you are,
> That war against your own affections
> And the huge army of the world's desires (5. 1. 8–10)

and its optimistically vainglorious 'wonder of the world' (12), to his over-dramatization of Berowne's cruel anti-academic apostasy:

> Berowne is like an envious sneaping frost
> That bites the first-born infants of the spring (100–1)

and his obligatory glorification of the Princess's charms ('So sweet a kiss the golden sun gives not', 4. 3. 24ff.), gives a lead that is not only followed in the ritual adulation of the other poems ('the heavenly rhetoric' of the eye, 'Thou for whom Jove would swear', 'Thy eye Jove's lightning bears', etc.). Berowne, adept in pushing the whimsical amorous conceit to the confines of the ludicrous –

> Of all complexions the cull'd sovereignty
> Do meet, as at a fair, in her fair cheek;
> Where several worthies make one dignity (4. 3. 230ff.) –

exercises his knack for exorbitance in a monologue that is in effect the comedy's most original, and certainly most determined, bout of figural inflation, a catalogue or rather cataract of hypercritical hyperbolism that altogether reverses the standard pattern of polite compliment. Casting himself in the stagy role of the defeated scourge of Eros ('I, that have been love's whip . . . A domineering pedant o'er the boy'), itself figured forth in a chain of carefully chosen superlatives ('Than whom no mortal so magnificent! . . . Regent of love rhymes, lord of folded arms / The anointed sovereign of sighs and groans'), Berowne brings off his true rhetorical *coup de main* (or *de foudre*, not to say *de théâtre*) in a brilliantly grotesque portrait (not so much warts-and-all as all-warts) of the veritable gallery of defects for which he has so perversely fallen:

> A woman that is like a German clock,
> Still a-repairing, ever out of frame,
> And never going aright . . .
> A whitely wanton with a velvet brow
> With two pitch-balls stuck in her face for eyes;
> Ay and by heaven, one that will do the deed
> Though Argus were her eunuch and her guard. (3. 1. 185ff.)

In this comedy of excesses, the hyperbole, trope of extremes, becomes virtually the expressive norm.

It is of course the very notion of norm that is implied in the conception of the trope as a semantic swerving or deviation: 'A Trope or turning is when a word is turned from his naturall signification, to some other' (Fraunce 1588b: A2ᵛ). The point of figural departure is the 'naturalness' or 'propriety' of the meaning tropically abused ('an alteration of a worde or sentence, from the proper and naturall siginification, to an other not proper', Peacham 1577: Biᵛ). A number of metaphors for this relationship – tropes for tropes – appear in Elizabethan figural commentary. All have to do with adorning, decking, painting, making-up, dressing-up or disguising, the base metaphor being that of the naked body or simple cloth (literal meaning) upon which the optional figural operations are conducted: 'This ornament we speake of is given by figures and figurative speaches which be the flowers as it were and colours that a Poet setteth upon his language by arte, as the embroderer doth his stone and perle, or passements of gold upon the stuffe of a Princely garment' (Puttenham 1589: 115). The most recurrent terms are listed in the title-page to Puttenham's *Arte*: 'Flowers, Colours, Ornaments, Exornations'.

This imagery has a prominent place in the rich meta-rhetoric of *LLL*: from the 'odoriferous flowers of fancy' ornamenting the poetry of the nasal Ovid (4. 2. 119–20) to the 'colourable colours' that Holofernes detects in Nathaniel's speech (143–4), to the exornational hyperboles, duly mocked by the Princess, with which the ladies deck out their introductory descriptions of the men:

> God bless my ladies! are they all in love,
> That every one her own hath garnished
> With such bedecking ornaments of praise? (2. 1. 77–9)

The colouring, or 'painting', metaphor for tropical language is ambiguous, having both a pictorial force, as in Orlando's jibe on Jaques's facile clichés in *AYLI* –

> I answer you right painted cloth, from whence you have studied your questions (3. 2. 269–70) –

and, more commonly, a cosmetic sense: the 'native blood is counted pinting now' of Berowne's (painted) defence of Rosaline, and the Princess's 'Nay, never paint me now: Where fair is not, praise cannot mend the brow' arresting the Forester's faltering flattery (4. 1. 16f.). This is the most persistent of the play's metaphors for metaphor and her sister tropes, together with the image of textual-vestual finery, silk being the privileged tropical weave (it is similarly chosen by Jonson in his figure of the 'skein of silk' wherewith to 'apparel fair and good matter', 1641: 43): 'Beauties no richer than rich taffeta' responds Boyet to the lords' collective hyperbole (see above), a comparison recalled in the 'damask sweet commixture' of his own conceit on the ladies' (unpainted) charms (5. 2. 296).

As representations of the kinds of departure from semantic rules present in tropological operations, these metaphors undoubtedly have a certain descriptive colour of their own, and may be seen to connote an attractive and decorous process of melioration (pictorial ornamentation, after all, or dressing- and making-up are perfectly respectable, and in varying degrees necessary, aspects of the predominant Elizabethan culture). But it is also evident that the same meta-tropical tropes very readily degenerate, given an extra touch of metaphorical emphasis, into the imagery of decadence. 'Exornation' becomes luxurious and deceptive disguise, dressing vain dressiness – or worse, a variety of transvestism – and cosmesis a masquerading of natural features that represents at an extreme the insignia of prostitution: 'so is that honny-flowing Matron Eloquence', warns Sidney of over-coloured language, 'apparelled, or rather disguised, in a curtizan-like painted affectation' (1595: K4ʳ); and Cornwallis of rhetorical vanity: 'As many there are of pretty abilities, that trust as much to the sounding of their wordes as some women doe to white and red for the pinting of their faces' (1601: 221). The ethically ambiguous career of this imagery is best illustrated in Puttenham, whose favourite 'colour' metaphor declines later into repellent mis-rouging: 'no lesse than if the crimson tainte, which should by some oversight or mishap be applied to her forehead or chinne, it would make (ye woulde say) but a very ridiculous bewtie' (1589: 115); and in Jonson, whose 'skein of silk' not only apparels fair matter but also furnishes the opulent and over-adorned fabrics preferred by the vainglorious to 'natural' coarse cloth (note the implication of transvestism):

> But now nothing is good that is natural: right and natural language seems to have least of the wit in it . . . Cloth of bodkin or tissue must be embroidered, as if no face were that were not powdered or painted . . . All must be affected and preposterous as our gallants' clothes, sweet bags and night-dressings, in which you would think our men laymen, like ladies, it is so curious. (1641: 53)

It is such an austerely censorious view of figural making- and dressing-up that appears to prevail in *LLL*. Cosmetic colouring, if not the emblem of 'a curtizan-like painted affectation', is for the Princess of France in the comedy at least the sign of the speakers' narcissistic trusting 'to the sounding of their wordes'. The Princess's 'never paint me' gesture towards the Forester (who instead is rewarded for simple 'foul words', 4. 1. 19) is confirmed as a decided and definite position in this rhetorical matter by her articulate refusal of the altogether more expertly exornated flattery of Boyet:

> Good Lord Boyet, my beauty, though but mean,
> Needs not the painted flourish of your praise:
> Beauty is bought by judgment of the eye,
> Not utter'd by base sale of chapmen's tongues.

> I am less proud to hear you tell my worth
> Than you much willing to be counted wise
> In spending your wit in the praise of mine. (2. 1. 13–19)

'Counted wise/In spending your wit': like the sober Cornwallis, the Princess upbraids the honey-tongued speaker with his 'pretty abilities' for using the complimentary colouring addressed to her (Boyet's overreaching 'And prodigally [nature] gave them all [= her graces] to you', 12) as a pretext for *self*-painting. Both the metaphor and the rationale of the Princess's stand are echoed in Berowne's first and passing repudiation of rhetorical devices (although in his case, it must be added, the rejection itself is a canny means of out-hyperbolizing the hyperbole by suggesting that his lady's graces render superfluous all figural cosmetics):

> Lend me the flourish of all gentle tongues, –
> Fie, painted rhetoric! O! she needs it not:
> To things of sale a seller's praise belongs;
> She passes praise; then praise too short doth blot. (4. 3. 235–8)

And so it is with the metaphor of apparel, or as it were tropical dress. If Armado and his epistolary style are reduced to the cruel metonymy of an ornamental 'plume of feathers' (4. 1. 95), the lords instead are found guilty of outright and outrageous bodily-discursive transvestism. The proximity between their masking gear and their would-be persuasive speech is insistent in the play's final scene: '[they] are apparell'd thus,/Like Muscovites, or Russians, as I guess', sneers Boyet, 'their purpose is to parle, to court and dance/And every one his love-feat will advance' (5. 2. 120ff.); and the ladies: 'four/In Russian habit: here they stay'd an hour'/And talk'd apace; and in that hour, my lord,/They did not bless us with one happy word' (367ff.). The point is effectively epitomized in Rosaline's brutally axiomatic 'well, better wits have worn plain statute-caps' (281): cloth of bodkin seems to have, as Jonson observes (implying the exact opposite) 'least of the wit in it'.

The lowest point in this downward parabola of the trope and its fortunes in LLL would appear unquestionably to be Berowne's great rhetorical repentance speech, marking the comedy's first false climax, in which the kindred promises to 'never more in Russian habit wait', 'trust to speeches penn'd', 'come in visor to my friend' or 'woo in rhyme' prelude a spectacular renunciation of the figure-as-overdressing. With a terminological explicitness rare in Shakespeare, Berowne brings the skein-of-silk versus cloth-of-bodkin opposition to an anti-rhetorical culmination whose severity would gratify the most virulent of figure-hating moralists:

Taffeta phrases, silken terms precise,
Three-pil'd hyperboles, spruce affection,
Figures pedantical; these summer flies
Have blown me full of maggot ostentation;
I do forswear them; and I here protest,
By this white glove (how white the hand, God knows),
Henceforth my wooing mind shall be express'd
In russet yeas and honest kersey noes (5. 2. 406–13)

The fierce tone and uncompromising terms of Berowne's dissociation
from luxurious figural apparel have two main historical correlates. The
first is Montaigne's ruthless reduction of the rhetoricians' most prized
tropological items to the status of vulgar and gossipy *vox* (NB the trope
as trick again): 'Doe but heare one pronounce "Metonimia",
"Metaphore", "Allegory" . . . and other such trash-names of Grammer,
would you not thinke, they meant some form of a rare and strange
language? They are titles and wordes, that concern your chamber-
maides tittle-tattles. It is a foppery and cheating tricke' (1603: 167). And
the second, closer and probably more directly pertinent to the language
and metalanguage of the comedy, is the 'Puritan' abhorrence for
figurality, expressed most vehemently in the so-called Paul's Cross
sermons of the late 1570s. To the straightforwardly and unbendingly
righteous Nonconformist, the semantic turn represents a deviation
from the path of truth and of moral restraint; the preacher Henry Crosse
identifies the trope – especially when it decorates the sermons of his
Conformist counterparts – with actual wantonness and sexual corruption of youth:

> fine phrases . . . swelling words, bumbasted out . . . with much
> pollished and new-made eloquence: with these daintie cates they
> furnish and set out their filthy and vicious books; now what do they,
> but tye youth in ye fetters of lust, and keepe them in thoughts of
> loue? . . . many [preachers] become affected to their phrases,
> Metaphors, Allegories, and such figuratiue and superlatiue termes,
> and so much vaine eloquence, as they yeeld no fruite at all to their
> auditors, but drive them to amazement. (1603: N4ʳ, O2ʳ)

The strategic Nonconformist gesture – akin to Berowne's – is that of the
absolute abjuring of the deceitful and captivating twists and turns of
style, such as to create a transparently unfigured homiletic mode: 'you
are not to expect', warns (or exults) Bartimaeus Andrewes with
reference to his sermons on the (figure-laden) Songs of Solomon, 'any
flourishing speeches garnish'd with Rhetoricall flowers and figures, or
any cunning sleightes of mans wisedome, or paynted eloquence with
affected wordes, but having an eye to the matter and not to the maner, to

expect a simple and plaine handling of that which is intreated of' (1583: A5r).

Now although the righteous odium unleashed by the Paul's Cross preachers, and dutifully rehearsed by the supposedly penitent Berowne, is directed against tropical aberrations in general ('Metaphors, Allegories'), there are clear indications that the worst offender in the defilement of the once innocently naked tongue is hyperbole. Berowne's 'three-pil'd hyperboles' – his one specific figural reference – represents the maximum of textural finesse, a triply woven and so triply sinful luxury that outdoes all the other silken and taffeta items in the collection. And the repellent dipterous metaphor that follows ('these summer flies / Have blown me full of maggot ostentation') suggests precisely the process of stylistic *inflation* peculiar to hyperbolic operations. It is the same figural swelling that is refused by the ladies in *their* anti-rhetorical sermons; their dismissal of the lords' advances 'As bombast and as lining to the time' (5. 2. 773) takes the first term both in its original sense of padding or stuffing for shaped garments (from Latin *bombax*, cotton) and in its derived sense of grandiloquent (stuffed) speech: 'swelling words, bumbasted out', as Crosse, somewhat less urbanely, puts it. In short, tropical excess in general – over-dressing, over-painting or any of their vicious variants – is liable to be identified with hyperbole, and (the pun is unavoidable) vice versa. Commending and recommending tropical finery in general, Dudley Fenner warns parenthetically that 'sometimes this fine manner of speech swerveth from this perfection'; he proceeds to identify the culprit: 'The excesse of this finesse [is] called Hyperbole' (1584: C4v).

The real trouble with hyperbole is that it surpasses (or 'throws beyond') the limits of *sense* and invades the territory of *reference*. The deviation at work is often not so much semantic as epistemic, having to do with the verifiable properties of the object: it is an 'ostensive falsification', in Alessandro Serpieri's phrase (1980a: 153). Hyperbole, like litotes, irony and other referential or 'metalogical' figures, 'implies acquaintanceship with the referent in order to contradict its faithful description' (Groupe μ 1970: v; on metalogisms in the drama, see Serpieri 1980a). Of these figures it is hyperbole that provides the most blatantly and shamelessly *unfaithful* mode of description. Berowne's 'German clock' or 'pitch-balls' derive their figural energy from their demonstrable (or 'ostensive') non-correspondence with the – presumably fine, albeit dark – facial features of his lady. For moral absolutists, little impressed by distinctions between strategically open falsification on the one hand and simple falsehood on the other, the descriptive infidelity of hyperbole is tantamount to lying. Even Puttenham's alternative English label for the 'Overreacher', indeed, is the 'loud lyer': 'when I speake that which neither I my selfe thinke to be true, nor would haue any other body beleeue, it must needs be a great dissimulation' (1589: Yii$^v$).

A great dissimilation; the hyperbole–mendacity equation is invoked frankly enough and happily enough by the lords in *LLL*. 'But I protest I love to hear him lie', confesses Navarre of Armado's 'high-born words' (1. 1. 172). 'By earth, she is not, corporal, there you lie', objects Berowne to one of Dumain's 'wonder' compliments (4. 3. 84), admitting of his own overblown discourse that 'I do nothing in the world but lie, and lie in my throat' (4. 3. 10–11).

This is where the clash over the acceptability of figural deviations took on crucial ethical, epistemological and especially theological aspects. The Puritan battle-cry of 'plain speech' (an ideal sanctioned by St Paul in the First Epistle to the Corinthians: 'I did not come proclaiming to you the testimony of God in lofty words . . . my speech and my message were not in plausible words of wisdom, but in demonstration of the Spirit and power' (ii. 1–4); and by Christ himself in the Sermon on the Mount: 'Let your communication be yea, yea; nay, nay' (Matthew v. 37), echoed in Berowne's 'russet yeas and honest kersey noes') represented not merely a stylistic preference but a cognitive and hermeneutic *absolute*. Naked language is synonymous with *nuda veritas*, unadorned truth, and is sacrosanct not only in all worldly discourse but most impellingly in the (severely literal) reading of the Bible. The Marprelate tracts make considerable play with the supposed exegetic and stylistic niceties of Anglican theologians (Richard Hooker being an exemplary case in point); 'Martin Junior', titular protagonist of one pamphlet, is at once admonished and admired by his brother Marprelate for the brutal veracity that he opposes to the Anglican arabesque: 'Neither doe I deny, boy, but that thou arte Tom tell-truth, euen like thy father, and that thou canst not abide, to speake unto thine unckle Cantur-by circumloquutions and paraphrases, and simply and plainely thou breakest thy minde unto him, and tellest him unto his face, without al these frivolous circumstances' (1589: Biii$^r$).

Marprelate's 'simply and plainely thou breakest thy minde' recalls Andrewes's 'a simple and plaine handling of that which is intreated of', which in turn recalls John Stockwood's 'my plaine and simpl handling of this Texte' (1578: 4): the (plain and simple) terms of the Puritan campaign against the figures remain perfectly unvaried from tract to tract. And it is these terms that are repeatedly echoed in the anti-figural strain of the rhetorical commentary in *LLL*: in the 'plain statute-caps' of

SHAKESPEARE'S UNIVERSE OF DISCOURSE

Rosaline's jibe, together with her wish 'That some plain man recount their purposes' (5. 2. 177); in Dumain's 'something else more plain', to send as an alternative to his figured ode (4. 3. 118); in Longaville's 'Now to plain-dealing', putting an end to Berowne's oratorical flourishes (4. 3. 366); and above all in Berowne's reprimand to Navarre over his last and disastrously ill-timed effort to win the Princess by rhetorical means immediately after the news of her father's death:

Prin.      I understand you not: my griefs are double.
Ber.      Honest plain words best pierce the ear of grief. (5. 2. 744–5)

Plain speech, *nuda veritas*, fie painted rhetoric . . . *LLL* appears to encode a confidently and nakedly anti-figural moral, demonstrated dramatically in the final rhetorical debacle and expounded unambiguously in Berowne's goodbye-to-all-that oration. This has become a standard reading of the comedy, whose recent critical history is full of expressions like 'from illusion to reality' (McLay 1967: 125), 'Respect for words as symbols of reality' (Berry 1972: 66) or '[the rejection of wit] virtually unrelated to nature, to reality' (Westlund 1967: 43) with reference to the lesson that the lords are forced to digest. There is frequent talk, in this critical tradition, of the punishing of rhetorical excess, be it the 'chastisement' and 'chastening' or 'progressive and painful exorcism of the gentlemen's pretenses and pretensions', especially their 'deplorable affectations, their wayward rhetoric', of which Thomas M. Greene writes (1971: 322); or the penalizing of Berowne because, in Joseph Westlund's words, he 'fails to realize that language is not just something to give one an exhilarating sense of power' (1967: 43); or the penance for the sin that Stanley Wells describes as 'an excessive concern for the means of communication' that 'may inhibit true communication' (1972: 69). Dramatically, the moral is supposedly worked out as a straight opposition between the sinfully excessive rhetoricians and the soberly realistic ladies, who provide 'a built-in corrective to [the lords'] attitude' (Calderwood 1969: 66): 'In the wit of the ladies themselves [there] is a certain edge of reality . . . Unlike the women, the King and his companions play, not with facts themselves, but with words, with nice phrases and antithetical statements' (Barton 1971: 23). And its practical upshot is what Robert Y. Turner terms 'a calling into question of all disproportionate style' (thus hyperbole in particular ) (1974: 215), and with it the affirmation of the Paul's Cross principle of plain and simple handling: '[the comedy's] resolution may be a proposal for therapy', argues William Matthews, accepting Berowne's anti-rhetorical gesture as the play's own: 'Plain speech becomes the battle-cry' (1964: 10).

Now there is no question that the play does invite this straight-forward (one might say 'literal') moral reading on the Hobbesian grounds of 'reality' and verbal sobriety. But the invited interpretation itself sets up so many ironies within the play and its (Elizabethan) performance conditions as to become no longer literal at all, but indeed impossibly paradoxical. The first of these ironies has to do with the figural make-up of the comedy itself, whose language, as we have seen, thrives on the very abuses that Berowne claims to refuse, from the three-piled hyperboles down. The stylistic – and thus dramaturgic and general – self-annihilation that the play's putative rejection of the figures entails has certainly not escaped the notice of the 'plain speech' school of critics. Pater's restrained attribution to the comedy of 'a delicate raillery by Shakespeare at his own chosen manner' (1889: 166) is amplified by more recent critics into a severer and more programmatic act of rhetorical self-castigation: 'The final attitude which the play takes toward [its] dalliance of wit and language', asserts Calderwood, 'is suggested in its own punning title, for when words do duty for reality love's labour is truly without issue' (1969: 60), while Greene discerns a last-minute stylistic retreat: 'In these closing moments of the last scene, one has the impression of the comedy turning back upon itself, withdrawing from those modes of speech and laughter which have in fact constituted its distinctiveness' (1971: 325).

Any such retrospective auto-auto-da-fé, however, presupposes an actual *break* with the play's verbal past, setting up a two-phase stylistic development ('figural' versus 'plain') that allows the withdrawal to be measured. In the event, not only does no such rhetorical reversal take place in the post-renunciation phase of the final act, but the figural (and specifically hyperbolical) colouring is if anything stepped up. Berowne's 'never more' speech itself, with its blind harper, its summer flies, its maggot ostentation (and of course its passing compliment, irresistible still, on the inconceivable whiteness of Rosaline's hand) represents one of the highest achievements of his customary over-painting. And so it is with his later contributions along the same ascetic lines: the 'rage' of his stylistic disease (417); the 'plague' caught from the ladies' eyes (421); and the 'deform'd', 'wanton as a child', 'skipping and vain', 'party-coated' behaviour he attributes oratorically to the effects of love (748ff.). As for the therapy prescribed for this malady, it too can only be described as hyperbolic both in the picturesque extremity of the austere conditions that the ladies prescribe ('some forlorn and naked hermitage', 'remote from all the pleasures of the world', 'frosts and fasts, hard lodging and thin weeds' (787ff.), and more particularly in the exuberant exaggerations of Rosaline's figural diagnosis:

303

> the world's large tongue
> Proclaims you for a man replete with mocks;
> Full of comparisons and wounding flouts, . . .
> To weed this wormwood from your fruitful brain. (834ff.)

Rosaline's strictures over Berowne's excessive irony ('mocks', 'wounding flouts') may be, given speaker and circumstances, one of the play's finer ironies in itself.

What this suggests, of course, is that the comedy's anti-figural gesture may itself be a purely figural move, a suspicion that is more than confirmed by the use to which the 'plain speech' slogan itself is put in other comedies. Launcelot Gobbo, for example, invokes the principle twice as a mode of outright mystification, first in his sadistic dealings with his father:

> Ergo Master Launcelot, – talk not of Master Launcelot father, for the young gentleman (according to fates and destinies, and such odd sayings, the Sisters Three, and such branches of learning), is indeed deceased, or as you would say in plain terms, gone to heaven (2. 2. 57–62);

and then in the malapropistic nonsense he offers Jessica:

> Yes truly, for look you, the sins of the father are to be laid upon the children, therefore (I promise you), I fear you, – I was always plain with you, and so now I speak my agitation of the matter. (3. 5. 1ff.)

And Falstaff prefixes his attempted seduction of Mistress Ford with a purely notional fie-painted-rhetoric disclaimer on the model of the prefaces to the Paul's Cross texts ('I wil use no fore-speech or entraunce, garnished and set out with some Rhetoricall flourishe, to winne at youre handes . . . curious and picked out words and termes', Stockwood 1578: 4):

*Fal.*   Mistress Ford, I cannot cog, I cannot prate, Mistress Ford. . . . Come, I cannot cog and say thou art this and that, like a many of these lisping hawthorn-buds that come like women in men's apparel, and smell like Bucklebury in simple time; I cannot; but I love thee, none but thee. (3. 3. 62ff.)

(Note Falstaff's skilful mimesis of the Puritan horror at rhetorical transvestism, 'like women in men's apparel'.)

Within the Elizabethan religious debate, the argument that the rejection of the figures itself qualifies as a sheer figural illusion becomes one of the principal theological and epistemological moves in the Church's response to the Nonconformist plain-speech campaign. In defence not only of Church-of-England style but more crucially of Church-of-England exegesis, polemicists like Richard Bernard affirm

that language is by its very nature tropical, whereby rhetoric and its
devices are seen to be indispensable to all acts of interpretation, not
least because the Holy Texts themselves manifest in abundance the
whole range of schematic and tropical deviations reviled by the
Nonconformists (not excluding the ineffably iniquitous hyperbolic
lie):

> Rhetoricke ... is necessarie, because euerie where a Diuine shall
> meet with figuratiue speeches in holy Scripture, which without
> Rhetoricke hee cannot explaine. ... This Art sheweth him all the
> tropes wheresoeuer hee meeteth with them, as these foure,
> Metaphora, Metonymia, Synecdoche, Ironia, with their three
> common affections, Allegoria, Catachresis, and Hyperbole, both in
> the figure Auxesis increasing, or Meiosis in diminishing, raise many
> lessons, and apply them for strengthening of faith. (1607: 47)

This is a bold and striking reversal of contemporary moralistic pieties:
far from being impious superfluities to be cleansed from the surface of
speech, the figures become precious hermeneutic instruments and
direct aids to faith. And the most radical aspect of this argument,
sustained even by so austere a preacher and theologian as William
Perkins, is that the language of the Logos itself is by no means plain and
literal as Crosse and his colleagues insist, but eminently and
persistently figured; God reveals himself to man through 'sacred
tropes': 'An Anthropopathia', for example, 'is a sacred Metaphor,
whereby those things that are properly spoken of a man, are by a
similitude attributed to God' (1600: 656). Like Bernard, Perkins upholds
tropical language as the only path affording effective access to the Word:
'All tropes emphaticall, ... besides delight and ornament, they doe also
afford matter for the nourishment of faith: as when Christ is put for a
Christian Man, or for the Church of God' (659).

The inevitability of the trope features, beyond the bounds of religious
polemic, within the epistemology of Bacon, who not only takes up the
argument concerning the tropicality of biblical and thus of theological
discourse ('in Divine learning, wee see howe frequent Parables and
Tropes are'), but admits the crucial importance of tropological modes of
thought and of expression in the foundation of scientific discourse: 'For
it is a Rule, That whatsoever Science is not consonant to presuppositions, must pray in ayde of Similitudes' (1605: 64ʳ). Bacon proceeds to
elaborate an evolutionary history of language in which tropical modes
of conception actually precede 'literal' language and make possible the
acquisition of knowledge in the earliest stages of human consciousness:
'And therefore in the Infancie of learning, and in rude times, the World
was full of Parables and Similitudes; for else would men either haue

305

passed ouer without Marke, or else reiected for Paradoxes, that which was offered' (*ibid.*).

This notion of the priority of the trope over 'scientific' or literally descriptive linguistic modes (anticipated in less explicit fashion by Puttenham's Ciceronian claim that poetic language arises 'before any civil society was among men', 1589: 3, and by Sidney's analogous assertion that poetry had 'priority' (his term) over other linguistic forms, 1595: B2$^r$–B2$^v$) is reworked by a line of later thinkers from Vico to Rousseau to Nietzsche, who gives the *topos* its most radical expression ('Tropes are not something that can be added or subtracted from language at will; they are its truest nature' (quoted in De Man 1974: 35).

In such an epistemological perspective, the position of the women in *LLL*, like that of the Nonconformists whose arguments they echo, cannot be taken too seriously, or better too literally. The language of Elizabethan anti-tropicality is indeed subject to the inevitable laws of the trope, even if the tropes concerned are of a codified (or as Nietzsche would put it, 'forgotten') nature: not only the dressing and painting terminology for the rejected figures, but the very notion of 'plainness' espoused as an alternative to figurality (and itself a dead metaphor or catachresis), are fatally ironized by their own inescapable semantic trickiness.

The final and decisive irony or paradox in the comedy's repudiation of the trope, however, is of a strictly theatrical character. For of all the targets for the Nonconformist abomination of wanton deviancy, nothing excited more violent revulsion than the theatrical representations of the time. Theatre is a twofold epitome of abuses: its language, reinforced by the performers' emphatic *actio*, presents in particularly heightened form, as Henry Crosse underlines, the vile hyperbolical inflation of maggot ostentation: 'for are not their Dialogues puft up with swelling wordes? are not theyr arguments pleasing and rauishing? and made more forcible by gesture and outward action? surely this must needes attract the minde to imitate such vices as are portrayed out, whereby the soule is tainted with impietie' (1603: 2$^r$); and the actors' bodies translate into direct corporeal terms the over-dressing and over-painting metaphors applied to the tropes. The Puritans' condemnation of the players' 'swelling wordes' is thus invariably accompanied by – and is in the end equivalent to – their repugnance at the actual transvestism perpetrated on stage, whether it be of a costumic kind: 'But if . . . all men are abomination that put on wemens raiment, Players are abomination that put on wemens raiment' (Rainolds 1599: 16); or of a cosmetic variety: 'for that face that is slubbred and starched with so many ointments and dregs, is more like a sore and surff then a naturall

face. God hath giuen the face, and thou defilest it with myre and dirt'
(Crosse 1603: K4ʳ); 'these plyers . . . will raher weare a visarde than a
naturall face' (Northbrooke 1577: 101).

The aberrations achieved by verbal figures and bodily figures alike (so
fatally united in the playhouse) represent transgressions against the
same principle, namely that of 'natural' propriety. Phillip Stubs in his
*Anatomy of Abuses* upholds the principle as a divine semiotic law:

> It is written in the 22. of Deuteronomie, that *what man soeuer*
> *weareth womans apparell is accursed, and what woman weareth*
> *mans apparell is accursed also.* . . . Our apparell was giuen as a signe
> distinctiue, to discerne betwixt sexe and sexe, and therefore one to
> wear the apparell of an other sexe, is to participate with the same,
> and to adulterate the veritie of his owne kinde. (1584: 38ʳ)

Any number of Church fathers are (ironically, given the Nonconformist
pretensions of the authors) cited by Northbrooke and followers in
support of the outright abolition of the stage display on such religious
grounds – from Augustine to Cyprian, to Tertullian, to Chrysostom to
Salvianus – although the main point of reference in the call for natural
bodily propriety remains St Paul (again, in a sense, ironically, since it
may have been Paul's veto against women preachers – 'the women
should keep silence in the churches', 1 Corinthians xiv. 34 – that led to
the prohibition of actresses and so to the very institution of
transvestism on the Elizabethan stage, see d'Amico 1981: 16). The
victory of these arguments over the putative persuasive or seductive
force of theatre itself is sadly demonstrated by the course of events in
mid-seventeenth-century England.

Now the implications of this anti-theatrical polemic for the *nuda*
*veritas* issues in *LLL* are not too far to seek. For in performance – at least
on the Elizabethan stage – the play's supposed spokesmen against
over-dressing and over-painting (including, it might be noted, the
physical disguising of the rejected masque) are *themselves* the chief
transgressors in this very vicious direction: boys in women's apparel
who strategically adulterate the verity of their own kind as part of the
unchaste fiction (or lie) in which they are caught. Thus the call for
honest kersey amounts not only to a rhetorical self-annihilation but to a
theatrical impossibility, given the acting conventions in play. When
John Rainolds, at the close of the century, describes the kind of dramatic
performance that ought to be the first to be damned, he might be
decreeing – like the women and the penitent Berowne within the
comedy – the damnation precisely of *LLL* and its spectacular
dénouement: 'such playes as bring in wooers masked, and dansing,
using much unmodest behaviour in woordes and deedes; young men in

307

wemens raiment, and supposed to be gentlewemen, ... such
stageplayes, I say, you ought in my judgment acknowledge to be iustly
charged and condemned' (1599: 20–1).

In a word, the dispensability of tropical deviation both in the language
and in the performance of the drama proves to be the most powerful of
tropes or fictions, just as it is the very fiction (that 'feigning' so much
reviled by the puritanical) that founds the entire rhetoric of the dramatic
representation: the naked truth, as the seventeenth-century Puritan
successors to Northbrooke efficaciously demonstrated, means no less
than the death of the dramatic theatre. The trope – hyperbolic
heightening above all – is the necessary condition of comic (and not only
comic) drama. In *LLL* – and this is the comedy's final irony in the matter
– only one speaker can claim in the end to be un- or under-dressed, and
thus to represent (as he himself points out) *nuda veritas*: namely, and
paradoxically, the overreaching plume of feathers himself:

*Armado.*   The naked truth of it is, I have no shirt. (5. 2. 701)

But then even this true nudity is, naturally (and unnaturally), disguised.

# Glossary

The field in which each word or expression originates is indicated in parentheses; the following abbreviations are used:

Ling. Linguistics
Phil. Philosophy of Language
Rhet. Rhetoric
Sem. Semiotic theory
Soc. Sociology

'Coin.' indicates a term introduced here for the first time, or used for the first time in a given sense.

Where appropriate, the etymology of the term is given (F. = French; Ger. = German; G. = Greek; I. = Italian; L. = Latin; lit. = literal meaning).

*Actantial Scheme (or Model)* (Sem.) The configuration of the six roles or functions (*actants*) fulfilled by characters in narrative; the roles are arranged in three oppositions: subject/object; sender/receiver; helper/opponent (Greimas 1966, 1970).

*Actio* (Rhet.; L., lit. 'action'; G. *hypocrisis*) Delivery: the fifth of the five traditional parts of rhetoric, consisting in the vocal and gestural performance of the oration.

*Ad placitum* (Phil.; L., lit. 'at pleasure') Expression used within the conventionalist (q.v.) account of meaning to denote the arbitrary imposition of names.

*Amplification* (Rhet.) The process of elaborating and expanding a particular argument or topic; or the figural means to such elaboration.

*Anaphora* (Ling./Rhet.; G., lit. 'carrying back') (i) In linguistics, a mode of reference, normally pronominal, that picks up the referent of an antecedent expression ('it', 'he', etc.); (ii) in rhetoric, the repetition of a word or phrase at the beginning of successive verses, clauses, etc.

*Anastrophe* (Rhet.; G., lit. 'inversion') Unusual word or clause order within a sentence.

*Antanaclasis* (Rhet.; G., lit. 'reflection') A pun of a strictly homonymic nature ('son'/'sun').

*Antimetabole* (Rhet.; G., lit. 'turn-about') The specular inversion of word or clause order, usually within a sentence or verse (AB:BA).

*Apostrophe* (Rhet.; G., lit. 'turning away') A digression from the discourse in progress in order to address a present, absent or imaginary object or person.

*Apostrophus* (Rhet.; L., from G. *apostrophe*, q.v.) The omission of a phoneme or letter from a word (marked graphically by ').

*Archaism* (Rhet.) An archaic or outmoded term or expression used for stylistic effect.

*Authentication* (Soc.) The use of conventional character-to-character signals in the dialogue in order to render it authentic as 'conversation' (Burns 1972).

*Back-channel signals* (Soc.) The responses (normally non-lexical) given by the listener during a speaking turn (Goffman 1975).

*Battle for the floor* (Soc.) A conversational situation in which all speakers strive to gain the speaking floor.

*Boosters* (Soc.) Signals (normally lexical) of encouragement from the listener to the speaker (Goffman 1975).

*Chiasmus* (Rhet.; G., lit. 'cross-shape') X-shaped specular inversion of word order in parallel verses or phrases.

*Climax* (Rhet.; G., lit. 'ladder') The arrangement of a series of words, phrases, clauses or sentences in order of increasing intensity.

*Commissive* (Phil.) An illocutionary act (q.v.) that commits the speaker to a given course of action (a promise, vow, undertaking, etc.) (Searle 1975b).

*Compound word* (Ling.) A word made up of two existing words or combining forms ('outrun').

*Connotation* (Phil./Sem.) The secondary sense or implication conveyed by a lexeme (q.v.) or other sign-unit.

*Context of utterance* (Ling.) The set of constraints on the utterance – relating to the speaker, the listener, the time and the location of discourse – that determine its form, meaning and appropriateness (Lyons 1977).

*Conventionalism, semantic* (Phil.) The theory or body of theories according to which the meaning of words is established on purely conventional grounds.

*Conversational fiction* (Coin.) The conventional principle whereby the *dramatis personae* are taken to be engaged in talk exchanges.

*Conversational rules* (Soc.) The pragmatic principles regulating the succession, quality, length, etc. of speaking turns in conversation.

*Copia verborum* (Rhet.; L., lit. 'abundance of words') The ideal of discursive richness or eloquence expounded by Erasmus and cultivated by Renaissance figurists.

*Co-text* (Ling./Sem.) The verbal context of an utterance or expression (Petöfi 1975)

*Declaration* (Phil.) An illocutionary act (q.v.) which, if performed in appropriate conditions, brings about the state of affairs referred to (e.g. court sentences, the naming of ships, declarations of war, etc.) (Searle 1975b).

*Deixis* (Ling.; G., lit. 'Showing') The use of deictic terms – such as personal and demonstrative pronouns, verb tenses, spatial and temporal adverbs (*here/now*) – that relate the utterance to its pragmatic context.

*Deixis, textual* (Ling.) Demonstrative pronouns and other deictic terms used to indicate aspects not of the context but of the verbal co-text (q.v.) (Lyons 1977).

*Denotation* (Phil./Sem.) The relationship between a lexeme (q.v.) or other sign-unit and the class of objects, properties, etc. to which it is applied (e.g. the lexeme 'table' and the class of objects 'table').

*Dicaeologia* (Rhet.; G., lit. 'plea in defence') Figure in which the speaker excuses his deeds or words on the grounds of necessity.

*Directive* (Phil.) An illocutionary act (q.v.) that attempts to induce the listener to do something (e.g. commands, requests, advice, etc.) (Searle 1975b).

*Discourse, dramatic* (Sem.) The dialogue considered particularly with respect to its functions within the dramatic narrative (Elam 1980).

*Discourse, theatrical* (Sem.) The set of signals – verbal and non-verbal – that make up the overall theatrical performance.

*Discourse time* (Sem.) The fictional moment (*now*) at which the utterance is produced within the dramatic world (Elam 1980)

*Dispositio* (Rhet.; L.; G. *taxis*) Arrangement: the second of the five traditional parts of rhetoric, comprising the ordering and amplification (q.v.) of arguments within the oration.

*Ecphonesis* (Rhet.; G., lit. 'outcry') Figure involving the passionate vocal – but normally non-lexical – expression of emotion ('O!').

*Ellipsis* (Rhet.; G., lit. 'omit') The omission of a word or expression that can be readily understood from the verbal co-text (q.v.).

*Elocutio* (Rhet.; L.; G. *lexis*) Style: the third of the five traditional parts of rhetoric, comprising the elaboration of discourse by means of rhetorical figures.

*Embedding* (Ling./Sem.) The insertion of subordinate textual units into the main textual structure (subordinate clauses in sentences; poems, letters, performances, etc. within the main play).

*Emblem* (Rhet.; G., lit. 'insertion') A picture bearing an allegorical significance, normally accompanied in emblem books by a motto and verse moral.

*Energia* (Rhet.; G., lit. 'activity, vigour') Class of vivid verbal description, especially of a pictorial kind.

*Énoncé* (Ling./Sem.; F., lit. 'statement') The utterance considered as a structured (syntactic/semantic/propositional) message, removed from the particular circumstances of its delivery (contrast *énonciation*).

*Énonciation* (Ling./Sem.; F., lit. 'delivery') The act of utterance considered in relationship to its context, and especially with regard to its deictic elements.

*Epenthesis* (Rhet.; G., lit. 'placing in addition') The addition of a phoneme, syllable or letter to the middle of a word.

*Epimone* (Rhet.; G., lit. 'delay') The insistent repetition of a given phrase.

*Epistrophe* (Rhet.; G., lit. 'additional turning') Repetition of final word or phrase over a series of verses, clauses or sentences.

*Ethopoeia* (Rhet.; G., lit. 'character description') A vivid verbal depiction of the personal features, traits and behaviour of an individual (species of *energia*, q.v.).

*Ethos* (Rhet.; lit. 'character') The emotional, psychological and moral character of the speaker, both influential on and represented by his discourse.

*Expressive* (Phil.) A convention-bound illocutionary act (q.v.) – such as greeting, congratulating, thanking – that presupposes a particular psychological state (Searle 1975b).

*Fabula* (Sem.; L., lit. 'fable') Russian formalists' term for the narrative material – agents, actions, etc. – in its logical and chronological order, as opposed to the order in which it is presented in the plot.

*Fabula time* (Coin.) The chronology of the underlying narrative sequence.

*Flatus vocis* (Phil.; L., lit. 'blowing of the voice') Expression adopted by extreme nominalists (v. nominalism) to denote empty universal terms.

*Flyting* (Scottish and Northern Engl. dialect) A ritual dispute between two opponents, consisting in an exchange of invective and abuse.

*Foregrounding* (Sem.) Prague formalists' term (Czech *aktualisace*) for the bringing to attention of some component of a text or message, rather than its content (Garvin 1964; Elam 1977).

*Form of the content* (Sem.) The formal organization of the information contained in discourse (Hjelmslev 1943).

*Form of the expression* (Sem.) The formal organization – phonic, graphic or syntactic – of the structure of discourse (Hjelmslev 1943).

*Frame dispute* (Soc.) Disagreement between two or more participants as to the kind of activity being engaged in (Goffman 1974).

*Frame, metadiscursive* (Coin.) Direct commentary – in the form of definition, description, etc. – on the (linguistic) activity in progress.

*Frame, presentational* (Coin.) Conventional dramaturgic device – prologue, induction, epilogue, etc. – designed to present the dramatic fiction or theatrical representation as such.

*Hyperbaton* (Rhet.; G., lit. 'overstepping') A class of schemes (q.v.) involving any form of departure from normal word order.

*Hyperbole* (Rhet.; G., lit. 'throwing beyond') Figure involving the use of exaggerated terms not intended to be taken literally.

*Hypertext* (Sem.) A text that transforms, imitates, parodies, dramatizes or otherwise derives from another text (the hypotext, q.v.) (Genette 1982).

*Hypostasization of language* (Phil.) The act or process of taking words as the exact equivalents to, or embodiments of, objects.

*Hypotext* (Sem.) A text that serves as source or primary text for a hypertext (q.v.).

*Hysteron proteron* (Rhet.; G., lit. 'the latter (placed as) the former') A scheme (q.v.) comprising the reversal of the logical, temporal or syntactic order of discourse (a form of *hyperbaton*, q.v.).

*Icon* (Rhet./Sem.; G., lit. 'image') (i) (Rhet.) Evocation of the resemblance of a person or object by means of simile or metaphor; (ii) (Sem.) a sign that denotes its object by means of resemblance (Peirce 1931–58).

*Icon, symbolic* (Phil.) In Renaissance Platonic-Hermetic theory, a visual image that directly expresses the essence or idea of what it represents (see Gombrich 1948).

*Idiolect* (Ling./Sem.) The characteristic mode or style of speech employed by a particular speaker.

*Illocutionary act (or illocution)* (Phil./Ling.) A social act performed in saying something, consisting in the fulfilment of a communicative goal (e.g. asking a question, making a statement, issuing a command, etc.) (Austin 1962).

*Illocutionary force* (Phil./Ling.) The pragmatic function or status of an utterance (as question, statement, command, etc.) (Austin 1962).

*Illocutionary sequel* (Phil./Ling.) An act entailed as the direct consequence of an illocution (the answer, e.g. to a question) (Austin 1962).

*Impresa* (Rhet.; I., lit. 'undertaking') An emblematic device or motto, usually represented on a coat of arms.

*Index* (Sem.; G., lit. 'pointer') A sign that denotes its object through direct physical connection or contiguity, or through cause–effect association (smoke as a sign of fire, etc.) (Peirce 1931–58).

*Indirect speech act* (Phil./Ling.) An implicit illocutionary act (q.v.) performed in the guise of another type of act (e.g. an order in the form of a question) (Searle 1975a).

*Infelicity* (Phil./Ling.) An error or violation in the performance of a speech act (q.v.) (Austin 1962).

*Interlinguistic games* (Coin.) Uses of language involving the relationship between at least two different languages (thus translating, code-switching, soriasmus (q.v.), etc.).

*Intertextuality* (Sem.) (i) The relations arising between texts; (ii) the notion

312

whereby every text is necessarily an intersection of other texts (Kristeva 1968).

*Intralinguistic functions* (Coin.) Uses of language that foreground the internal (especially semantic) relations between words or other discourse units (puns, etc.).

*Introjection of the referent* (Sem.) The process whereby objects referred to in artistic texts come to belong to the universe of the text, even when they correspond to extra-textual entities (Pagnini 1980).

*Inventio* (Rhet.; L.; G. *heuresis*) Invention: the first of the five traditional parts of rhetoric, comprising the finding or creating of arguments and proofs.

*Isocolon* (Rhet.; G., lit. 'equivalent limbs / clauses') Scheme (q.v.) which balances two or more clauses of similar length within a sentence.

*Kinesic factors* (Sem.) Body-movement and gesture as communicative elements.

*Language-game* (Phil.; Ger. *Sprachspiel*) Ludwig Wittgenstein's term (1953) for a linguistic activity considered in relationship with the context or form of life of which it is part.

*Lexeme* (Ling.; from G. *lexis*, 'word') A minimal unit within the vocabulary of the language (vocabulary word, stem, etc.).

*Locus communis* (Rhet.; L.; G. *topos*) Commonplace: an argument or theme of wide and repeated application, readily inserted into a speech.

*Locutionary act* (Phil. / Ling.) The act of saying something in a given language (Austin 1962).

*Memoria* (Rhet.; L.; G. *mneme*) Memory: The fourth of the five traditional parts of rhetoric, consisting in the memorization of the oration, with the help of a number of mnemonic aids.

*Mention* (Phil. / Ling.) A reflexive – as opposed to directly referential – expression ('the word "black" has five letters') (contrast use, q.v.).

*Metacommunication* (Sem.) Verbal commentary or non-verbal signals concerning some aspect of the process of communication (its production, reception, circumstances, etc.) (see Habermas 1970; Bateson 1972).

*Metadiscourse* (Sem.) Discourse which has as its object some aspect of discourse itself (speech acts, style, reference, etc.).

*Metadrama* Drama which has as its theme or point of reference either its own dramaturgic make-up or some internal dramatic structure (play-within-the-play, etc.) (see Calderwood 1969).

*Metalanguage* (Phil. / Sem.) Language used to describe or otherwise comment on language itself (the object language) (see Carnap 1947; Jakobson 1956).

*Metalogism* (Rhet.; G., lit. 'altered reasoning') Class of figures that bring the object or referent directly into play by giving an unfaithful description of it (includes hyperbole (q.v.), irony, paradox, etc.) (Groupe μ 1970).

*Metaplasm* (Rhet.; G., lit. 're-moulding') The transposition of phonemes (q.v.), syllables or letters within a word (includes *prosthesis, aphoresis, paragoge* (q.v.), etc.).

*Metatheatre* Theatrical representation which has as its object or theme the representation in progress or some internal performance (compare metadrama, q.v.) (see Abel 1963).

*Metonymy* (Rhet.; G., lit. 'name-change') Figure of contiguity, involving the substitution of cause for effect, or vice versa, or of proper name for personal quality, or vice versa.

*Mise en abyme* (F., lit. 'placing in the central blazon'; from heraldry) André

Gide's term for the embedding (q.v.) within a work of art of an internal structure that reflects certain qualities of the main work.

*Modality* (Phil.) The qualification of the propositional content of discourse according to its possibility, impossibility, contingency or necessity (expressed through modal verbs such as 'can', 'must', etc.).

*Morpheme* (Ling.; from G. *morphē*, 'form') A grammatical unit that cannot be broken down into smaller units (e.g. in the lexeme 'writings' the elements 'write'–'ing'–'s').

*Naturalism, semantic* (Phil.) The theory or body of theories according to which the relationship between signs, objects and meanings is naturally motivated rather than arbitrary.

*Nominalism* (Phil.) The late-medieval philosophical movement according to which universal terms are merely names denoting individuals, and only individuals – not universal concepts – exist.

*Numen* (Phil.; L., lit. 'divine power') A guiding force or spirit supposed, in certain occult theories, to preside over phenomena and hence over names.

*Object of discourse* (Phil.) An entity, quality or event referred to in discourse.

*Ornatus difficilis* (Rhet.; L.) Difficult ornament: a figure (specifically a trope, q.v.) that entails semantic and conceptual as well as formal operations.

*Ornatus facilis* (Rhet.; L.) Easy ornament: a figure (especially a scheme, q.v.) that involves only formal or structural transformations.

*Ostension* (Phil./Sem.; from L., lit. 'showing') The displaying of an object or event as the expression of the class of which it is a member (an actual stone, say, as member of the class 'stone').

*Ostensive definition* (Phil.) A definition that consists not in verbal explanation but in the showing (ostension) of the object denoted by the word in question.

*Paragoge* (Rhet.; G., lit. 'leading past') The addition of a phoneme (q.v.), syllable or letter to the end of a word.

*Paralinguistic features* (Ling.) Variable vocal qualities produced during the utterance of speech: pitch, volume, etc. (Trager 1958).

*Paratext* (Sem.) A marginal or peripheral aspect of textual structure, usually preceding or following the text proper (title, preface, afterword, marginal notes, etc.) (Genette 1982).

*Parimion* (Rhet.; G., lit. 'close resemblance') Alliteration, especially of an emphatic and insistent kind.

*Paroemia* (Rhet.; G., lit. 'byword') The quoting of proverbs.

*Paronomasia* (Rhet.; G., lit. 'change of name') A pun involving two or more words that are close in sound but not exactly homonymic (e.g. 'Ship'/'Sheep').

*Pathos* (Rhet.; G., lit. 'suffering') The emotional effects that the speaker arouses, or strives to arouse, in his listeners.

*Performative* (Phil./Ling.) An utterance that constitutes the very act it refers to (e.g. 'I pronounce you man and wife') (Austin 1962).

*Performative verb* A verb ('pronounce' in the above example) that may be used in a performative utterance.

*Perlocutionary act* (Phil./Ling.) A social act performed by saying something, entailing certain effects (perlocutionary effects) upon the listener (e.g. convincing, alarming, deterring, etc.) (Austin 1962).

*Perlocutionary sequel* The behaviour produced as the direct consequence of a perlocutionary act (e.g. the act of shooting as a result of the persuasion to shoot) (Austin 1962).

*Phoneme* (Ling.; from G. *phonema*, 'sound') A distinctive sound class of a given language, serving to distinguish one word from another (e.g. /d/ and /t/ in the words 'den' and 'ten').

*Ploce* (Rhet.; G., lit. 'plait') The repetition of a word in a different sense or function after an interval (e.g. 'light (n.) . . . light (adj.)')

*Pragmatic* (Ling. / Sem.; from G. *pragma*, 'act') adj.) Concerning the relationship between linguistic and other signs and their context (senders, receivers, circumstances); *pragmatics* (n.) the study of the relationship between signs and their context.

*Pragmatographia* (Rhet.; G., lit. 'description of an act') Vivid verbal depiction of an action or event (species of *energia*, q.v.).

*Predicate* (Phil. / Ling.) (v.) To assert or affirm (a property) of the subject of a proposition (e.g. 'Boyet is wit's pedlar'); (n.) the property that is affirmed of the subject ('wit's pedlar').

*Presupposition* (Phil. / Ling.) That (a proposition or predicate) which is taken for granted in an utterance.

*Presupposition, existential* (Phil.) The principle whereby any object of discourse, in order to be referred to, is taken to exist within the universe of discourse (q.v.) (e.g. Father Christmas in the utterance 'Father Christmas is coming tomorrow').

*Presupposition, pragmatic* (Ling.) Those aspects of the speaking situation that are taken for granted in talk (e.g. the identity, sex, status etc. of the participants when these are known to all).

*Proairesis* (Sem.; G.) Action: especially the sequence of actions in narrative texts.

*Proof, artificial* (Rhet.) A mode of persuasion achieved by the orator through his own art or invention (comprehends *ethos* and *pathos* (q.v.) and logical proof).

*Proof, inartificial* (Rhet.) External support for a given argument or cause (testimonies, documents, etc.).

*Proposition* (Phil. / Ling.) That which is expressed by a declarative sentence, in the form of a statement, and which may be true or false (as in the sentence 'Shakespeare was really Elizabeth I').

*Propositional act* (Phil.) The act – prerequisite to the full speech act (q.v.) – of expressing a proposition (Searle 1969).

*Propositional attitude* (Phil.) The attitude of the speaker with regard to the proposition he expresses (e.g. belief, doubt, uncertainty, etc.).

*Prosopographia* (Rhet.; G., lit. 'depiction of face') Vivid description of a person, real or imaginary (type of *energia*, q.v.).

*Prosopopeia* (Rhet.; G., lit. 'face-making; dramatization') The representation of an absent or imaginary person speaking or acting.

*Prosthesis* (Rhet.; G., lit. 'placing before') The addition of a phoneme (q.v.), syllable or letter to the beginning of a word.

*Province* (Ling.) The features of language that serve to identify discourse with a particular occupational or professional activity (Crystal and Davy 1969).

*Recursion* (Ling.) The property or process whereby an overall discourse structure (e.g. a sentence) may contain an indefinitely extendible series of subordinate structures (e.g. clauses or phrases).

*Reference act* (Phil.) The act – prerequisite to the speech act proper (q.v.) – of referring to an object (Searle 1969).

*Reference, singular definite* (Phil.) The use of an expression which identifies a single object or entity ('you', 'the dramatist Shakespeare').

*Referent* (Phil./Sem.) The object to which an expression (or gesture or other communicative act) refers.

*Reflexivity* (Ling.) The property of language whereby it is able to refer to, or describe, itself.

*Regression* (Sem.) The process of perpetuation of a structure or event in an indefinite series of repetitions.

*Repair mechanism* (Soc.) Means whereby participants in a talk exchange may correct turn-taking errors and violations (Sacks *et al.* 1974).

*Representative* (Phil./Ling.) An illocutionary act (q.v.) that commits the speaker to the truth of the proposition asserted (statement, denial, etc.) (Searle 1975b).

*Rerun signal* (Soc.) Request from the listener to the speaker to repeat or reformulate an utterance that has not been understood (Goffman 1975).

*Role, deictic* (Ling.) The position occupied by a participant in a speech exchange, indicated especially by personal pronouns (speaker 'I', addressee 'you', etc.) and by the person of the verb (see Lyons 1977).

*Scheme* (Rhet.; from G. *skhēma*, 'form') Class of figures that involves the transformation of phonetic, graphic or syntactic structure, but not of sense.

*Semantics* (Ling.) (i) The meaning structure of language; (ii) the study of meaning and its production.

*Semiosis* (Sem.; G.) The process of signification.

*Semiotic* (G. *sēmeiōtikos*, lit. 'taking note of signs') (adj.) Relating to signs and sign systems; *semiotics* (n.) the study of signs and sign systems.

*Sententia* (Rhet.; L., lit. 'judgment, opinion') A brief axiom or statement of universal truth.

*Situation of utterance* (Ling.) The configuration of material and circumstantial elements – participants, time, place, occasion, etc. – within which an utterance is issued.

*Size marker* (Coin.) A comment or other signal regarding the length of a speaking turn.

*Soriasmus* (Rhet.; G., lit. 'heaping') A vice of language (q.v.) consisting in the mixing of languages as a show of supposed learning.

*Speech act* (Phil./Ling.) An utterance viewed as a goal-oriented social event, serving to express the speaker's attitude or intentions (illocutionary act, q.v.) or to achieve some effect on the listener (perlocutionary act, q.v.) (Austin 1962; Searle 1969).

*Syllepsis* (Rhet.; G., lit. 'taking together') The use of one verb or adjective, etc., to cover two distinct syntactic functions (e.g. the verb 'were' in 'I and my friends were happy').

*Synecdoche* (Rhet.; G., lit. 'interpreting (one thing) with (another)') Figure in which the whole is substituted for a part, or vice versa, or a genus for a species, or vice versa ('twenty *head* of cattle').

*Synonymia* (Rhet.) A mode of amplifying a discourse through the accumulation of synonymous epithets.

*Tetragrammaton* (G., lit. 'having four letters') The Hebrew name for God, consisting of the four consonants YHWH, considered in the Cabalistic tradition as unpronounceable and sacred in itself.

*Topic* (Rhet.; from G. *topos*, 'place') (i) The material from which an argument is constructed (ii) a stock theme to be inserted into discourse (compare, in this sense, *locus comunis*).

*Transformability of the sign* (Sem.) The capacity of theatrical sign-vehicles to bear a range of non-literal denotations (Bogatyrev 1938; Honzl 1940; Elam 1980).

*Trope* (Rhet.; G., lit. 'turn') A class of figures that entails a change in the sense or application of a word or phrase.

*Turn, conversational* (Soc.) (i) The right or opportunity to speak during a talk exchange; (ii) an actual contribution made during such an exchange (see Sacks *et al.* 1974).

*Turn signal* (Soc.) Any of a number of means whereby participants in talk exchanges regulate the succession of contributions (Sacks *et al.* 1974).

*Universe of discourse* (Phil.) Term introduced by the logician Augustus De Morgan (1847) to denote the set of objects, individuals, events, attributes, propositions, etc., created by a given body of discourse.

*Uptake* (Phil.) The correct understanding of the illocutionary force of an utterance on the part of the listener (Austin 1962).

*Use* (Phil./Ling.) The employment of a given word or expression in a referential rather than reflexive fashion (contrast mention, q.v.).

*Vice of language* (Rhet.) Excessive or indecorous departure from the norm, especially by way of stylistic affectation.

*Vis verborum* (Phil.; L., lit. 'power of words') Doctrine espoused in the occult sciences according to which verbal formulae may acquire directly efficacious force in magical operations.

*World, actual* (or *reference*) (Phil.) A state of affairs – set of individuals, events, attributes, etc. – defined as actually existing or having actually existed.

*World, possible* (Phil.) A state of affairs defined as possible with respect to, but not realized in, the actual world (q.v.).

*World-creating expression* (Ling.) Modal verb or adjective (v. modality) that expresses a possible state of affairs ('can', 'might', 'probable', etc.) (see McCawley 1978).

*World-creating games* (Coin.) The referential, predicative and other functions of language responsible for setting up the individuals, properties and events of the dramatic world.

*Zeugma* (Rhet.; G., lit. 'yoking') Scheme (q.v.) in which one verb governs two or more objects or clauses, especially when they are semantically incompatible ('John ate his supper and then his words').

# References

The date given after each author's name in the text and in the references is that of the first edition. When a later edition has been used, the date is given at the end of the reference.

Abbott, E. A. 1881. *A Shakespearian Grammar.* London: Macmillan.

Abel, Lionel 1963. *Metatheatre: A New View of Dramatic Form.* New York: Hill and Wang.

Agrippa Von Nettesheim, Henry Cornelius 1533. *De occulta philosophia libri tre,* trans. 'J. F.' (1651), *Three Books of Occult Philosophy or Magic,* ed. W. F. Whitehead. Chicago: Hahn and Whitehead, 1898.

Alciati, Andrea 1547. *Emblemata.* Lyons.

Anagnostopoulos, Georgios 1972. Plato's *Cratylus:* the two theories of the correctness of names. *Review of Metaphysics,* xxv, 4, 691–736.

Andrewes, Bartimaeus 1583. *Certaine Verie Worthie, Godly and Profitable Sermons, upon the Fifth Chapter of the Songs of Solomon.* London.

Arbeau, Thoinot 1588. *Orchesography,* trans. C. W. Beaumont. London: C. W. Beaumont, 1925.

Aristotle *Rhetoric,* trans. J. H. Freese. London: Heinemann, 1926.

    *De interpretatione,* trans. E. M. Edghill. In R. McKeon (ed.), *The Basic Works of Aristotle.* New York: Random House, 1941.

    *Poetics,* trans. Gerald F. Else. Ann Arbor: University of Michigan Press, 1967.

Ascham, Roger 1545. *Toxophilus: The School of Shooting Conteyned in Two Bookes.* London.

Ashworth, E. J. 1974. *Language and Logic in the Post-Medieval Period.* Dordrecht: Reidel.

Austin, J. L. 1962. *How to Do Things with Words,* second edition. London: Oxford University Press, 1976.

Bacon, Francis 1605. *The Proficiencie and Aduancement of Learning, Diuine and Humane.* London.

    1625. *Essayes,* third edition, ed. M. J. Hawkins. London: Dent, 1972.

Barber, C. L. 1959. *Shakespeare's Festive Comedy.* Princeton University Press.

Barish, Jonas A. 1966. The antitheatrical prejudice. *Critical Quarterly,* viii, 329–46.

Barton, Anne 1971. Shakespeare and the limits of language. *Shakespeare Survey,* 24, pp. 19–30.

    1978. A source for *Love's Labour's Lost. Times Literary Supplement,* 24 November, pp. 1373–4.

Bateson, Gregory 1972. *Steps to an Ecology of Mind.* London: Intertext.

Baugh, A. C. 1970. *A History of the English Language.* New York: Appleton-Century-Crofts.

REFERENCES

Bellinghausen, Anton M. 1955. Die Wortkulisse bei Shakespeare. *Shakespeare-Jahrbuch*, XCI, 182–95.

Bernard, Richard 1607. *The Faithfull Shepherd*, second edition. London, 1621.

Berry, Ralph 1972. *Shakespeare's Comedies: Explorations in Form*. Princeton University Press.

Bindella, Maria Teresa 1971. Sir Thomas Elyot e la danza. *Miscellanea*, I (Udine), 67–82.

Blau, J. L. 1944. *The Christian Interpretation of the Cabala in the Renaissance*. New York: Columbia University Press.

Boas, F. S. (ed.) 1950. *The Hieroglyphics of Horapollo*. New York: Pantheon.

Bocchi, Achille 1555. *Symbolicae quaestiones*. Bologna, 1574.

Bogatyrcv, Petr 1938. Les signes du théâtre. *Poétique*, 8 (1971), 517–30.

Bonazza, Blaze O., 1966. *Shakespeare's Early Comedies: A Structural Analysis*. The Hague: Mouton.

Bonomi, Andrea 1979. *Universi di discorso*. Milan: Feltrinelli.

Boorde, Andrew 1542. *A Compendyous Regyment or a Dyetary of Helth*. London.

  1552. *The Breuiary of Healthe*. London.

Borgmann, Albert 1974. *The Philosophy of Language: Historical Foundations and Contemporary Issues*. The Hague: Mouton.

Bradbrook, Muriel C. 1936. *The School of Night: A Study in the Literary Relationships of Sir Walter Raleigh*. Cambridge University Press.

  1955. *The Growth and Structure of Elizabethan Comedy*, new edition. Cambridge University Press, 1979.

Brown, Roger and Gilman, Albert 1960. The pronouns of power and solidarity. In T. A. Sebeok (ed.), *Style in Language*, pp. 253–76. Cambridge, Mass.: MIT Press.

Bruno, Giordano 1585. *The Heroic Frenzies*, trans. P. E. Memmo Jr. Chapel Hill: University of North Carolina Press, 1964.

Bullokar, William 1580. *The Booke at Large*, ed. J. R. Turner. University of Leeds Press, 1970.

Bullough, Geoffrey 1957. *Narrative and Dramatic Sources of Shakespeare*, vol. I. London: Routledge and Kegan Paul.

Burns, Elizabeth 1972. *Theatricality: A Study of Convention in the Theatre and in Social Life*. London: Longman.

Calderwood, James L. 1969. *Shakespearean Metadrama*. Minneapolis: University of Minnesota Press.

  1979. *Metadrama in Shakespeare's Henriad: Richard II to Henry V*. Berkeley and Los Angeles: University of California Press.

Camden, William 1605. *Remaines concerning Britaine*, second edition. London, 1614.

Camillo, Giulio 1550. *L'idea del teatro*. Florence, 1579.

Carnap, Rudolf 1947. *Meaning and Necessity*. Chicago University Press.

Carroll, William C. 1976. *The Great Feast of Language in 'Love's Labour's Lost'*. Princeton University Press

Cassirer, Ernst 1932. *The Platonic Renaissance in England*, trans. J. P. Pettigrew. New York: Nelson, 1953.

Cercignani, Fausto 1981. *Shakespeare's Works and Elizabethan Pronunciation*. London: Oxford University Press.

REFERENCES

Chambers, Edmund K. 1930. *William Shakespeare: A Study of Facts and Problems*. London: Oxford University Press.

Chambers, Ross 1980. Le masque et le miroir. Vers une théorie relationelle du théâtre. *Etudes littéraires*, XIII, 3, 397–412.

Chapman, George 1595. *Ovids Banquet of Sence*. London.

Charlton, H. B. 1938. *Shakespearean Comedy*. London: Methuen.

Charney, Maurice 1961. *Shakespeare's Roman Plays: The Function of Imagery in the Drama*. Cambridge, Mass.: Harvard University Press.

Charron, Pierre 1601. *Of Wisdom*, trans. George Stanhope, third edition. London, 1729.

Cicero *De oratore*, trans. E. W. Sutton and H. Rackham. London: Heinemann, 1942.

Clark, H. H. and Haviland, S. E. 1977. Comprehension and the given–new contract. In R. O. Freedle (ed.), *Discourse Production and Comprehension*, pp. 1–38. Norwood, NJ: Ablex.

Clemen, Wolfgang 1951. *The Development of Shakespeare's Imagery*. London: Methuen.

Cody, Richard 1969. *The Landscape of the Mind: Pastoralism and Platonic Theory in Tasso's Aminta and Shakespeare's Early Comedies*. Oxford: Clarendon Press.

Coleridge, Samuel Taylor *Shakespearean Criticism*, ed. T. M. Raysor. London: Dent, 1960.

Cornwallis, William 1601. *Essayes (Second Parte)*, ed. D. C. Allen. Baltimore: Johns Hopkins University Press, 1946.

Croll, Oswald 1608. *Basilica chymica*. Geneva, 1643.

Crosse, Henry 1603. *Vertues Common-wealth*. London.

Crystal, David and Davy, Donald 1969. *Investigating English Style*. London: Longman.

Cusanus, Nicolaus (Nicholas of Cusa) 1453. *De visione Dei*, trans. Giles Randall, *The Single Eye*. London, 1646.

d'Amico, Masolino 1974. *Scena e parola in Shakespeare*. Turin: Einaudi.

1981. *Dieci secoli di teatro inglese: 970–1980*. Milan: Mondadori.

Daniel, Samuel 1599. *Musophilus: Containing a Generall Defence of Learning*. London.

1603. *A Defence of Rhyme*, ed. G. B. Harrison. London: Bodley Head, 1925.

Day, Angel 1586. *The English Secretorie*, ed. R. O. Evans, Gainsville, Fla.: Scholars Facsimiles and Reprints, 1967.

della Casa, Giovanni 1559. *Galateo*, ed. C. Milanini, Milan: Rizzoli, 1950.

Del Rio, Martin 1633. *Disquisitiorum magicorum libri sex*. Cologne.

De Man, Paul 1974. Nietzsche's theory of rhetoric. *Symposium* (Spring), pp. 33–51.

De Morgan, Augustus 1847. *Formal Logic*. London: Taylor and Walton.

Deonna, W. 1954. The crab and the butterfly: a study in animal symbolism. *Journal of the Warburg and Courtauld Institutes*, XVII, 47–86.

Dixon, Peter 1971. *Rhetoric*. London: Methuen.

Dodd, William 1979. 'Misura per Misura': la trasparenza della commedia. Milan: Il Formichiere.

Duncan, Starkey 1973. Toward a grammar for dyadic conversation. *Semiotica*, IX, 1, 29–46.

Elam, Keir 1977. Language in the theater. *Sub-stance*, 18/19, 139–62.
    1980. *The Semiotics of Theatre and Drama*. London: Methuen.
Elyot, Thomas 1531. *The Book Named the Governor*, ed. S. E. Lehmberg. London: Dent, 1962.
Erasmus, Desiderius 1513. *On Copia of Words and Ideas*, trans. D. B. King and H. B. Rix. Milwaukee: Marquette University Press, 1963.
Evans, Malcolm 1975. Mercury versus Apollo: a reading of *Love's Labour's Lost*. *Shakespeare Quarterly*, XXVI, 113–27.
Fenner, Dudley 1584. *The Artes of Logicke and Rethorike*. London.
Ficino, Marsilio 1475. *Commentary on Plato's Symposium*, trans. Sears R. Jayne. Columbia, Missouri: *University of Missouri Studies*, XIX, 1 (1944). 1561. *Opera omnia*. Basle.
Fornari, Franco 1979. *Coinema e icona: nuova proposta per la psicoanalisi dell'arte*. Milan: Il Saggiatore.
Foucault, Michel 1966. *The Order of Things* (trans.). New York: Vintage, 1973.
Fraser, Russell 1970. *The War against Poetry*. Princeton University Press.
Fraunce, Abraham 1588a. *Insignium, armorum, emblematum, hieroglyphicorum, et symbolorum, quae ab italis nominantur, explicatio*. London. 1588b. *The Arcadian Rhetoric*. London.
Frazer, James G. 1936. *The Golden Bough*, third edition. London: Macmillan.
Freeman, Rosemary 1948. *English Emblem Books*. London: Chatto and Windus.
Gadamer, Hans-Georg 1960. *Truth and Method*, trans. and ed. G. Barden and J. Cumming. New York: Seabury Press, 1975.
Gale, R. M. 1971. The fictive use of language. *Philosophy*, 46, 324–40.
Galway, Margaret 1935. Flyting in Shakespere's comedies. *Shakespeare Association Bulletin*, X, 4, 183–91.
Garvin, Paul L. (ed.) 1964. *A Prague School Reader on Esthetics, Literary Structure and Style*. Washington, DC: Georgetown University Press.
Genette, Gérard 1982. *Palimpsestes: la littérature au second degré*. Paris: Seuil.
Giehlow, Karl 1915. Die Hieroglyphenkunde des Humanismus in der Allegorie der Renaissance. *Jahrbuch der kunsthistorischen Sammlungen in Wien*, XXXII, 1–232.
Giovio, Paolo 1555. *Dialogo dell'imprese militari et amorose*. Rome. Trans. Samuel Daniel, *The Worthy Tract of Paulus Iouius, contayning a Discourse of Rare Inuentions, both Militarie and Amorous called Imprese*. London, 1585.
Goffman, Erving 1974. *Frame Analysis*. Harmondsworth: Penguin. 1975. Replies and responses. Working Papers 46–7 of the Centro Internazionale di Semiotica e di Linguistica, Urbino (now in *Forms of Talk*, pp. 5–77. Oxford: Basil Blackwell, 1981).
Goldstein, Neal 1974. *Love's Labour's Lost* and the Renaissance vision of love. *Shakespeare Quarterly*, XXV, 3, 335–50.
Gombrich, Ernst H. 1948. Icones symbolicae: the visual image in Neo-Platonic thought. *Journal of the Courtauld and Warburg Institutes*, XI, 163–92.
Granville-Barker, Harley 1927. *Prefaces to Shakespeare (First Series)*. London: Batsford.
Greene, Thomas M. 1971. *Love's Labour's Lost*: the grace of society. *Shakespeare Quarterly*, XXII, 4, 315–28.
Greimas, A. J. 1966. *Sémantique structurale*. Paris: Larousse. 1970. *Du sens*. Paris: Seuil.

Grice, H. P. 1967. Logic and conversation. In Peter Cole and Jerry L. Morgan (eds.), *Syntax and Semantics. 3: Speech Acts*, pp. 41–58. New York: Academic Press, 1975.

Groupe μ 1970. *Rhétorique générale*. Paris: Larousse.

Guthrie, W. K. C. 1935. *Orpheus and Greek Religion: A Study of the Orphic Movement*. London: Methuen.

Habermas, Jürgen 1970. Toward a theory of communicative competence. In H. P. Dreitzel (ed.), *Recent Sociology No. 2.: Patterns of Communicative Behaviour*, pp. 114–48. New York: Macmillan.

Hamilton, A. C. 1967. *The Early Shakespeare*. San Marino, Cal.: The Huntington Library.

Hart, John 1569. *An Orthographie*. London.

Helmes, Henry 1594. *Gesta Grayorum: Or, the History of the High and Mighty Prince, Henry, Prince of Purpoole*. London, 1688.

Heraclitus *The Cosmic Fragments*, ed. G. S. Kirk. Cambridge University Press, 1970.

Heywood, John 1562. *Woorkes (Proverbes and Epigrams)*. London.

Heywood, Thomas 1612. *An Apology for Actors*. In G. E. Bentley (ed.), *The Seventeenth-Century Stage*, pp. 10–22. Chicago University Press, 1968.

Hjelmslev, Louis 1943. *Prologomena to a Theory of Language*, trans. F. J. Whitfield. Bloomington: Indiana University Press, 1953.

Hofstadter, Douglas R. 1979. *Gödel, Escher, Bach: An Eternal Golden Braid*. Harmondsworth: Penguin, 1980.

Honzl, Jindřich 1940. Dynamics of the sign in the theater. In L. Matejka and I. R. Titunik (eds.), *Semiotics of Art: Prague School Contributions*, pp. 74–93. Cambridge, Mass.: MIT Press, 1976.

Huarte, Juan 1594. *The Examination of Men's Wits*, trans. M. Camillo Camilli and Englished by R[ichard] C[arew]. Gainesville, Fla.: Scholars Facsimiles and Reprints, 1959.

Hulme, Hilda 1962. *Explorations in Shakespeare's Language*. London: Longman.

Jakobson, Roman 1956. Metalanguage as a linguistic problem (lecture unpublished in English), trans. Il metalinguaggio come problema linguistico. In R. Jakobson, *Lo sviluppo della semiotica*, pp. 85–98. Milan: Bompiani, 1978.

   1957. Shifters, verbal categories, and the Russian verb. in *Selected Writings*, vol. II, pp. 130–47. The Hague: Mouton, 1971.

Jones, R. F. 1953. *The Triumph of the English Language*. London: Oxford University Press.

Jonson, Ben 1641. *Timber, or Discoveries*, ed. Ralph S. Walker. Syracuse University Press, 1953.

Joos, M. 1962. *The Five Clocks*. Publications of the Indiana University Research Center in Anthropology, Folklore and Linguistics, 22. Bloomington, Ind.

Kahn, Coppélia 1977. *The Taming of the Shrew*: Shakespeare's mirror of marriage. In Arlyn Diamond and Lee R. Edwards (eds.), *The Authority of Experience: Essays in Feminist Criticism*, pp. 84–100. Amherst: University of Massachussetts Press

Kempson, R. M. 1977. *Semantic Theory*. Cambridge University Press.

Kenny, Anthony 1973. *Wittgenstein*. Harmondsworth: Penguin.

## REFERENCES

Kökeritz, Helge 1953. *Shakespeare's Pronunciation*. New Haven: Yale University Press.

Kowzan, Tadeusz 1976. Art 'en abyme'. *Diogenes*, 96, 67–92.

Krieger, Elliot 1979. *A Marxist Study of Shakespeare's Comedies*. London: Macmillan.

Kristeva, Julia 1968. Σημειωτικὴ: *Recherches pour une sémanalyse*. Paris: Seuil.

Langer, Susanne K. 1953. *Feeling and Form*. New York: Scribner.

Lausberg, Heinrich 1967. *Elemente der literarischen Rhetorik*, second edition. Munich: Hueber Verlag.

Lee, Rensselaer W. 1977. *Names on Trees: Ariosto into Art*. Princeton University Press.

Lever, Ralph 1573. *The Arte of Reason*. London.

Levin, Harry 1965. Shakespeare's nomenclature. In W. Gerald (ed.), *Essays on Shakespeare*, pp. 59–90. Princeton.

Levinson, Ronald B. 1957. Language and the *Cratylus*: four questions. *Review of Metaphysics*, IX, 1, 28–41.

Luther, Martin 1520. *The Babylonian Captivity of the Church*, trans. A. T. W. Steinhauser and revised by F. C. Ahrens and A. B. Wentz, *Works*, vol. 36, pp. 11–126. Philadelphia: Muhlenberg Press, 1959.

Lyly, John 1578. *Euphues: The Anatomy of Wit*, ed. M. Croll and H. Clemons. London: Routledge, 1916.

1580. *Euphues and his England*, ed. M. Croll and H. Clemons. London: Routledge, 1916.

Lyons, John 1977. *Semantics*. Cambridge University Press.

McCawley, James D. 1978. 'World-creating' predicates. *Versus*, 19/20, 77–93.

McHugh, Roland 1980. *Annotations to 'Finnegans Wake'*. London: Routledge and Kegan Paul.

McKie, W. S. 1936. Shakespeare's English: and how far it can be investigated with the help of the *New English Dictionary*. *Modern Language Review*, 31, 1–10.

McLay, Catherine M. 1967. The dialogues of spring and winter: a key to the unity of *Love's Labour's Lost*. *Shakespeare Quarterly*, XVIII, 2, 119–27.

Mahood, Molly M. 1957. *Shakespeare's Wordplay*. London: Methuen.

Manly, John Matthews 1897. *Specimens of the Pre-Shakespearean Drama*, vol. 1. Boston: The Athenaeum Press.

Marprelate, Martin 1589. *The Iust Censure and Reproofe of Martin Iunior*. (Wolston?)

Matthews, William 1964. Language in *Love's Labour's Lost*. *Essays and Studies*, XVII, 1–11.

Montaigne, Michel de 1603. *Essayes*, trans. John Florio. London.

More, Thomas 1532. *The Confutation of Tyndale's Answer*. *Complete Works*, vol. VIII, part 1, ed. L. A. Schuster, R. C. Marius, J. P. Lusardi and R. J. Schoeck. New Haven: Yale University Press, 1973.

Morris, Charles 1946. *Signs, Language and Behaviour*. Englewood Cliffs, NJ: Prentice-Hall.

Mulcaster, Richard 1582. *The First Part of the Elementarie*, ed. E. T. Campagnac. London: Oxford University Press, 1925.

Mullini, Roberta 1979. *Much Ado About Nothing*: L'orientamento della comunicazione nell'eavesdropping. *Quaderni di Teatro*, II, 5, 113–53.

REFERENCES

Munday, Anthony 1586. *A Second and Third Blast of Retrait from Plaies and Theatres*. New York and London: Garland, 1973.

Nagler, A. M. 1958. *Shakespeare's Stage*. New Haven: Yale University Press.

Nashe, Thomas 1592. *Pierce Penniless his Supplication to the Diuell*. London.

    1593. *Christ's Tears over Jerusalem*, second edition. London, 1594.

    1600. *Summer's Last Will and Testament*. In J. B. Steane (ed.), *The Unfortunate Traveller and Other Works*, pp. 146–207. Harmondsworth: Penguin, 1972.

Northbrooke, John 1577. *A Treatise against Dicing, Dancing, Plays, and Interludes*. London: Shakespeare Society, 1843.

Nosworthy, J. M. 1979. The importance of being Marcade. *Shakespeare Survey*, 32, 105–14.

Ohmann, Richard 1971. Speech, action and style. In Seymour Chatman (ed.), *Literary Style*, pp. 241–54. London: Oxford University Press.

    1973. Literature as act. In Seymour Chatman (ed.), *Approaches to Poetics*, pp. 81–107. New York: Columbia University Press.

Pachter, Henry M. 1951. *Paracelsus: Magic into Science*. New York: Schuman.

Pagnini, Marcello 1974. *Lingua e musica*. Bologna: Il Mulino.

    1976. *Shakespeare e il paradigma della specularità*. Pisa: Pacini.

    1980. *Pragmatica della letteratura*. Palermo: Sellerio.

Pater, Walter 1889. *Appreciations*. London: Macmillan.

Peacham, Henry 1577. *The Garden of Eloquence*. London.

Peirce, Charles S. 1931–58. *Collected Papers*. Cambridge, Mass.: Harvard University Press.

Perkins, William 1600. *Works*, fourth edition. Cambridge, 1608.

Petöfi, Janos S. 1975. *Vers une théorie partielle du texte*. Hamburg: Buske.

Phialas, Peter G. 1966. *Shakespeare's Romantic Comedies*. Chapel Hill: University of North Carolina Press.

Pico della Mirandola, Giovanni 1486a. *Conclusiones nongentae*. Rome, 1532.

    1486b. Of the dignity of man, trans. Elizabeth L. Forbes. *Journal of the History of Ideas*, III, 3 (1942), 347–54.

    1489. *Heptaplus*, ed. Eugenio Garin. Florence: Reale Istituto di Studi Filosofici, 1942.

    1510. *The Lyfe of Johan Picus [by G. F. Pico] . . . with Dyvers Epistles and Other Werkes of ye Said Johan Picus*, trans. Thomas More. London.

Plato *Cratylus*, trans. B. Jowett, London: Oxford University Press, 1953.

Plautus *The Swaggering Soldier (Miles gloriosus)*, trans. E. F. Watling. In *The Pot of Gold and other Plays*, pp. 147–212. Harmondsworth: Penguin, 1965.

Potter, Lois 1980. The plays and playwrights. *The Revels History of Drama in English. Vol. II: 1500–1576*, pp. 141–257. London: Methuen.

Pratt, Mary Louise 1977. *Toward a Speech Act Theory of Literary Discourse*. Bloomington: Indiana University Press.

Praz, Mario 1964. *Studies in Seventeenth-Century Imagery*, second edition. Rome: Edizioni di Storia e Letteratura.

Primaudaye, Pierre de la 1586. *The French Academie*, trans. T[homas] B[owes]. London.

Proclus *Proclus on the Theology of Plato*, trans. Thomas Taylor. London, 1787.

Puttenham, George 1589. *The Arte of Englishe Poesie*. London.

Quintilian *Institutio oratoria*, trans. H. E. Butler. London: Heinemann, 1922–4.

REFERENCES

Quirk, Randolph 1970. Shakespeare and the English language. In Kenneth Muir and Samuel Schoenbaum (eds.), *A New Companion to Shakespeare Studies*, pp. 67–82. Cambridge University Press.

Rainolds, John 1599. *Th'Ouerthrow of Stage-Playes*. Middleburg.

Reuchlin, Johannes 1494. *De arte cabalistica*. Basle.

Righter, Anne 1962. *Shakespeare and the Idea of the Play*. Harmondsworth: Penguin, 1967.

Ryle, Gilbert 1957. The theory of meaning. In T. M. Olshewsky (ed.), *Problems in the Philosophy of Language*, pp. 131–50. New York: Holt, Rinehart and Winston, 1969.

Sacks, Harvey, Schegloff, Emanuel A. and Jefferson, Gail 1974. A simplest systematics for the organization of turn-taking in conversation. *Language*, 50, 696–735.

Sanchez, Francesco 1581. *Quod nihil scitur*. Rotterdam, 1649.

Savona, Jeannette Laillou 1980. Narration et actes de parole dans le texte dramatique. *Études Littéraires*, XIII, 3, 471–94.

Schlauch, Margaret 1965. The social background of Shakespeare's malapropisms. In S. Helsztynski (ed.), *Poland's Homage to Shakespeare*, pp. 203–31. Warsaw: Neophilological Committee of Polish Academy of Sciences.

Scot, Reginald 1584. *The Discoverie of Witchcraft*, ed. Brinsley Nicholson. London: E. Stock, 1886.

Searle, John R. 1969. *Speech Acts: An Essay in the Philosophy of Language*. Cambridge University Press.

1975a. Indirect speech acts. In Peter Cole and Jerry L. Morgan (eds.), *Syntax and Semantics. 3: Speech Acts*, pp. 59–82. New York: Academic Press.

1975b A taxonomy of illocutionary acts. In K. Gunderson (ed.), *Language, Mind and Knowledge*, pp. 344–69. Minneapolis: University of Minnesota Press.

Secret, F. 1969. *Les kabbalistes chrétiens de la Renaissance*. Paris: Dunod.

Segre, Cesare 1982. Intertestuale/interdiscorsivo. Paper presented at the Tenth National Conference of the Italian Association of Semiotic Studies (AISS), Como, 8–10 October.

Serpieri, Alessandro 1978a. Ipotesi teorica di segmentazione del testo teatrale. In *Come comunica il teatro: dal testo alla scena*, pp. 11–54. Milan: Il Formichiere.

1978b. *Otello: l'eros negato*. Milan: Il Formichiere.

1980a. La retorica a teatro. *Strumenti critici*, 41, 146–63.

1980b. Introduzione. In *Amleto*, pp. 5–19. Milan: Feltrinelli.

Sextus Empiricus *Outlines of Pyrrhonism*, trans. R. G. Bury. London: Heinemann, 1933.

Sherry, Richard 1550. *A Treatise of Schemes and Tropes*. London.

Short, M. H. 1981. Discourse analysis and the analysis of drama. *Applied Linguistics*, XI, 2, 181–202.

Sidney, Philip 1595. *An Apology for Poetry*. London.

Smith, Charles G. 1963. *Shakespeare's Proverb Lore: His Use of the 'Sententiae' of Leonard Culman and Publius Syrus*. Cambridge, Mass.: Harvard University Press.

Smith, G. Gregory (ed.) 1904. *Elizabethan Critical Essays*. London: Oxford University Press.

✓Sonnino, Lee A. 1968. *A Handbook to Sixteenth-Century Rhetoric*. London: Routledge and Kegan Paul.

Stamm, Rudolf 1954. *Shakespeare's Word-Scenery, with Some Remarks on Stage-History and the Interpretation of his Plays*. Zurich and St Gallen: Polygraphischer Verlag.

Stockwood, John 1578. *A Sermon Preached at Paules Crosse*. London.

Stubs, Phillip 1584. *The Anatomie of Abuses*. London.

Susenbrotus, Joannes 1540. *Epitome troporum ac schematum et grammaticarum et rhetorum*. London, 1570.

Swinburne, Algernon Charles 1880. *A Study of Shakespeare*. London: Chatto.

Swinden, Patrick 1973. *An Introduction to Shakespeare's Comedies*. London: Macmillan.

Symeone, Gabriele 1560. *Le sententiose imprese*. Lyons.

Tasso, Torquato 1573. *Aminta*. Milan: Rizzoli, 1976.

Thomas, Thomas 1588. *Dictionarium linguae Latinae et Anglicanae*. London.

Tilley, M. P. 1950. *The Proverbs in England in the Sixteenth and Seventeenth Centuries*. Ann Arbor: University of Michigan Press.

Top, Alexander 1603. *The Oliue Leafe*. Menston: Scolar Press, 1971.

Trager, George L. 1958. Paralanguage: a first approximation. In Dell Hymes (ed.), *Language in Culture and Society*, pp. 274–88. New York: Harper and Row, 1964.

Turner, Robert Y. 1974. *Shakespeare's Apprenticeship*. Chicago University Press.

Uhlig, Claus 1970. 'The sobbing deer': *As You Like It*, II. i. 21–66, and the historical context. *Renaissance Drama*, pp. 79–110.

Urmson, James O. 1972. Dramatic representation. *Philosophical Quarterly*, XXII, 333–43.

Verstegen, Richard (pseud. of Richard Rowlands) 1605. *A Restitution of Decayed Intelligence*. Antwerp.

Vickers, Brian 1970. Shakespeare's use of rhetoric. In Kenneth Muir and Samuel Schoenbaum (eds.), *A New Companion to Shakespeare Studies*, pp. 83–98. Cambridge University Press.

Viswanathan, S. 1969. 'Illeism with a difference' in certain middle plays of Shakespeare. *Shakespeare Quarterly*, XX, 4, 407–15.

Volli, Ugo 1982. Che pene d'amore con la clausura. *La Repubblica*, 6 November.

Walker, D. P. 1953. Orpheus the theologian and Renaissance Platonists. *Journal of the Warburg and Courtauld Institutes*, XVI, 100–20.
1954. The *Prisca Theologia* in France. *Journal of the Warburg and Courtauld Institutes*, XVII, 204–59.

Wells, Stanley 1972. Shakespeare without sources. *Stratford-upon-Avon Studies*, 14, 58–74.

Westlund, Joseph 1967. Fancy and achievement in *Love's Labour's Lost. Shakespeare Quarterly*, XVIII, 1, 37–46.

Whiting, B. J. 1932. The nature of the proverb. *Harvard Studies and Notes in Philology and Literature*, XIV, 273–307.

Whitney, Geffrey 1586. *A Choice of Emblemes and Other Devises*. London.

Wikberg, Kay 1975. *Yes–No Questions and Answers in Shakespeare's Plays: A Study in Text Linguistics*. Åbo, Finland: Åbo Akademi.

Willcock, Gladys D. 1934. *Shakespeare as Critic of Language*. London: Oxford University Press.

REFERENCES

Wilson, F. P. 1969. *Shakespearean and Other Studies*, ed. Helen Gardner. London: Oxford University Press.

Wilson, K. J. 1976. Ascham's *Toxophilus* and the Rules of Art. *Renaissance Quarterly*, 1, 30–51.

Wilson, Thomas 1553. *The Arte of Rhetorique*. London.

Wind, Edgar 1967. *Pagan Mysteries in the Renaissance*. Harmondsworth: Penguin.

Wittgenstein, Ludwig 1953. *Philosophical Investigations*, trans. G. E. M. Anscombe. Oxford: Basil Blackwell.

1958. *The Blue and Brown Brooks*. Oxford: Basil Blackwell.

Woodward, William H. (ed.) 1904. *Desiderius Erasmus Concerning the Aim and Method of Education*. Cambridge University Press.

Wright, Thomas 1601. *The Passions of the Minde*. London.

Yates, Frances 1936. *A Study of 'Love's Labour's Lost'*. Cambridge University Press.

1947. *The French Academies of the Sixteenth Century*. London: The Warburg Institute.

1964. *Giordano Bruno and the Hermetic Tradition*. London: Routledge and Kegan Paul.

1979. *The Occult Philosophy in the Elizabethan Age*. London: Routledge and Kegan Paul.

Yngve, Victor H. 1971. On getting a word in edgewise. *Papers from the Sixth Regional Meeting of the Chicago Linguistic Society*, pp. 567–78. Chicago.

OTHER EDITIONS OF SHAKESPEARE'S COMEDIES
REFERRED TO IN TEXT

*A Midsummer Night's Dream*, ed. W. J. Rolfe. New York: Harper and Brothers, 1877.
*The Taming of the Shrew*, ed. G. R. Hibbard. Harmondsworth: Penguin, 1968.
*The Two Gentlemen of Verona*, ed. Warwick Bond. London: Methuen, 1906.

# Index

Page numbers in bold type indicate glossary entries.

actantial scheme, 202, 255–6, **309**
action, dramatic, 6, 177
actor: body of, 50; body-movement of,
236; costume of, 51; and orator
compared, 235; outdone by description,
60; speaker as, 66–7; speech acts and,
200, 219; vocal delivery by, 33, 48
address, direct, 40, 44, 252
addressee, 86, 179–80, 184–5, 189, 233–4;
doubling as topic, 183
*ad placitum* theory of names, 123,
166–7, 168, 170, 172, **309**
Agrippa Von Nettesheim, Henry
Cornelius (*De occulta philosophia*),
124, 131, 161, 163
Alciati, Andrea: *Emblemata*, 155
allusion, 27; contextualized, 28
anagrams, 162, 164, 262
anaphora (linguistic), 80–1, 86, 90, 102–3,
248, 309; anaphoric chains, 80, 102–4;
anaphoric space, 84, 102, 103 (anaphora
(rhetorical): see scheme)
Andrewes, Bartimaeus: *Sermons*,
299–300
Arbeau, Thoinot: *Orchesography*, 237,
238
*Arden of Faversham*, epilogue, 37
Ariosto, Ludovico, 28, 133, 136: *Orlando
Furioso*, 137
Aristotle: *De interpretatione*, theory of
sign in, 1, 166, 170; *Poetics*:
dramaturgic criteria in, 3, 6, 72, *ethos*
in, 218, *pathos* in, 233; *Rhetoric*: *ethos*
in, 217–18, 229, *pathos* in, 230
Ascham, Roger: *Toxophilus*, 238
audience: identity of, 40, 86; 'inner',
response of, 44, 54–5, 66;
interpretation by, 33, 78–9, 83, 184,
188, 190
Augustine, Saint: *Confessions*, 118, 119
Austin, J. L.: on illocutionary acts,
typology of, 201, 312; on illocutionary
force, 312; on illocutionary sequel,
312; on infelicity, 226, 312; on
locutionary acts, 10, 18, 33, 313; on

performative verbs, 201, 314; on
perlocutionary act, 231, 314; on
perlocutionary sequel, 314; on
sincerity condition, 216; on speech
acts, 6, 11, on stage, 199–200; on
uptake, 210, 317; on verbal bond, 229
authentication (of dialogue), 68–9, 189,
**309**

Bacon, Francis: *Advancement of
Learning*: *actio* in, 235, *copia
verborum* in, 267, critique of linguistic
idolatry in, 166, 169–70, priority of
trope in, 305–6; *Essays*: garden as
figure in, 94
Barton, Anne, 149, 302 (*see also* Righter,
Anne)
beginnings: of comedies, 89–92; *in media
verba*, 89–91; opening configurations,
179–80; opening exchanges, 91–2; of
other Shakespearean plays, 91
Bernard, Richard: *Faithful Shepherd*,
304–5
Bocchi, Achille: *Symbolicae quaestiones*,
158, 159
body, human: figurality of, 236–8, 240;
relations with language, 50–3, 60, 241;
signifying power of, 114
Bonomi, Andrea, 80, 84, 101–2
Boorde, Andrew: *Dietary of Health*,
268–9
Borges, Jorge Luis, 32
Bruno, Giordano, 156, 169; *Degli eroici
furori*, 152, 163
Bullokar, William: *Book at Large*, 262–3
burlesque: hyperbole, 291; hypertextual,
28; icon, 63–4; illocutionary, 208–12;
index, 52–6; literary, 19, 291;
narrative, 74, 84; predication, 99–101;
proverbs, 278, 282; reference, 92–4;
rejection of trope, 304
Burns, Elizabeth, 34, 189, 309

Cabalism, 123, 131, 141, 162–4, **316**; in
England, 163–4

329

# INDEX

*As You Like It*: anaphora (rhetorical) in, 248–9; *asteismus* in, 130; burlesque in 28–9, 62, 73–4, 89; context in, 73–5; dance in, 257; *elocutio* in, 240–1; ending of, 112, 248–9, 257; epilogue of, 35, 38–40, 44; 'figure' in, 241; gesture in, 51; graphism in, 160; icon, verbal in, 59, 62, hyperbole in 291; hypertextual signals in 28–9, 73–4; insincerity in, 219; language as 'theme' in, 22; magic in, 165; mention in, 30; metadiscourse in, 25; metatheatre in, 20, 69–70; modes of discourse in, 69–70; music in, 144; name, motivated in, 133–4; opening configuration of, 180; parody in, 27; pastoralism in, 136–9; *pathos* in, 230–1; proverbs in 283, 285, 286–7; reference in, 20, 94–5; replay signals (semantic) in, 114; scene in, 115; signs, behavioural, in, 115; space in, 94–5; speaker as actor in, 67, 69–70; text, embedded, in, 25; title of 85–6; transvestism in, 47; turn signals in, 189, 192; uptake in, 210–11; voice in, 47; word, deflation of, in, 173–4; 'world' in, 83; world-creating frames in, 20; world-creating games in, 14, 73–6

*The Comedy of Errors*: actantial scheme of, 256; anaphora (linguistic) in, 102–4; beginning of, 8, 90; *chiasmus* in, 256–7; context in, 77; deixis in, 50; 'discourse' in, 1; ending of, 112; gesture in, 51, 53–4; magic in, 165; name, 'natural', in, 135; object of discourse in, 102–4; opening configuration of, 180; proverbs in, 277, 281, 283, 286; quotation in, 26–7, reference in, 32; time in, 106–8; title of, 88; turn signal in, 191, 195; voice in, 49; word, deflation of, in, 174; world-creating games in, 14

*Love's Labour's Lost*: actantial scheme of, 255–6; alliteration in, 10, 16, 88, 244, 259; allusion in, 27; alphabetic disposition of names in, 263; *anastrophe* in, 249; *antanaclasis* in, 119; *antimetabole* in, 254; apostrophe in, 252; *apostrophus* in, 260–1; archaism in, 261, 274–5; aside in, 252; *asteismus* in, 81, 241; as baroque text, 32; beginning of, 90; body in, 114; *chiasmus* in, 253–7; climax in, 252–3; code-switching in, 18, 272–3; compounding in, 269–70; *congeries* in, 267; context foregrounded in, 77–8; *copia verborum* in, 267–8; dance in, 236; *dicaeologia* in, 228;

'discourse' in, 1; *ecphonesis* in, 263–4; *ellipsis* in, 270; emblems parodied in, 152–5; ending of, 70–1, 109–11, 112, 158–9; English language in, 266; enigma in, 148, 155–8; *epenthesis* in, 260; *euche* in, 228; event, embedded, in, 24–5; exposition in, 40–1, 44–6; *fabula* of, 250–1; fashion, lexical, in, 273–4; *festina lente* in, 152–5, 235–6, 241; figural frame in, 21; figure in, 211, 235–6, 241; floor, battle for, in, 198–9; frame-breaking in, 45; graphic/phonetic priority in, 262–4; Hermes in, 148–9, 150–1; Hermetism in, 29, 149–51, 163, 175; hyperbole in, 293–5, 300; *hysteron proteron* in, 250–1; icon, verbal, in, 59–60, 62, 63–4; idiolects in, 238–9; infelicity in, 91, 226–9; index, verbal, in, 54–5; intertextuality in, 26, 105, 268–9; language as 'theme' in, 22; language-game, 'primitive', in, 118–19; language–mind relationship in, 213–14; Latin in, 212–13; letter in, 25–6, 263–4; listener in, 233–4; metacommunication in, 25–6; metadiscourse in, 25; metadrama in, 20, 67, 70–1, 251–3; metaplasm in, 258, 259; metatheatre in, 20, 199, 307–8; *mise en abyme* in, 32; misframing in, 45; morpheme, breakdown of, in, 270; mysteries, pagan, in, 145–6, 152; name, proper, in, 120, 121–2, 126, 133; naming rites in, 17, 120–1; naturalism, semantic, in, 122; neologisms in, 18–19, 118, 119, 266, 268–9, 270–2; opening exchange of, 91; Orphic effects in, 144–7, 165; orthographic pun in, 262; ostensive definition in, 118–19; overspying scene in, 24–5, 67, 156; *paragoge* in, 259–60; *parimion* in, 259; *paronomasia* in, 64, 261; pastoralism in, 138, 139–40; *pathos* in, 231, 252; perlocutionary failure in, 232–4; phonetic games in, 10, 259–62; 'plain speech' in, 297, 301–4, 307–8; Platonism in, 125–8; *ploce* in, 244; plot of, 234; predication in, 99, 101; prologue, 'inner', in, 40–1, 44; *prosthesis* in, 260; proverbs in, 277–8, 279, 280, 281–2, 286; quotation in, 26; reference in, 46, 93–4: reflexivity in, 31, 250, 253–4; replay signals (semantic) in, 114; rhetoric in, 235–6, 238; scepticism in, 172; 'School of Night' in, 157; semantic frames in, 21, 114; *serio ludere* in, 138, 156–7, 159; sign: arbitrary, 175–6, cultivation of, 126–9, graphic, 172; sincerity

335